WOMEN ADMINISTRATORS AND PROFESSIONALS A GLOBAL PERSPECTIVE

With an Extended Bibliography

WOMEN ADMINISTRATORS AND PROFESSIONALS A GLOBAL PERSPECTIVE

With an Extended Bibliography

Pramod Mishra
Urmila Mohapatra

Research Monograph (4)
of
Academy for Asia Pacific Studies
New Delhi

KALINGA PUBLICATIONS
DELHI
2003

Women Administrators and Professionals
A Global Perspective
With an extended Bibliography

ISBN 81-87644-49-4

Rs. 850.00
$ 150.00
£ 75.00

Research Monograph (4)
of
Academy for Asia Pacific Studies
New Delhi

Published by:
Rajat Sood
KALINGA PUBLICATIONS
10A, Pocket-I, Phase-I,
Mayur Vihar, Delhi-110091
Tel.: 2794060, 2754881
Fax : 91-11-2494060

Lasertypeset at :
FLASH PHOTOCOMPOSERS
38, Suryadeep Building,
Ring Road, Delhi-110052
Tel.: 7377527

Printed at :
SHOBI OFFSET
Kucha Chelan, Daryaganj,
New Delhi-110002

Contents

Forward iii

Preface i

PART I

Introduction 1

1. The status of Women Administrators in the World At Large 3

2. Women Entrepreneurs in Business Enterprises: A Global Perspective 13

3. Challenges and Remedies for Women Executives 21

4. The Managerial Profession for Women : The Changing Norms 37

5. Societal Attitude Towards Women Managers 61

6. Women Managers Outshine their Male Counterparts 75

7. Job Satisfaction of Women Managers: Glass Ceiling Effect 81

8. Corporate Restructuring and Reduction of Jobs for Women 103

9. Women Administrators Professionals of USA 115
   - 9.1 Some Success Stories 121
   - 9.2 Profiles of Successful Managers in the US 128
   - 9.3 From Pulpits to Judicial Benches : Influx of Women Transformed Workplaces in the 1990s 133
   - 9.4 Glass Ceiling at Top Level 139
   - 9.5 Scarcity of Black Women Managers at the Top Level 140

10. Women Executives of Canada 143
    - 10.1 Health Status of Canadian Women Managers 162

11. The British Women Managers and Professionals (With Special Focus on South Asian Immigrants) 163

11.1 A Comparison of French and British Women Professionals 183

12. Women Managers of Eastern Europe 185

12.1 Situation in Poland 192

13. The Asian Women Managers 193

13.1 The Status of Women Administrators in Bangladesh 195

14. Women Managers of Africa : The Case of Nigeria 205

15. The Situation in Latin America : A Pilot Study of Mexico 211

Select References 213

PART II

AN EXTENDED BIBLIOGRAPHY

I. Theoritical Concerns about Women Administrators and Professionals 217

II. Anticipatory Socialization of Women toward Managerial and Professional Careers 224

III. Professional Socialization of Women Across Organizations 231

IV. Barriers against the upward Mobility of Women Managers and professionals 232

V. Recruitment of Women into Managerial Systems 234

VI. Performance Evaluation of Women Managers and Professionals 237

VII. Women & Men Administrators: Variations in Leadership Attributes 244

VIII. Role Perceptions of Managerial Women and Role Expectations of Others 248

IX. The Family Environment of Women Managers 254

X. Discriminatory Practices toward Women Administrators and Professionals 258

XI. Sexual Harassment of Women Managers 259

XII. Salary Differences Between Men and Women Managers and Professionals 262

XIII. Minority Women Administrators and Professionals 264

XIV. Managerial Women in Cross-National Perspective 266

XV. Women Managers in Corporate Workplace 272

XVI. Women Administrators in Academic Settings 276

XVII. Women in Police Leadership 280

XVIII. Women in Military Leadership 283

XIX. Women in Voluntary Organization Leadership 288

XX. Women in Library Administration System 290

XXI. Women in Social Service Administration 292

XXII. Women Professionals in Media 294

XXIII. Women in the Legal Professions 296

XXIV. Women Engineers and Scientists 298

XXV. Women in Public Administration 305

XXVI. Women in Federal Administration 307

XXVII. Women in State Administration 309

XXVIII. Women in Local Administration 311

XXIX. Women Professionals in Health Care System 313

XXX. Women Social Scientists 316

XXXI. Strategies of Success for Women Managers 318

XXXII. Empowerment of Women Managers and Professionals 325

XXXIII. Stress Management and Managerial Women 329
XXXIV. Managerial Training for Women Professionals 332
XXXV. Mentoring the Women Managers and Professionals 337
XXXVI. Profession of Women Administrators & Professionals 339
XXXVII. Women and Power in Organisations 342
XXXVIII. Glass Ceilings for Women Professionals & Administrators 348
XXXIX. Job Satisfaction of Women Managers 351
XXXX. Women Managers & Professionals in USA & Canada 356
XXXXI. Women Administrators & Professionals in UK in a Multicultural Perspective 359
XXXXII. Women Administrators & Professionals in the Afro-Asian Regions 363
XXXXIII. Women Managers & Professionals in Russia 366
Index 369

Foreword

This book on women Administrators and Professionals: A Global Perspective (With an extended bibliography) was completed in the Center for Government Services by the co-authors: Dr. Pramod Mishra and Mrs. Urmila Mohapatra. It is one of our Cultural Diversity Projects. It should serve as a guide to the future researchers interested in the attitudes, behavior, and perceptions of the women professionals. I wish the co-authors all success.

Manindra K. Mohapatra
Director,
Center for Governmental Services
Indiana State University
Terre Haute, IN

August 15, 2002
Indian Independence Day

Preface

In the last two decades, some women around the world have entered the diverse workplaces as administrators, managers, and other types of professions. The social science researchers have also begun studying systematically the workplace and cultural changes following the entry of women personnels. This book is an attempt to provide some reflections on women administrators & professionals all over the world and to classify a large number of studies by scholars in the field.

Many individuals and organizations have provided support services to us during this project. The Centre for Governmental Services of Indiana State University provided the setting for our work. The inter-library loan service of the Cunningham Memorial Library, Indiana State University promptly delivered books, articles, and working papers. Electronic access to library reference made it possible for us to assemble the research material and do this collaborative research. The distance between India and America was considerably shortened.

As our several review essays indicate, research in social science has created new knowledge about women administrators and professionals. Yet, there are many new unexplored areas of research. We hope that the future researchers will explore these new areas.

We extend our thanks to Professor Manindra K. Mohapatra, Kathy Comp, and Ruchi Tyagi of the Center for Governmental Services for their extended support for this program. Some library research for this book was done in the Library of Congress, British Library (London), D Montfort University Library (Leicester) and India International Center Library, Indian Institute of Public Administration Library and Jawaharlal Nehru University Library, New Delhi. We are thankful to the staff members of these libraries for their support.

Pramod Mishra (New Delhi, India)
Urmila Mohapatra (Terre Haute, USA)

Part I

Introduction

Gender sensitivity has been a crucial issue since the mid-twentieth century. Hereafter nation after nation have not only accorded equal status to both men and women, but also have passed several legislative acts to enhance the status of women. With the dramatic rise of female literacy in all parts of the world beginning with North America and Europe, one also notices a considerable growth of women administrators, managers and professionals all over the world. However, in spite of their significant representation in the public and private services, the women have often undergone the agonizing experience of overt and covert discrimination by their employers that is often institutionalized by the practice of "Glass Ceiling". Besides, one also comes across a number of instances of violence against women managers and professionals often perpetrated by their seniors and even by their own colleagues.

The purpose of the present study co-authored by us is two-fold. First, although there are a number of independent research works available on feminism and gender-senstive issues, one does not come across many well-documented and comprehensive studies on women administrators and professionals. Our purpose is to generate a wide ranging debate on the present status of women leaders in public and private services and on the formidable challenges faced by them.

Second, although the second half of the book is a classified bibliography on women administrators and professionals, we are also attempting to highlight some of the formidable challenges faced by the nation-states in their efforts to eliminate any traces of discrimination against the women managers and opinion-builders at the dawn of the twenty-first century.

As the readers will find in due course, our Part I will explore the quest for theory building on gender sensitive issues related to women managers in the changing global realities, sexual discrimination of women decision-makers, corporate restructuring, reduction of jobs for women all over the world, asymmetry in power equations in business organizations, the test of proficiency of women managers and entrepreneurs vis-à-vis their male counterparts, the biased societal outlook to deny decision-making powers to competent women managers, glass ceiling and job satisfaction of women employees/administrators

It will also focuss on the role, status and evaluation of the performance of women administrators and professionals in different global regions like North America, South America, Western Europe, Eastern Europe, Asia, Africa, and Australia. Part II is an extended bibliography and we have taken care to update it as far as possible. For the convenience of the researchers, we have given a broad classification of these resource materials.

1

The status of Women Administrators in the World At Large

Although women represent more than 50% of the world population, in no country do women represent half or even close to half of the corporate managers. The anticipated breakthrough into the centers of organizational power seems even less likely than it did 20 years ago. Women's increased investment in higher education and greater commitment to management as a career, as well as new equal opportunity legislation and the shortage - or expected shortage - of high quality managers, did not result in a significant breakthrough into the executive suite. The intensification of global competition has become a major influence compelling firms to view women managers as a competitive advantage rather than as a legislated necessity.[1] Such companies approach the decision to send women managers abroad in new ways, which may be discussed as follows : First, the companies do not assume that it will not work. Second, they do not assume that a woman will not want to go abroad. Guidelines they consider in hiring local women managers include taking advantage of the low demand for women managers.

What has prevented women's movement into management and, especially, into the executive suite? What have countries, companies, and women themselves done to increase women's representation in management? Until the late 1970s, women were virtually invisible as managers, and their absence was generally considered a non-issue. Since then, women managers have become increasingly visible in many countries. From one perspective the picture is positive. In each country, changing societal patterns have resulted in significant increases in the number of women managers. These patterns include favorable economic and demographic conditions, supportive government policies, changing family roles and emerging support systems. In addition, women show positive responses to their new opportunities. Form another perspective the picture is not so rosy. Each country tells a similar story of a society in which men control the centers of political and economic power, and of a profession controlled primarily by men—a profession in which women remain relative newcomers, especially at the top. In all countries, major barriers still hold back women's progress in management. Beyond the international commonalities underlying women's exclusion from the centres of managerial power and authority lies the uniqueness of local conditions in each country that has produced the variety of women's experiences worldwide.

Systematic investigation of women's progress in management is new. It began in North America, primarily in the U.S., in the early 1970s, in Western Europe in the early 1980s, in Asia toward the mid-1980s, and in the former Eastern European communist countries and the People's Republic of China only toward the end of the 1980s.

In all countries, broad societal forces during recent decades have led to more women entering lower-level managerial positions. For example, in both the industrialized and industrializing worlds, the expansion of banking and other financial services opened opportunities for women in lower-and middle-level management. In most countries in the 1970s and 1980s, the growing public sector also absorbed many of the increasingly educated women into lower-level managerial positions. In both the industrialized and industrializing worlds, economic growth and increasing global competition heightened the demand for top quality managers. Economic enterprises began to take advantage of the growing availability of qualified women to fill the new positions.

In each country, the specific processes used to bring about change differed. In the U.S., powerful women's groups used the political process and the courts to help establish regulations that held employers responsible for implementing equal opportunity within their organizations. Such political and legal changes made it in organizations' self-interest to open their doors to women for lower-level managerial positions. Neither the political nor the legal changes were sufficiently powerful, however, to counter resistance to women entering the most senior levels. In France, legislation passed in the 1980s gave unions responsibility for negotiating equal opportunity on behalf of women. But progress was very limited.

The French unions appear to have lacked enough motivation to affect the previously legislated societal changes. In Hong Kong, where government intervention in commerce has been minimal and sex discrimination in employment continues to be legal, the proportion of women among corporate managers remains negligible. In the social welfare states of Western Europe and Israel, social democratic parties created large public service bureaucracies that became the main employers of women, thereby providing major channels for women moving into management. Not surprisingly, in these countries gender segregation emerged along sectorial lines, with women managers concentrated in the public sector and men in the private sector.

The case of Erstwhile Communist States

Under communist rule, Eastern European countries and the former Soviet Union set quotas as for women in local management. Women remained highly underrepresented in more senior and national positions, however. In the former Yugoslavia, for example, opportunities for women managers depended on the political interests of the Communist Party. Women's chances for promotion were best during periods of economic growth and political calm. When political unrest was greatest, the proportion of women promoted into and within management dropped. In Poland, since women rarely filled managerial positions in state enterprises, few now have enough experience to draw upon for managing in the new market-oriented economy. The large women's organizations in a few former communist countries, such as Poland and Russia, operated essentially as extensions of the Communist Party. As such, they served primarily a social control function for the Party rather than an-advocacy role for women. Countries recently freed from communist rule are experiencing a backlash against many of the policies that were supportive of women's employment, professional advancement and general freedoms.

Other countries, such as India, Singapore, Malaysia, Indonesia and Zimbabwe, have only recently emerged from extended periods of colonial rule. Colonialism's impact on women differed in important ways from its impact on men. For example, in colonial Indonesia, the Dutch recruited upper-class men for roles in the civil service, and reinforced women's exclusion from public life. In

Zimbabwe, where white men control the private business sector and black men control family life, black women continue to face a double challenge both as women and as blacks, a challenge also faced by women in South Africa. In most post-colonial countries, women participated in the struggle for liberation. Some later became members of their country's new government, thus providing role models for other women. Because they were brought into government positions by these unusual circumstances, however, the token women leaders did not necessarily become harbingers for succeeding women's continued involvement in the centres of economic or political power. More commonly, these women emerged as exceptions to a pattern that continues to exclude women from power.

Present Position is rather gloomy

In recent years, the proportion of women managers has increased significantly in all countries for which data are available, although at a faster rate in some countries than in others. Yet, the anticipated beakthrough into the centres of organizational power seems even less likely today than it did 20 years ago when Rosalind Loring and Theodora Wells noted in their groundbreaking book, *Breakthrough: Women into Management*, "It's when and how, not if women move up. The groundwork has been laid." This optimism was reflected in many countries, where people believed that the developments that had led to women's entry into the labor force and later their entry into management had unleashed a dynamic that would lead to more nearly equal distribution of women throughout the profession.

Whereas the optimism about women's movement into management appears to have been well-grounded, the optimism about women moving up into the executive suite now appears to have been premature. Conditions that we, like other observers, expected would remove the barriers to women's progress in management left most women well below the glass ceiling, where they could glimpse the executive suite but not quite enter it. Women's increased investment in higher education and greater commitment to management as a career, as well as new equal opportunity legislation and the shortage—or expected shortage—of high quality managers, did not result in a significant breakthrough into the executive suite. Regardless of the proportion of women managers at lower levels, in every country women remain only a tiny action of people in senior positions.

Although there is no systematic research on the few executive women of most nationalities who have succeeded in assuming very senior positions, female executives appear to come from the same societal groups as do male executives. For example, in cultures in which executives are drawn primarily from the upper classes, the few women executives, like their male counterparts, are most likely to come from elite families in which family connections smooth the way for business success. Similarly, in cultures such as Hong Kong, in which the dominant enterprise structure is the family business, senior women, like their male counterparts, are most likely to run their families' businesses. In such cultures, executives view themselves as working in the service of their family. For a woman, however, being an executive in a family business is not necessarily recognized as qualifying her to assume an executive position in a non-family enterprise. For example, in the Malaysian province of Kelantin, where women have traditionally dominated both business activity and family finances, the proportion of women who are promoted into upper-level managerial positions in non-family enterprises and government organizations remains negligible.

Given these patterns, women's promotion into senior positions is related to their access to the channels from which firms recruit executives —channels that tend to be different from those from which firms recruit entry-level managers. Becoming a manager requires the proper credentials, while becoming an executive requires, among other things, belonging to the appropriate networks. For example, in Israel, women's near total exclusion from the senior ranks of the military has deprived them of experiences that firms in the civilian economy consider crucial for managing complex organizations. Because of such exclusion, Israeli women remain unlikely to obtain significantly more powerful positions in the near future. Such definitions of appropriate experience eliminate women from consideration for senior corporate positions in other ways. For example, the requirement of many British firms that candidates for board member positions must have had prior board experience in a public company—which few women have had—eliminates most British women from consideration, and explains, in part, the paucity of women board members in the U.K.

Until recently, a single theme dominated questions about women managers worldwide: the concern for understanding women's under-representation, under-utilization and skewed distribution among the levels of management. Only in the 1990s, has the question of global competitiveness and transnational efficacy begun to transform and complement these equity-based concerns. To appreciate the organizational reality faced by today's women managers worldwide, our understanding of the issues must expand to include the business dynamics of the 1990s and the 21st century. The intensification of global competition has become a major influence compelling firms to view women managers as a competitive advantage rather than as a legislated necessity. Global competition challenges corporations to maximize the effectiveness of their human resources. The opportunity cost of prejudice of rejecting women and limiting selection to men is much higher than in previous economic environments. As A. Fisher wrote in Fortune in 1992, "The best reason for believing that more women will be in charge before long is that in a ferociously competitive global economy, no company can afford to waste valuable brainpower simply because it's wearing a skirt."

The successful performance of growing numbers of women managers offers firms an opportunity to out-perform their more prejudiced competitors by better using women's capabilities. For example, leading management scholars, such as Chris Bartlett, Sumantra Ghoshal and Michael Porter, have identified innovation as a key factor in global competitiveness. An inherent source of innovation is well-managed diversity, including gender diversity. Women bring diversity to transnational corporations whose management has heretofore been primarily male. In addition, today's transnational firms have greater flexibility in hiring women than most of their predecessors have had. For example, whereas domestic and multi-domestic companies hire primarily local nationals, and therefore must closely follow local norms on hiring or not hiring women managers, transnational corporations are not similarly limited. Because the corporate culture of transnational firms is not coincident with the local culture of any particular country, transnationals have greater flexibility in defining selection and promotion criteria that best fit the firm's needs rather than those that most closely mimic the historic patterns of a particular country. Said simply, transnationals can and do hire local women managers even in countries in which the local companies rarely do so. In Japan, for instance, North American firms have led the way in hiring excellent Japanese women, while Japanese firms remain extremely reluctant to hire them.

Similarly, North American transnationals have begun to send women abroad as international managers, thereby benefitting from the greater flexibility that many cultures afford foreign women. Since most countries do not hold foreign women to the same professionally limiting roles that restrict local women, most women expatriate managers have been outstandingly successful in all geographies—Africa, the Americas, Asia, Europe and the Middle East. Additional advantages come from the fit between many women's approaches to management and the structural changes in today's corporations. Whereas firms previously have been characterized by steep hierarchies, today's emerging transnationals are increasingly characterized by flattened networks of equals. Recent research suggests that women work particularly well in such networks. Transnational firms thus see women managers as bringing needed collaborative and participative skills to the workplace.

Actions taken by Transnational Firms

It is in executives' and their companies' best interest to welcome more women into the executive suite. Some leading transnational firms have already accepted this reality and begun to benefit from acting accordingly. They follow a few consistent approaches. For example, in considering North American women managers for international assignments, such companies approach the decision to send women managers abroad in several new ways:

1. The companies do not assume that it will not work. They do not assume that North American women managers on international assignments will be treated the same way that local women are treated. They do not use the presence or absence of local women managers to predict the potential success of foreign women managers. Outside North America, North American women managers are treated as foreigners

who happen to be women, not as women who happen to be foreigners, and are therefore accorded the respect necessary for success.

2. They do not assume that a woman will not want to go abroad. They ask her. Both single and married women need to balance their private and professional lives, and many are very interested in taking international assignments. Moreover, the proportion of North American women interested in working abroad is identical to that of men, and can be predicted to increase over the coming decade.
3. They offer women every opportunity to succeed. They accord a woman full status at the outset, not that of a temporary or experimental expatriate, with the appropriate title to communicate the home office's commitment to her. They are not surprised if local colleagues and clients initially direct their comments to male managers rather than to the new woman international manager during their first meeting with her, and do not accept such behavior. They redirect discussion, where appropriate, to the woman. Such behavior from foreign colleagues should not be interpreted as prejudice, but rather as a reaction to a new, ambiguous and unexpected situation.
4. Companies or flexible benefits packages. Since most benefits packages for international managers have been designed to meet the needs of traditional families (employed husband, non-employed wife and children), transnationals modify benefits packages to meet the needs of international managers who are single—female or male—or in dual-career relationships. Such modifications might include increased lead time in announcing assignments, executive search services for the partner in dual-career couples and payment for "staying connected"—including telephone and airfare expenses—for couples who choose some form of commuting rather than both simultaneously relocating abroad.

Guidelines in Hiring Local Women Managers

In considering hiring local women managers, leading North American companies also follow a few consistent guidelines to increase their chances of success:

1. Companies use the flexibility afforded foreign firms, which need not limit their hiring and promotion practices to those of the local culture. Foreign firms have considerably more flexibility to tailor human resource decisions to those that best fit the firm's needs, including hiring both women and men for managerial and executive positions, even in countries whose local companies hire primarily men.

2. Companies take advantage of the low demand for women managers. They do not limit their selection pool to those people targeted by most other local and foreign firms that is, they do not limit their recruitment to men; they draw from the best people available, including both women and men. Because of the lower demand, it is often easier to attract a top quality woman manager than a top quality man.

3. They do not confuse women managers and executives with women workers. The family and educational background of most potential managerial and executive candidates is completely different from that of most women in a country. They do not use general population characteristics, such as literacy rates, to predict the potential availability of women managers and executives.

4. They offer a working environment that is attractive to women managers and executives. Professional women working outside North America often find different organizational and career characteristics attractive from those valued by North American women. For example, in many parts of the world, highly educated women—those targeted for potential managerial and executive positions—come from upper class families in which they have relatively easy access to household help. Therefore, work-family dilemmas are neither the same as they are for most North American women nor the same as they are for less advantaged local women workers. Offering day-care centres in such environments, for example, might not be as highly valued as it would be in similar North American settings.

Until recently, a single theme dominated questions about women managers worldwide: the concern for understanding women's under-representation, under-utilization and skewed distribution among the levels of management. Now the question of global competitiveness and transnational efficacy has begun to transform and complement these equity-based concerns. To understand the organizational reality faced by today's women managers, our appreciation of the issues must expand to include the business dynamics of the 1990s and the 21st century.

The intensification of global competition has become a major influence compelling firms to view women managers as a competitive advantage rather than as a legislated necessity. Global competition challenges corporations to maximize the effectiveness of their human resources. The successful performance of growing numbers of women managers offers firms an opportunity to outperform their more prejudiced competitors by better using women's capabilities. It is in executives' and their companies' own best interest to welcome more women into the executive suite.

2

Women Enterpreneurs in Business Enterprises: A Global Perspective

In 1997 at the OECD Conference in Paris on "Women Enterpreneurs in small and Medium Enterprises" representatives from forty countries actively participated. Let us briefly highlight on that momentous meeting.

The phenomenal growth of businesses owned by women is not just an American trend. The women are making significant contributions to their national economies as well as to the world's. The White House invited 22 American women, representing a cross-section of businesses, government and women's organizations. NAFE, along with other women's organizations, was asked to help assess the role of associations in supporting women in business.

"It's exciting to see how much is happening globally for women. Women's associations could play an important role in supporting the growth of woman-owned businesses if they can find ways to pool their resources," said Barbara Weller, head of strategic planning and product development for NAFE. In her view, "Affordable technology is creating incredible opportunities for women everywhere, allowing them to build businesses in record time on a worldwide scale. They will need a tremendous amount of support, mentoring and encouragement."

In her speech to the Paris delegation, Louise Guay, president of Canada-based Public Technologies Multimedia, Inc., predicted that technology will play an important role for woman-owned businesses in the next millennium: "The future economy will look like a mosaic where traditional, artistic and digital economies will reappear in the virtual community... Women's businesses and their invisible power have a future here that can propel them on to new horizons."

To help honor Nafe's 25 Years as the leading membership association for businesswomen, we wanted to recap some of the best tips we've learned that have made NAFE members the best networkers ever! At the dawn of the 21st century effective and caring networking plays an immense role in our success. Sophisticated networkers want to brush up on the tools that have become second nature, or want new ideas to bring their networking to a new level. And new networkers seek the basics, and the reassurance that their first forays will pay off. Here are some networking tips—NAFE style:

Building a solid foundation

Understand How Networking Works

The concept of networking is simple: It is planning and making contacts and sharing information for professional and personal gain. The key words in that definition are planning and personal. Networking doesn't just happen, and quality networking happens only when supportive relationships, as well as business contacts, are built.

Networking is a 24-hour process that's about giving as well as getting. You can't expect to attend one network meeting every six months and get results. You must always be on the lookout for people you can include in your network, and whose networks you can join. Understand that you may not benefit immediately. It may take years to see results. Then again, you may get a phone call overnight.

It's best to constantly work at building your network, even when things are going well. Avoid networking only when you're in crisis—you want your network in place before you suddenly lose your job or have to take a transfer to a new town. Keeping your network intact means you won't have to scramble for a support system; it will be there for you.

Set Your Goals

Decide who you want in your network and how you will contact them. Some people prefer making telephone calls to writing letters; others feel just the opposite. Try doing what makes you most uncomfortable. After all, networking is about pushing yourself forward and learning new skills. Also decide how your "networking rendezvous" will take place. Over coffee, at lunch, at someone's place of business, or over the telephone? Maybe vou'll concentrate on joining organizations and attending meetings.

Plan Your Strategy

Make lists of names. Go through your Rolodex and list the people with whom you haven't talked in six months. Perhaps you want to reconnect with people from more than a year ago; list them. And don't forget to make cold calls. Maybe you've read articles about "stars" in your profession or friends have told you about wonderful speakers or authors they've heard. Many of these people could be included in your network. List them, too.

Take Action

Set a timetable to achieve your goals; perhaps you can aim for one cold call, one lunch and two reconnecting calls a week. Create a computer or paper file or notebook to record who you've called and what the outcome or response was. Stick to your schedule to stay on track. Read over your responses from time to time. You'll be surprised and encouraged by how many contacts you are making.

It helps to set aside a special networking time, such as 3 to 5 PM on Thursdays, if your work schedule allows. Quiet Sunday evenings at home can be good times for telephone networking, often the only way to make long-distance contacts. If you put yourself on a mental schedule, you're more likely to really make those contacts. When attending meetings, set goals to meet a certain number of people or leave with a certain number of business cards. Then, do it!

Overcoming networking Jitters

Prepare

The first few dreaded minutes of a networking meeting can work for you with some preparation. Before arriving, find out as much as you can about the agenda and organization. It's a good idea to make contact with someone at group headquarters beforehand and request a brochure. Ask a question about the speaker or the length or the program, for example. This way, you will have forged a connection and will have a friendly face to look for when you arrive.

Psyche Yourself Up

Your attitude is your most important asset. Refocus your preoccupation with your own anxieties by thinking about the other attendees. Pretend you're having a party and concentrate on helping others have a good time. Don't think of the people at the event as a mass entity (you'll be overwhelmed) but as individuals whom you can meet one-on-one. Rehearse what you'll say.

Talk Small

Have at least three "small talk" questions in mind that will serve as conversation openers. ("How did you find out about the meeting tonight?" "What do you enjoy most about your job?") Ask open-ended questions that draw people out, then turn their answers into two-way conversations.

Seek Opportunities to Meet People

Don't wait until you actually walk into the meeting room to begin networking. If you arrive at the meeting place by car and notice a group of women in the parking lot, take the opportunity to strike up a conversation. "Are you going to the women's networking meeting?" "Did you run into that traffic on the freeway?" Whether you are in the elevator, the ladies room or waiting at the bar, start talking.

Use Your Name Tag to Your Advantage.

Attach your name tag to your right lapel. This way, when you extend your hand to meet someone, the person's eye moves easily to your name tag. Make sure the name tag itself is not only easy to read but stands out.

When you meet someone new, use her name tag to establish common ground and strike up a conversation. Comments such as "My sister's name is Eileen, too," or "I went to high school in that town" can do wonders for opening the lines of communication.

Find Kindred Spirits

Making eye contact is one of the most crucial tools for successful mingling. When you are seeking out people to talk with, scan the reception area for eye contact and friendly smiles. A person who averts her eyes and turns her head will not be easily approachable.

Also, seek out people who are by themselves. Instead of going up to a group of five people gathered around the bar laughing, find someone on equal footing—standing alone, looking like she would be appreciative if you approached her.

Seat Yourself Strategically

If seats are not assigned at the event you are attending use this opportunity to meet new people. Do not approach a round table where nine people are seated and there is one empty seat left. The group will already be engaged in conversation and may not notice your arrival. But if you approach a table where few people are seated, you'll find them eager (and grateful) to welcome you.

Maintaining your network

Be Organized

All your contacts won't do you any good unless you organize them. Think about how all this information will be most helpful to you. Many people use a multiple Rolodex system. The one on top of your desk is for current, frequently used contacts. A second business-card file is for the names of people you want access to, but know you won't be speaking with more than every few months. An optional third file can be for the "old-timers," people you haven't contacted in a year or more.

You can also organize your network on color-coded or alphabetized index cards as well as special computer software developed for this purpose, categorizing your contacts and keeping track of the calls you make to each. Give your network a checkup of least once a year. Weed out and reorganize, keeping your list of active contacts close at hand. Don't discard old contacts—you never know when you (or someone you know) may want to reconnect with them.

Caring for your contacts

Foster a Giving Attitude

Remember, nobody likes a loser, or a taker. Call contacts every few months to say hello and to offer your help. For most people, a no-strings-attached phone call from a colleague will be a pleasant surprise. Genuine concern and support showed to others will pay off when you need help.

Remember the Little Things

Send colleagues copies of newspaper and magazine articles that you think will interest them. Include a short handwritten note that can be as simple as "FYI" or "Thought you'd like to read this." If the article relates to your mutual profession, this will raise your professional credibility because it shows that you keep abreast of industry happenings.

Enhance Your Connections

Put your contacts on the mailing list for your company's publications. You'll cement your connections and may even provide useful information. This could also lead to new business opportunities for your firm.

Broaden Your Scope

Refer executive recruiters to qualified people within your network if you aren't interested in certain jobs. Your contacts (and the recruiters) will appreciate—and remember—such generosity.

Practicing network etiquette

Always Respect Your Contacts Names

Get an OK before you use a person's name as a referral to get to someone else. If you don't, it will surely backfire and the person will hesitate to ever help you again.

Keep an Eye on the Clock

Make sure you call people at appropriate times that are convenient for them. Don't wake someone at midnight just to "touch base." Always check that the person has several minutes to talk to you before you start your conversation.

Follow Through on Your Promises

If someone asks for a copy of an article you've mentioned, jot that request on the back of her business card and send her the article within ten working days (the sooner the better!). If you offer to give someone a phone number, make sure you get it to her.

Even if you haven't made specific commitments to your contacts, communicate to stay visible. Send them cards at holiday time, ask them to lunch "for no reason at all," and remember birthdays. Think of creative ways to keep in touch.

Thank Everyone Who Helps You

At any given meeting, you're bound to come away with at least three ideas or tips. Thank the people who offered them, with a one-minute phone call or a brief handwritten note Its wise to thank people for leads even if their suggestions do not pan out; your contacts will appreciate the follow-up.

Remember: Networking is a challenge

Always push yourself. Approach new people at meetings and start a conversation. Taking the initiative does pay off. Whether you're a novice or an expert, you get only as much out of networking as you put into it!

Catalyst, the nonprofit research and business advisory organization I which works to advance women, has launched the first large-scale, national research project to examine the career mobility of women of color in corporations. I Catalyst invited NAFE members of color to participate in the study. They were seeking, women of Asian/Pacific Islander, Black/African and Hispanic descent currently working for large corporations to help them learn what women of color think about their career opportunities in American companies. They raised some querries like these. What are the success factors and barriers that affect career mobility? Are diversity programs effective? Do women of color camouflage their cultural identity to succeed in the corporate world? Based on their findings, Catalyst has develop strategies for companies to improve the recruitment, retention and advancement of women of color. Results were released in later 1998.

3

Challenges and Remedies for Women Executives

Men have power in organizations that women often lack. Male power is a feature of the society in which we live, as well as the organizations in which we work, and the interpersonal encounters that happen there. Owing to power relations that differentiate society at large, women's work experience is different from that of men. During the last 20 years in Britain, the number of women employees has grown; there has been a 2.8 million fall in the number of men, and a two million rise in the number of women who work. One might think that, as more women have entered the labour force, they have gained more positions of power. But, as the numbers increase, the proportion of women in positions of power has decreased. There was, for example, a drop of 3.5 per cent of women in senior management 1975 and 1984. There are around three million managers in Britain, but only about one-fifth are women.

Job Segregation

Looking generally at men's and women's employment it is clear that there are enormous differences in the types of job which women and men do, the pay they receive, the hours they work, the skills they acquire and their patterns of employment. Women's work is almost always lower paid, lacks a craft tradition, has weaker trade union organization and is of unskilled status. The work is often deemed inferior because women do it. All these differences help to contribute towards women's lack of power in employment. Women are segregated into jobs that are sex-typed "women's jobs". Men's and women's jobs are "horizontally" segregated. Women most commonly work in different types of occupation. For example, where women predominate in occupations such as data preparation and as chambermaids, men are computer operators and kitchen porters. It is usually the case that male jobs are ranked higher than female jobs. There are clear distinctions between men's and women's work.

Men's and women's work is also differentiated by "vertical segregation". Men are usually working in higher grade occupations and women in lower grades. This happens even in occupations where women predominate, for example in nursing. In 1986 it was found that 9 per cent of nurses were men, but they held 45 per cent of the top nursing jobs. Women make up only about 2 per cent of management. In manual employment they are under-represented in the ranks of skilled but increasingly segregated into semi-and unskilled work like packing and light assembly. Segregation is maintained either by differential recruitment or by confining women to lower grades. Segregation has in some respects increased in the last two decades.

Part-time working tends to be sex-typed. Part-time jobs are seen as 'women's jobs"; 42 per cent of women employed work part time, the number of part-time jobs having expanded. Women do not necessarily prefer part-time work. For many it is a matter of compelled circumstance, not a matter of preference. Some women do two part-time jobs; the number of women with second jobs doubled between 1983 and 1988, suggesting that women want, or need, more paid work hours. As a result of increases in part-time and low-paid jobs only a minority of women earn enough to enjoy full economic independence and many women do not earn sufficient wages to keep their families above the poverty level.

Barriers to women's progress

Women face a number of barriers to their progress in organizations, and to the gaining of power. The first barrier is the role women have been socialized to adopt, that is, passive. Women's paid work is regarded as marginal and temporary and is inextricably linked to women's unpaid work in the household. There is a set of "rules" that militate against women in organizations. The second is lack of support including limited financial resources, education and training, lack of childcare arrangements, networks, role models, mentors and domestic constraints. A third barrier is attitudes such as employer biases, negative perceptions of women, sex-segregated jobs, sexual harassment and pay inequalities. Further. subconscious barriers could emerge in stereotyping and attribution of female behaviour and use of language. Women may be reluctant, or sometimes ambivalent, about achieving power in an organization. Both men and women help to maintain these barriers to women's progress. Each of these sets of barriers are intertwined and interlinked.

The attitudes that differentiate men and women, and lead to differing socialization, develop at a very early stage. Traditional stereotyping starts from the moment of birth because the child is handled differently according to whether the child is a boy or a girl. Childhood socialization and the games children play may have a consequence for women's failure to notice the informal power network, take part in power struggles and create alliances. Socialization shapes individual work expectations, for example, what kind of jobs are accessible, and also other priorities in life, such as the importance of family.

The very latest research reflects the effects of parents' traditional sex-role attitudes; despite girls and boys having the same school grades and being scored similarly in maths tests, parents of girls express less confidence in their child's competence compared with the parents of boys. In fact studies of school grades show that girls do better in maths as well as other subjects. This undervaluation of women's capabilities limits women's career choices so that they develop their abilities only in sex-appropriate areas by choosing arts subjects instead of maths or computing. This leads women into low-paid jobs like nursing or teaching.

Teachers too have a role to play in gender socialization. Many studies show that teachers perceive pupils differently according to their gender. A study by Stanworth showed that teachers are more pre-occupied with and concerned about boys than girls. Boys' futures were seen as involving more responsibility and jobs with authority, such as managers. This was the case even when boys had less success in school. For girls, teachers offered only stereotyped occupations, like nurse or secretary, in spite of the fact that these occupational predictions did not match girls' success in school. This extra attention towards boys leads males to develop better self-esteem and to be more individualistic and authoritative, which in turn can make boys seek more responsible work in the future. In other words, teachers can transfer their own ideas about sex-role stereotypes to their pupils. In future, girls without positive encouragement might not perceive themselves as being as competent as males to work as managers.

The barriers to women's power are maintained because of the restricted choices facing school leavers. Career choices made by women reflect traditional stereotyping and the tendency to be narrower. One survey showed that 7 per cent of girls chose jobs in three groupings — clerical, nursing and selling occupations while the same proportion of boys had jobs in seven groupings. It would be difficult to argue that men and women are exercising free choice when jobs are so sex-typed. Free choice is not so free when it is made in an environment in which tradition dictates what employment is appropriate for men and women or where jobs have become labelled as men's or women's jobs.

It is often assumed that women lack power because they lack qualifications. Women leaving school have comparable, if not better, qualifications than men and have almost equal levels of participation in universities and the labour force. There is evidence to show that more women managers have degree-level qualifications than men but only achieve similar status positions. Women, however, fail to obtain the specific occupational and professional qualifications needed for progress. This can be because they are actively discouraged from taking exams. Then, within the professions, women fail to reach the profession's ruling elites.

The problems facing women managers have been well documented. Women are confronted by a "glass ceiling" when it comes to entering positions of power in senior executive levels and government. The glass ceiling may seem to be invisible but it is a real barrier for women when they vie for promotion to top jobs. Of what does this glass ceiling consist? Are men or women, or both, to blame for its existence? One in three female directors blames male attitudes for poor opportunities for women in business. Scottish business women are documented as saying that male chauvinism is the main obstacle but low self-esteem and lack of confidence are also strong contributing factors to slow female advancement. Women's progress is slowed because their companies force them to perform to higher standards than men. Women are expected to have more strengths and fewer faults than their male counterparts.

It is also clear that the attributes of male and female managers are perceived as different.

Negative perceptions of Women

The majority of managers are men and judgements about effective management tend to be based on an adherence to a masculine gender stereotype. It is assumed that women's domestic commitments will take precedence. This assumption leads to prejudice against them, detracts from the notion that-women can be committed professionals, and damages promotion prospects. Almost half of men in one survey said they believed mothers should not work. If women do choose a career in management they have to make a total long-term commitment in which family responsibilities are subordinated. A survey by Gold and Pringle of women managers shows that this is the case and that work was central to their lives; any interruptions to work were mostly of short duration.

There is, however a myth of pregnancy in the minds of employers; the myth is the belief that women will leave to have babies and that wastage due to the pregnancy is greater than any other reason, yet pregnancy was not found to be the main cause of wastage. Mothers are not less committed to their work and careers than fathers. In fact some employers have found that women are more committed to work than men. One explanation is that women have fewer opportunities to move jobs and so tend to become restricted. Other research shows that women managers are more committed to their careers, as opposed to family or home lives, than male managers with equivalent ages, salaries, education and managerial levels. The myth of lack of commitment may have come about because men do not want to accept women into management posts.

Many women managers feel that their male colleagues create stress for them and seem to be threatened by them. There is a masculine consciousness, which feels threatened and so often they exclude women from their social interactions. Some men feel particularly threatened because they think their organizations are increasingly promoting a few women as "tokens". One might assume that, as the proportion of women increases in an organization, the sex bias and "threatened male colleague" syndrome decreases. But, while there is high resistance from male managers at first, then a rapid decrease in resistance, there is a rapid increase again when the proportion of women becomes large enough to be powerful and threatening.

The rules that militate Against Women

Ultimately the "rules" of organizations militate against women (e.g. women are not employed in that job; women have a certain set of skills associated with caring and dexterity; men would not want to do that kind of work: we don't want to hire and train a woman for that job as she might become pregnant. These rules reflect the social worth of women in ways that reproduce and maintain those values. Organizations segment opportunity structures and job markets in ways which enable men to achieve positions of power and prestige more easily than women. These rules, the way they are structured and maintained, have a profound impact on the way we come to view ourselves, our identity and our sense of self.

Stereotyping of men and women is one of the social processes taking place of which we have little awareness. Women are seen to be different from men and are often evaluated less favourably. As we have so little awareness of the extent to which sex stereotypes influence our evaluations of others, we have little opportunity to challenge these beliefs because they are both unrecognized and universally shared. As long as women are seen as having different capabilities from men, and this is not questioned, women will remain typecast and disadvantaged.

Here is an example of how the "rules" and stereotyping operate in recruitment. A study on recruitment to fill 101 job vacancies in the North-East of England in retail sales and clerical work showed that the "personal qualities" of the candidate were most important (for example, common sense, confidence, liveliness). These qualities are not amenable to measurement and are totally dependent on the subjective judgement of the interviewer. Almost half the employers indicated that gender was a significant element in their requirements and preferences. Fourteen per cent wanted to appoint men while 33 per cent wanted to appoint women. About half of those who wanted to appoint women identified the job as a "woman's job", as the job was of low status, unworthy of a man and, therefore, suitable for a woman. A number of respondents regarded women as having particular aptitudes for meticulous clerical work and as having "feminine skills" of gentle persuasion, physical attractiveness or in fostering a co-operative and non-threatening atmosphere.

Other research has demonstrated clear bias against women in personnel decisions related to promotion, development and supervision. In general women are seen as being warm, kind, emotional, gentle, understanding, aware of others" feelings and helpful to others where men are aggressive, forceful, strong, rational, self-confident, competitive and independent. Women and men appear to be remarkably similar, in the extent to which they see men and women as different, yet have little awareness of the extent to which these stereotypes influence our evaluations of others. The female traits are less valued so women are denied the developmental tasks, which could have helped in their promotion. As a result, they are excluded from the organization's power network.

Women's chances of success are likely to be less than those of men because of stereotyping. Women are often evaluated as less acceptable candidates for stimulating, challenging jobs and are not perceived as having the necessary attributes for success in high status positions within their organizations. There are some excellent views in the literature on the devaluation of women's competence (see, for example). Lott concludes that the tendency to devalue a competent woman is the rule rather than the exception. If we accept that women are being evaluated less favourably than men, then we understand why so few women are selected for middle and senior management posts and why so few women have power in organizations. The recruitment and selection process is social and subjective and, therefore, open to bias against women. Collinson found that a lot of informal recruitment was used which favoured male applicants.

There is no shortage of examples of how professional groups, and the "rules" they generate, can protect the power and influence of men so that men dominate. They can be found in medicine, management, the civil service, insurance, television, teaching, law and others.

The language of power

Women have learned gender roles. Differences in men's and women's behaviour come about as they are playing out gender roles, roles where men have more power. These differences are reflected in our language. Women's language has been characterized as lacking forcefulness; women demonstrate politeness and uncertainty using, for example, tag questions (statements with little questions on the end as in "It's a nice day, isn't it"). People expect women to use tags. Tag questions are not used because the speaker is unsure of herself, or does not know the answer, but to facilitate communication. Yet it can be interpreted as avoiding conflict, being weak. It weakens women's image, but not men's. Further, women speak more tentatively than men only when they speak with men. With men they offer more disclaimers ("I'm no expert", "I may be wrong"). Using tentative language makes men listen; men are more influenced by women who speak tentatively, so it is no wonder that they do.

A study on the right to speak shows that men use a set of "devices", apparently with women's consent, to maintain male control of topics of conversation. Men tend, for example, to complete women's sentences, give minimal responses to topics initiated by women and interrupt without being sanctioned. Women also get the "shit work" in conversations, feeding men lines, drawing them out, responding to topics that men determine and acting as an audience. Women are, then, less powerful in conversations.

If gaining power means advancing yourself and controlling or limiting the power of others, then this does not fit with how women see themselves. The stereotypical base of women's power is "relational". Relational power is concerned with taking care, being supportive and facilitative. This is socially acceptable behaviour for women and does not fit easily with what might be defined as powerful behaviour. Women who have reached the higher echelons of management have used particular strategies in behaviour management to get there. They have to blend in with the organizational culture, trying to be feminine but business-like and showing stereotypical male characteristics of rationality and instrumentality.

The primacy of women's domestic role

Structural constraints prevent women from pursuing the uninterrupted career often necessary for achievement of long term success. Combining family responsibilities with young children is difficult, especially owing to lack of adequate child care in the UK. Despite the increasing proportion of female employment in the UK, the level of child care facilities for children under three years old is very low; only 2 per cent of UK children use local authority day nurseries. Similar facilities are available in France for 20 per cent and in Denmark 48 per cent. Furthermore, for slightly older children in France, nursery education is available on a full-time basis for 95 per cent of them, contrary to the UK in which only a quarter of three-and four-year-olds take part in nursery education, mainly on a part-time basis.

Women's lives involve trade-offs between home and work. Obviously lack of child care facilities is not the only problem faced by working women. The dilemma arises also from childhood illnesses. Two-thirds of children had consulted a doctor at least once a year; 21 per cent had seen a doctor once, 14 per cent twice, 9 per cent three times and 20 per cent more than three times. Keeping in mind that a family often has more than one child and up to 90 per cent of minor illnesses are treated at home by mothers; mothers have exceptional responsibility. Only a small minority of fathers took time off from work. The responsibility for a sick child was left to the mother, which reflects traditional sex-role attitudes.

Approaches to helping women in their carreers

What are the implications of this inquiry? Few women get far in business despite celebrated and rare examples. That is not just their loss, but a loss to companies. As we have seen, women meet enormous conscious and unconscious barriers hindering them from advancing in management positions. More fundamentally, women have less power than men.

What should women, men and organizations do in order to get more women managers and balance the skewed power structure? The rest of this article will focus on what approaches could be taken by women, organizations and governments in order to facilitate women's way to the top.

Equal parenting and responsibilities could help women in their career development. The ultimate goal for women is to break the glass ceiling which requires first, improving institutional arrangements — child care arrangements, flexible working hours and family leave. Many companies now offer alternative work arrangements, such as job sharing, flexitime and part-time work. Such practices can facilitate women's career advancement. Equal parenting and division of housework constitute the key issues, which must be addressed if the conditions are to be created in which women and men have equal power relations. As we move towards the next decade, there should be a growing awareness that the fundamental issue is not changes in the respective roles of men and women but the nature of the relationship between work and family life.

Legislation is one route to change perhaps the most disturbing structural barrier — job segregation — but achieving equality that way seems to be a dream. Evaluating jobs on the basis of comparable worth should be a more beneficial way of achieving equality. Work should be valued and rewarded according to the actual skill and abilities required regardless of gender. Work done by women should not be paid less than equivalent work done by men. The other important structural barrier emerges in the selection process. Therefore, recruitment practices should be monitored and made more consistent and equitable. Abolishing structural barriers is not, by itself, sufficient to effect changes in social attitudes. Positive action towards women is needed. Change does not happen in a social vacuum. Structural and attitudinal barriers need to be attacked together. We will discuss next what could be done with the attitudinal barriers which women face.

Why focus on the attitudinal barriers?

Are attitudes concerning the roles of men and women changing? Despite the Equal Opportunities Act 1975, which outlawed most forms of occupational discrimination, few real changes have taken place to improve women's career prospects in the UK. Traditional sex-role thinking still exists. Legislation cannot by itself change the embedded power structure of organizations in which women are in a subordinate position. What is really needed is a fundamental change in attitude towards women and employment. Studies of work attitudes show that employment experience influences attitudes and vice versa. For example, as women gained work experience, they tended to have less traditional attitudes towards women's roles. Further, males with experience of female managers have more favourable attitudes towards them than men without such an experience. However, women's work experiences are flavoured by the sex segregation of labour markets. This pattern produce typical stereotyping in which some jobs are accepted to be designed mainly for female or for male. Hackett and Betz stated that, mainly owing to socialization experiences, women lack strong expectations and fail to understand fully their capabilities and talent in career pursuits.

Positive action is required in schools to encourage girls to pursue nontraditional career paths. Further awareness of the problems arising from sex-stereotyping at an early age is needed. However, changes have been slow. By way of example, the proportion of female applicants for undergraduate-level computer science courses dropped from 28 per cent in 1976 to 13 per cent in 1986. Why does new technology like computers conform to traditional sex-role division, being seen as a more masculine domain? Wajcman claimed that the trend seems to be geared to traditional sex-role stereotyping in, which computers are linked in school to science and maths, traditionally male subjects. These attitudes would have to change. However, mentors could provide women with much-needed encouragement to enter masculine domains.

Why do women need mentoring?

Educating people about stereotyping can help women in the short term, but more fundamental change is needed to alter power structures. It is argued that because men have more social power, women have become the "out group". Group studies show that in group members favour in groups (men) over out groups (women). Therefore, through mentoring, women could have access to the "in group" or women could create their own groupings.

White et al. found that successful women did have a promotion strategy, which involved the use of an informal network and an active approach. Women's lack of advancement to high levels has been said to be a result of not having access to inside information.

Having a mentor significantly affects individuals' perceptions of power in organizations and women could have acquired more power in those organizations through mentoring.

Mentors are usually higher-level managers who encourage, guide, support and facilitate a junior executive/protégé career advancement. They could be a key for women to advance in their careers. Most top female executives have had mentors who were vital to their success. Mentoring received by women could lead them to experience less discrimination and speed up women's careers. Noe suggests that mentors are important in helping women to understand the realities of the male dominated business culture. Mentors are essential for introducing women to the formal network of power relations in the organization. Through mentoring women would have better access to power networks and could receive more promotion. Dreher and Ash found that employees with mentors have more promotions and higher incomes. However, women experience difficulties in entering the "old boy networks".

Raggins et al. suggested mentoring may give women better access to these information channels. Further, women could create their own power networks. Bronstein et al. investigated psychologists' academic jobs in the USA. They found a hint of this "old girls network" pattern emerged; the greater proportion of recommendation letters were written by women to women and praise and support were higher than in cross-sex recommendation letters. White et al., however, studied successful women managers and felt that a mentor was a sign of weakness because it showed stereotypical dependency on the part of the female protege. Women experience more barriers in achieving a mentoring relationship. Role expectations may lead women to be more passive in starting such relationships, and men to take a more aggressive role, which speeds up their advancement through the mentoring relationship. Therefore, women need to take a more active role to initiate such a relationship. Women have less access to informal and formal opportunities for developing mentoring relationships. In practical terms, women do not go to men's clubs or participate in sport with male groups. Cross-sex mentoring may produce jealousy and gossip. One way to get round these problems is same-sex mentoring.

An alternative to mentoring : peer mentoring

Mentoring can emerge among co-workers; this is called peer mentoring. It is also called "network mentoring". Peers play the roles of mentors, depending on their level of expertise. This type of mentoring is not power oriented and hierarchical as a typical mentoring relationship might be. Therefore, peer mentoring can be a better alternative for women.

According to Haring-Hidore and Paludi in traditional cross-sex mentoring relationships where there is a female protege and a male mentor there is the greatest possibility of exploiting women in terms of sexuality. However, peer mentoring could cover a large proportion of mentoring functions. Peer mentoring as an alternative to the mentoring relationship at managerial level can be problematic. Peer mentoring can function very well at shop floor level in which mentoring may be used as a teaching tool and give psychological support to co-workers. Managers need role modelling and career-related help in order to advance, but peer mentoring might lack these components of mentoring. Mostly, peer mentoring lacks power. Therefore, it could be suggested that combining them could facilitate women's advancement best.

Peer mentoring and mentoring offer partial gateways to power networks, but women have to act against their passive sex-role stereotype in order to go further. Organization theory has neglected gender issues and, as a consequence, critical debates surrounding the importance of female qualities in organizations have been stifled. To address this we have to turn to a selective examination of the importance of feminine and masculine personality traits in organizations.

What could women do to achieve personal power?

Women are seen differently and judged by traditional male standards in the organization. Women are compared with stereotypes of femininity and expected to be supportive and caring. In short, women are seen to be in a subordinate position. Therefore, women could enhance their personal power by adapting the masculine, instrumental behaviour. It is argued that women who have an instrumental personality are assertive; they feel themselves to be more powerful. Morrison et al. studied female senior executives who were regarded as "high flyers". These women clearly demonstrated instrumental personality traits — an ability to manage subordinates, to be aggressive, make hard decisions and say what they think. Female passivity emerges, however, when women managers attribute their success to luck or hard work, which reflects women's stereotypical image of being non-aggressive and waiting to be chosen. Women hold themselves back because they have learned to do so. The ambivalence of women towards power and competition could be confronted through women's groups and assertiveness training. Women may learn helpful strategies on how to be more assertive and deal with their fear of success.

Popular assertiveness training may assist a small minority of women, but there is little evidence that women as a whole lack achievement motivation, fear success or lack instrumental abilities. Therefore, the value of assertiveness training in increasing women's power is perhaps questionable. How helpful is assertiveness training if the assertive woman manager is judged less favourably than the equally assertive male manager? Under valuation of feminine qualities causes negative consequences for women and for whole organizations. Feminine qualities include many superior qualities, for example, collaboration. Collaboration is increasingly valued in the changing work environment. Hierarchical, masculine-based power structures do not meet contemporary demands for flexible and collaborative management. In fact, feminine qualities are the qualities supposed necessary for tomorrow's successful manager.

One basic question in this article has been: What is the best route to achieve more power? The answers can be looked at from many different angles different causes of inequality lead to different ideas about the changes. This article dealt with three different tools structural (laws), individuals (assertiveness training) and inter group (mentoring). These could surmount one of the major barriers for women about which we are most concerned sex-role stereotyping, most of which takes place at an unconscious level. In spite of the fact that stereotyping seems to be an unsolvable puzzle, an increased awareness of the factors leading to stereotyping will reduce barriers facing women entering managerial posts. Fortunately, stereotypical images can change, even if slowly.

The main channel for changing stereotypes is the mass media: TV, magazines, and newspapers. Understanding the determinants affecting our perceptions will reduce questionable personal assessments. This understanding will be a pathway for acquiring a positive and equal stereotype of a woman in the future.

In short, what is required is a fundamental re-examination of asymmetrical power relations, which is a crucial but often neglected factor, which contributes to the reproduction of job segregation. To make equality a reality in organizations it is essential to raise stereotyping to the level of awareness in order to make fundamental changes in values, attitudes and procedures Furthermore, there is a need to monitor recruitment practices, and companies should conduct periodic reviews to assess the impact of strategies designed to reduce job segregation. However, this is not itself sufficient; what should be stressed is the importance of training, mentoring, flexible working patterns, and the provision of child care facilities for all employees.

[illegible]

[illegible] mass media [illegible] large [illegible] ... regulated ... [illegible] ... [illegible] ... take [illegible] ... [illegible] ... [illegible]

4

The Managerial Profession for Women : The Changing Norms

A survey by the Institute of Management in 1994 reveals that, after 20 years of steady growth, the proportion of women managers in the UK has fallen. With increasing numbers of women entering the labour market and many more employers publicly committed to equal opportunities policies, this halt in female progression would appear anomalous and requires explanation. In seeking such an explanation this analysis challenges the assumption implicit in much of the literature on women managers that their failure to progress can be explained solely in terms of the individual behaviour of women and their employers. Instead, it examines the characteristics of organizations in which women make their careers, which are potent factors impeding female advancement. While acknowledging the importance of discriminatory behaviour and prejudice, it also draws attention to the effects of radical organizational change. Such change has wrought havoc with the careers of both men and women in management. This chapter explores some of the consequences of organizational change for women managers through the in-depth analysis of a "typical" case. It reveals that in the organization studied, restructuring in response to a rapidly changing business environment, has profound and often negative consequences for women managers. It explores the complex process by which restructuring and managerial policy and practice eventually combined to undermine the organization's stated intent to expand significantly the number of women in management. It is suggested that in-depth analysis over time is required to understand the complex processes of change and its often unanticipated consequences for management careers.

The discussion starts with a review of research into women managers and identifies a number of organizational factors which could influence their careers. It then moves on to a detailed examination of the research findings, ending with some discussion of the implications of these for the future of women in management.

Explaining women managers' careers: individual and organizational perspectives

Women in the UK have been entering the labour market in increasing numbers. However, while the number of women managers has also risen, it is at a much slower rate and their penetration into management is modest even in those industries, which largely employ women. Where they have been successful in acquiring management positions these are mostly confined to lower and middle management level and few have succeeded in achieving senior management posts. For example, the 1994 Institute of Management survey revealed an overall increase of above 8 per cent in female managers over the last 20 years (from 1.8 per cent in 1974 to 9.5 per cent in 1994). Those at director level, however, increased by less than 2 per cent, from 0.6 per cent to 2.8 per cent, over the same period (Institute of Management, 1994).

There is a growing literature, which attempts to explain women's under-representation in management. For example, a variety of research has shown that women's career paths are different from those of men. Women have made careers in marketing, personnel, administration and advertising, rather than general management or the specialist areas, which offer the best opportunities for progress (Evetts, 1993; Nicholson and West, 1988). Prejudice against women has been found in recruitment and selection procedures (Motram, 1987), promotion and appraisal processes (Alimo-Metcalfe, 1994) and in their less favourable access to career development opportunities (Jackson and Hirsh, 1991). The attitudes and behaviour of the women themselves, their family roles (Cooper and Davidson, 1984; White et al., 1992) and even their speech patterns (Schick-Case, 1994) have also been cited as a problem.

Academic writing and research attempt to explain women's under-representation therefore focuses mainly on the behaviour of individual women - their career choices, attitudes, family commitments, etc., or the prejudice of their male superiors or colleagues. Their prescriptions for change also follow this individual perspective, concentrating on how management development, career planning and equal opportunities policies can assist women in their careers (see for example, Flanders, 1994). As yet, however, there has been little consideration of the way in which characteristics of the organizations in which they work may facilitate or impede the progress of women in their attempts to enter management. There are some grounds for believing that women find career advancement easier in public sector bureaucracies (Davidson and Cooper, 1992) and some writers have argued that women are more likely to progress in the new leaner and flatter organizations (Cooper and Davidson, 1984). Moreover, a recent large-scale cross-industry survey in the USA (Bum et al., 1994) found significant relationships between the proportion of women in managerial posts and a number of organizational characteristics. The authors conclude that "organizational measures of social structure, resource needs and institutional tendencies" account for almost half of the variation in the percentage of management positions filled by women in the organizations in their sample.

The discussion so far has drawn attention to the need to analyse the effect of organizational context in the study of women managers' careers. This factor would seem particularly salient given the radical organizational change, which has taken place in large numbers of public and private sector companies. Most commercial organizations have undergone significant change in their structure and culture, prompted by business strategies designed to meet the demands of an increasingly competitive market environment. Those in the public sector have not been sheltered from such organizational turbulence. Government policies and resource constraint have dictated a more "business like" or market orientation leading to many of the organizational changes found in the private sector. This change has generally involved a move away from an organization based on functional or divisional hierarchies to one based on strategic business units. The consequences of such restructuring have been a devolution of responsibility accompanied by a significant delayering and downsizing. Middle management have been particularly affected in these lean, flattened and decentralized organizations, experiencing significant changes in their role and a reduction in their career opportunities and job security. The last decade has seen a steady increase in women managers at this middle management level, although as we have noted earlier, the most senior positions have remained stubbornly resistant to female entry.

This raises a question as to whether changes in career conditions as a result of organizational restructuring have gender implications. Does such restructuring provide a route for women through the barriers that hold glass ceilings in place or do glass ceilings remain, but in different places? Are they more or less vulnerable as a result of organizational restructuring? Answers to these questions require systematic analysis of the relationship between these features of organizational change and managerial careers.

A review of current writing on organizational change reveals a wide range of potential effects on women managers careers. These can be broadly divided into five main categories. The first concerns the external and internal market for managerial labour. The second and third are the effect of organizational delayering on managerial roles and on managerial career paths. Fourth is the role of management development processes in assisting managers to adapt to change. Finally, there is the question of the role of equal opportunities policies and practice in mediating the consequences of organizational change.

Changes in the market for managerial labour

Managerial work has grown as a proportion of total employment and the 1980s saw a steady increase in the demand for managers. Where companies experienced difficulty in attracting and retaining high calibre staff they turned to nontraditional candidates as a source of managerial talent. Such a trend might be more pronounced where the rewards offered to managers are uncompetitive (notably in the public sector) and where a strong internal labour market is operating. The increase in the number of well-qualified women entering the labour market during this period also provided an under-utilized pool of potential managers and their entry into management expanded significantly. Their growing presence in the world of work, however, may have had an influence beyond merely providing a "reserve army" to make up for a shortage of male managers. Whereas there may be some reluctance to appoint women to positions of authority over men, a female boss might be considered more appropriate for a predominately female workforce. Blum et al.'s (1994) study confirms this general trend showing a positive association between the percentage of non-management jobs filled by women in companies and the percentage of women in management positions.

The more recent effect of "downsizing" and the loss of managerial jobs is less clear. The most recent Institute of Management survey (Institute of Management, 1994) revealed a decline in the proportion of women managers at almost all levels of management and noted that women were twice as likely as men to resign their positions. However, many down-sized companies have curtailed external recruitment and strengthened their commitment to management development in order to exploit their existing talent. At least one survey has found that women can benefit from such "grow your-own" policies (Blum et al., 1994). Increased dependence on an internal labour market could, *ceteris paribus*, advantage internal women candidates.

A more significant labour market trend reflects factors, which changed the demand for particular kinds of managerial or professional expertise. Most notable of these is a reorientation of companies towards the needs of internal and external customers in response to the increasing competitive environment for private companies, and a government-led imperative for those in the public sector. Where the customer base consists of a large proportion of women, or, where women are thought to possess the kind of interpersonal skills needed to relate to customers, then women managers may find advancement easier. Allied to this growth in the "cult of the customer" is the expansion of a number of specialisms customer relations, advertising and marketing - where women are better represented. Growth in management posts in these areas, therefore, is likely to increase the number of women in management. A further major feature of management in the 1980s was the emphasis on the management of human resources within organizations and growth in employment in the personnel function (Storey, 1992). Personnel is another specialism with higher numbers of women managers.

The growth of a professional specialisms where women have typically made careers, accounts for a significant proportion of the growth in female managers. Any change in the position of these organization specialisms, such as the break up of corporate personnel departments and associated decentralization noted by Storey (1992) and Purcell and Ahlstrand (1994), could have a negative impact on the overall number of women managers.

Changes in managerial roles and styles

The combined effect of decentralization and delayering on middle management roles has been widely commented (Storey, 1992). Dopson and Stuart (1993), for example, found that management jobs had become more generalist with increased responsibilities, a wider range of tasks and a greater span of control and mix of subordinates. They also identified a shift from technical to general skills and an emphasis on managing people. Other writers, e.g. Bowen and Lawler (1992) have argued that successful managers need to replace the "command and control" management style associated with the traditional, large-scale bureaucracy and adopt that of coach, counsellor, team leader and facilitator. A move away from technical expertise to a general one based on a more people-centred approach would appear at first sight to benefit women. Some writers, for example, maintain that women are more concerned with relationships and have better interpersonal skills than men (Marshall, 1984). However, it is uncertain how far managerial selection is made on the basis of these "new" characteristics. Drath (1990), Bowen and Lawler (1992), for example, suggest that managers are still promoted on the basis of individualistic, competitive and assertive behaviour. A point supported by Hirsh and Bevan (1991) who concluded that the employers they surveyed still tended to look for "macho" characteristics in managers and that "managers who are well inclined towards other people are seen as rather cissy!".

Changing career paths

A typical feature of the traditional large-scale bureaucracy was a division between line and staff management. In the past these represented two distinct career paths for managers - general managers who moved between line and staff in a spiral or a "Y" form in order to progress their careers, and support staff who advanced exclusively within their own specialism.

Women have typically made their careers in support functions rather than through the line and, as we have noted above, advancement through these specialist "functional chimneys" may be threatened by organizational restructuring. However, restructuring has also significantly changed career paths for general management. In the large-scale, multi-layered organization, the general managers gained experience by spiralling round the organization through relatively fast and frequent promotions. The path to senior management, in particular, usually entailed geographical mobility, continuity of service and substantial experience of the central function. All these factors put women, especially those with partners and families, at a disadvantage (Nicholson and West, 1988). As we have noted earlier, in flattened organizations middle management roles have become wider and there is often an increased use of project teams. This implies that the broad experience gained by spiralling could now be gathered without recourse to changing jobs and location. Moreover, with the break-up of large central corporate departments and devolution of responsibilities to middle management, it could be argued that the kind of responsibilities and status formerly associated with senior management roles are now relocated in the middle levels of the organization. Thus, it could be that future women managers may be content to remain where they are and the significance of the glass ceiling will have diminished. However, devolution may have its disadvantages. Dopson and Stuart (1993), for example, report an increased workload and longer hours associated with these middle management positions, factors, which are said to deter women with families from seeking senior management posts. Moreover, there is, of course, increased competition for the senior management jobs that remain. How women managers might fare in this new scenario therefore demands clarification.

Management development and career planning

Changes in managerial responsibilities, role and style, suggest a central place for management development in any organizational strategy for change. Career planning also has greater significance in the absence of clearly defined career paths. Furthermore, it could be argued that access to appropriate management development opportunities and career advice may be critical to long-term employment, let alone career advancement, in the more competitive environment of the 1990s.

There is much research evidence that women lose out on access to formal training opportunities (Tharenou et al., 1994). Access to organizationally sponsored training and development schemes and to education opportunities is unequal and, while women are not under-represented at the start of graduate trainee "fast tracks", they are likely to "leak out" as they receive assignments further away from the core business. Fast tracks are also exclusionary for those women who are late entrants to management. Generally, it seems that women are less likely to benefit from formal processes of management development than men (Jackson and Hirsh, 1991). However, most management development is achieved through work experience and it may be that access to a variety of work assignments is more significant for career progression than formal training (Campion et al., 1994).

How successful women managers are in acquiring such appropriate experience in order to survive organizational change has yet to be established.

Equal opportunities policies and organizational change

Finally, there is the question as to how far equal opportunities policies and practice is able to ensure the equal treatment of women at a time of organizational change. One of the main characteristics of organizational change has been a desire to sweep away bureaucratic rules and procedures in order to achieve flexibility and encourage innovation. How far equal opportunities regulation might survive this process is unclear. The break up of strong central personnel departments may also have reduced organizations' capacity to enforce equal opportunities good practice. While their effect may have been considered marginal in the past, these aspects of organizational change would appear to reduce even further the impact of equal opportunities policies on women managers' careers.

The discussion so far has identified a number of organizational factors which could account for the growth in the numbers of women managers in the 1970s and 1980s and a flattening of this trend, or even possible decline, in the 1990s. The trends reported, however, tend to be general and there is little understanding of how these factors interact to affect the careers of women in a specific organizational context. Such an understanding requires a study of particular cases to explore these processes in depth. This analysis reports on one such in-depth case study investigation of a public service utility (PSU) that has experienced substantial restructuring over the past ten years. The case is one in a larger comparative research project examining career outcomes in different organizations.

The case study at PSU

PSU is an example of a male-dominated bureaucracy, which prior to radical restructuring, had few women in managerial positions and none in senior posts. It is typical of many public sector organizations, which have undergone an extensive period of restructuring as aspects of their operations have been successively opened up to market influences.

The information on which the analysis is based is drawn from a variety of sources: employee statistics; internal company documents; interviews with personnel specialists and senior managers. In addition, a matched sample of ten male and ten female senior managers were interviewed in depth in the spring of 1994. The women interviewed constituted two-thirds of female senior managers within the organization. Interviews covered a range of topics related to managerial roles, career experience and managerial career development.

Examining the outcomes of organizational change and restructuring of management appears to be a straight toward exercise involving comparisons before and after change is introduced. However, the task is often made much more difficult by the absence of detailed human resource planning data and by the inevitable changes in job classification and grading systems which take place as companies restructure. However, reliable comparative data were available at PSU from 1990 onwards and, with the help of our interviews, it is possible to identify the impact of restructuring on managerial jobs and the position of women managers over main periods of recent change.

Restructuring at PSU

Restructuring has become a continuous process in large-scale organizations and PSU is no exception to this rule. Despite constant reorganization, until 1988, PSU management still reflected the functional dominance of engineers in an organization characterised by a military culture with a centralized system of command and control. There was a strong internal labour market for managers and less than 5 per cent were recruited externally. Managerial careers were based on seniority and experience within the organization rather than qualifications and most managers had worked their way up from the technical or operative grades. The organization employed very few women, and none were in senior management posts.

In 1988, a major organizational crisis prompted radical changes in organization and management. A programme of resfructuring commenced involving adoption of a policy of responsiveness to customers, delegation of authority, reduction in the chain of command to five levels between the chief executive and the workforce, and broader spans of control for management and supervision. The formerly dominant engineering department was relegated to a servicing role with a glum acceptance on the part of senior engineers "that engineering is not an end in itself - the services our customers buy are the reason for our existence". A newly-created operations department became the central focus of the organization and management was devolved into ten business units operating on a project centre basis. The role of other support functions, finance, personnel, development and marketing, were also enhanced. This period of change saw modest but significant growth in the numbers of women in management and, by 1991, seven had penetrated the glass ceiling into senior management.

The beginning of 1991 saw further radical change with the devolution of significant responsibilities to the business units, including major capital expenditure and the day-to-day operation of engineering and personnel. During this period, the company also experienced a radical downsizing and over one4ifth of the workforce left the organization. However, management continued to grow and women made some modest increases in their representation in management.

PSU typifies many of the changes that have taken place in large-scale public and private organizations in recent years. In the case of PSU, it resulted in a shift in organizational power away from engineering to operations and finance, and has resulted in a major change in management roles as the organization has flattened and responsibilities devolved. It therefore provides a useful site in which to investigate some of the hypothesis concerning the effect of organizational change on women in management discussed at the beginning of this analysis.

Internal labour markets and women managers

The period of restructuring following the 1988 crisis involved a considerable downsizing of the workforce, reducing numbers by 4,045 posts between 1991 and 1993/1994. A government-initiated enquiry into the organization and management of PSU in 1988 had concluded that it was "over-supervised and under-managed". In consequence, while the workforce diminished, management increased both in actual numbers (by 534) and, as a percentage of the workforce. It was therefore a period of significant growth in managerial posts.

Our earlier discussion would suggest that growth in managerial posts, combined with a strong internal labour market and a diminishing pool of male candidates, might, ceteris paribus, increase the organization's dependence on non-traditional sources of labour such as women. There is some evidence to support this proposition at PSU. Also proportion of women managers grew from 7.6 to 9.1 per cent of the total, between 1991 and 1993/94 - a modest increase of 1.5 per cent.

Thus, there was an opening up of opportunities for women during this period and further analysis shows that some had even penetrated the previously impervious layers of senior management. By 1990 there were seven senior female managers and by 1993/1994 their numbers had more than doubled, with one woman joining the directorate. As one of the respondents remarked: "This progress would have been unthinkable prior to 1988". The increase in women as a proportion of senior management over this period was 2.6 per cent, greater than that for women management as a whole. This faster progress at senior levels was attributed by some respondents to the direct personal influence of a chief executive committed to equal opportunities policies. Women, however, still remained a very small proportion of management.

Why then did women fail to capitalize more on the opportunities offered by managerial growth? In our discussion earlier, it was suggested that internal labour markets may benefit women. At PSU, however, it appears that a strong internal labour market, combined with an insufficient pool of females within the organization, conspired to limit women's representation in management.

PSU traditionally operated an internal labour market with managers working their way up the organization from the operational and technical grades. It was, as we have noted, a male-dominated organization. However, there was a steady increase in the number of women, from 9 per cent of employees in 1991 to 12 per cent by 1993/1994, but, as we have seen, this was not matched by a proportionate growth in women managers who increased their representation by only 1.5 per cent. The explanation lies in the fact that in 1990, women only constituted 3 per cent of the supervisory grades from which managers were traditionally drawn, and were particularly under-represented in the operations division where the most significant increase in management took place. It was the view of many of respondents that the supervisor's role, especially in operations where shift work and long hours were endemic, was unattractive to women with caring responsibilities. Furthermore, in a culture where length of service was a major criteria for promotion, few women had sufficient experience at this time to compete for a supervisory post. In many respects the "glass ceiling" in this organization had existed at supervisory level ensuring there were few promotion candidates for managerial posts. Thus, only extensive external recruitment directly into management could have substantially altered the gender balance. In fact, the expansion in management generally was not achieved by open competition, but by upgrading supervisory posts, excluding any possibility of significant change in the proportion of women.

Feminization of the workforce and internal labour markets

The argument that women may find it easier to achieve posts in areas where there are higher proportions of women employees finds some support. It can be seen that women managers constitute a greater proportion of managers in departments with a higher percentage of women employees.

The relationship between these two variables, however, is far from straightforward. Reference to the figures for 1991 to 1993 for the Human Resource Division (H RD), in particular, shows that despite an increase of women staff to almost two-thirds of the total by 1993/1994, the proportion of women who were managers actually fell back from 41 per cent to 25 per cent during this period. In finance, moreover, although just over one half of the staff was female in 1991, only 19 per cent of managers were women. The position had changed marginally by 1993/1994, but women still only constituted 23 per cent of managers in that division.

Career paths and managerial roles

The argument above suggests that the relationship between management growth, the feminization of the workforce and the proportion of women managers is complex. It is clear that these factors alone do not automatically prompt an expansion in women managers. In the case of PSU, the interviews revealed the break-up of the existing power structures and consequent change in career paths following the post-1 988 radical restructuring exercise as a significant factor, especially in relation to senior management posts. This resulted in a redefinition of management roles and the qualities and experience required in order to achieve them. The impact of these redefinitions were different for general management and for specialist management posts, so it is important to examine these two trends separately.

As far as general management posts were concerned, prior to 1988, long experience in the organization, and in the engineering function in particular, was a passport to career success. After 1988, however, as in other "restructured" organizations, the newly-appointed management team emphasized the importance of general management skills, a customer focus and business orientation rather than technical expertise. In the view of one respondent, in the ten key appointments made to head the business units, only four went to managers who under the former system might have expected promotion. The main criterion for selection was, in the reported words of the chief executive, "being a person who can make things happen". In consequence, another respondent explained: "People who under the old regime had their careers paths mapped out for them saw them disappear overnight... it was a very strange time and caused very high stress for everyone - all hierarchical barriers were broken down". The most extraordinary appointment to a business manager's post, was that of woman - an HRD specialist with no direct operational experience, who had worked her way up the organization from a secretarial position. Such an appointment was unprecedented in the history of the organization.

The interviews with senior managers confirmed a continuing trend for engineering experience to be less important from 1990 onwards. When asked what kind of skills were necessary for their current jobs, both men and women managers placed emphasis on the less "masculine" aspects of management - people management, team building, communications, counselling, coaching, etc. However, they also pointed out that there was increased need for negotiating and political skills, financial awareness, stamina and determination. Furthermore, many said that direct engineering or operational experience (of the new central function) remained a prerequisite for a general management post, despite some notable departures from this rule in the 1989-1991 restructuring period. There was a feeling that the more open system experienced since 1988 was closing up. Thus, the degree to which the redefinition of managerial roles made these posts more accessible to women in the organization is therefore questionable, as few had direct operational experience. Nonetheless, there were a number of appointments of external candidates with no previous experience of the industry made on the basis of commercial or service industry expertise. A very few of these appointments were women.

While the skill requirements of a general management post may have made them more accessible to women candidates, other factors also associated with the restructuring were operating against them. All the senior general managers interviewed reported extremely long hours of work and feelings of pressure in the job. There is no doubt that the pressure of work has intensified as a result of devolution, but long hours have always been a characteristic at all levels within the organization stemming from the need to cover shifts. It was official policy to reduce what was often a 12-hour day, six-days-a-week job, but managers were also encouraged to "walk the floor" more often and engage in more direct forms of performance management. Thus any significant reduction in hours was extremely difficult, especially if all shift personnel were to be covered. It is interesting to note that only two of the ten men and one of the ten women managers interviewed had children. One male manager explained that the job was incompatible with family life and that as a single man he could only just manage. These posts, therefore, are unlikely to attract or retain women with family commitments.

Statistics on the exact job destinations of men and women by professional specialism, are not available, but an indication of general trends can be found in the broad divisional classification. General managers were located in the engineering and operations divisions and comprised the majority of managers in the company. The main areas of growth in management was in operations with an overall increase of 549 posts.

It can be seen that despite a loosening in the technical requirements for operations and engineering posts, noted which might have opened entry to female candidates, there was minimal growth in women managers over the 1991-1993 period. In operations, only 5 per cent of managers were women in 1991, growing to 7 per cent by 1993. As one can see this was because expansion in management was achieved by upgrading supervisory posts and there were very few women at this level.

Women at PSU had not benefited significantly from the expansion in general management posts. Their position in the support functions, such as personnel, where women have made most inroads into management, however, might be different. The HRD division was the second fastest area of managerial growth. It was also the area where, at 41 per cent of the function's total, women managers were most strongly represented in 1991. By 1993, however, women's share of management posts had actually fallen to 25 per cent. It seems, therefore, that women failed to capitalize on the opportunities offered by management growth even in the specialist areas where they might be expected to compete most effectively.

This failure cannot be accounted for by a shortage of women in the function. In HRD in 1993/1994 virtually two-thirds of staff in this department were women. Moreover, almost three-quarters of the men in HRD in 1993 wêre managers, the highest ratio of all the divisions, but only one-third of the women. This finding is consistent with the research of Long (1984) and Monks (1993) who also found men to be over-represented at the management level in personnel departments.

The other division where women managers are better represented, 19 per cent of managers in 1991, is finance. Here the regrading process also favoured men, but to a lesser degree.

These findings have bearing on some of the hypotheses about the effect of devolution and delayering on women managers. First, it appears in this case that women are just as disadvantaged when it comes to regrading within a post as they are when they apply for a promotion. Thus internal labour markets do not necessarily lead to an expansion in female managers. This is most obviously the case where there are small proportions of women in the workforce. However, even where they are present in large numbers, they do not automatically benefit from internal recruitment practices. Second, and perhaps more surprising, is the fact that growth in professional specialisms in which women are well qualified and represented does not necessarily increase proportionately the number of women managers in that specialism.

Changes in specialist career paths

Why then did women lose out on the opportunities afforded by managerial growth? In the case of the HRD it would be tempting to adopt Legge's (1987) proposition that there is an inverse relationship between the power of personnel and women's representation within it. The HRD function had become significantly more central to the strategic concerns of the senior management, as had finance, where women also failed to make much headway. However, in order to explore this point further it is important to examine in greater depth the changes that were taking place in professional specialisms within the organization at that time.

The main factor affecting the professional specialist during this period was the break up of central departments and devolution to the local level. This often included integration into the general management team. At the time of the research, this devolution process was almost complete for financial experts and was increasingly affecting central personnel. All of the specialist professional managers interviewed had experienced considerable changes in their job as a result of this trend. However, the experience of devolution may vary for the different specialist functions. For example, the general managers interviewed were all very keen on acquiring financial management skills and saw this as a new and essential component of their job as business managers. Integration into the management team, therefore, may be eased for the financial specialist, as other members of the team perceived this function to be particularly important. As one women financial manager commented: "Sometimes being a woman and financial specialist is a help - people tend to be more polite and disarmed by your technical knowledge".

The experience of those in the personnel function was less positive and many of the women interviewed felt that their contribution to management tended to be overlooked. This was confirmed by the interviews with general managers, who, while they recognized the importance of people management skills, put little emphasis on the formal aspects of personnel management. Women in this specialism, therefore, may be at a double disadvantage in attempting to become integrated into predominantly male general management teams: disadvantaged both as a woman and a personnel professional.

Isolation from other women was felt and the supportive environment provided by a "critical mass" of other professional colleagues missed by those who had been moved out of the central departments. Furthermore, devolution entails adopting the working patterns of the general management team, which as we have seen, involved very long hours. The professional specialists, so placed, found that they were experiencing the pressures of work complained about by the general managers in these posts. As one explained: "The job has broadened enormously, but everything has been added and nothing taken away".

All these factors, therefore, could deter women from seeking these devolved posts in the future. It may also be the case that a narrow expertise does not equip the personnel or other specialists well for taking on these new posts which are perceived as being more strategic and business driven. As one explained: "Now the business unit sets the agenda and formulates policy rather than the centre". Long's (1984) study moreover suggests that in personnel broad organizational experience has always been an advantage and that this was more likely to be gained by men rather than women. As a result, Long suggests male personnel managers tend to be more politically aware and to operate from a broader organizational perspective than women. Devolution therefore may merely be exacerbating a trend that was always present. One consequence of this change in orientation felt by some of the personnel specialists was that general management experience is more appropriate to this kind of post than their own expertise and one pointed out that either a general manager or a specialist personnel person would be equipped for his job. Thus there is a dilution of specialist expertise, and a growing requirement for general management skills in these posts. Such a change in orientation would clearly benefit men who tend to have a wider range of managerial experience rather than women. Few women have the broad general management experience, which might now be considered necessary for the devolved specialist jobs of the future.

Management and career development at PSU

The discussion so far has identified significant changes in managerial roles and career paths as a result of the process of restructuring. Management development and training might be expected to have a central role in assisting managers to adapt to change and in acquiring the broader range of skills and competences required. This significance is enhanced in the case of PSU as it was largely dependent on internal recruitment to feed its managerial expansion. There was a growing emphasis on formal management development processes over the period studied, but the review of the experiences of the managers interviewed showed it to be fragmented and haphazard. There has been some discussion in the literature as to how far women managers can be assisted by formal management development programmes. However, there were no management courses at PSU specifically aimed at women and there was a marginal tendency for men to have had more access to formal management training. As formal training and development have been found to be associated with career success for both men and women, this clearly puts women at a disadvantage (Tharenou et al., 1994). It also confirms Kanter's contention (1977) that women are more likely to miss out on training opportunities where the formal hierarchy is dominated by men.

The assessment center proceedings, which in earlier days focused on selection rather than development, were felt to be a daunting and often dispiriting experience by both men and women - a process unlikely to build up the self-confidence of women managers who often cited this as a problem in advancing their careers. The main advantage of the assessment center, as far as career progression was concerned, was said to be the networking opportunities it afforded and "being visible" to the senior managers who participated. However, this advantage was exclusively mentioned by our male rather than our female respondents.

There was no formal system of mentoring (a system which has been shown to advance both male and female careers (Ragins and Sundstrom, 1989), but most managers had acquired sponsors who had helped them in their careers from time to time. Fast track and graduate management programmes were also useful in this respect, both in providing a broad experience across the organization and by appointing formal mentors. However, only a few graduate and young manager trainees are taken on each year (140 in total for 1990-1993). Furthermore, while just over one-third of these manager traineeships have been female there was a tendency for women to drop out from the programme faster than men. One did not investigate this phenomenon in depth, but the male culture, long hours and the problems of combining work and family life in the organization mentioned above, were quoted by some of the respondents as the most likely causes.

The most significant development activities for all the managers came from the work itself. For line managers a variety of experience in a broad range of engineering or operating positions was important and, for the specialists, attachment to these key functions was often a critical factor. Deputizing for a superior was mentioned, but more significant was secondment to a high profile project, which brought strategic business planning experience and the opportunity to work with key senior managers. It was clear that spiralling around the organization and involvement in projects was not only instrumental to career progression in terms of gaining experience, but also in providing increased visibility and networking opportunities. In the view of several respondents, these latter were particularly important during this period of flexibility in appointments, restructuring and change. A proposition amply supported by other researchers, see, for example, Coe (1992); Kanter (1977); Marshall (1984). However, women have difficulty in establishing networks in predominantly male environments, and the women interviewed also complained that they had to struggle harder than their male colleagues to achieve visibility and avoid being shunted into organizational "backwaters". As broad organizational experience, especially in a central function, was gaining even more significance for entry to management posts, women were finding themselves at an increasing disadvantage.

Formal management and career development processes, therefore, have not been instrumental in the career progression of women managers at PSU. It is the informal processes of job experience, sponsorship and networks, which are more important to advancement in the organization. Research has shown that these processes tend to work to the benefit of men (Coe, 1992; Marshall, 1984).

Equal opportunities at PSU

So far it has been argued that the growth in management posts, the break-up of traditional career paths and a partial redefinition of management roles did provide some, albeit limited, opportunity for the advancement of women into management. This leads to a consideration of the role of equal opportunities policy and practice in the support of female managers.

It was the view of the women interviewed that equal opportunities measures were necessary. Most spontaneously mentioned examples of discrimination and prejudice that they had encountered in their careers. As one explained: "If I were a man it would be different - there is an amazing set of patronizing and condescending men here". Another woman commented: "We are always fighting to establish our credibility and I've seen many women fall along the wayside".

While formal equal opportunities procedures were in place they remained somewhat marginal to the main business. What remains the central personnel department is currently responsible for monitoring of these policies. However, the intended total devolution of responsibility for equal opportunities to the business units could well weaken their implementation. Collinson (1991), Storey (1992) and Purcell and Ahlstrand (1994), all suggest that devolution to local discretion may result in a dilution of policies decided at corporate level and that the loss of a co-ordinating authoritative corporate personnel department, can lead to a weakening of professional personnel standards.

Another potent factor with implications for equal opportunities practice concerns the way in which experience relevant to management posts is gained. In the past this experience was largely gained through frequent promotion - a process subject to equal opportunities regulation. As promotion opportunities diminish, allocation to projects and lateral shifts become the main vehicle for gaining the experience and challenge formerly associated with promotion. In the past such moves, particularly allocation to projects, have been made by invitation and have not been subject to formal equal opportunities procedures or monitoring. If access to such critical developmental experience remain unregulated, women are likely to be even more disadvantaged in their attempts to progress their careers in the future.

The influence of equal opportunities policies on the fate of future women managers at PSU is uncertain. However, there is a good reason for arguing that, in any case, traditional equal opportunity policy and procedures would be ineffective given the major impact of structural changes that are taking place.

Discussion

This discussion has explored the complex processes by which organizational change can impede or support the careers of women managers. The analysis demonstrates how the organizational and cultural change experienced by many large-scale organizations in recent years can provide both opportunities and penalties for women managers.

The investigation at PSU has shown that growth in management jobs, combined with a process of breaking up existing organizational power structures and career paths, opened up some opportunities for women in the period under study. A reduction in emphasis on length of service and engineering experience as criteria for entry into management, and changing definitions of the skills and expertise required for managerial roles, were significant factors in this process. In particular, the relegation of the previously dominant engineering department to a servicing role destroyed its monopoly of the main paths into key management posts. Restructuring also brought significant changes in managerial roles and the skills and experience needed to fulfil them. A loosening of the technical requirements for general management and the inclusion of business and "people management" skills allowed some women to enter these posts in the initial restructuring period. Sponsorship by the chief executive and other senior managers committed to equal opportunities policies also assisted a very small number of women into senior positions formerly exclusively occupied by men.

Despite some gains, the analysis also shows that women's advancement, especially at middle manager levels, was severely limited. It was more modest than the expansion of women in the workforce as a whole, suggesting that feminization alone does not necessarily lead to a proportionate growth in women managers.

Not only was the increase in numbers small, but women had largely failed to establish themselves in the line management posts central to the organization. This is partly because there were very few women employed in these central areas and expansion in management was for the most part the result of upgrading existing staff. Thus, this case study shows that the operation of a strong internal labour market in a male dominated organization excludes the possibility of remedying the gender imbalance through external recruitment.

Women have typically made their careers in the support functions of organizations, often using professional qualifications as a means of progression. A significant finding of the research therefore was the failure of women to capitalize on expansion in the professional specialisms, notably personnel, in which they were most strongly represented. This is directly attributable, at least in part, to the process of decentralization which devolved significant corporate responsibilities to the local level during the research period. Decentralization of central support functions, most notably personnel, to the business units, resulted in a demand for a broader range of skills and general management experience than that normally held by women who had followed highly specialized and narrowly focused careers in the organization.

An additional factor stemming from devolution was the long hours and pressure of work experienced by management and the supervisor grades from which managers were recruited. This made these posts unattractive to men and women with family commitments.

Moreover, while unsocial hours and work overload had always been a feature of general managers' posts, its extension to the support functions is likely to prove a deterrent to some women seeking promotion or joining the organization in the future.

Despite significant changes in career paths, neither men nor women had received systematic assistance with their career planning and development. Delayering and devolution had resulted in changes to both specialist and general management roles and broad organizational experience was found to be essential to career success. However, access to the key developmental experiences - lateral moves, projects and secondment - was gained through sponsorship, networking and "being visible": processes where women have been shown to fare badly.

The research did not investigate discrimination per se, but it no doubt played its part in the women's limited progress. PSU did have equal opportunities policies in place but these lacked teeth and in any case were unlikely to have much effect on the complex processes of exclusion identified above. Moreover, while PSU was attempting to strengthen its equal opportunities policies, devolvement of responsibility for them to the local level where local managers may lack the will, and personnel specialists the authority, to enforce them, may dilute their effect.

Writers on women managers often propose management development, career planning and equal opportunities practice as the primary means by which employers can assist women in their careers. This research suggests that such remedies are unlikely to have much effect in the face of the major barriers posed by much of the organizational change that we have examined.

Conclusion

This study clearly demonstrates that analyses based on individual behaviour and perspectives are unlikely to explain the current under-representation of women in management, or the recently reported drop in their number. Explanations must take into account the organizational context, which can both facilitate and frustrate women's career progression.

The case study at PSU reveals organizational context and restructuring to have important, but conflicting implications for the advancement of women into management. While the break up of existing power structures may open the door to management, other countervailing factors will ensure that only a few women will enter.

PSU typifies much of the organizational restructuring, which has taken place as companies attempt to prosper in an increasingly competitive business environment. In the struggle to survive, the gender implications of such change have hardly been considered. Traditional equal opportunities practice and policy seems unlikely to have teeth in the decentralized, delayered and deregulated organization to which many top executives aspire. However, the unanticipated consequence of change could lead to a loss of the very skills and qualities which many organizations consider essential to their success.

5

Societal Attitude Towards Women Managers

Despite the apparent strides made by professional women in their respective fields, gender discrimination continues to persist the workplace. Research has documented the existence of discrimination against women in terms of the devaluation of their performance and unfavorable attribution to their work as well as its manifestation in selection, placement, salary fixation, and appraisal decisions in organizations. Women often receive lower levels of remuneration compared to men, are less often assigned prestigious and challenging work than men and report greater barriers to gaining mentors at the workplace than men. Their gender is reported as major obstacle to women's advancement in organizations. This indicates the pervasiveness in organizations of gender discrimination or what Harvey (1986) calls a "stigmatized difference" in which women are perceived not merely as being different from but inferior to men.

Understanding Discrimination

Discrimination can be viewed as a differential treatment of people on the basis of ascribed social attributes such as gender and race rather than achieved attributes such as ability and skill. Gender discrimination as a social phenomenon has been studied from a variety of perspectives. In trying to understand discrimination, a key question is: Do men and women indeed differ significantly? The possibility of biological differences leading to differences in personality development has been explored by social psychologists like Eysenck (1957), Garai and Scheinfeld (1968), and Maccoby (1966). In 1974, Maccoby and Jacklin published their comprehensive book, The Psychology of Sex Differences, which led to a reassessment of such differences reported in earlier studies because of problems in measurement, methodology, etc. Later social scientists like Connell (1985) rejected biological determinism as being naive: "Natural difference is a passively-suffered condition, like being subject to gravity. If human life were in its basic structures (including gender) so conditioned, human history would be unthinkable".

In a related approach which Nieva and Gutek (1981) call the individual deficit model, gender differences seen as arising from innate biological factors or early socialization, which is supposed to leave permanent impressions on the individual. Men according to this perspective are viewed as possessing desirable traits in appropriate degrees and deviations from such standards in women represent deficits. Certain supposedly female traits such as being more emotional than men and not being assertive like men are examples of such comparisons using men as reference points. Women's lower positions in organizations are explained in terms of their deficits in motivation, personality development and traits, which make them unsuitable for certain functions such as leadership (Nieva & Gutek, 1981). Research evidence on gender differences in various attributes, particularly leadership, has been mixed. Some studies found evidence to indicate that men and women may have different personality characteristics, which could influence leadership styles (Jacobson & Effertz, 1974; Maier, 1970) whereas other studies reported no such differences (Adams, 1978; Osborn & Vicars, 1976). To make sense of such conflicting findings, Dobbings and Platz (1986) carried out a meta-analytic review of 17 studies examining sex differences in leadership. They found no such differences and in fact proposed a moratorium on research comparing male and female leaders on measures of initiating structure, consideration, and effectiveness. Indeed in many other areas relevant to work such as problem-solving abilities and motivation to manage, men and women appear to be more alike than different (Heilman, 1983).

Another perspective can be called the structural-institutional model. It studies the impact of structural and workplace factor on people. Gender differences in attributes and dispositions are analyzed in terms of social structural factors. For example, the belief that men are more influential and women are more easily influenced is explained in terms of differences arising from status inequalities by which men are more likely than women to have high-status roles (Eagly, 1983). Differences are viewed as stemming largely from the existing distribution of men and women into social roles. Role relationships are hierarchical in nature with men enjoying an overall advantage in power and status (Hartmann, 1981). In the organizational context this status differential is perpetuated in a variety of ways. In fact, the expectations and aspirations of women are reported to be influenced by the attributes of the organizations where they work (Kanter, 1977a): The work structure often offers to women low stimulation and little real opportunity, thus constraining their aspirations and motivations. Women are often consigned to dead-end or peripheral jobs and the sex-structuring of organizations itself suggests discrimination (Bartol, 1978). The distribution of men and women in the organizational hierarchy is another important structural factor. If women are in a small minority at the workplace, it not only influences adversely their feelings and attitudes, but also the way others treat them (Kanter, 1977a). As members of a minority group in male-dominated organizations, women are viewed not as individuals, but as tokens representing their entire category. The token position and visibility associated with it make heavy demands on women for a consistently high and flawless performance. Also their "small minority" status results in the exclusion of women from informal sources of information and networks of alliances; their differences from men are accentuated and their attributes and behavior are distorted to fit the stereotypes. Consequences of such structural factors have been reported to be severely adverse for women (Yoder, 1983).

A related perspective deals with the social expectations of sex-appropriate behavior and can be called the sex-role model. As proposed by Mead and Parsons, different agencies of socialization pass on to their members the social scripts of expected "female" and "male" roles which people learn, internalize, and enact. Such sex-linked role scripts and assignments associate women with family roles (the expressive wife) and men with work-roles (the instrumental husband). Sex-role prescriptions govern a wide range of human behavior, conditioning career-oriented women to opt for traditional work fields—even when overcrowded and monetarily unattractive—to enable women to have enough space for their supposedly major roles of wife and mother. Such expectations make the entry and acceptance of women difficult in areas regarded traditionally as male preserves (Nieva & Gutek, 1981). Moreover, the sex-role expectations are carried over into the workplace where they are irrelevant and inappropriate. As a result of the spillover of expectations of nurturance and passivity from their family to work roles, women, including those professionally-equipped for challenging assignments, are often side-tracked. Expected to provide support to others, women are assigned enabling, "service" roles in which they are required to render assistance to "performing" roles meant usually for men (Bhatnagar, 1988a). Because roles do not offer a comparable opportunity to prove the incumbents' skills and potential, competent women are bypassed by men of similar ability who get a chance to demonstrate it in their "performing roles. Sex-role spillover also occurs for men, but the fallout of such spillover has been found to be more visibly negative for women than for men (Gutek & Cohen, 1987).

Implicit in the above approaches is an assumption that men and women represent two internally homogeneous but mutually dissimilar social categories. The inter group model provides another useful framework for understanding the process of discrimination. Its basic premise is that by virtue of their membership, the perceptions and interactions between men and women get characterized by processes that typically occur within and between groups, which contest for limited resources and rewards. To retain their identity and supremacy, groups emphasize within-group similarities and between-group differences. Negative discrimination against the out group helps in strengthening the solidarity within the group (Tajfel, 1978). Stereotypes further bolster the group identity. Indeed psychologists like All port (1954) viewed stereotypes as a functional part of the process of discrimination which enable individuals to identify a salient feature of a person as member of a group and regard it as the only attribute of consequence for that person, and generalize it to all the other members of the group.

Stereotypes result in labeling or pigeon-holing others in terms of the prominent attribute, despite noticeable within-group differences with regard to that attribute, the presence of other prominent attributes in the group, and in the face of disconfirming evidence. A classic study by Broverman, Vogel, Broverman, Clarkson, and Rosencrantz (1972) showed the existence of strong stereotypes about different characteristics of men and women. The possitively-valued traits for men appeared to form a cluster of related behaviors that entail competence, rationality, and assertiveness; and the positively-value feminine traits formed another cluster reflecting warmth and expressiveness. The stereotype seems to be that the general competence, which is expected on a job is not expected of women. Since the intergroup model shows that the treatment of an individual depends primarily on group membership, individual women, irrespective of their competence level, are treated as though they lack general competence, or what it takes to be successful in a job. Gender, like other visible indicators such as skin color, is treated as a "signal" of the future performance of people aspiring to join an organization (Spence, 1973). Gender stereotypes, as "efficient" aids in decision-making help the male decision-makers in organizations to simplify the complex reality of individual differences. Problems such as overgeneralization, inaccuracy, and inapplicability of gender stereotypes lead to faulty pre-entry and post-entry decisions and discriminatory treatment against women. They are thus disadvantaged "not because of who they are or what they have done but because of what group they belong to" (Heilman, 1983, p.271).

Initiating Change: The Role of Exposure

If discriminatory behavior has to change, the underlying stereotyped attitudes need modification. One way of affecting such changes is through exposure to experiences that are incongruent with the established stereotypes (the book-keeping model in Weber & Crocker, 1983). Such a change can be facilitated if male managers are exposed to experiences with women, which deviate from the stereotype of nonperformance and incompetence.

Exposure can be defined as a condition whereby the stimulus (such as a woman manager) becomes accessible to a person's perception (adapted from Zajonc, 1968). Exposure can range from access to information about the stimulus, and passive observation, to interactions with the stimulus. Some studies, which examine the exposure-attitudes relationship report a positive relation between the two variables (e.g., Johnson, Thomson, & Fríncke, 1960; Zajonc, 1968). Zajonc, for instance, varied the frequency with which respondents were visually exposed to novel stimuli such as nonsense words, Chinese characters and photographs. He found that greater visual exposure was associated with more positive attitudes toward the stimulus. He hypothesized that with greater exposure, the respondent's initial anxiety toward or fear of the stimulus would gradually decrease.

Coming to gender stereotypes, through a series of experiments Eagly and Steffen (1984) demonstrated that information about the presence of women in nontraditional roles mitigated against stereotypic conceptions about these women. Heilman and Martell (1986) found that exposure to information about successful women in heretofore male-dominated occupations could reduce sex bias in personnel decisions. Thus, the above studies explored the effect of greater cognitive exposure on stereotypic attitudes.

A related important issue, which needs to be researched, is the effect of experiential exposure or actual interaction on stereotypic attitudes. If mere exposure to information helps modify attitudes, it makes sense to assume that actual interaction would also influence attitudes. However, this assumption needs to be tested empirically.

In one study, some scholars explored the relationship between greater experiential exposure, i.e., interaction and attitudes. They argue more information can influence attitudes toward women favorably (Eagly & Steffen, 1984; Heilman & Martell, 1986), greater interaction should have the same influence. Earlier studies (Kanter, 1977b) have suggested that structural changes such as presence of women in larger numbers can help make male managers' attitudes more positive toward women.

Hypothesis 1 In this study, they have tested the hypothesis that greater work-related interaction of male managers with women managers is associated with more positive attitudes toward women as managers. The work of Tversky and Kahneman (cited in Heilman & Martell, 1986) suggests that the bias against women persists partly because of lack of exposure to behavioral examples of women who have been successful in male-dominated occupations Heilman and Martell (1986) found support for the proposition that exposure to successful women in traditionally male occupations mitigates against subsequent sex bias. Thus it was not merely the fact of additional information but the positive nature of information, which reportedly influenced the attitudes. In another study, it was argued that if task-related interactions with women managers generate a feeling of satisfaction among male managers, it should lead to more positive attitudes towards women as managers.

Hypothesis 2. They have tested the hypothesis that greater satisfaction reported with work-related interaction with women managers is associated with more positive attitudes toward women as managers.

Research Setting

The study was conducted in the main branches of six banks. Banks were chosen because (a) they employ a large number of women in managerial positions, and (b) the physical layout of branches—with several employees working in close proximity to each other—provides ample opportunity for employee interaction. The six banks were randomly chosen from a standard list of banks.

Respondents

Data were collected from 101 male managers who were approached personally at their worksites. About 90% of them were over 30 years old and married. Eighty seven percent were college graduates. Eighty percent occupied junior or middle management positions.

Measures

1. Interaction: In that study, interaction was measured in terms of number of times women managers and male managers interacted within the organization on task matters.
   (a) The extent of interaction : This was measured using two scales. In one, the participant was asked to indicate the total number of women managers he had met on task matters in his career. The other scale asked the participant to rate how frequently he interacted with women managers on task matters, on a 7-point scale. The rating of 1

indicated low level (very low frequency) of interactions, while the rating of 7 indicated a high level of interaction.

(b) Satisfaction with interaction : This refers to the extent to which interactions with women managers on task matters were perceived as rewarding or satisfying. A single item 7-point scale was used to measure this. A rating of 2 indicated that the task interactions with women managers were perceived to be extremely unsatisfactory. A rating of 7 indicated the task interactions with women managers were perceived to be extremely satisfactory.

2. Attitudes Toward Women as Managers : This was defined as the evaluative beliefs held by male managers about women in the role of a manager. Attitudes were measured using two scales. The first scale was the Women As Managers Scale (WAMS) developed by Peters, Terborg, and Taynor (1974). The original scale had 21 items. Another item was added, based on the data collected by Bhatnagar (1987) from a similar respondent sample. Of these 22 items, 11 were negatively worded. Each item was scored from I to 7. Negatively worded statements were reverse scored. The participant's total score was obtained by summing his scores on the 22 items.

The second instrument was a 21-point measure (Overall Assessment). Participants rated their overall assessment of women as managers on this scale. The scale ranged from -10 through 0 to +10. The rating of -10 indicated that the participant believed men to be far superior to women as managers. The rating of 0 indicated that the participant believed women were as good managers as were men. The rating of +10 indicated that the participants believed women to be far superior to men as managers. This measure was included to determine the face validity of the WAMS. A relatively high correlation between the two measures would indicate that WAMS had face validity.

In conversations with participants, it appeared that despite specific instructions, some of them had evaluated women's managerial capabilities, based on their exposure to women clerks. In other words, on the basis of their experience with one category of women (namely, women clerks), respondents appeared to be making evaluations about another category of women (namely, women managers). This behavior appears similar to behavior observed in the field of consumer behavior. Howard and Sheth (1969) argue that in the absence of much experience with a product class, consumers tend to generalize their experiences with other physically or semantically similar products to make a purchase decision. Such a generalization could be occurring in respect to women managers also. Taylor and llgen (1981) have demonstrated that exposure to competent women in one field has favorable consequences for the personnel decisions made about a woman in a different field. In our study, such transference from clerks to officers was quite likely to occur. In Indian banks, where 83.2% of women employees are clerks and only 9.1% are officers (Bhatnagar, 1 988b), it is likely that male managers get greater exposure to women clerks than to women managers. In the absence of exposure to women managers, they may be generalizing from their experiences with women clerk.

It is important to examine if interaction with women clerks can predict attitudes toward women as managers. For, if it does, the focus of change attempts must include women clerks also. A second study was proposed, partly to reexamine the earlier hypotheses and partly also to examine if the extent of exposure and satisfaction with exposure to women clerks predicted attitudes.

Extending the earlier argument about interaction with women managers to interaction with women clerks, it as proposed that (a) greater interaction with women clerks would be associated with more positive attitudes toward women as managers (H3), and (b) greater satisfaction with interaction with women clerks would be associated with more positive attitudes toward women as managers (H4).

Summary of finding of the two studies

The two studies correlated measures of the extent of interaction and satisfaction with interaction, with measures of attitudes toward women as managers. The findings of the two studies in respect to these relationships are summarized below:

Only three of the eight correlations between the number of women managers met and attitudes were significant and positive as hypothesized. Results showed no relationship between the frequency of interactions with women managers and attitudes. Thus, H1 hypothesizing a positive relation between interaction and attitudes received weak support.

All four correlations between satisfaction with interaction with women managers and attitudes were positive and significant. H2, which predicted a positive relation between satisfaction with interaction and favorable attitudes toward women as managers, was fully supported.

Implications

The study suggests that the extent of interaction with women employees (managers and clerks) does not predict attitudes toward women as managers. It is the satisfaction with interaction with women managers and (to a much lesser extent) women clerks that predicts attitudes toward women as managers. Our results indicate that mere increase in exposure and attitude do not correlate. Thus Zajonc's (1968) proposition is not supported. Zajonc found that mere increase in exposure to a stimulus was sufficient to create more positive attitudes toward the stimulus. He had wondered whether this relationship could be generalized. Our findings suggest that such a generalization does not occur.

Moreover, it appears that a mere increase in exposure to the stimuli in terms of increased interactions is not sufficient to create positive attitudes toward all stimuli belonging to the same or similar category. In her study of exposure to successful women as an antidote to sex discrimination, Heilman (1986) argued that only under certain circumstances does exposure lead to a weakening of stereotypes, which mediate discrimination. The relevance of the information presented and its representativeness of women as a group were two important factors, which influenced the impact of exposure to successful women in her simulation study with college students as subjects. She observed that even greater restrictiveness may operate in an actual situation.

The study could be described as a snapshot of reality in the sense that responses were based on actual interaction of respondents with women in work situations. Therefore, Heilman's (1986) concerns about relevance and representativeness as essential elements of information were taken care of. Our findings show that exposure through interaction indeed gets associated with favorable attitude toward women, but under a very specific condition: when such work-related interactions are experienced as being satisfactory. The study suggests a refinement of the mere exposure hypothesis: it is not mere exposure through interaction, but the positive nature of interaction that softens stereotypes and makes attitudes more favorable. Satisfaction with exposure emerges as an important variable associated with less discriminatory and more positive attitudes.

After the main study was over, they conducted interviews to understand further our findings. Since satisfaction with interaction emerged as a significant variable, we carried out a preliminary exploration as to the nature of interactions with women managers, which were regarded by male managers as satisfactory. Ten male managers from four banks were interviewed (six of them had responded to their questionnaire in the earlier part of the study). They were asked to describe satisfactory and unsatisfactory interactions with women employees and give examples. As an interesting aside, respondents tended to be more prolific in their recall of unsatisfactory interactions than satisfactory interactions. Content analysis of caselets developed from interviews indicated that when women managers met the task-related expectations, the interactions were perceived as being satisfactory. Thus these interviews suggested that satisfaction was dependent upon women accomplishing the concerned tasks, and following procedures and norms in "the expected" manner.

If satisfaction with interactions leads to the development of more positive attitudes toward women as managers, the following practical implications follow:

Increasing the exposure to women managers appears to be a necessary but not a sufficient condition to reduce the discriminatory behavior of male managers. Affirmative policies which aim at increasing the presence of women in organizations by reserving a proportion of managerial positions for women or recruiting women in large numbers at lower levels may by themselves not be sufficient to improve attitudes toward women. Such measures are a necessary first step to ensue women's entry and presence in managerial positions at the workplace. Organizations need to take a proactive next step to create enabling conditions so that competent women can perform well. This study suggests that the larger the number of women managers evoking satisfaction of their male colleagues about task-related interaction, the more favorable male attitudes would become.

The study suggests that women managers have a significant role to play in reducing the discrimination against them. If they can meet work-related expectations, others will experience satisfaction with work-related interactions with women managers. As the book-keeping model of revision of stereotypic beliefs (Weber & Crocker, 1983) suggests, each instance of stereotype-relevant favorable experience will contribute to mod the stereotype and make the attitudes of male managers toward women managers more positive. Hopefully, more positive attitudes will lead to less discriminatory behavior, for as Heilman and Stopeck (1985) and Heilman and Martell (1986) report, stereotypic characterizations mediate gender discrimination.

For making male managers' attitudes more positive, women managers need to meet work-related expectations. In order to do this women managers need to have information and clarity about the expectations held of them, and frequent feedback about how well they are meeting these expectations.

In organizations where there is some degree of overlap in the tasks of junior officers and clerks, women clerks can similarly facilitate a change in the overall impressions of men regarding women's competence. This may result in less discriminatory behavior against women.

For weakening the gender stereotypes, such findings suggest a multipronged strategy. Organizations need to create greater opportunities for exposure of women members through proactive recruitment policies, and appropriate placement, so that men get much greater opportunities to interact with women on work-related matters. Also organizations need to create opportunities and climates, which facilitate performance. Women need to utilize these opportunities effectively to convert interaction into satisfying work-related experiences for others. Cognitive inputs such as giving information about competence of women to male managers may not be sufficient to weaken the negative stereotypes; emotive reactions such as satisfaction arising out of personal experience of competent performance by women may help significantly in making male managers' attitudes more favorable.

Limitations and Future Research. They discuss some limitations of the present study and suggest areas in which future research can throw useful light.

The study had some limitations. Admittedly, there are difficulties associated with measuring feelings and attitudes within the habitual interaction at workplaces such as the ones studied in our research. This study examined male respondents' attitudes at a single point in time in the backdrop of ongoing work-related interactions with women managers and clerks.

The possibility of recent interactions transiently influencing expressed satisfaction favorably or unfavorably cannot be ruled out. Future research can incorporate measures to obviate such contamination.

Future research can use alternative, less explicit measures of attitudes toward women as managers, so as to overcome the bias of socially-desirable responses. For instance, projective tests can be developed to measure attitudes toward women as managers.

In this study, satisfaction with interaction was explored subsequent to the main study. This exploration indicated that in order to be characterized as satisfactory interaction, women's performance needs to meet the expectations of the male managers: if these expectations are not met, the interactions are perceived as unsatisfactory. This relationship raises the complex issue about expectations and conformity. In order to reduce discrimination, should women conform to all the expectations of male managers? To what extent and at what cost? Hennig and Jardim (1977) report that successful women managers in American organizations spent a considerable part of their time dressing, talking, and behaving like men. Such an expectation may require women to suppress their individuality. Also, does the onus for attitude change rest only on women and organizations, or do male managers too have a key role to play?

Also, the determinants of attitudes toward women as managers were examined with main focus on women-related interaction variables. Future research needs to enrich our understanding further by exploring the role of perceiver-related variables in determining male managers' attitudes toward women as managers. For example, the role of "perceived threat" in the minds of male managers in determining attitudes toward women managers can be studied. It can be speculated that male managers may feel dissatisfied if women managers' competence is perceived as posing a threat to male managers personally or collectively. If such a relationship holds true, then it is possible to think of a "competence tolerance range" among male managers for women managers. Interactions that confirm women's performance within the competence tolerance range may evoke satisfaction, and performance and satisfaction may covary within the range Performance falling below the threshold of tolerance may be perceived as unsatisfactory. It is likely that women's performance which exceeds the upper threshold of the range may pose a threat, evoke anxieties among male managers and lead to the perception of interaction as being did not explore perceived threat and other possible determinants of satisfaction. This important constellation of issues is in need of investigation by future research.

6

Women Managers Outshine their Male Counterparts

New studies find that female managers outshine their male counterparts in almost every measure Several years after women first started pouring into the labor force—and trying to be more like men in every wearing power suits to picking up golf clubs—new research is showing that men ought to be the ones doing more of the imitatings. In fact, after years of analyzing what makes leaders most effective and figuring out who's got the Right Stuff, management gurus now know how to boost the odds of getting a great executive: Hire a female.

That's the essential finding of a growing number of comprehensive management studies conducted by consultants across the country for companies ranging from high-tech to manufacturing to consumer services. By and large, the studies show that women executives, when rated by their peers, underlings, and bosses, score higher than their male counterparts on a wide variety of measures—from producing high-quality work to goal-setting to mentoring employees. Using elaborate performance evaluations of executives, researchers found that women got higher ratings than men on almost every skill measured. Ironically, the researchers weren't looking to ferret out gender differences. They accidentally stumbled on the findings when they were compiling hundreds of routine performance evaluations and then analyzing the results.

The gender differences were often small, and men sometimes earned higher marks in some critical areas, such as strategic ability and technical analysis. But overall, female executives were judged more effective than their male counterparts. "Women are scoring higher on almost everything we look at," says Shirley Ross, an industrial psychologist who helped oversee a study performed by Hagberg Consulting Group in Foster City, California. Hagberg conducts in-depth performance evaluations of senior managers for its diverse clients, including technology, health care, financial-service, and consumer-goods companies. Of the 425 high-level executives (execs) evaluated, each by about 25 people, women execs won higher ratings on 42 of the 52 skills measured.

The growing body of new research comes at a time when talent-hungry recruiters are scrambling to find execs who can retain workers and who can excel in the smaller bureaucracies of New Economy companies. Women think through decisions better than men, are more collaborative, and seek less personal glory, says the head of IBM's Global Services Div., Douglas Elix, who hired two managers within a year—both women. Instead of being motivated by self-interest, women are more driven by "what they can do for the company," Elix says. Adds Harvard Business School Professor Rasabeth Moss Kanter, author of the 20-year-old management classic, Men and Women of the Corporation: Women get high ratings on exactly those skills needed to succeed in the global Information Age, where teamwork and partnering are so important."

It's no surprise, then, that some executives say they're beginning to develop a new hiring bias. If forced to choose between equally qualified male and female candidates for a top-level job, they say they often pick the woman—not because of affirmative action or any particular desire to give the female a chance but because they believe she will do a better job." I would rather hire a woman," says Anu Shukla, who sold her Internet marketing-software company Rubric Inc. earlier this year for $390 million." I know I'm going to get a certain quality of work, I know I'm going to get a certain dedication," she says, quickly adding that she's fully aware that not all women execs excel. Similarly, Brent Clark, CEO of Grand Rapids-based Pell Inc., the nation's largest foot-care chain, says he would choose a woman over a man, too. Women are more stable, he says, less turf-conscious and better at "all sorts of intangibles that can help an organization."

But if women are so great, why aren't more of them running the big companies? Thousands of talented women now graduate from business schools and hold substantive middle-management jobs at major corporations—45% of all managerial posts are held by females, according to the Labor Dept. Yet only two of the nation's

500 biggest companies have female CEOs: Hewlett-Packard Co.'s Carly Fiorina and Avon Products' Andrea Jung. And of the 1,000 largest corporations, only six are run by women.

For one thing, there's still a pipeline problem: Most women get stuck in jobs that involve human resources or public relations—posts that rarely lead to the tap. At the same time, female managers' strengths have long been undervalued, and their contributions in the workplace have gone largely unnoticed and unrewarded. Companies are now saying they want the skills women typically bring to the job, but such rhetoric doesn't always translate into reality. Some businesses view women only as workhorses, well-suited for demanding careers in middle management but not far prime jobs. These undercurrents at bias in Corporate America infuriate many women, who then bail out rather than navigate unsupportive terrain. "They're doing the work, but they don't make it to the tap," says Lyn Andrews, president of Web MD Health, a consumer unit of Web MD Carp. in New York. Many start their own companies, while others seek a different work/family balance than many corporations offer. There are now more than 9 million women-owned businesses in the U.S., double the number 12 years ago.

The new studies offer some clues about why the cultural mismatch between women and large companies persists and why it's so critical to keep women on board. What makes the new research more compelling than other such data is that it is based an results culled from executives' actual performance evaluations rather than an opinion surveys or experiments that simulate business situations.

Because the participants had no idea that their evaluations would end up as part of a study on gender, the data are untainted, says Janet Irwin, a California management consultant who conducted one of the studies. "We were startled by the results," she says.

Irwin and her colleagues discovered that women ranked higher than men on 28 of 31 measures. Irwin was stunned by women's consistently high ratings and how the scores defied conventional wisdom. Contrary to stereotypes, women outperformed men in all kinds of intellectual areas, such as producing high-quality work, recognizing trends, and generating new ideas and acting on them. "Women's strengths are stronger than men's," says Irwin, "and their weaknesses are not as pronounced."

Several other studies showed similar patterns. Personnel Decisions International, a consulting firm in Minneapolis, looked at a huge sample—58, 000 managers—and found that women outranked men in 20 of 23 areas. Larry Pfaff, a Michigan management consultant, examined evaluations from 2,482 executives from a variety of companies and found that women outperformed men on 17 of 20 measures.

Certainly, many women managers are keenly aware that they inhabit a different reality at the office than men. Nancy Hawthorne, farmer chief financial officer at Continental Cablevision Inc., who subsequently became a consultant, says she often felt her basses "wandered what the heck I was doing." At meetings, she often allowed subordinates to explain the details of ongoing projects. She felt her role was to delegate tasks to people around her to help them be mare effective. "I was being traffic cap and coach and facilitator," she said." I was always into building a department that hummed."

Kiely bristles at some research that concluded that women aren't perceived as strategic or vision-oriented. Her strategy, she says, is to make people think something is their idea so she can get them to buy into a plan. Another potential trap: Women's biggest strengths can also become their biggest weaknesses, says Vivian Eyre, a New York management consultant. By working so hard to get great results, they often take away time from building critical business alliances. "Given the opportunity to stay in their offices and make sure their report is perfect or going out of their office and talking to Joe about his business, women are more likely to do their own work," says Eyre.

What's more, she adds, women still suffer from a lack mentoring and being kept outside informal networks of communication. Many women admit that because they spend so much time focusing on getting results, they don't think enough about strategy and vision—qualities that Harvard's Kanter says are still the most important in a top executive. "If women are seen as only glorified office facilitators but not as tough-minded risk-takers," says Kanter, "they will be held back from the CEO jobs."

In the end, it takes a lot more than competence to make it to the top. Getting the best performance evaluations in the company's history may not be nearly enough. "When you actually sit down in a selection committee to choose the CEO, lots of subtle assumptions come into play," said Deborah Merrill Sands, co-director of Simmons' Center on Gender & Organization. Companies may say they want collaborative leaders, but they still hold deep-seated beliefs that top managers need to be heroic figures. Interpersonal skills may be recognized as important, she said, but they aren't explicitly seen as corner-office skills. "We are in the process of changing our concepts of says. "But organizations haven't evolved that much yet."

One recent study shows how CEOs and corporate boards view upper management, and he found a clear double standard. Male CEOs and senior vice-presidents got high marks from their bosses when they were forceful and assertive and lower scores if they were cooperative and empathic. The opposite was true for women: Female CEOs got downgraded for being assertive and got better scores when they were cooperative. Kabacoff's conclusion? "At the highest levels, bosses are still evaluating people in the most stereotypical ways." That means that even though women have proven their readiness to lead companies into the future, they're not likely to get a shot until their bosses are ready to stop living in the past.

What's more, she adds, women still suffer from a lack of mentoring and being kept outside informal networks of communication. Many women admit that because they spend so much time focusing on getting results, they don't think enough about strategy and vision—qualities that Harvard's Kanter says are still the most important in a top executive. "If women are seen as only glorified office facilitators but not as tough-minded risk-takers," says Kanter, "they will be held back from the CEO jobs."

Table 6.1

Where Female Executives Do Better: A Scorecard

None of the studies set out to find gender differences. They stumbled on them while compiling and analyzing performance evaluations.

SKILL (Each X denotes which group scored higher on the respective studies)	Men	Women
Motivating Others		X X X X X
Fostering communication		X X X X*
Producing high-quality work		X X X X X
StrategicPlanning	X X	X X*
Listening to others		X X X X X
Analyzing issues	X X	X X*

*In one study, women's and men's scores in these categories were statistically even

DATA: Hagberg Consulting Group, Management Research Group, Lawrence A. Pfaff, Personnel decisions international Inc., advanced teamware Inc.

7

Job Satisfaction of Women Managers: Glass Ceiling Effect

A recent study examines differences between men's and women's job satisfaction. Although there is ample literature that addresses the general likes and dislikes of workers towards their employment, there is less research related to gender differences regarding job satisfaction. And there is limited research that examines male versus female job satisfaction and other career-related issues—among transportation/logistic managers.

To accomplish this objective some researchers have surveyed 500 male and 500 female transportation/logistic managers, and received completed survey instruments from 146 women and 155 men. The findings from these respondents form the basis of this study. Specifically, this chapter address the following topics: (a) a literature review of gender-based job satisfaction; (b) a description of the methodology used in this study; (c) an examination of the demographic differences between male and female respondents, including how they thought their income compared to what they felt it should be; (d) male versus female reaction to the concept of a "glass ceiling" for women executives; (e) a discussion of male versus female job satisfaction based on the Andrews and Withey Index of Job Satisfaction; (f) a look at the gender-based responses to the question, "If you could start your career over, would you still choose to work in the transportation/logistics industry?"; (g) a discussion of the findings; and (h) an examination of the managerial implications that emerged from this study.

Literature Review

The first question they asked the respondents dealt with their income expectations. Historically, this has been an area of concern to female workers. In 1991 Susan Faludi, in her influential book, Backlash: The Undeclared War Against American Women declared,

"Why do American women, in fact, face one of the worst gender-based gaps in the developed world?" More recent studies seem to indicate that gender-based pay inequality, for doing the same work, appears to be lessening. Because women are being paid more equitably for their work efforts, it is becoming more common that women are generating the larger income in dual-income families. The U.S. Bureau of Labor Statistics noted that in 1970, for two-income households, women had the higher incomes in 4.4 percent of the families. This number increased to 22.0 percent in 1997. Logisticians appear to be doing relatively well in terms of their compensation. A salary survey in 1997 by William Mercer Inc found that senior logisticians had their salaries advance 7.8 percent in 1997. Since inflation from 1996 to 1997 was in the range of 3 percent, this indicates that employers recognized the value of the logistics function and were willing to compensate these managers with substantial salary advances. One recent study of women logisticians at all levels of management found that since they were relatively younger than their male logistician counterparts, their salaries were on the average lower than for all logisticians. Nevertheless, their average annual compensation for 1997 was $92,000.

Another aspect relating to job satisfaction was addressed in this study. It involved the "glass ceiling" for women executives, which is the idea that the predominantly male hierarchy rarely allows women to become members of the highest levels of management. This phenomenon is controversial because it is more ethereal to men and more real to women executives. Nevertheless, the U.S. Labor Department has created a Federal Glass Ceiling Commission, a bipartisan study group trying to encourage diversity in the workplace.

How prevalent is the "glass ceiling?" One study by Catalyst, a women's research and advocacy group, found that for the 500 largest publicly traded companies, women account for 47 percent of all workers, but they held at least one of the five highest positions in only forty-seven of these companies. Another potential problem is where these women executives are working. Of the 978 women who were at the vice-presidential level, only about 28 percent were in positions involved directly with revenue generation, which are generally thought to be the positions that best lead to the highest levels of management. The majority of female vice-presidents were clustered in staff positions, such as public relations and human resources. Catalyst president Sheila Wellington, when reviewing this study, stated that its findings clearly indicate the fallaciousness of people who say, "The glass ceiling has been cracked by a Niagara of women flowing to the top of corporate America."

Why has the "glass ceiling" taken place? There are a number of possible explanations, including the following: women's ideas are not clearly understood by men because women and men communicate in different ways, men's egos are threatened by successful women, the "invisible woman syndrome," where men just ignore or discount the ideas of women, and the assumption by men that all women desire to be on the "mommy track" because their first loyalty is not to their employer, but to their children and family. Even with these potential roadblocks to a woman's success, the business press still regularly reports on women achieving great success in reaching the highest levels of corporate management.

One study specifically addressed the "glass ceiling" in the transportation/logistics industry. Male and female transportation/logistics managers were asked to react to this statement: "The opportunities for advancement within the logistics profession are the same for women and men." There were statistically significant differences based on gender. Only about 15 percent of females agreed to this statement to either a "great extent" or a very great extent." About 45 percent of males, however, believed the validity of this statement to a "great extent" or a "very great extent."

A third issue addressed in this study is the overall level of job satisfaction of men and women in the work force. A 1994 study by Roper Starch Worldwide reported that in 1973, 41 percent of women and 37 percent of men stated they were "very satisfied" with their jobs. By 1994 these percentages had declined to 26 percent of women and 28 percent of men. A more recent survey by The Wall Street Journal/NBC News found that 37 percent of men and women reported they were" completely satisfied" with their jobs and another 47 percent stated they were "somewhat satisfied" with their current positions. A 1996 study of male and female transportation/logistics managers asked each respondent to rate their job satisfaction on a five-point Likert type scale: very satisfied, satisfied, neutral, dissatisfied, and very dissatisfied. Male respondents were somewhat more satisfied with their careers than were the females. Almost 85 percent of the males selected either "very satisfied" or "satisfied," compared to about 69 percent of the females who selected the same responses. However, only about 6 percent of the men chose "dissatisfied or very dissatisfied," compared to approximately 17 percent of the women who selected these alternatives.

Although both men and women appear to hold generally positive attitudes towards their jobs, substantial numbers of Americans are leaving the corporate work environment to start their own businesses. In addition, others are taking positions that allow more personal time.

A number of studies have addressed female workers' job satisfaction issues. While some writers believe women are not satisfied in their work, other studies seem to disprove this idea. One recent study of women transportation and logistics managers found that 32.8 percent strongly agreed and another 42.2 percent agreed with the statement, "I am generally satisfied with my current position." Another study of women in transportation and logistics managerial positions found 68.6 percent were either "satisfied" or "very satisfied" with their current positions. Other research has indicated that women are less committed to their jobs relative to men and that women who have had their careers interrupted, typically for maternity leaves, are less satisfied with their positions compared to workers who have not had interruptions in their careers.

In summary, there appears to be a general consensus—based on the eleven studies cited above—that when men and women are asked about their job satisfaction, they do not have statistically significant differences in their responses.

A final issue addressed in this study is whether men and women would start their careers over again in the area of transportation and logistics. One study addressed this issue directly by asking male and female transportation/logistics managers to respond to this statement: "I really care about continuing my career in logistics." Almost 72 percent of the male and female respondents—with no statistically significant gender-based difference—stated that they either agreed to a "great extent" or a "very great extent." A number of additional studies asked related questions of men and women who are employed in the transportation and logistics areas. These findings were consistently favorable towards the employees' chosen area of employment. The study just mentioned also asked males and females working in the logistics area to react to this statement: "I talk up my company to my friends as a great place to work." About 54 percent of the respondents stated that they agreed with this statement to a "great extent" or a "very great extent." There was no statistically significant difference between the responses of men and women. Among traffic managers, one study of men and women found that 25.9 percent of the respondents rated their jobs as "terrific" and another 65.7 percent stated their level of job satisfaction as "good." In another study of male and female traffic managers, 82 percent either agreed or strongly agreed with this statement: "The corporate traffic function will grow more important during the 1 990s." The one potentially negative factor is the issue of job security because of the growing trend to outsource the transportation and logistics function. Illustrative of this trend is that in recent years many companies are using third-party providers to perform the transportation and logistics functions that were previously performed by the company's own employees. For example, Dell Computer outsourced both inbound and outbound logistics activities to Roadway Logistics, while Whirlpool Corporation decided to outsource its entire inbound materials management to Ryder Dedicated Logistics.

Research Methodology

To gather primary information for this study, a sample of logistics and transportation professionals was surveyed. Independent systematic random samples of 500 male and 500 female logisticians were selected from the 1997 Council of Logistics Management Membership Directory. We eliminated all individuals who were either consultants or professors at a college or university. Each potential respondent was first sent a copy of the twopage questionnaire along with a cover letter urging his or her participation. Approximately ten days later a second copy of the questionnaire was sent with a cover letter thanking those who had responded and reminding others to please do so.

Altogether, usable responses were received from 146 female professionals, representing 29.2 percent of the initial sample. Also, usable responses were received from 155 male professionals, representing 31.0 percent of the initial sample. These response rates are considered very good. Responses from these 146 female and 155 male logistics professionals, then, form the database for the results to follow.

Comparison of male and female logisticians

Each respondent was queried as to his or her age range (under 30, 30 to 39, 40 to 49, 50 and over), educational level (no college degree, college degree, graduate degree) and approximate annual salary ($40,000, $60,000, $80,000, $100,000, $1 20,000+).

The following trends were observed.

First, women logisticians tend to be significantly younger than men ($p < .01$).(n37) In particular, there is a paucity of women age 50 and over: just one in ten women in this age range, compared to about one in three men. This no doubt reflects the scarcity of women entering the profession prior to approximately twenty years ago. It is equally interesting that, in the youngest age group (under 30), women out number men by about a three to one margin, perhaps reflecting positively on affirmative action efforts within the profession.

Second, women logisticians are significantly less likely to have a four-year degree (by 5.3 percentage points) or an advanced degree (by 7.4 percentage points) than men ($p <.01$). As the profession enters the 2000s, continuing education for its younger female managers will be an issue of growing importance.

Finally, salaries for women lag significantly behind those for men in the logistics field ($p <.01$). This differential is particularly striking if one splits annual salary at about the $70,000 range: 55.8 percent of women earn less than this amount per year, compared with just 30.3 percent of men. It would be instructive to explore possible explanations for this salary gap. One plausible reason involves the demographic differences just discussed. If indeed female logistics managers are younger and, to date at least, less educated than their male counterparts, it is logical to expect some salary differential.

This explanation is also supported by responses to the question, "How has your personal annual income compared to what you expected it would be?" The respondent could select one of the following five answers-much better, somewhat better, about what I expected, somewhat lower, and much lower. The results of this query are found in Table 7.1. There were no statistically different responses based on gender (p = 48). One might have expected much more disappointment with salary among women than men if the sizable gender differences in annual salary were based on what women perceived as gender discrimination.

Gender perception of the "glass ceiling"

Another question asked each respondent, "Based on your personal opinion, is there a "glass ceiling" (i.e., an invisible barrier generally barring women from career advancement beyond some point) in the logistics/transportation industry?" The respondent could select one of five possible answers: definitely yes, probably yes, unsure, probably no, and definitely no. As can be seen clearly in Table 7.2, there is a significant gender difference (p <.01) in the responses to this question. Nearly one-half (46.9 percent) of women professionals think there probably is such a barrier, and another one-fourth (28.3 percent) believe there definitely is one. While this is a stronger response pattern than among men, even one-third of men think there definitely or probably is a "glass ceiling" in logistics. This is certainly a troubling finding, one that strongly suggests further investigation into the extent of the problem within the field, as well as study into possible avenues of remedy.

Male versus female job satisfaction

Job satisfaction among male and female logistics professionals was measured with the Andrews and Withey Job Satisfaction Questionnaire. This general index of job satisfaction has been validated and utilized in a variety of previous studies. The instrument is reproduced in Figure 4 and consists of five questions or items, each scored on a seven-point scale, from 1 (delighted) to 7 (terrible).

Overall job satisfaction is measured by averaging each manager's responses to the five items. Table 7.4 presents polygons that display the responses for men and women logistics professionals. The mean job satisfaction score for men is 2.48 and the mean score for women is 2.65, a difference that is not significant ($p = .08$), at least not at the 5 percent level or less.

These results indicate that both men and women are reasonably well satisfied with their jobs. Notice that a midpoint score of 3.5 on the seven-point scale would indicate that the worker is neither delighted nor terribly unhappy about his or her job. That is, a 3.5 score indicates that a worker takes an "average" position regarding job satisfaction. From this perspective of the midpoint of the scale, the polygons suggest that about four out of every five female and male managers take an "average" or better than "average" position about their job satisfaction.

Career choice satisfaction

Each respondent was asked, "If you could start your career over, would you still choose to work in the transportation/logistics field?" There were five possible answers to select from: definitely yes, probably yes, unsure, probably no, and definitely no. Responses to this question, by gender, appear in Table 7.5. The differences between men and women when responding to this question were not significant; that is, male and female logistics managers do not differ with respect to career choice satisfaction.

Altogether, most logistics and transportation personnel are reasonably content in their careers. About two out of every three managers surveyed indicated that they either probably or definitely would still choose to work in the logistics area if they could start over in their careers. While only very few said they definitely would pick a different career, about one in ten admitted that they probably would do so, and another one in five said they were unsure what they would do. So, not everyone now employed as a logistics professional is satisfied with his or her career choice, but differences based on gender are minimal.

To better understand why some logistics personnel are happy in their choice of career but others are not, each respondent was invited to provide a narrative response explaining their answer to this question. Most did so, and the reasons are discussed below.

First we separated male and female responses. Then we combined their answers "definitely yes" and "probably yes"—in response to each person's likelihood of staying in transportation and logistics—into one group and then categorized the responses by broad themes. We also combined the answers "unsure," "probably no," and "definitely no" into another group and categorized these responses into similar categories of responses. A discussion of the top three pluses and minuses—by gender--regarding career choice satisfaction follows.

Males: Career Benefits

Of the 55 men who participated in our study, 146 told us in their owns words why they answered the way they did. Of these 146 respondents, 103 men, when asked if they would remain in transportation/logistics if they could start their careers over, answered "definitely yes" or "probably yes." We will now examine the top three reasons why males like their jobs in the descending order of frequency that they appeared. We will also include a number of verbatim statements so the reader can grdsp the flavor of the respondents' comments.

Excellent Career Advancement Opportunities

The most common reason males like their career choice is that it provides exceptional opportunities for career advancement. This benefit was stated by 36 respondents (35.0 percent of those men who selected "definitely yes" or "probably yes"). Respondents said:

- "Transportation/distribution is a new and evolving discipline. I believe that as our society changes, supply chain issues will continue to increase in importance especially for companies that recognize it as a tool to differentiate itself from its competitors. Managers, like myself, who are in the forefront of distribution activities, can only become more important to our employers. I am at the right place at the right time to benefit from the growing importance of the logistics function."
- "The excitement of technological advances doesn't diminish the role of human innovation and creativity. Because logistics is at the leading edge of decreasing costs while increasing

customer service standards, my advancement potential has never been greater."

- "It is an area of expertise that continues to expand and evolve into one of the most critical areas of business management."
- "Today's senior management is paying more attention to logistics. As the retail industry matures there are less and less ways to distinguish one company's products or services from competitors. Logistics separates the winners from the losers."

Fast-Paced Environment

The second greatest benefit of a career in transportation/logistics—as noted by thirty-one male respondents (30.1 percent)—was that it was a fast-paced work environment that was constantly offering a variety of work activities. Here are three typical observations:

- "Very interesting work, with lots of variety. Literally every day is different and that's why I look forward to going to work each day."
- "Exciting, adventurous, always something new or changing. I like the opportunities to work in various areas, such as inventory management, systems operations and transportation."
- "Transportation/logistics is relentlessly becoming more efficient. Everyday there are new opportunities to help my company become more competitive."

Intellectually Challenging

Thirty male respondents (29.1 percent) stated that they would stay in the transportation/logistics career area because it was mentally challenging to select the optimum logistics package of costs versus customer service levels. Below are three of their statements:

- "Transportation and logistics are intellectually fascinating areas, because they apply much of what we know (management, math, engineering) and they affect so many lives."

- "It offers a dynamic atmosphere. You can be extremely creative in this career. It is like being an artist." "The challenges and opportunities are what you make them. In logistics, there is not one way to do anything: there are a 1,000 ways. Your job is to think of all the alternatives and select the best."

Females: Career Benefits

There were 146 female transportation/logistics managers who participated in our survey. Of these, 139 told us in their own words their thoughts about transportation/logistics as a career choice. For these 139 women respondents, 88 stated they would either "definitely yes" or "probably yes" stay in their present career. We will now look at the top three reasons why these women like their careers. Also included will be a number of their comments so the reader can better appreciate their statements.

Intellectually Challenging

The most prevalent reason women desired to stay in the transportation/logistics career area is the intellectual challenge that this position offers. This point was made by thirty female respondents (34.1 percent). Below are four of their statements:

- "The creativity you are able to express in designing innovative solutions to unique problems. I really enjoy working on problems where there is no 'standard' solution, each situation requires its own analysis and problem solving."
- "Logistics is a very exciting work environment. I enjoy the stress of solving problems that seem intractable to others. I perform best when the problems appear most difficult."
- "I love challenges and supply chain management offers lots of them! This area is so new that we are all trying to define the best paradigm in each channel situation."
- "I love to question 'why' we have always done things the way we do. In many cases, no one can remember why we had, for example, a warehouse in Cleveland and also in Gary, IN. By closing the Gary facility, our costs decreased substantially with no change in customer service standards."

Excellent Career Advancement Opportunities

Twenty-four women respondents (27.3 percent) would remain in their present job because it offered excellent promotion opportunities. Here are three of their comments:

- "I feel that since I am a female I've been put on a fast track and can, and have, really advanced quickly in this field. I hope to be a good role model for other women in my company. I want to prove that women can excel in senior management positions."
- "This career area is very momentarily rewarding because there are so few managers who really understand supply chain management. Managers, like myself, are in great demand and therefore this is a wonderful career choice."

Fast-Paced Environment

The third most common reason women are satisfied in their career choice is their fast-paced work environment. This benefit was noted by eighteen female respondents (20.5 percent), and here are three of their observations:

- "Variety, variety, and variety! No day is ever the same. Not too many managers can make that statement."
- "Logistics is constantly challenging and offers something different every day. This is especially true in the transportation aspect of logistics. What a change I have observed since deregulation!"
- "Logistics offers a daily opportunity to solve problems. Each problem is different than the last, which is why this is the least boring job I can imagine."

Males: Career Negatives

Of the 146 men who answered the open-ended question about their career satisfaction, 43 selected one of these three alternatives regarding their desire to continue working in the transportation/logistics career area: "unsure," "probably no," or "definitely no." Their responses were categorized into broad categories and the three most numerous are examined below.

Prefer Other Occupations

The most common reason male respondents were less than enthusiastic about their career choice was that they desired to work in another occupation. Fifteen men (34.9 percent) took this position and here are four of their statements:

- "It is an industry overrun with morons, who lack vision, but they do possess petty egos. Although I have been very successful, it has not been fulfilling other than financially—I'd rather make less money and do something I love."
- "Marketing is where the action is at my company. If I worked there, I wouldn't have to worry about being outsourced, the way a number of my friends who work in logistics at other companies have been in recent months."
- "I am very money oriented, and therefore I should have been in sales. In sales, if you perform and work very hard, the results show up very quickly in your pay check. In my area, it is mainly group projects and it is hard to tell who did what and therefore one is not directly compensated for one's efforts."

"I love to travel overseas and should be in international sales and marketing activities." Limited Promotion Opportunities Outside of Logistics

Eleven male respondents (25.6 percent), who were not devoted to transportation/logistics, noted that other career choices offer greater promotion potential. Here are three of their comments:

- "Logistics is considered a necessary evil. We are not valued and are thought of as employees who do not see the big picture, just our small, and generally unimportant, function. Since we are so specialized, once you are in logistics, it is almost impossible to get out."
- "I am considered exclusively a technical nerd. Because of this perception, I will never be given more managerial responsibility outside of transportation."
- "Logistics is a career limiting choice. If I could start over, I would guide my career towards a more generalist approach that stresses a line (not staff) position in either finance or marketing."

Too Much Stress

Six male respondents (14.0 percent) stated they were less than enamored with their career because it involves excessive stress. Here are two of their observations:

- "I am stressed all day long. We have had a number of rounds of layoffs and I am now doing the work that three people did as recently as two years ago.
- "I work too many hours with no job security. Every month I hear about another distribution man or woman I know who lost their job to outsourcing. My biggest regret is that I'm only 39 years old and can't afford to retire."

Females: Career Negatives

Of the 139 female respondents who answered in their own words about their career choice satisfaction, 51 selected one of the following choices in terms of their likelihood of remaining in the transportation/logistics area: "unsure," "probably no," or "definitely no." We were able to categorize their reasons into a number of broad themes. The three most common reasons will be examined below in the descending order of frequency that they appeared.

Prefer Other Occupations

The most common reason for women's lack of enthusiasm for transportation/logistics career was that they would have preferred to work in another occupation. Twenty-four respondents (47.1 percent) took this position, and here are four of their comments:

- "Sales and marketing managers are the 'heros' in our company, as shown by their salary and perks and by whose opinions are really listened to when strategic management decisions are made."
- "I was pre-law, and knowing what I know now, I'd pursue law and work as an advocate for women's rights."
- "I would work in production control or industrial engineering. Manufacturing is more fun and has more respect."

- "I would prefer to be in a field that is a bit more creative, i.e., marketing." Limited Promotion Opportunities Outside of Logistics

The second most common reason for women's lack of ardor about their present career choice is that transportation/logistics lacks career advancement except in the same area. Thus eight females (15.7 percent) stated they were perceived as "technocrats" that probably were not being considered for promotions outside of their present work environment. Here are three of their statements:

- "Transportation management represents such a specific set of skills that I have become pigeonholed as only capable of working in this area. While I enjoy what I am doing, I didn't think I would be doing it the rest of my life, which is appearing more probable as each year passes.
- "I would prefer to work in a field where the expertise that you develop is more transferable to other management situations."
- "If I could do it over, I would not work in the logistics area. Most logisticians are too specialized and focused in their area to be considered for more general management positions. At least in my company, which is in the Fortune 500, once in logistics management, you are there forever."

Desire More People-Oriented Position

The third most common reason for women's lack of fervor about their careers is that their job lacks enough interaction with other people. This point was noted by five females (9.8 percent), and here are two of their statements:

- "I would prefer to work in a field that is more personal—one that touches the heart rather than the artificial regimentation of the corporate life. I'm a people-person in an area that lives by computer print-outs."
- "I have no job satisfaction because I have limited interaction with people I don t see any connection between what I do and helping people."

Glass Celing Effect

John Gray wrote the best seller "Men Are From Mars, Women Are from Venus" which outlines basic psychological differences between men and women. Gray would probably be disappointed by the data from the present study, because it has found that men and women managers in the transportation/logistics workplace are not substantially different from each other in terms of attitudes towards their jobs and careers. Thus, it was found that there was not a significant difference between men and women in terms of their actual salaries compared to their expectations. There was also not a significant difference between women and men in terms of their job satisfaction as measured by the Andrews and Withey Job Satisfaction Questionnaire. In addition, there was not a significant difference between men and women in terms of whether they would choose to start their careers over in the transportation/logistics area. And, when asked why they would or would not select the same career again, both men and women again had similar answers. In terms of the positive aspects of their careers, they each listed the same three factors (although the order was different). For the negative aspects of their career choice, men and women listed exactly the same first and second dislikes. They disagreed for their third most common complaint—women stated that they desired jobs with more personal relations, while men commented that they desired positions that were less stressful.

The one statistically significant difference between men and women in this study was their perception of the existence of the "glass ceiling" in the transportation/logistics sector of the economy. Women overwhelmingly thought it was present in many companies, while males were much less sure of its existence. Specifically, about 75 percent of women thought there was a "glass ceiling" in the transportation/logistics sector of the economy, compared to only about 33 percent of the male respondents.

Of course, the above findings represent the results of only a single survey. In many ways, the results support those previously reported in the literature. In other ways, they do not. As always, it is important to recommend that attitude research, such as reported here, be replicated with other samples, procedures, and/or questionnaires, and that the final conclusion of the profession be guided by the preponderance of results as reported across numerous studies.

One believes there are three managerial implications for improvement that emerge from this study. The first involves women's perceptions of the "glass ceiling" in the transportation/logistics industry. Since over three-fourths of the female respondents either definitely or probably believe this situation exists, it is imperative that senior management addresses their concern. As noted in the literature search, this conundrum is not found just in the transportation/logistics sector of the economy. It is so prevalent that the federal government has established the Federal Glass Ceiling Commission, which tries to encourage gender diversity among all levels of management. One believe that this problem will not be corrected until the senior management of each firm makes a strong commitment to helping women achieve greater success. An example is General Electric, where CEO Jack Welch is determined to increase the number of women in top management positions. There is a paucity of females at present. No woman possesses one of the top twenty jobs at GE, and of the 120 highest ranking positions, only four are held by women. When meeting his senior managers, Welch insists they bring the women and minority managers they are mentoring, so Welch can get to know them better. When it comes to promotions and new assignments, Welsh again becomes an advocate for women and minorities. Why does Welch take such an active position? Because, he says, "Guys will pick guys ...."

A second managerial implication gleaned from the responses of women managers involved the positive and negative aspects of their career choice. One takes take it as a given that top-level executives in transportation and logistics honestly desire to attract more women into the field and to retain in the organization a higher percentage of those women who find the work initially attractive. From the benefits side, recruiters should be aware that women logisticians find their work intellectually challenging (the top cited benefit), that it offers excellent promotion opportunities within the logistics function, as well as offering a fast-paced environment (which is perhaps closely related to the intellectual challenge). All of these positive aspects can be used to point out to potential new hires what current female logistics managers find most satisfying about their jobs and careers.

In addition, to help insure that women managers stay in the field, firms need to address the concerns raised by those who are not particularly satisfied with their jobs. Of course, if in the end a particular female employee finds another occupation more appealing, there is little that can be done to prevent her leaving the logistics discipline. However, providing promotion opportunities outside of the logistics field can be accomplished, and this will be discussed next. Finally, desiring a more people-oriented position was noted by several unsatisfied women logistics managers. It may be possible to alter the culture of the logistics work environment at the margin, certainly not by transforming it into a "helping" profession, but at least by providing enhanced employee opportunity for interacting with other managers, working as a team, developing a more caring, problem-solving approach to dealing with customers, and the like. There is much that top management can do to encourage and nurture a corporate culture that values interpersonal contact and decision making, perhaps not for every management decision, but at least for those that tend to be more important.

The third idea that emerges from this study is the issue of transportation/logistics managers—men and women—perceiving that they are not promotable outside of their present area of expertise. This situation was noted equally by both male and female respondents. It appears to be a contradiction with another finding from this study. When transportation/logistics managers were asked about the reasons why they liked their present career, both men and women stated that the excellent promotion potential was a major benefit. One believes these differing positions can be explained. Those managers who reveled in the promotion potential were referring to advancement within the overall area of transportation/logistics. As this function becomes more important, because of its ability to both decrease costs and improve levels of customer service, the distribution area will provide qualified managers with upward mobility. The managers who complained about promotion potential were referring to being promoted outside of the transportation/logistics function. This concern is real, and senior management should be aware that they are limiting their search for future top management if managers in transportation/ logistics are not considered for these positions. One would propose a career model that has been used in sales and marketing for decades.

Thus, a high percentage of college graduates who desire to work in marketing start out in field or outside sales. The idea is that there is no better way for new employees to understand and empathize with their customers than to call on them face-to-face. In most cases, these new salespeople perform this function for two to four years. After that time, they meet with their career counselors, and each salesperson must make a decision. If they like field sales, then they can stay in the area and eventually become a sales manager for cities, states, regions, etc. However, if they would like to experience other areas of marketing, they can then be rotated into other marketing positions, such as marketing research, product and service development, brand management, etc. For transportation/ logistics managers, we propose a similar idea. After new managers spend their first one or two assignments in transportation/logistics, they should be able to decide if they desire to stay in this area, or if they would like to experience other positions in marketing, production, finance, etc. This would allow each individual the chance to broaden their mental and professional horizons. Of course, managers in other areas would also be offered the same opportunities, that is, they might start in marketing and finance and later be rotated into the transportation/logistics area. The advantage to this system is that men and women can experience various managerial activities and therefore be better prepared for the top senior management positions, which tend to be more generalist in nature.

Table 7.1
Career Benefits and Negatives

Legend for Chart:
A - Benefit
B - Percentage

A	B
Career Benefits	
Males	
1. Excellent career advancement opportunities	35 0%
2. Fast-paced environment	30.1%
3. Intellectually challenging	29.1%
Females	
1. Intellectually challenging	34.1%
2. Excellent career advancement opportunities	27.3%
3. Fast-paced environment	20.5%

Legend for Chart:
A - Negatives
B - Percentage

A	B
Career Negatives	
Males	
1. Prefer other occupations	34.9%
2. Limited promotion opportunities outside of logistics	25.6%
3. Too much stress	14.0%
Females	
1. Prefer other occupations	47.1%
2. Limited promotion opportunities outside of logistics	15.7%
3. Desire more people-oriented position	9.8%

Table 7.2

Gender-based Differences Among Transportation and Logistics Professionals

Legend for Chart:
B - Female
C - Male

A	B	C
Age ($p<.01$)		
Under 30	13.2%	4.5%
30 to 39	34.7%	20.6%
40 to 49	41.7%	43.9%
50 and Over	10.4%	31.0%
Education ($p<.01$)		
No College Degree	19.2%	6.5%
College Degree	42.4%	47.7%
Graduate Degree	38.4%	45.8%
Salary ($p<.01$)		
\$40,000	22.5%	8.6%
\$60,000	33.3%	21.7%
\$80,000	15.9%	21.7%
\$100,000	13.8%	22.4%
\$120,000+	14.5%	25.6%

Table 7.3

Annual Salary Compared to What Respondent Expected It Would Be

Legend for Chart:
B - Female
C - Male

A	B	C
Much Higher	9.7%	9.0%
Somewhat Higher	25.5%	29.1%
About As Expected	36.5%	40.7%
Somewhat Lower	25.5%	20.6%
Much Lower	2.8%	0.6%

Table 7.4

Perceived Presence of a 'Glass Ceiling" in Field of Logistics and Transportation by Gender

Legend for Chart:
B - Female
C - Male

A	B	C
Definitely Yes	28.3%	6.5%
Probably Yes	46.9%	26.4%
Unsure	9.0%	22.6%
Probably No	11.7%	25.8%
Definitely No	4.1%	18.7%

Figure 7.5

Likelihood of Staying in Field Transportation and Logistics by Gender

Legend for Chart:
B - Female
C - Male

A	B	C
Definitely Yes	25.7%	30.3%
Probably Yes	37.5%	40.1%
Unsure	22.2%	17.4%
Probably No	11.8%	10.3%
Definitely No	2.8%	1.9%

8

Corporate Restructuring and Reduction of Jobs for Women

An emerging body of work on women in organizations provides diverse and often conflicting data on the organizational experiences of women and their responses to them. Two sets of issues are being hotly debated. First, are rates of voluntary attrition higher among women than among their male counterparts? Second, why are women leaving organizational life? Some work in this area suggests that women are indeed bailing out of corporate life at proportionately higher rates than men ("Fed Up," 1986; Schwartz, 1989; Stroh, Brett, & Reilly, 1993; "Why Women Managers," 1986). Other work reports that the rates of attrition are not significantly different for professional men and women (Rosin & Korabik, 1995).

Three types of explanations are commonly provided to explain the attrition of women managers from organizations: first, women may be more prone to work-family conflicts because they are more likely to carry the load of a "second shift" (Hochschild, 1989) or family work; second, women are more likely to find themselves in work environments that are "chilly" and even discriminatory (Gutek, Cohen, & Konrad, 1990; Marshall, 1995; Rosin & Korabik, 1991); and third, the first wave of successful women may be reaching the top echelons of management and finding that corporate life is not as fulfilling as they had expected it to be ("Fed Up," 1995). Very little empirical work actually compares attrition among male and female managers or explores their reasons for leaving organizations (see Rosin & Korabik, 1995, for an exception).

Eploration of women's reasons for leaving organizations appear to belie popular stereotypes that women are leaving for family reasons or because they are not committed to work. Brett and Stroh (1994) suggested that women managers experience higher levels of stress at work and are leaving organizations to seek better career opportunities elsewhere. Women may also be less tolerant than men of unfavourable career situations and less optimistic that their current career situations will change significantly for the better. Thus corporate women are more likely than male managers to consciously manage their own careers (Brett & Stroh, 1994; White, Cox, & Cooper, 1992).

Conceptual and empirical work on women in organizations and on organizational restructuring have very rarely crossed paths. One notable exception is the recent work of Goffee and Nicholson (1994). In an attempt to compare the careers of male and female managers, they examined the effects of organizational restructuring on the psychological contracts between employers and employees. They concluded that the traditional male contract is based on long-term loyalty to the organization and work-centered life interests. In return for loyalty and commitment from employees the organization is expected to provide stability and upward mobility. Goffee and Nicholson suggested that women have had to modify such contracts to adapt them to their own multi-faceted life interests and limited access to extrinsic rewards. Thus women may have very diverse psychological contracts based on intrinsic rewards, lateral rather than upward mobility, and self-directed rather than organization-driven career choices. Goffee and Nicholson proposed that women may have been forced to develop strategies to deal with uncertainty and insecurity in part because their organizations have never been hospitable and welcoming. They concluded that restructuring may not appear to be as threatening to female managers as to their male counterparts and may not represent a significant change in their corporate environments.

Others (Maddock & Parkin, 1994; Marshall, 1995) pointed out that restructuring may be particularly difficult for women because the values that drive the "lean, mean organization" encourage economic efficiency and intense competitiveness at the expense of all other criteria. Maddock and Parkin referred to this culture as the "smart macho" culture. Such cultures require overwhelming commitment to the bottom line and may not tolerate managers who favour multidimensional performance measures or have diverse interests and responsibilities outside work.

Method and Findings

This research was undertaken to address some of the conflicts and limitations of prior research on women and their experience of organizational restructuring. Three specific questions were addressed:

1. Are women more likely to leave an organization involved in restructuring?
2. Is their departure prompted primarily by organizational or personal factors?
3. Is organizational restructuring inherently a gendered process that is experienced differently by women?

For this study, undertaken in the summer of 1995, 15 senior women managers who had voluntarily left a large crown corporation during its restructuring process were interviewed in order to explore the factors that had influenced their decisions. The corporation had undergone several rounds of restructuring and downsizing in the previous 5 years. In late 1994, it offered its employees a voluntary severance package as part of its downsizing strategy.

The representation of women at senior levels of the corporation had seen gains in the previous few years, peaking at 9.3% in 1994. The corporate restructuring, employment equity initiatives, and retirement of senior males have been proposed as factors contributing to that trend. Unfortunately, the severance packages eroded those gains. Women opted for them at significantly higher rates than their representation at all levels in the corporation. For example, one third of managerial subscribers to the package were women, while they accounted for only around 12% of employees at those levels. Overall, 46% of the subscribers were women, although they accounted for less than 20% of employees overall. As a consequence, representation of women in every staff category suffered. The overall representation of women in the corporation was projected to fall to 18.7%, which is a pre-1987 level. Most troubling is the fact that there are few definitive explanations for this phenomenon.

Procedures

The decision to limit this study to senior women was made primarily to make the number of interviews manageable and to reflect the fact that the already limited representation of women at those levels is particularly vulnerable to turnover. Each senior woman who opted for the voluntary package was sent a letter describing the study and inviting her to participate in it. Of the 29 women on that list, 14 were managerial staff and 15 executive staff. Of those, 16 indicated their willingness to participate in this study. Fifteen women were interviewed individually. The interviews lasted between 45 minutes and 2/2 hours, with the average interview lasting II/2 hours.

The study and its likely outcomes were described to each participant, and she was assured of the confidentiality of her responses. An interview guide was followed that focussed on each woman's experience at the corporation. Participants were asked about their decision to leave the organization and the nature of the factors that contributed to that decision. They were also asked more general questions about the organizational culture, the types of issues faced by professional women there, and the sources of career support available to them. The guide was used to open discussion; participants were encouraged to direct the interview to issues and incidents that they thought were relevant to the study. Each respondent was offered a copy of the report if she so desired.

Respondent Profile

Every attempt was made to encourage participation in this study. However, any interpretation of the results must be tempered by a recognition that this is a small sample that may not be completely representative of senior women at this organization. Of the 29 senior women who elected to leave during the last separation package, almost equal numbers came from managerial and executive ranks. However, of the IS women interviewed, only 5 were managerial staff. While 4 of the 29 who left were designated as visible minorities, none of them participated in the study.

The women who participated in this study had between 4 and 25 years of service at the corporation and were earning between $70,000 and $120,000 a year. They ranged in age from their mid-thirties to their mid-fifties. Most stated that they held staff or support positions. Only 4 referred to their jobs as having direct line responsibility. Almost half of the respondents had held positions in human resources or related functions. Four of the women had engineering degrees. Most of the participants were married and had children, although only a few had young children. Four were married to men who either still work at the corporation or had recently left.

Of these 15 women, 5 had moved directly into other large corporations. One had decided to work in the nonprofit sector, three were employed as consultants, and two had decided to take some time off for family reasons and intended to begin looking for work shortly. Several were involved in setting up their own consulting practices, one intended to complete a university degree, and another had decided to semi-retire.

Study Findings

While the respondensts cited a variety of reasons for leaving the organization, a series of common themes began to emerge after just a few interviews. This study focuses exclusively on the issues raised by respondents that were attributed, directly or indirectly, to the restructuring process. Although a number of women referred to the financial incentives associated with the package, in no case was that the primary factor. The most often cited factors were he lack of opportunities for career advancement and the stress brought on by the restructuring process.

It also appeared that while the restructuring process had taken its toll, it was also indicative of a new set of values that did not match the respondents' personal values. It is important to emphasize here that most of the participants in the study agreed that the restructuring was inevitable and that the corporation needed to move towards greater public accountability and cost effectiveness. However many of the women disapproved of the processes used to restructure and expressed doubts about whether these processes would achieve the stated goals

Although some of these women felt that they had not experienced gender bias, most were aware that it existed and had seen evidence of it. Many reported that the restructuring process had exacerbated gender issues that had existed prior to it. Most reflected that the bias was subtle and difficult to fight and that it was likely to increase as they moved up in the corporate hierarchy.

Since this is a small qualitative study, the voices of these women are most important. In this study, quotes from these women are frequently used because they described their experience very well.

Asked about their reasons for leaving the organization, this is what some of them had to say:

> "I loved my job, I loved the people I worked with, for the most part. But that wasn't enough. You really need to believe in what you are doing." "We [had] a lean, mean, fighting machine kind of approach. I felt that the commitment was gone. . . I started to get disconnected from the values of the organization. There were a couple of instances that were chilling.... I knew I was not going anywhere." "I left a job I loved, in a company that I felt committed to, but in a company that I felt was spiralling out."

This study touches on the dominant organizational themes related to the restructuring effort. For purposes of discussion, these themes have been grouped into categories. It is clear that these categories are interdependent, even symbiotic.

Limited opportunities : Almost all the respondents noted that opportunities for professional growth and mobility were very limited. Senior-level women have always been faced with a glass ceiling, but in this study lateral as well as upward mobility became very unlikely while the organization was downsizing. It also became very clear that most of the women occupied positions that were considered staff or support positions, and these positions were particularly vulnerable during the downsizing effort:

> "After the restructuring, there was a new executive pay plan. And this new pay plan was going to really pay for the value of the job . . . I could predict which jobs would be at the higher level, and which ones would be at a lower level. The ones at the higher level were the 'hard' jobs . . . the lower were the 'soft' jobs. And guess which ones were occupied by women!"

Almost all of the women interviewed were not hopeful for the future, although they felt they had done well in the past. In addition to the reality of downsizing and restructuring, many felt that corporate strategy and values were likely to hurt senior managers in general and women in particular. They also realized that with restructuring came a noticeable backlash against women that was likely to hurt their career prospects.

"It is an insidious kind of thing. They do promote women to senior positions. They don't promote a lot of women to senior positions.... I believe that as a woman I always had to try harder. I am not one to look for sexist things. I just don't.... I have a fairly tough skin. I don't get uptight. But there was no doubt at all that I could see that all the women had to struggle somehow, and I don't think they were all paranoid. I just always thought that they had to go an extra mile. I also always felt that when women were appointed to positions, I don't know if it was the underground network, because I never heard it from senior managers, but people always thought they got appointed because of employment equity. I very rarely ever heard the lower rank and file, I mean middle management, ever, when a woman got the job, say she deserved the job."

The restructuring process : All of these senior women recognized the need for corporate restructuring and its possible benefits. Most were of the opinion that the means used to achieve greater cost effectiveness and public accountability were seriously flawed. They described the process as demoralizing and dehumanizing. The restructuring had destroyed their psychological contract with their employer and had not replaced it with another that was acceptable to them. Several felt that the organizations and its leaders were not "walking the talk," that the values they professed were inconsistent with the decisions they made:

> "It is quite frustrating, sitting in a corporate group, watching this perceived need to downsize and cut costs, and yet [there was] this huge duplication of effort that was so clearly going on around the organization . . . So a lot of [us] were doing this on the one hand, and seeing a lot of actions that didn't necessarily jive. I found that incredibly frustrating to deal with. A lot of 'speak.'"

Respondents also pointed out that the process was taking inordinately long and that they were hit with another wave of change before they had recovered from the first one. They thought the process of change was unnecessarily hard on people. Morale appeared to be at an all-time low, and restructuring had exacted a heavy price on the personal and professional lives of employees:

"Part of it was just how chaotic the organization was. The organization was trying enormous changes in a really short period of time, with no one really in control . . . It was replete with a million details. . . Everyone was overworked, overstressed." "It was almost depressing. We had gone through so many years of being told, 'Change, change! Downsize, downsize!' There's only so much of that anyone can take and retain a level of pride."

At the beginning, most of these women were hopeful that change would come and that it would be for the better. After 2 years of restructuring they were less hopeful and much more tired. The work-load had increased, stress levels were higher, and intrinsic and extrinsic rewards did not appear to exist anymore.

"The managers who are left are overworked, and they have lost their sense of where they are heading. You just cannot do everything you are expected to do in the time you have without eating yourself alive."

The restructuring was not going the way these women thought it should, and they were unwilling to pay the personal price it demanded. In the final analysis, they felt excluded and unappreciated. There was no clear logic or strategic direction that appeared to be driving the restructuring effort. A lot of unpredictability was associated with the future and with future career prospects. Some reflected that the corporate direction was inconsistent with their own values, and they were unable to support and implement changes they could not believe in.

"It is the 'flavour du moment.' It is not even the flavour du jour or the flavour of the month. It is literally the flavour du moment. The tide changes from day to day. You're in, you're out!" "We went through tremendous pain in 1993, all with this optimism, only to find that it was falsely placed optimism. And we were going to do it all over again to get it right this time. I couldn't go into the process again, having been so optimistic and full of energy the first time and being so emptied of optimism and so tired the second time."

Changing culture : The restructuring was accompanied by shifts in organizational culture that were almost always viewed in negative terms. With the restructuring and the threats that it brought, senior management appeared to close ranks and was perceived as becoming more and more of an old boys' club. That obviously hurt women in the corporation, but also excluded men who were not part of the dominant network. "Whose person you were" became very important. One woman said she got "tired of never being in the loop." The culture was described by these women in extremely negative terms such as "cowboy management," "macho," and a "banana republic." It appeared to be a culture based on fear rather than empowerment. People had begun to feel disenfranchised and cynical about the restructuring process, often electing to "play the game" while looking out for their own interests.

In the words of the respondents: "You stayed in the trenches and didn't put your head up, because you were going to get a rubber bullet in your brain."

"It makes it schizophrenic because they mouth the words, they talk the talk, but they do not walk the talk. If tomorrow [the CEO] says it will all be green, I can tell you that half the people will be saying bullshit it's green. We'll pretend it's green, but we all know that it's yellow and it will stay yellow."

The old boys' club also had implications for the direction of the change process. Challenges to corporate decisions and direction were few and far between, and when they were raised they were rarely tolerated. There appeared to be very little consideration and compassion for people. Attempts to champion those who were struggling led to being discounted and marginalized as a "fringe loony or a whining woman

"One of things that brought me to the feeling that I couldn't work there anymore is that I couldn't make a difference anymore. For a long time, even though it was slow and cumbersome and it made me crazy, I could make a difference... In the last year, I just couldn't get through. I was out of sync with the values ... getting out of the loop.... One of things at [-] was that there was always a large capacity for dissent... no more."

Discussion and Conclusions

Two broad sets of findings emerge from this study, one related to restructuring in general and its effects on all employees, and another related to its effects on women and their careers.

These respondents reported that organizational restructuring is chaotic, disorienting, and extremely painful. Several inherent paradoxes were revealed in respondents' descriptions. Some of these are familiar to researchers and organizations involved in restructuring. Most common is that the organization was cutting staff without reorganizing work. The obvious result was increased workloads for restructuring survivors. In addition, the organization demanded extraordinary commitment from its members during restructuring. Their workload often increased, and load they were sometimes asked to engage in activity that was incompatible with their values. They were also asked to take the decisions of top management on faith and were offered no justification for these decisions and no indication of future direction. Yet there was no recognition of their efforts, and no assurance that their careers would survive the restructuring.

The organization appeared to have made the decision to downsize through across-the-board cutbacks without considering the consequences. The people who were most likely to take voluntary separation packages were often those with the most job mobility, not the low performers that the organization most wanted to get rid of. It also became clear that downsizing itself increased workloads in some areas-most noticeably in human resources-yet they were also subjected to the same cuts as other organizational units.

The experiences reported here also suggest that it may be overly simplistic to assume that voluntary separation is a less painful option than layoffs or terminations. Although none of these women appeared to regret their decision to leave the organization, their descriptions reflect the fact that the experience of restructuring was extremely unpleasant, even though they were not fired. Voluntary separation from the organization is not necessarily an option that they would have chosen under other circumstances. It is also clear that they saw the restructuring as a major event in their lives. They used it as a marker in their careers and remembered it vividly.

It is also evident that the restructuring process itself was a source of much of the dissatisfaction these women experienced. They were asked to pay an enormous personal price to remain with the organization, without any indication of future benefit. In its attempts to become more "bottom-line oriented," the organization became ruthless and intolerant in its treatment of employees. Restructuring decisions and the information related to them were closely guarded. Survival appeared to centre around who you knew, rather than what you knew. The leaders were seen as an elitist group of "old boys" who were disconnected from employees. The atmosphere became intensely competitive, pitting employees against each other and against management at a time when the organization needed everyone to pull together.

Women faced a set of special challenges during the restructuring. They were over-represented in support function, which were targets of cost-cutting. They were the most recent entrants into senior ranks and did not have personal and professional networks to rely on. They were also faced with a backlash against employment equity and forced to justify their positions in the organization by overachieving. At the same time, they felt increasingly threatened and unable to voice criticism or make a difference. The value of the organization were antithetical to their personal values. Restructuring appeared to have a dehumanizing effect on the workplace. The corporate culture set a very high value on exclusive commitment to career and organization, and appeared to equate effectiveness with impersonal and intolerant treatment and unrelenting adherence to unrealistic performance standards.

Although this is a small qualitative study that cannot be considered representative of organizational restructuring efforts, it raises a number of questions about the effectiveness of restructuring in this case. It also makes a case for studying the effects of restructuring on employees at various levels-those who leave an organization, as well as those who elect to stay. Finally, it suggests that women may be particularly vulnerable to the effects of organizational restructuring.

It is also evident that the restructuring process itself was a source of much of the dissatisfaction these women experienced. They were asked to pay an enormous personal price to remain with the organization, without any indication of future benefit. In its attempts to become more "bottom-line oriented", the organization became ruthless and intolerant in its treatment of employees. Restructuring decisions and the information related to them were closely guarded. Survival appeared to rest on whom you knew rather than what you knew. The leaders were seen as an elite group of old boys who were disconnected from employees. The atmosphere became increasingly competitive, pitting employees against each other and against management at a time when the organization needed everyone to pull together.

Women faced a set of special challenges during the restructuring. They were over-represented in support functions which were targets of cost-cutting. They were the most recent entrants into senior ranks and did not have personal and professional networks to rely on. They were also faced with a backlash against employment equity and forced to justify their positions in the organization by overachieving. At the same time, they felt increasingly threatened and unable to voice criticism or make a difference. The values of the organization were antithetical to their personal values. Restructuring appeared to have a dehumanizing effect on the workplace. The corporate culture set a very high value on exclusive commitment to career and organization, and appeared to equate effectiveness with impersonal and intolerant treatment and unrelenting adherence to unrealistic performance standards.

Although this is a small qualitative study that cannot be considered representative of organizational restructuring efforts, it raises a number of questions about the effectiveness of restructuring in this case. It also makes a case for studying the effects of restructuring on employees at various levels: those who leave an organization as well as those who elect to stay. Finally, it suggests that women may be particularly vulnerable to the effects of organizational restructuring.

9

Women Administrators and Professionals of USA

Numerous studies have examined the role of American women in the public sector. All have agreed that while there has been a small amount of progress, women are still substantially underrepresented as a population in the higher levels of management (Hays and Kearney, 1992; Blau, 1978 and most severely in the 5% of all jobs with the highest prestige rating (Bose, 1983). These results are particularly disturbing in light of two widely known factors: (1) the conditions persist despite long term efforts to practice equal employment opportunity and affirmative action ideals; and (2) preparatory degrees for public service, especially the Master's degree in public administration, have been awarded roughly equally across gender categories.

Women are severely underrepresented in the United States at the middle and upper levels of management at all levels of the government. On the surface, the statistics may be deceiving. For example, the New York State work force of 1981 was 50% female. However, only one management or policy making position in five was occupied by a female. In addition, 95% of these women were in the lowest level of management (Gottfried, 1988).

At the federal level, only 32% of managerial positions and 10% of Senior Executive Service positions are held by women (U.S. Department of Commerce, 1989). This is only a marginal increase from the 1985 level of 7.2% of the Senior Executive Service (Rehfuss, 1986); of this group, only 13% were in professional positions, 21% in technical, and 23% in administrative positions in 1987 (EEOC, 1988)— again, only a marginal increase. The state level has also seen minimal progress in the last decade. While only 10% of state agency heads were women in the mid 1980s, the total proportion of women occupying these positions rose to 20% in 1993 (Bullard and White, 1993).

Unfortunately, research attributes this increase directly to a circumventing, rather than breaking, of the glass ceiling (Bullard and Wright, 1993). These gains were largely obtained in very specific types of agencies — those already heavily dominated by women. In addition, Neuse (1978) found longevity to explain only part of the under representation of women managers at the state level.

City and county management is also an occupation with few women in its ranks. Only 7% of city managers were women in 1987, with only 4.3% of newly promoted city managers being women in 1987 (Barber, 1988; Slack, 1987). By 1991, 18.6% of county CEOs and managerial positions and 34% of assistant city managers were held by women (Cunningham, 1992). Of the three levels of government, the local level has apparently had the greatest progress toward gender equity.

Recent literature also highlights a more alarming fact than the slow advancement of women in the public sector. Guy (1993) found that modest advances by women often result in a "backlash" against females in which recent gains are lost or significantly reduced. In this environment, women who advance tend to be unique in a number of ways. First, successful women managers tend to come from a higher socio-economic status than men in comparable management positions (Guy, 1993). Second, they often display greater educational attainments and are more likely to be "overachievers" (Kornegay-Clarke, 1986; Neuse, 1978) than men in comparable management positions.

Of course, the lack of women managers is not unique to the public sector. The under representation of women in the public sector is but a reflection of the record of the private sector. However, it can be argued that the record of the public sector is much worse in some respects (Cayer and Sigelman, 1980). It can also be argued that the public sector, the enforcer of equal employment opportunity, has a moral obligation to set an example and obtain a higher degree of equality than the private sector.

Primary Explanations for the Under representation of Women in Management Positions

Very little literature exists on why women themselves feel they are underrepresented in management positions; however, there is a large body of speculation that attempts to address the problem of the persistent under representation of women in mid and upper levels of organizations. Although widely divergent, these theories fall within three broad, but not mutually exclusive, categories: (1) women lack the qualities requisite for advancement; (2) organizational barriers prevent the advancement of women; and (3) societal factors impede the upward mobility of women.

Questions concerning the qualifications of women usually emphasize their limited knowledge base or a negative perception of their sense of professional commitment. For example, mid-level managers often believe that women are less committed to their chosen profession than men (Huckel, 1985; Lepper, 1986). It is also widely believed that women still lack the education required to succeed at higher positions. Some argue that the number of women in elite positions is proportional to the total number of women in elite pools (Ward et al.1990). City managers have attributed occupational segregation in their profession to the lack of adequate education and career orientation among women (Huckel, 1985). However, recent data show that the proportion of managerial positions held by women in the public service has been significantly lower than the proportion of women obtaining degrees in this area of study.

Organizational factors are also often used to explain the difficulties faced by women in the workplace. Research clearly shows that policies such as veterans preference are discriminatory toward women (Elliot, 1986). With only 25% of the workforce being veterans and 98% of veterans being male, one study found 50% of all federal positions and 65%o of all top positions were veteran preference hires (Tummala, 1987). For example, in the state government of Montana, 61% of all professional and managerial positions were veteran hires and only 8% of the clerical staff were veterans; however, this constituted 79% of the hire rate at the clerical level during that year (Tummala, 1987).

The structure of bureaucracies is hypo-thesized to further hamper the advancement of women. Bureaucracies tend to reflect and hold on to stereotypes long after they have been disproven (Kornegay- Clarke, 1986). Many of these stereotypes contribute to the continued presence of sexual harassment and discrimination in the workplace. Multiple surveys of government employees have found that approximately 20% of women personally experienced gender discrimination on the job (US. Merit Systems Protection Board, 1988 and 1994; Hopkins, 1980). Women at higher levels of management report more instances of sexual harassment and discrimination than those at lower levels, perhaps due to such issues as a greater awareness of the problem; instances of harassment escalate when women work outside of their traditional fields; and women in lower positions have fewer safe avenues of complaint and resolution, and therefore, are less likely to report harassment (Vertz, 1985).

Social theories of occupational segregation include socialization, role values, and the career preferences of women. Considerable evidence supports the contention that women are channeled into traditional or supportive roles regardless of their educational attainment. There exists a tendency for women performing the same tasks as men to be classified in a different and lower position than their male counterpart (Gottfreid, 1988). This difference in classification systems further solidifies occupational segregation and perpetuates discrimination by forcing women onto shorter career ladders in traditionally female positions (Rosenfeld, 1980).

It is also believed that women in the workplace, specifically women in managerial positions, experience serious conflict between family and work roles and this results in less career advancement. The attribution of work/family conflict is called into question by studies that compare women who have never married to married women with children. In terms of occupational attainment, however, Roos (1983) found little difference between the groups. While never married women were more like men in terms of having a continuous full-time work history, they advanced no further than those women who left for periods to have children.

Other role conflicts, such as managing a two career family, may affect career advancement (McClendon, 1976). The career of a married women often takes a back seat to that of her spouse although this is less true of woman in higher position (Vertz, 1985). what, then, can be concluded about the experiences and attainment levels of women managers in the public sector? While a significant change in the regulatory and legal environment governing the workplace has occurred empirical evidence suggests that women have made only marginal career path progress. Potential explanations in terms of qualification, organizational factors, and role theory provide a framework for further analysis, although many uncertainties persist.

These suppositions concerning the under representation of women in the public sector derive from data collected from numerous sources. Virtually every other actor within the public sector employment picture has addressed this issue except the professional women with the educational qualifications and experience required to fill these positions. This type of sample voids the applicability of the first theory (which states that women lack the qualifications to assume management positions) and allows us to question women managers presently working at all levels of the government to determine their perceptions and attitudes toward occupational segregation, and assess how they may either validate or call into question the other two groups of theories.

Conclusions and Implications

How do women perceive the workplace conditions in the public sector and how do these perceptions reflect our theoretical understanding of occupational segregation and sector differences? First, many women—and men—are being forced out of the public sector because of economic disincentives. Both the quantitative and qualitative data display the concern over the funneling of the best professionals to the private sector. As stated by one respondent, "the public sector desperately needs intelligent, committed public servants." While the Federal Employee Pay Comparability Act has increased the satisfaction with pay levels in the federal service to 42% (U.S. Merit Systems Protection Board 1994), this neither completely dealt with the problems associated with federal employment nor served to address pay disparity problems at the state and local levels.

The public and private sectors provide rather stark differences in terms of employment benefits for administrative ranks. The disincentives of the public sector-pay, working conditions, and poor job offers-are the primary advantages of the private sector. The primary advantages of the public sector are the ability to make a contribution to society, job security and health and retirement benefits. Factors such as past work experience clearly influence women's perception of workplace conditions.

Unfortunately, some aspects of employment transcend sector barriers. Sexual harassment and racial and sexual discrimination appear strongly in both sectors. Over 50% of the women stated that they had personally experienced discrimination, and 30% had experienced sexual harassment. Many respondents drew correlations between their experiences of discrimination and dominant workplace values. These comments included "working twice as hard to prove I'm not a token;" perception of co-workers that a family will hurt her professionalism; paternalism; veterans' preference; and the existence of a "glass ceiling" that prevents movement into top management.

Despite the negative perceptions of the conditions existing in the public sector, women still felt that these conditions, by-and-large, had not become significant barriers to advancement in the public sector. Even in the case of discrimination, while the number of incidents was unacceptably high, the public sector was still considered superior in this regard to private institutions.

Nonetheless, such conditions have profound organizational and policy implications. Given the federal legislation passed in the last twenty-five years promoting equal employment opportunity, why is the government (the regulator of discriminatory actions) also a place where half of the female workforce qualified for administrator rank perceives unequal treatment on a fairly regular basis?

It is also obvious that many dedicated and efficient individuals are prevented from entering or discouraged from staying in the government service. These individuals then turn to the private sector for economic and professional gain.

Many of the issues raised in this study are already part of our understanding of public/private sector differences and reinforces past research in this area. However, it is noteworthy that outside of the issues of sexual harassment and sexual discrimination, the other theorized explanations of occupational segregation theory are not perceived as barriers by this sample group.

Based on these outcomes, it is perhaps time for researchers and practitioners to stop looking at the progress of the past and look toward reviving progress in the future. This task begins by ceasing to debate whether these types of employee perceptions are based on reality or constitute misconceptions. The fact remains that such perceptions have, and are, affecting the public sector workforce — in terms of attitude, commitment, and/or future employment — and therefore must be confronted.

9.1 Some Success Stories

From corporate America to health care to the halls of academe women are initiating sweeping changes in the workplace. Here are several women's stories of professional goals and in making their work environments more responsive to their needs.

Georgia Landrum still remembers those cold, dark winter mornings when she rose at 5 A.M. to dress her four little girls. She left them at the bus stop before dawn and headed off, lunch pail in hand, to the 7 A.M. shift at DuPont's agricultural plant in Wilmington, Delaware. Back then, in the early 1980's, the buzzwords on-site day care and flextime weren't yet part of the national lexicon.

Despite the hellacious hours, Landrum, now 47, had jumped at the chance to get out of her low-paying clerk's job to go work as a maintenance technician, repairing centrifuges, pumps and other equipment. One of a handful of female DuPont workers to hold such a nontraditional job, Landrum didn't have much of a choice. She had two daughters and had taken custody of her two nieces after her sister's death. "I could earn 100 percent more, plus overtime," Landrum recalls.

By 1986, when Landrum was moving up to her next nontraditional job at DuPont, as a purchasing supervisor, Dreama Jackson was engaged in her own private battle with management. Jackson, now 52, was a product coordinator, responsible for the smooth transfer of DuPont products from the plant to warehouses around the country. The position had been a man's job, and at staff meetings she was like the odd one out at the ol' boys' club. "I would make a suggestion or answer a question and would get no response," Jackson recalls. "Then a man would make the same suggestion or give the same answer, and it was 'Year, why don't we do that.'"

Landrum and Jackson suffered alone until an employee conference in 1987 brought together many of the women in the company's large agricultural division. Talking among themselves, they found that all of them-Black, White, Latino and Asian—had similar job frustrations, feelings of isolation and family needs that were not being addressed by DuPont. The women decided to do something about it.

That year they formed the U.S. Businesswomen's Network, an organization within DuPont. Today more than 150 DuPont employees belong, with a core team of 13 women who keep abreast of the issues.

Networks like the one at DuPont are becoming more common across the country, as increasingly; women take the initiative to balance work and family in their search for career-advancement opportunities. Even where there are no formal groups, women are still sending employers the message that they want day-care options, revamped sick leave, policies that allow time for children and elderly relatives, flexible work schedules and the same consideration for promotion traditionally given to men.

"Employers need to understand that you can be both a good family person and a good employee," asserts Ellen Bravo, executive director of the 15,000-member 9 to 5, National Association of Working Women. Bravo suggests that women should first outline the issues that need to be addressed, then plan carefully how they want to proceed.

That was the strategy employed by the women at DuPont, where workers now have access to flexible work schedules day care referral services extended family leave, multicultural-awareness workshops and, in some cases the option to work from home—as Landrum does now.

The case for diversity

DnPont's story aside, getting companies to become more sensitive to promoting women and people of color into management positions remains a fundamental problem. Bobbi Gutman, 50, shocked management at Motorola in suburban Chicago when she quit her job as a personnel director in 1986 after only one year because she felt women and people of color weren't moving fast enough within the company. At that time the company had fewer than six women and people of color who were vice-presidents, out of a pool of more than 300 officers.

The situation at Motorola keenly reflected the national picture: Women have fared poorly in making the executive ranks, comprising only 5 percent of senior managers in Fortune 1,000 companies, claims Catalyst, an organization that monitors women's progress in business. Women of color have fared even worse: According to Catalyst, they make up only 3 to 5 percent of all female managers nationwide.

Gutman, a forthright African-American woman, wasn't afraid to speak her mind at the exit interview. "I felt obliged to tell the truth instead of the old saw that I had found a better opportunity," she says. "The good news is that the people I talked to were very surprised at what I was saying."

You couldn't have told Gutman then that she would wind up back at the company three years later, this time in a position to bring about change as director of executive and management development. "In December 1988 I bumped into the CEO at a social function, and we talked about how we could make Motorola stronger," she says. "I was so taken by the commitment to changing this organization that I agreed to come in and help them."

Today as vice-president and director of global diversity, she works with the office of the CEO to ensure that women and people of color with the potential to move up the corporate ladder are identified and groomed. When she returned to Motorola in 1989, the company had two female vice-presidents and six vice-presidents were not White. Six years later, the number has grown to 31 women, nine Blacks and 30 other people of color. Motorola's current goal is to add at least three women and three people of color at the vice-president level each year. For its efforts, in 1993 the company won the government's highest award for diversity, and Gutman is much sought after as a speaker at other companies seeking to improve the representation of women and people of color on their staffs.

Gutman takes care to point out that diversity is not about quotas. "This is not some altruistic endeavor to make people feel good," she says. "This is hard, cold business. The birthrate in this country for Blacks is nearly twice that of Whites. For Latinos it's also two times that of Whites. It doesn't take a rocket scientist to figure out what this country is going to look like in years to come."

Unfortunately conservative attacks on affirmative action could seriously reverse the trend toward diversity. But American companies, Gutman asserts cannot allow racism and sexism to stand in the way, or we'll lose against global competition."

Seizing the power

Attorney Ava N. Jackson, the first female executive director of the North Mississippi Rural Legal Services in Oxford, took on a fight similar to Gutman's. Jackson, 38, had done all the right things required to make it in the rouqh-and-tumble southern law community. In 1981 she earned a law degree from the University of Mississippi, or "Ole Miss," the breeding ground for good-ol-boy lawyers, and logged grueling hours as a young staff attorney for Rural Legal Services. But like most Black female lawyers in the Magnolia State, she had never practiced with the "right" firm nor been admitted into the unofficial old-boy network Nevertheless, she worked her way up to managing attorney of the Oxford office

Then in 1990 she was hired as acting director of the office, and she saw a chance to grab the golden gavel. Of course there was a catch. When hired, she has been informed that her acting directorship would "be a temporary things." She immediately understood what that really meant: The job was hers until the right man could be found.

Jackson searched for a loophole, one that would make her job permanent, something that would force the good ol' boys to stand up and take notice. "I saw that they were having problems with the national funding agency," she recalls. "I stayed on it. I hired consultants to correct the deficiencies. I worked continuously with the federal government. Eventually we overcame that problem."

With that victory under her belt, she networked like crazy within the state bar associations. Perhaps most important, she forged connections with other women board members. She got the job.

As head honcho, Jackson remains on the lookout for qualified women to hire. Bringing in other women behind you is crucial, she says, demonstrating how well she has learned the good ol' boys' game. "By the time positions have been advertised, the people have been picked and chosen for those positions," she explains. "The deals have already been cut."

Marching back from disappointment

Marilyn Kern-Foxworth was a precocious student who graduated from college by 20. Before she was 30, she became the first African-American to earn a Ph.D. with a concentration in advertising. She began her teaching career at the University of Tennessee at Knoxville in 1980 with the same expectation of moving quickly, this time through the ranks of academia into tenure.

Kern-Foxworth threw herself into her work. She served as a student adviser and began building her portfolio of scholarly research, a necessity fortenure consideration. She contributed to a dictionary of biographies of African-American writers and traveled to Africa to research how the media formulates images of Africa for Americans. Articulate, dedicated, charismatic and bright, Kern-Foxworth seemed to have it all.

Yet when she came up for tenure in 1986, she was turned down cold. The entire tenure committee had voted against her. The gifted A-student for whom everything had come so easily was shattered.

Looking back, Kern-Foxworth can see what went wrong. She lacked a mentor to guide her through the system, and she had neglected to make the round of parties so crucial to academic mobility because, as a single woman and the only Black, she'd felt uncomfortable. The chairman even told her she was "socially isolating herself." She had few relationships with her peers.

Even though Kern-Foxworth appealed the tenure committee's decision and was ultimately granted tenure, she felt the need to move on. Fortunately, when she left to teach at Texas A&M University in 1987, she had analyzed the academic culture. "I changed everything when I came here," she says. "I got mentors. I went to almost every event sponsored by the department.

I coauthored papers with other colleagues, I developed relationships."

By then she was also married and the mother of a young son. Recalls Kern-Foxworth: "My husband told me I was like a madwoman. I came home, cooked dinner, put the dishes in the dishwasher, got my son into bed and headed for the computer."

Kern-Foxworth, 42, and the author of Aunt Jemima, Uncle Ben and Rastus: Blacks in Advertising, Yesterday, Today and Tomorrow, is now a tenured professor in the university's journalism department. The secret of her success this time around? "I had a clear strategy she says.

The struggle for equal benefits

A clear sense of one's purpose can make all the difference. In New York City, labor leader Josephine LeBean found a cause worth fighting for securing benefits for the army of mostly Black and Hispanic women who go to the homes of the sick and elderly to feed and bathe them, perform simple errands and administer medicine Ironically, these women were denied the very health care they spend their lives giving others, for the city had failed to provide its home-care attendants with medical insurance and retirement benefits.

Then, in the late 1970's, Josephine LeBeau entered the picture. LeBeau had just become a labor leader in the ranks of New York's District Council 1707. A switchboard operator, evening college student and single parent of two sons, she was poor and living with her family in public housing when she took up the cause of home health-care workers. 'They didn't see me a far removed from them," LeBeau says. "They really had nobody who would listen or help."

Their despair was evident. LeBeau hasn't forgotten the call she received from a hopeless young health-care worker who was diabetic, who had high blood pressure, was in an abusive marriage anti whose child was on drugs: "She said, 'If I don't speak yon I'm going to kill myself."'

Such experiences fueled the fire within LeBeau. She relentlessly worked to unionize the women, advertising in newspapers and waging a grassroots campaign. She finally succeeded in pressuring the government into providing medical and retirement benefits. Today more than 80,000 home-care workers enjoy the fruits of LeBeau's labors But the battle continues. 'The biggest challenge we face now is budget cuts that begin at the federal level trickle down to the state and then to the city," says LeBeau, who at 52 is executive director of District Council 1707 and the grandmother of five. "The cuts mean a percentage of workers will lose their jobs." But LeBeau vows not to give up the fight. "It's a human-rights issue," she says simply.

A long way to go

Working women have come a long way, but it's a short distance in relation to where we have to go. Nine to 5's toll-free hot line (see sidebar) receives some 25,000 calls a year, many of them from women who fear losing their jobs. Hot-line staffers offer women advice and, if necessary, refer them to an attorney in their area.

"We're hearing stories from women who go to work and tell their boss they're pregnant and two weeks later the boss is telling them how their work is suffering," Bravo says. "They're being primed for dismissal. We also hear from women fired from work when their children have cancer and they need to take them for treatment. Many women are scared to death when the school calls them at work." Adds Bravo soberly: "In the end, as long as they don't blatantly violate the law, employers can still do pretty much what they want."

But as so man women the country have demonstrated, lasting change is possible, both through organized group efforts and individual acts of courage. The first step is to believe in the possibilities. The second is to recognize that the responsibility for changing the workplace is in your hands. Many companies are showing themselves to be more open than ever to the needs of working women. So claim your power. Get together with other women who share the same concerns, devise a plan of action, and go for it!

9.2 Profiles of Successful Managers in the US

The first female executives adhered to many of the rules of conduct that spelled success for men. Women were told that in order to succeed, they must play the corporate game the way men play it. Up to now, women's ways of thinking, doing and feeling did not have much pace in the business world. However, according to Fortune Magazine, less than 0.5 percent of the highest paid officers and directors in America's largest public companies are women. Could it be that this first wave of thought was wrong?

Women are entering the American work force in record numbers. Today, women constitute 45 percent of the labour force. Two-thirds of the expected work force growth in the next decade will be female, with a third of all middle-management positions held by women.

At the same time the work place is changing. Pressed by competition and a "fast-changing technology characterised by flexibility and innovation, companies are casting aside old-culture values". Most success companies today will be those that aggressively hire, train and promote women, and allow these women to express, not give up, their personal feminine values.

Studies in success

As the national director of the Girl Scouts of the USA, Francis Hesselbein holds the equivalent of the CEO's post in the largest nonprofit organisation for girls and women in the non-Communist world. The Girl Scouts have more than three million members and a paid professional staff of 500. The yearly operating budget $26 million.

Hesselbein is the first chief executive from within the Girl Scouts' ranks, having begun her career in the fifties as a temporary leader of a thirty-girl troop. While working with her troop, Hesselbein was chosen president of the local council. Soon afterward, she was asked by the national organisation to train board members. She then became the executive director for her local council. In 1976, the board named her National Executive Director.

During her tenure Hesselbein instituted a common planning and management system to unite the local councils. She developed and defined guidelines for financial reporting, equal employment, delivery systems and nine other areas of concern. These guidelines have since been adopted by public schools, not-for-profit organisations and several major corporations. These and other accomplishments have resulted in the Girl Scout organisation being described as one of the best-managed organisations around

Barbara Grogan, forty-three, is founder and president of Western Industrial Contractors, a $6 million millwriting firm in Denver Colorado. She started the company with $50,000 and an old pickup truck in 1972. At that time construction companies were losing their business base, and many have not survived to this day. But Grogan, one of less than a dozen women among the nearly 5,000 millwrighting contractors nationwide, has not only survived but flourished, attracting such clients as AT&T, United Airlines and IBM.

In 1986, Grogan added a consulting division to provide clients with estimating, scheduling and cost-control services in all phases of the construction business. The consulting company recently won a $1 million contract to do the scheduling for Denver's new international airport.

Millwrighting involves the moving and installation of industrial equipment. Grogan's company has installed the world's largest underground baggage sorting system at United's Hare terminal, hung a four-storey theatre screen and relocated $7 million flight simulators used to train airline pilots.

Nancy Badore is the executive director of the Ford Motor Company's Executive Development Centre, which is responsible for training the company's top two thousand managers worldwide in the "new culture" values based on quality and customer orientation. It is this new culture that is credited with enabling Ford to emerge from its near collapse in the early eighties.

Nearly forty-three, Badore joined the company in 1979 as a member of the corporate employee relations staff, where she worked on establishing Ford's Employee Involvement programme, an approach which focused on getting union stewards and plant managers talking with one another.

Soon after, Badore took charge of a project to bring division heads together with plant managers so that division managers could listen to and learn from them. The programme worked so well that her next assignment was to develop a model for permanent structure within Ford that would train the company's executive managers in the programme and keep training them on a continuing basis.

Badore now reports to an executive vice president just below the chairman. Her Executive Development Centre, with its $5 million budget, educates the very top layer of managers and plays a pivotal role in defining the company's direction of change.

The new style of successful women managers

Why have Hesselbein, Grogan and Badore succeeded while other women have not? All three women have brought a unique woman's perspective to the working environment. No longer advocating the command-and-control style of management long associated with men, these women are drawing on styles and habits that they have developed "from their shared experience as women". They recognise that women managers no longer need to act, talk, dress and think like men.

Women, like those profiled, are succeeding because of—not in spite of—certain characteristics generally considered to be feminine and inappropriate in leaders. Those women who assume leadership roles in today's business world are bringing their distinctly feminine values with them. These values include an attention to process instead of a focus on the bottom line; a willingness to look at how an action will affect other people instead of asking, "What's in it for me?"; a concern for the wider needs of the community; a disposition to draw on personal, private experience when dealing in the public arena; an appreciation of diversity; and a outsider's impatience with rituals and symbols of status that divide people who work together and reinforce hierarchies.

This new management style has been labeled "interactive leadership". So termed because these women actively work to "make their interactions with subordinates and superiors positive for everyone involved."(S) Women who employ an interactive leadership style encourage participation, share power and information, enhance other people's self-worth and get others excited about their work. All these things reflect their values and beliefs that allowing employees to contribute and to feel powerful and important is a win-win situation.

Shared characteristics and work patterns make for successful women managers

Successful women managers work at a steady pace, but take small breaks scheduled throughout the day. Forty to sixty percent of successful women managers spend time in formal scheduled meetings with unscheduled tasks quickly filling up what remains of the rest of the day. The pace is steady and fast but geared to cause a minimum of stress because these women schedule in very small breaks at various times during the work day. Hesselbein reads and relaxes on her sofa during lunch. Badore has her secretary leave fifteen-minute breaks between back-to-back meetings when possible.

The women do not view unscheduled tasks and encounters as interruptions. Today's successful women managers make it a point to be accessible, particularly to immediate subordinates. They employ an open-door policy. They care, enjoy being involved and make it a point to help others. Successful women managers give others credit and praise and send small signals of recognition. They refrain from asserting their own superiority.

Successful interactive leaders make time for activities not directly related to their work. Although the open-ended nature of their jobs demands long hours, none permit this to mean the sacrifice of important family time. Women are no longer duty-bound to put career ahead of family. Badore is strict about her hours. She comes into the office at 8.30 am and makes sure she is out of the office by 6.00 pm, so that she and her husband can enjoy quality time with her children. Grogan never goes to the office on weekends and discourages her employees from doing so. They all are willing to put off work-related tasks that did not demand immediate attention in order to prevent business responsibilities from infringing on family time. In fact, "general family happiness and fulfillment (contentment) was noted as away of providing balance and perspective to life, thereby fostering or permitting greater effort and productivity at work."

Successful women managers schedule time to attend to mail. Successful women do not view mail as a burden, rather as a way to keep in touch with the outside world as well as with personal and professional contacts. Mail, including periodicals, is a way to keep up-to-date with current events and industry trends. Successful women managers attend to mail immediately and set aside time to do so. Badore reserves an hour each day to go over the mail with her secretary. Hesselbein personally answers every letter she receives within three days.

Successful women managers maintain a complex network of relationships with people outside their organisation. They consider representing their companies a major aspect of their jobs. In addition, successful women managers are aware of themselves as role models and make use of that position to help other women internal or external to the corporate environment.

The women focus on the ecology of leadership. In other words, they keep the long-term in constant focus. They are always looking at what people are doing and noting trends that could have an effect on their jobs and organisations. They are big-picture oriented.

Successful women managers schedule in time for sharing information rather than guarding it. Knowing that communication flows in two directions, these women encourage dialogues, signalling to their employees that they are trusted and that their ideas are respected. They allow subordinates to reach conclusions, solve problems and see the results of the decisions made.

Successful women managers know that what people really want is to feel they are contributing to a higher purpose and have the opportunity as individuals to learn and grow. Today's woman leader allows those around her to maximize contributions and potential.

Successful women form "centrearchies". Successful women are "not at the top, but in the centre; not reaching down, but reaching out. Successful women managers prefer the team approach to problem solving and try to make people feel part of the organisation by encouraging this team participation. Badore's entire career has been built on the notion that management is best done by the team approach. She helped develop this style on the factory floor and then brought it to the executive suite.

These feminine principles had little chance for influence in the days when business organisations were dominated by men. But corporations have changed—and are still changing. Today's corporation is "driven by fast-changing technologies, global competition, the shortage of skilled labour and the need to adjust to a diverse work force that includes a large percentage of women".

In order to survive, businesses need to take advantage of what women are able to provide. At the very time when women are surging into the work force, companies need to hire these women and take advantage of those values inherent to them - values that underlie the feminine principles of leadership and may guarantee the success of corporate America.

9.3 From Pulpits to Judicial Benches, Influx of Women Transformed Workplaces in the 1990s

When Carin Smith entered Oregon State University in 1976, the school of veterinary medicine had only a handful of female students. By 1980, when she joined that graduate program, she and other women made up half the vet school's entering class. Today, it's men who are becoming as quaint as James Herriot: They wield only one-fourth of the school's stethoscopes. The shift in Oregon symbolizes a dramatic change in the gender makeup of some of the nation's most traditionally male-dominated professions.

From dentistry to Dodge sales, women are taking over more jobs once held almost exclusively by men one of the last gender barriers in the American workplace.

True, many jobs remain male preserves. Fewer than 1 percent of the nation's pickling machine operators, stevedores, or movie projectionists, for instance, are women. Yet, in dozens of other fields, the numbers have changed dramatically, due to economic and social factors. "We have always been applauding these [occupational] milestones for women," says Claudia Golden, a Harvard University economist in Cambridge, Mass. "When we stop applauding, we will know we have made it."

The ovations have, in fact, grown softer since the 1970s and 1980s, when many of the most blatant barriers to women were shoved aside. But women continue to carve new career paths, building on those prior gains. Equal opportunity laws have opened doors, and a generation of girls has grown up being told by parents, "You can have any job you want."

Dr. Smith, now based in Leavenworth, Wash., who edits the Bulletin of the Association of Women Veterinarians, says she decided to become an animal doctor at age 5. Now, women account for 43 percent of all practicing vets up from just 2 percent in 1989.

In this field, even as women such as Smith were feeling freer to pursue a career that related to their love of animals, economic forces were also at work. Pay for vets was falling -, prompting many men to seek other occupations. Similar dynamics have transformed the gender makeup of other occupations. From 1989 to 2001, women increased their representation in 106 of 497 occupations tracked by the US Labor Department, finds a new study by the Employment Policy Foundation, a Washington research group.

In addition to veterinarians, the fields where women's participation increased the most were:

- Top public administrators: Women's share rose from 4 percent to 37 percent.
- Industrial engineers (efficiency experts): from 6 percent to 22 percent.
- Members of the clergy: from 6 percent to 18 percent.
- Math and science teachers: up six fold from a relatively small base. Chemistry teachers: up fourfold.
- Dentists: up fourfold.
- Car salespeople: up threefold.

Despite these statistics, Barbara Reskin, a Harvard University sociologist, believes the 1990s have been less a period of dramatic progress than a "solidification" of the "big leap" women made in the previous two decades in shrinking their occupational segregation.

Still, the shifts have come during a period when women's share of the overall labor force remained relatively flat: It rose from 57.4 percent of US workers in 1989 to 60.1 percent today. By contrast, in the 1970s and 80s the shape of the labor force was transformed by an influx of women. Since then, in hundreds of occupations there has been little change in the gender ratio. Indeed, women are still crowding, voluntarily or semi-voluntarily, into certain occupations they have dominated for many decades - sales workers, secretaries, cashiers, nurses, elementary school teachers, receptionists, hairdressers, and so on.

Just 20 occupations are home to almost half of all working women: nearly 30 million out of total 63 million women in the work force, according to the labor department. They account for 97 percent or more of all secretaries, receptionists, and registered nurses, for instance. Few men enter these areas, often seeing such jobs as ones that would compromise their masculinity. One exception is flight attendants, where a lawsuit opened the door to men lured by the travel perks the job offers.

Lone female at a dotcom

But women are venturing more and more into "male turf." When Vidya Sundaram last year joined Xtime, a start-up firm in San Mateo, Calif., that offers Internet-based software for scheduling appointments, she was the only woman among a dozen or so software engineers. In Silicon Valley, female programmers are almost rare. The young Stanford University graduate figures her arrival at Xtime brought a certain civilizing influence.

"It is a good balance to have a mix of men and women. It makes for a healthy work environment. It is pretty unhealthy if it's all men. I'm more open than the men." After a few months on the job, Ms. Sundaram started "making noises about wanting a sister" on the job. Management heeded her request, hiring a former colleague from a failed dotcom.

Sundaram says the team of software engineers works closely together, and "it doesn't faze me that people are sometimes working 20-hour days." For some women, especially those with children, long hours are an issue - causing them to avoid certain occupations.

Pay gap persists

This is also regarded as one reason why full-time working women get paid, on average, about 72.2 percent of men 5 annual earnings. Women often take on greater, more time-consuming family responsibilities than men. On average, they work 92 percent of the hours of men. Women physicians who are unmarried and have no children, for instance, earn 13 percent more per year than those who are married and 15 percent more than those with children, according to a study by Alicia Sasser, a Harvard economist. She attributes the difference to "time constraints imposed by work norms and family responsibilities."

In many industries, gender shifts have stemmed in part from changes in the supply of skilled laborers. Women were able to move into accounting in greater numbers as the supply of men became exhausted. Women like Sundaram are starting to find jobs in high-tech areas as more of them take computer science courses and other engineering courses in college. "There continue to be some barriers to e-commerce occupations," says Harvard Professor Reskin. Many people get these jobs through networking, for example, and women have fewer connections to tap.

In the blue-collar area, women didn't advance far in the 1 990s. One reason may be that the number of jobs in the crafts and in manufacturing have been declining as productivity rises and jobs are shifted abroad. Men still hold the vast majority of the least-desirable or most-dangerous jobs, such as loggers and miners. That's reflected in accident statistics. Thirteen men die on the job for every woman.

New law-school majority

In many professions, women are climbing fast, reflecting their increased education as well as the law banning gender discrimination. Today the majority of bachelor's degrees, and 40 percent of doctorates, go to women. "The professions in general have been blown wide open," says Harvard's Professor Golden.

In law, for example, women now account for almost one-third of the nation's lawyers, as well as the majority of entering law students. Over the past dozen years, the number of women law partners, general counsels, and federal judges has doubled. But an American Bar Association commission acknowledges: "Women in the legal profession remain underrepresented in positions of greatest status, influence, and economic reward. They account for only about 15 percent of federal judges and law firm partners, 10 percent of law school deans and general counsels, and 5 percent of managing partners of large firms." Women lawyers are often at nonprofits, government agencies, or smaller law firms, where they can better manage their hours.

A somewhat similar story could be told for other professions. Women constitute more than 40 percent of medical-school entrants. But highly paid surgeons and orthopedists tend to be men. More and more primary-care physicians are women.

Women make up 66 percent of public relations specialists, up from 27 percent in 1970. More and more women are becoming bank branch managers. In many newspapers, women journalists outnumber or almost outnumber men. But men tend to hold the most prestigious posts.

Rising entrepreneurs

More women are studying management, entering business, or starting their own businesses. Women are starting businesses at twice the rate of men, about half in the service sector and 19 percent in the retail area. Some 8.5 million women-owned businesses employ 24 million people.

One reason some women go into business for themselves: They figure that rising to the top in corporations is difficult. "The overt kinds of discrimination have been taken care of," but the more subtle ones have not, says Debra Kolb, a professor of management at Simmons College in Boston.

One example may be the assumption that the attributes required for leadership are more male than female. Ms. Kolb says such bias often makes it hard for women to move up the corporate ladder. Others say many women voluntarily opt off the fast track. Rather, in seeking time to raise a family, they choose flexibility, a friendly workplace environment, and other nonmonetary factors, argue Diana Furchtgott-Roth, now chief of staff at the Council of Economic Advisers, and Christine Stolba, at the American Enterprise Institute.

In Silicon Valley, Sonja Hoel is one of perhaps three women who have become a partner in one of the top 10 venture-capital firms there.

That job puts her on the executive board of seven firms - the only woman on each of those boards Being a woman," she says, "is only a handicap if you make it so".

Table 9.1
Leading US occupations for women

	millions of women	
1. Sales workers, retail, and personal services	4.3	*63.5%
2. Secretaries	2.6	98.9
3. Managers and administrators	2.4	31.0
4. Cashiers	2.3	77.5
5. Sales supervisors and proprietors	2.0	40.3

Table 9.2
Some Nontraditional Jobs for Women

	millions of women	
Atmospheric scientists	3	25.0%
Upholsterers	13	20.3
Dentists	31	18.7
Vehicle washers and equipment cleaners	43	13.7
Meter readers	6	13.0
Announcers	6	11.1
Pest-control occupants	4	5.6
Welders and cutters	29	4.9
Garbage collectors	2	3.7
Washing, cleaning, and pickling machine operators	0	less than 1%

*percent of women in category

SOURCE: Department of Labor, US Government, DC

9.4 Glass Ceiling at Top Level

In the US during the past few decades, an explosion has taken place in the number of women in high profile, high prestige, income professions. Many law and medical schools now have an almost equal number of men and women. In engineering, women now receive 20 percent of the degrees. But a far more basic change - what many refer to as 'the feminization of power' - has yet to occur. The top echelons of engineering, law, and medicine - the most influential, lucrative, prestigious positions remain overwhelmingly in the hands of men."

"'You have to be out there in the work force to begin to realize that our whole social fabric has been set up by and for mostly white middle-and upper-class men,' says Jane Dolkart, assistant professor of law at Southern Methodist University in Dallas, Texas, and an expert in discrimination law. Dolkart returned to academe three years ago, after 5 years in government and private practice in Washington. DC. Earlier, in the 1970s, she taught law at Catholic University."

'"Things have changed immensely since my student years and my teaching years,' Dolkart says. 'As a student in the 1960s I had few female classmates, but that was just part of it. The courses and subject matter and examples discussed bore no relationship to anything that seemed to reflect my life. On the most basic level, no one ever used the word 'she' ..."

"'At the time I came out of law school there was enormous discrimination in hiring,' Dolkart recalls. 'I was in a group of women law students at Columbia and New York University that brought the first lawsuit under the employment discrimination laws against 11 New York City Law firms. It's important to realize that the development of a theory of sex discrimination as a constitutional matter, a statutory matter, was done primarily by women attorneys. Employment discrimination laws had been on the books for years, but until there were women out there thinking about the impact of being female on jobs, not a lot happened. And it wouldn't have happened but for the fact that there were women lawyers who brought an entirely different perspective'..."

"Today, an the engineering front, large industrial firms seem to hire women engineering graduates with more regard to grades than gender. But women still face special challenges in the competition for academic posts. Today's environment — few openings and tight research funding —is hostile for everyone, but in some ways is more hostile to women. The whole tenure issue makes hiring women dangerous...

"The data suggests there's still a problem. In all three professions —law, medicine and engineering – women earn less than men with comparable training and years of practice. They hold fewer partnerships, judgeships upper management posts, full professorships. Law firms more and more are looking at the bottom line. What they most want or partners is people who can make a lot of money...

"There is beginning to be an 'old-girl' network, but it's still very much smaller. It is harder for women to have access to people power. If you are looking for work in large corporations, that is much harder for women Your contact are the people you meet along the way. These disadvantages, form important supports for the glass ceiling, the invisible barrier that keeps women from claiming their rightful share of top-level jobs..."

"Speaking of the future... overt employment discrimination is only one aspect of removing the inequalities that still persist The subtle barriers must also be attacked. Employers need to assure women that they will have opportunities to gain the contacts and mentors that help build careers. People need to heighten their awareness of women's issues. They need to learn to understand each others' value systems."

9.5 Scarcity of Black Women Managers at Top Level

A recent survey revealed minority women managers are not moving up in the ranks because they don't have ready access to role models, mentors and high-visibility projects.

Most Black women and other minority women in management are deeply dissatisfied with their chances for advancement in the workplace, a study recently reported.

Minority women managers say they're not moving up in the ranks because they don't have ready access to role models, mentors and high-visibility projects, the Catalyst research group said.

"The women surveyed are highly educated and believe themselves qualified to advance in corporations," said Sheila Wellington, president of Catalyst, which works to advance women in business.

Nearly a quarter of the women said they plan to leave their companies. About 1,700 of the women had graduate degrees. Corporations need to pay attention, according to Catalyst. Companies are risking the loss of talent in a tight labor market as well as the loss of market share of minority women consumers and business owners.

The survey was conducted by mail and has a margin of error of 2.4 percentage points

The women surveyed are highly educated and believe themselves qualified to advance in corporations," said Sheila Wellington, president of Catalyst, which tracks trends in women in business.

Nearly a quarter of the women said they plan to leave their companies. About [illegible] of the women had graduate degrees. Corporations need to pay attention, according to Catalyst. Companies face the loss of talent in a tight labor market as well as the loss of return on investment [illegible] and [illegible].

The survey [illegible] conducted [illegible] and has a margin of error of [illegible] 4 percentage points.

[illegible]

10

Women Executives of Canada

Employment equity has been an issue in Canada at both federal and provincial levels for several years. A Royal Commission on Equality in Employment (Abella, 1984) indicated that despite government efforts, certain groups continued to face discrimination in employment. These groups included women, natives, persons with disabilities and visible minorities. This report led to the 1986 federal Employment Equity Act. At the provincial level, education authorities respond to the under representation of women in leadership positions in very different ways. The Ministry of Education in Ontario is viewed as quite proactive in its formal recognition of the problem and in taking measures to address it, unlike provinces such as Alberta, where there has been no formal government response (Young, 1990).

Historically, the Ontario Ministry of Education has tended to focus on equity for women, although there has been increasing attention in recent years to the disadvantage faced by racial minorities, persons with disabilities, Francophones and aboriginals (Ministry of Education, 1989, p.2). The fact that provincial employment equity legislation has been introduced has also necessitated broadening the focus of the Ministry. The following study focuses on the effects of employment equity policies and programmes for women in Ontario school boards, since these initiatives have been in place for two decades.

In 1973, the Ontario Minister of Education recommended that there should be a policy of 'equal opportunity' for women, with respect to employment and promotion at the Ministry level. Since that time, the Ministry has received increasing pressure to focus more attention on equity for women within school boards. A Woman's Adviser was appointed within the Ministry in 1975; an employment equity unit within the Ministry was constituted in 1979 to provide information to boards; and in 1984, the Education Minister requested school boards in Ontario to develop affirmative action plans with goals and timetables (Focus on Leadership 1, 1984).

Starting in 1985, school boards were required to provide affirmative action data in their reports to the Ministry. Also in 1985, school boards began to participate in the Affirmative Action/ Employment Equity (AA/EE) Incentive Fund, a fund provided to boards at their request for up to 3 years to assist them to develop and implement employment equity programmes. It was expected that the first year of funding would be used toward employing an AA/EE coordinator who would oversee employment equity initiatives within the board.

In a memorandum to school boards in 1988, the Education Minister requested that school boards establish a goal of at least 30% representation of women in all positions by the year 2000. In February 1990, a memorandum from the Minister raised this goal to 50% representation by women for the positions of Supervisory Officer, Principal and Vice-Principal.

Most recently, in 1992, the Education Act was amended to require school boards to: Develop and implement a policy on employment equity for women and other groups designated by the Minister, to submit the policy to the Minister for approval and to implement changes to the policy as directed by the Minister. (Ministry of Education, 1993, p.12)

The Current Status of Women in Educational Administration

Since 1986, the Ministry of Education has produced an annual report entitled The Status of Women and Employment Equity in Ontario School Boards. This report contains statistical information, which includes the occupational and salary distribution by sex of all full-time board personnel; since part-time employees tend to be women, exclusion of this group is noteworthy.

All reports point to the continuing need to increase the representation and/or status of women in different occupational categories, but it is interesting to note that despite the clear concentration by sex amongst the non-teaching staff, employment equity tends to be focused on professional women's access to leadership positions. While this study replicates this focus it is recognised that there is a definite hierarchical ordering in the articulation of the policy.

It is clear that after almost two decades of Ministry attention, women are still not proportionately represented in educational administration. A recent report acknowledges that 'progress has been slow' and 'goals are still far from being realized' (Ministry of Education, 1991, p.7).

If one analyzes the statistics provided in the report the following scenario emerges. First, the proportion of women teachers at different levels is relevant; in 1991, women represented 76.8% of elementary school teachers and 44.8% of secondary teachers. However, while approximately three-quarters of elementary teachers were women in 1991, approximately three-quarters of elementary principals were men. Similarly, while almost half of secondary teachers were women in 1991, approximately 85% of secondary principals were men (Ministry of Education, 1993, p.54). At the same time, women could not be said to be lacking credentials since, in 1991, women made up 53% of all successful candidates for the Supervisory Officer's certificate and 62% of those achieving the Principal's qualification (Ministry of Education, 1993, p.48). Therefore, as the 1990 report comments, statistics from boards with respect to the status of women are particularly disappointing. However, to place these figures in a national context, a survey conducted in 1990 (King & Peart, 1992) found that, of the provinces, Ontario actually had the highest proportion of women in both principal and vice-principal positions. Again, Ontario is viewed as being at the forefront of change.

In other Western industrialised countries, the under representation of women in educational leadership is also apparent. For example, in the USA, a survey published annually in the American School Board journal indicated that, in 1993, women represented 10.9% of secondary principals and 43.1% of elementary principals (Leadership, 1993). In 1991 in England and Wales, women made up 18.3% of secondary head teachers and 48.5% of primary head teachers (Ouston, 1993, p.2). As Acker states: In most countries, men dominate in the higher reaches of education, as indicated both by the teaching of older students and by the disproportionate occupation of management positions.

The purpose of one case study in Canada was to explore how employment equity policy in education is experienced by women administrators in their daily lives. We begin with the particular experiences of a small group of women in order to consider how these experiences are connected to the broader policy and ideological context (Smith, 1987). The method, provides a means to address the relationship between structural oppression and the realities of individual lives (Weiler, 1988).

In this study, begins from the women subjects' comments about their experiences in administration and employment equity, and then the researcher draws on feminist discourses in order to provide a text that may be useful for them and in 'naming different realities' (Rossiter, 1988, p.21). As opposed to providing findings that are generalisable to all women administrators in Ontario schools, it is expected that the insights and understandings that are developed through this exploration may prompt other women to consider critically their own contexts.

Three women secondary school principals agreed to participate in the research. The researcher was interested in speaking to women principals because they could speak about their experience of entering administration and of promotion, and would also be able to speak about their day-to-day contact with teachers, as well as colleagues and senior administrators. The three women range in age from 40 to 53 years old, and work in boards located in rural, 'semi-urban' and urban contexts. Their family situations differ in terms of the number and ages of their children, occupations of partners, and changes (for example, in marital status) over time. These women were contacted through word of mouth.

At the time of the interviews, Jan was the youngest of the three women at 40 years of age, although she ad been in the position of Principal the longest. She became Vice-Principal when she was just 28, and Principal at 36. Diane is a Principal in the same board as Jan, although her school is in a more urban setting. She had been Principal for a year and was Vice-Principal for 5 years before that. She is 46 years of age. At 53, Marg has been employed in the education system the longest of the three women. She began teaching in an elementary school and switched to the secondary level when she became an administrator. All of her experience had taken place within the rural county where she grew up.

For each participant, the researcher collected and subsequently transcribed between 3 and 5 hours of taped interviews. She also spent a day 'shadowing' each woman, that is, following her around the school as she carried out her daily routine. Each interview took place in the Principal's Office at her school. For the first interview, She formulated questions that addressed her career history, transition to administration, and her perspectives on employment equity policy. Subsequent interviews pursued ideas that required elaboration or explanation. Interviews were semi-structured in that She had pre-formulated questions, but the dialogue moved away from this agenda as other issues arose in the interviews.

She began data analysis for each participant by listening to the interview tapes over and over until she could read the transcripts and hear the speaker. She wrote down topics that recurred and began to make connections between these topics. Then she wrote an outline of each woman's story. When she had finished, I sought to construct a dialogue between each participant, she and other theorists who could help me to make sense of their stories within a broader sociological context.

The organised data focussed on three themes: the first addresses the participants' experiences of gender inequity; the second explores their experiences of contradiction with respect to employment equity policy 'in practice' and the problematic scope of equity policy; and the third presents the participants as agents and considers the possibilities for resistance and change that they envision.

Experiences of Gender Inequity

(On the basis of analyzing the responses, the following scenario emerges)

If you were to go back... 15, 20 years ago, if you were male, you were promoted, and you might have represented 10 or 15% of the teaching population [in elementary schools]. (one respondent)

When they first started to emphasise that curriculum leadership role, some of our principals had been in the position for a number of years, and many of them men, male principals... were appointed without, perhaps, very much experience. (second respondent)

In this board... I've gone from being a minority of one, practically, to having about 15 other [women] comrades. (third respondent)

All three of the interview participants recognise that male preferment has long been part of common-sense practices when hiring administrators. The male-centredness of administrative structures, values and practices probably explains why the last two respondents describe aspects of their educational careers in terms of 'survival' rather than in terms of 'achievement'.

Virtually every quality that distinguishes men from women is already affirmatively compensated in this society... For each of their differences from women, what amounts to an affirmative action plan is in effect, otherwise known as the structure and values of American society. (MacKinnon, 1987, p.36)

Looking back on their application processes, the three respondents are acutely aware that existing ideas and practices operated to favour male administrative aspirants. They mention their discomfort with several aspects of this environment, including: competition, hierarchy and the assumed separation of professional and personal lives. For example, one talks about the competition at the vice-principal level. She suggests that because viceprincipals tend to be striving for promotion, there is less collaboration than she would like. Similarly, another one refers to the principals' group within her board:

All of these women would prefer to see a more collaboratie, co-operative environment and suggest that they ore working to create that; however, they feel that many of their male colleagues are quite comfortable with the existing competitive practices.

The competitive environment can be attributed to the fact that several people are vying for a few positions, and that the system is hierarchical. One has a number of problems with the resultant notions around 'upward mobility' in a career: she said :

"Most of my women friends... [are] not tied into a hierarchical move, they're interested in either lateral leadership opportunities, changes in pace, changes in direction. It just seems to be something the women are a little more comfortable with."

One of them is convinced that competence and satisfaction at one level do not necessarily mean competence and satisfaction at a higher level in the education system. She therefore rejects the idea that there should be specific career paths and a specific 'timetable of events' into which people are channelled. The writings of Rosemary Grant (1989) and Carol Shakeshaft (1987) echo some of her insights. Grant and Shakeshaft argue that definitions of career ambition, aspiration and timetables have generally been based on norms set by male administrators. Shakeshaft adds that many women educators question the valuing of administration over teaching. The three participants also express concern about moving further and further away from the learning environment of the school as they 'progress' in their careers.

Perhaps because of their traditionally greater commitments within the 'private sphere', women are also uncomfortable with the assumption that one can, and should, keep one's personal and professional life separate. Jan's (one of the principal interviewed) experience provides an example of how this assumption becomes part of practices that may be oppressive for women: [As a single Vice-Principal in a large high school] Iran the school within the first two months... And then, being a single parent, I had to make some requirements of meetings, so I could keep my family. So I became known as willing to do that, to take that risk. [emphasis added]

Jan is referring to the fact that these meetings had been traditionally held during evening mealtimes. The power of that norm is indicated by her reference to the 'risk' she took in breaking it; from this comment one infers that, by changing meeting times, she thought she may be perceived as lacking commitment (i.e. unwilling to work 'all hours'), and therefore as unworthy of promotion.

Marg (another Principal interviewed) also talks about her discomfort with the idea that aspects of one's life can be compartmentalised. She feels that her approach to administration is different from that of many males because she does not do this herself or when interacting with others. She said :

"Sometimes I relate to a situation as a mother; I think I know what that mother is going through now."

The difference in approach that Marg brings is tolerated because she is 'the Principal'. However, when Diane took a similar approach as Vice-Principal, she encountered resistance:

In addition to barriers posed by existing norms and practices, all three women mentioned a lack of institutional support networks. Marg comments that while she initially received encouragement from a couple of colleagues, 'in terms of a network that her male colleagues enjoy, it was not there'. Similarly, Kennington Edson (1988) reports that many women aspirants to educational administration view themselves as unable to gain access to traditional, informal male support systems. Jan also refers to the continuing power of the 'old boys' network', characterised by practices of selection and exclusion. Very early on, Diane recognised the male-centredness of administration and became a participant in a group of female administrative aspirants within her board.

Grant (1989) and Weiler (1988) mention research subjects who belong to similar support groups, for similar reasons. In Diane's case, the group formed initially to provide 'career-related' support to the women, and once in administrative positions, the women continued to give each other personal as well as professional support. This group has continued in different forms and at different times.

During interviews, it became clear that such groups are necessary for women administrators who often find it very difficult to 'fit into' the existing environment. Of course it is important to note, as did Jan, Marg and Diane, that many subtle barriers work to prevent women from even applying for positions of added responsibility. All three comment that many women teachers need encouragement to apply for administration; often they lack confidence and/or are constrained by family pressures. It is also found that domestic responsibilities were listed as a major difficulty for women who were attempting to move from teacher to administrator in the USA. As Diane says, for women it's 'never the right time':

Women educators and administrators must also demand access to the 'process of defining value' (cf. MacKinnon, 1987) in education, so that the environment is not so inhospitable for women. Jan, Marg and Diane recognise this, but also live with the resistance to the changes that they bring. In speaking about the responses of staff, students and colleagues to their appointments to administration, all three describe some form of opposition. For Marg, it was overt:

When I was made Principal they had a party, a Principals' Association party, and I was invited to it because I was entering administration at that time, I was becoming a Principal. And I tell you, [one of the administrators there] fold me exactly what he thought of women principals and where women should be and [pause] what he thought of them and [pause], anyway. All three Principals were conscious of being watched carefully for mistakes. However, it becomes a no-win' situation, as Marg comments: "But you're also walking such a tightrope because some of the traits that are considered to be acceptable in leadership are considered to be male traits, male acceptable, positive traits. And the same kinds of characteristics within a female are seen as less than positive."

Marg's comments are echoed by Grant (1989), who suggests that the practice of consistently appointing male candidates to management positions has led to the development of a management model based on traits stereotypically attributed to men, against which women are assessed unfavourably. Thus, women in traditionally male occupations tend to be judged as either 'competent and unfeminine or incompetent and feminine' (Biklen quoted in Shakeshaft, 1987, p.113).

Because of the resistance, women principals like Jan, Marg and Diane are careful about raising issues around gender equity in their boards. When I asked Marg about the possibility of becoming involved with employment equity for women in her board, she responded: "For me personally, I don't think it's a good idea [pause]. It may result in a time when I may be able to have more impact on that area. Right at this point I haven't felt it was wise."

While Jan and Diane feel somewhat more comfortable raising issues of gender in their boards, probably because of the larger proportion of women administrators there, they too are careful. Diane admits that she does not want to risk being viewed as a 'one-issue' person. All three women view change in gender relations as a long-term, evolutionary process.

Employment Equity in Practice

In their study of English colleges, Joan Cann et al. (1991) observe that there is a pervasive gap between the rhetoric and the reality of equal opportunity policies for women. Since it, is possible for liberal discourse to work against women's interests, 'it is only by looking at a discourse in operation, in a specific historical context, that it is possible to see whose interests it serves at a particular moment' (Weedon, 1987, p.111). In the next section one finds a discussion on the present and problematise the predominant discourse around employment equity, as articulated by the three participants when discussing their experiences of the Ministry's policy. Subsequent sections consider other problematic policy issues, namely, the implementation and scope of programmes.

Special Treatment for Women

It was quite revealing that, in the interviews, Jan, Marg and Diane all suggested that employment equity programmes were necessary for other women, but were not as necessary for themselves. In this way, they all distanced themselves from the programmes in their boards. One thinks that this practice can be attributed partly to the prevalent idea that employment equity provides 'special treatment' for women, and therefore contradicts the principle of merit.

For example, Marg talks about the reception to the Ministry's employment equity policy within her board. She says: "I hear both male and female colleagues really talking strongly against this whole mandate of 50%, which upsets me, particularly when I hear females talking about it, because their whole argument is based on people being in positions ... just because they're female as opposed to because they're capable.... saying, Hey, we shouldn't have any special treatment over anyone else". [emphasis added]

The discourse of employment equity as 'special treatment' reflects existing gender relations in , which female difference is constructed as inferiority or lack (MacKinnon, 1987). It also reflects the tendency to blame individuals for their situations rather than examining systemic constraints. Therefore, while the three Principals acknowledge that women aspirants generally have different experiences from men, they are afraid that responding to those experiences through employment equity programmes will only reinforce unequal gender relations. This contradiction between the policy's goal of improving the work environment for women administrators and the participants' reality of increased pressure and surveillance of those entering administration points to the need for more attention to what End Lee (1990) calls the 'invisible policy'—the existing practices and relations in the organisation. It is apparent from the comments of Jan, Marg and Diane that these practices present a formidable barrier to equity for women.

Unfortunately, the formal policy does little to challenge the prevailing liberal-individualist discourse. For example, there tends to be an equation of the status quo with merit hiring, and employment equity programmes with reverse discrimination. Marg starts to deconstruct the concept of merit in the following passage:

> Well I think that there's more that goes into hiring than just merit, I think we're all aware of that. There's the whole political scene that has to be considered, and [pause] certainly merit, certainly having earned the position is important. And ... I worked on a policy to try to ensure that there is equal opportunity for males and females so that the criteria, the screening points, everything is laid out very clearly, and so that is a step. But we all know that, even within that, there's all the other political kinds of things that go on around it where you have a male network, you have a female network which is different, you have the support systems which I think are different for both. So I don't think you can ever get a clean, merit appointment. I don't think you could ever do that. You just strive to, try to ensure that it becomes more feasible. [emphasis added]

Marg's comments indicate that there is a need to problematise merit in practice. Similarly, Alison Jaggar (1983) argues that the discourse of merit serves to justify the status quo, since those who currently occupy positions of power determine what is to count as meritorious performance and values. But while women who are experiencing contradictions and disjunctures between their realities and the prevailing rhetoric may be aware of the problematic discourse, moving outside of that discourse can represent a difficult challenge. For example, Jan uses the language of merit at the same time as she indicates an awareness of the double standard at work:

> The worst thing is to hire someone who is inadequate. Thank God, like at the moment, we haven't got that. We've got women

who are just dynamic, and they're giving 175%, so we've got good role models. But from my point of view, you get a couple of "duds" and they're going to be picked up on by, you know, the general teaching staff, saying, "Well that's the promotion of a woman. Look how..." ... And the irony of that is that you could do the same thing with a man and they wouldn't even care [laugh] you have to be so careful that you're promoting good women.

Her comments are ironic since it is clear that the discourse of merit is constantly used to undermine employment equity programmes to the extent that it is highly unlikely that 'unqualified' women would be hired. Perhaps because of their awareness of the pervasiveness of discourse and practices that favour the status quo, the interview participants view equity in employment for women as a long-term goal.

Design and Implementation

Comments made by Jan, Marg and Diane highlight the fact that although increase in the numbers of women in administration occurs slowly (Ministry of Education, 1991), those resisting employment equity in their boards imply that change is enormous. One is reminded of recent debates over 'political correctness' in which opponents of 'the politically correct movement' complain that women and minorities are taking over universities—this despite the fact that these groups continue to represent a small fraction of faculty numbers. Marg and Diane attribute the combination of little change and strong resistance to the lack of commitment to employment equity at both the Ministry and board levels.

At the time of the interviews, neither Marg's board, nor Jan and Diane's board had officially adopted goals and timetables for hiring women into positions of added responsibility. Diane speculates on the Ministry's motivation for introducing employment equity policy, in the following exchange:

D: I don't think [the Ministry] ever would have done it on their own. But it's because of the political force of two very strong unions: the Women's Federation, and the Secondary Teachers' Federation.

A: What do you think then, that the Ministry is setting out to do with employment equity?

D: Say that they're doing something.... All they can do is keep it as a visible issue.... I think it's very much a monitoring, you know, keep the lid on but make everybody feel happy kind of situation that the Ministry's in. I don't think they have any real concerns that they're prepared to, they can't do a whole lot about it, they don't have any clout. In Diane's view, the Ministry is not committed to change, and even if it were, would not have enough power to enforce change within the boards.

In support of her argument that the Ministry is not committed to change, Diane talks about the Affirmative Action Coordinator positions that were sponsored by the Ministry for a limited time. She comments that making an affirmative action position a consultant position is 'putting it in a very tenuous position' because coordinators and consultants have no power. The lack of power of these positions is highlighted by the lack of funding associated with them. As a result of the limited funding, many boards have made these positions part-time or have combined the position with a staff member's regular duties so that they spend half their time on each.

Diane suggests that the money might have been better spent by giving incentive funding to boards to put women into Administrator-In-Training positions:

You give some money to the board to release a teacher from part of their teaching schedule in order to... shadow a person in an administrative position and also do some of the tasks. So it's kind of an additional position of responsibility in the school that the school boards cannot afford.... If the Ministry gave some funding for, for example, women only, to be put into those positions, without making it too large scale, One thinks that Diane suggests that if the Ministry treated employment equity as it does other priorities it might be more effective. She suggests that the 'hand-in-hand relationship that the Ministry has with boards in the development of curriculum documents might be an appropriate model for their relationship with respect to employment equity policy. As it is, Diane suggests that boards are not required to demonstrate a strong commitment to employment equity, and that those few boards who do are considered to be revolutionary.

It says something about the 'invisible policy' within boards when the 'policy compliance' approach of this board is viewed as revolutionary by principals like Diane. Perhaps their approach is viewed as revolutionary because it is so uncommon for a board to demonstrate anything besides a formal commitment to employment equity policy. For example, Marg suggests that Ministry directives regarding employment equity are 'not received all that well' in her board.

It is evident from the preceding discussion that interview participants perceive there to be a lack of commitment to significant workplace change on the part of the Ministry and on the part of boards. They imply that opposition to the policy within their boards is considered to be acceptable, as is the 'exporting of blame' onto women (cf. Apple, 1986). Instead of blaming hierarchical structures and economic policies, there may be the tendency for male aspirants to blame women for their failure to 'get ahead' within the education system. In times of fiscal restraint and reduced career opportunity, one can expect this 'exporting of blame' to increase.

The Scope of Equity Policy

While employment equity programmes are thought to be necessary by the participants, they all mention that they are not sufficient. In other words, inequity for women is a result of patriarchal social structures, and change must therefore occur at a number of societal levels. However, the three participants convey a sense that many of the factors that are intricately connected with inequity for women are not acknowledged by employment equity programmes; that is, there tends be a decontextualisation of the problem.

Until the problem of inequity is placed within the context of a wider social and economic analysis, there will be a failure to address the full range of constraints faced by women teachers (Weiler 1988). For example, women's possibilities may be constrained by a lack of encouragement from superiors, colleagues and family, lack of access to political networks, and a lack of time and energy because of family and household responsibilities. In Diane's view, there must be societal supports in place for women before the pool of administrative aspirants will increase.

Jan suggests that we will not 'achieve the goal of equity until such time as all those societal issues are brought closer into line'.

Later, she elaborates: When the world is such that women aren't in poverty and women aren't being raped and abused, when there's equality of freedoms in the world, then at that point, we don't need employment equity programmes.... At the moment we're using them as interventions to bring the world back into balance.

Jan makes the interesting connections among issues of violence against women, the pauperisation of women, and inequities for women in the workplace; in her view, the various forms of oppression that women face are linked. At the same time, she recognises that there are differences among women. When asked whether employment equity policy is necessary for her and for other women, she responded:

For me personally, it's not necessary because I work in a board where the underlying philosophy is that women are valuable in their jobs as leaders.... But I think, in general, society is still not, one-third of, or two-thirds of single-family parents are women, poverty-level homes ... So the way Canadian society is now, there is still far too much inequity for women. You have to take some major political moves in order to change that.

Recognising differences among women (whether based on class, race, ability, etc.) forces us to contemplate the connections between various oppressions, as well as the disadvantages, which historically have not been addressed by employers such as the Ministry. For government, "affirmative action" promised a trendy, low-cost alternative to the enactment and enforcement of rigorous equal value legislation; selective promotion of a few both promotes individualism and serves the interests of formally qualified professional and managerial women. (quoted in Maroney & Luxton, 1987, p.88)

Resistance and Change

In previous sections one has discussed some of the career experiences of the three participants, and the concerns that they raise about employment equity policy. It is evident that the three women are somewhat constrained by their environments; as Sandra Acker (1989) suggests, there is often a tension between women's desire to progress in their careers and their desire to bring about feminist social change for women in education. However, it is important to point out that the participants definitely view themselves as agents of change within the system, albeit in different ways. Jan tends to construct herself as an 'implementer' of employment equity policy within her board rather than as a beneficiary; Marg refers to herself as a 'survivor' within the system, whose practices are slowly changing the negative attitudes toward women in administration; and Diane portrays herself as a 'negotiator' within her board, who is both a founder/participant in a women's support network and who actively works with colleagues and senior administrators to bring about change.

Jan views employment equity as one of many strategies required to bring about equality for women in the workplace She talks about change initiated at three levels: first, a change in the existing practices that are supported by those in power; second, change that may be initiated by women educators in general; and third change initiated through her own practices. When Jan speaks about change that must be supported by those in power, she refers to the importance of equitable hiring practices at all levels, and the necessity for boards to demonstrate that women do get hired into administration and do enjoy their jobs once there. But as well as change coming from above, Jan feels that women must take some responsibility for changing their own situations and those of other women. For example, she speaks about the importance of women encouraging other women.

The revolution, which women are making is a revolution from the ground up. It begins in their own lives, but its goal and direction is the radical transformation of all social relations.

Interestingly, by seeing herself as an implementer of the policy rather than a beneficiary, Jan is also distancing herself from the problematic 'special treatment' aspect of the policy that was referred to earlier.

Given the atmosphere in Marg's board, she is less certain about her ability to fight openly for change. Nevertheless, it is clear that Marg was aware of many of the contradictions between her experiences and the predominant rhetoric around gender equity and was doing all she could to improve the attitudes and the environment for women who followed her. In her own practices within her school, Marg is actively promoting change through her example and through dialogue. She considers it as part of her job to try to build support for some of the younger women who are currently aspiring to positions of added responsibility.

Marg prides herself on being a survivor within the system. on being the only female administrator in her county for many years. Marg also seeks to change attitudes through dialogue with staff and colleagues. For example, she talks about her response to the backlash to employment equity:

Marg thinks that it is important to engage with people's concerns about employment equity; as she says about the resistance that women entering administration face: 'It's necessary that women recognise the attitudes and deal with them'.

Of the three participants. Diane has been involved most formally with equity issues for women. She has been involved on the Status of Women Committees at both district and provincial levels and talks about consciously entering administration in order to bring about change for women. She says:

It not only seemed to be something I wanted to do It seemed to me became very clear to me it was something I had an obligation to do. That I didn't have the right to sort of sit back and say somebody else can do this and somebody else can speak for women But that there needed to be role models for the young women in our schools.

Diane's strategies for change are directed toward 'women-centered' activities as well as activities which involve negotiation with men within more formal structures. For example, Diane's membership in a female support group stems partly from her feeling that women need a space to affirm themselves without the presence of men.

Diane, seems to be suggesting that it is only when women treat one another as 'those who count' that we will break out of our silence. Therefore, for Diane, part of the work toward change for women must occur in isolation.

Diane's comments about the support group suggest that it was, in many respects, a consciousness-raising group where women could meet together to 'critically reconstitute the meaning of their social experience' (MacKinnon, 1982). Through their sharing and supporting, the group helped its members to adjust to the male-dominated administrative environment and to identify locations for change. Kathleen Weiler (1988) comments that such groups may provide the opportunity for women to change resistance into 'counter-hegemonic' activity. Cann et al. (1991) also talk about the important contribution that women's support groups can make to institutional development and change.

In addition to change through their own practices, Diane feels that women need to pressure senior administrators to create an environment that is receptive to women entering administration. In this regard, she views herself as a negotiator within her board. According to Diane, women in her board have 'bargaining power' with their Director because the board is not complying formally with the Ministry employment equity policy. Apparently, she and other women in her board initiated a number of programmes and workshops with the Director's support. Diane views this 'evolutionary way of bringing about change as a more effective long-run strategy.

Conclusion

This study set out to explore how employment equity policy in Ontario school boards is experienced by a small group of women administrators in their daily lives. It is expected that this research would enhance our theoretical understanding of how relations at the 'micro' level are organised by provincial practices and broader discourses within our capitalist, patriarchal society.

The study uses a 'materialist' approach, in starting from the experiences of women in particular contexts and drawing on relevant feminist theory to make sense of these experiences. While no claims to representativeness can be made, the data from this study provide insights into the context of employment equity policy in the Canadian schools. Since the Ontario Ministry of Education is considered to be at the forefront with respect to employment equity policy in Canada and perhaps in other countries, the issues raised here may be useful for other jurisdictions to consider. However, the primary intention of this study is to help other women to analyse how external discourses and policies penetrate and organise their own experiences (Smith, 1987) and to contemplate opportunities for counter-hegemonic work.

The data indicate that there is a disjuncture between the world experienced by the subject and the world that is organised in the abstract, conceptual mode of policy statements (Smith, 1987). The interview participants know from their experience what women aspiring to educational administration are up against: their 'upbringing' as women (psycho-social barriers); existing male-centred norms and practices, a lack of institutional support networks, overt opposition from colleagues, staff, and senior administrators, and a devaluing of the 'differences' that they bring.

At the same time, Jan, Marg and Diane are also aware of the pervasive discourse around employment equity as 'reverse discrimination'. The frequent references to this discourse by interview participants provide a good example of how 'externalized forms of organization' and 'discourse mediated by texts' regulate and penetrate the local and particular experiences of women (Smith, 1987, p.6). In this research, the existence of employment equity policy—within the context of existing institutional practices and relations, within the context of the predominant capitalist discourse of individualism, merit and competition, and within a society that devalues women—produces contradictory consciousnesses within all three participants. The disjuncture between their personal experiences and their discussion of employment equity policy is apparent.

Interview participants also perceive a disjuncture between Ministry policy statements and the actions of board personnel, i.e. the policy in practice. While policy goals are dearly and strongly stated, actual compliance by boards is viewed by participants as revolutionary. There is little statistical evidence for the common perception within their boards that significant change is occurring. Further, while employment equity is thought to provide benefits to women, Jan, Marg and Diane perceive that they are being scrutinised and must work even harder to achieve credibility in their positions.

Part of the explanation for these contradictions seems to lie in the invisible policy, the relations and practices which formal employment equity policy interrupts. The three women refer to the limited scope of employment equity in addressing the problems that women collectively face. At the same time, these women are struggling to resist oppressive practices and to make equity for themselves and others a reality. We see this in the ways in which Jan, Marg and Diane make sense of their situations and articulate their agendas for change. Therefore, one I would like to conclude with an image of these women as social agents who wield power and make choices, even as they are clearly situated within relations of power that constrain their possibilities.

10.1 Health Status of Canadian Women Managers

Most studies of the relationship between socioeconomic status (SES) and health have concentrated on disparities between the richest and poorest men; few studies have examined such relationships for women due to difficulties in measuring SES for women. In one study, data collected from Canadian Public Service middle and senior managers provided an opportunity to examine associations between SES and health within the upper end of the SES spectrum for both genders, since women managers can be assumed to have a relatively high SES. Demographic, health and lifestyle characteristics are compared for middle and senior managers for each gender separately to determine whether women experience the health benefits associated with higher SES that have been previously observed for men. The results support the hypothesis that achieving a higher SES through work is a more stressful process for women than for men and that women's upward mobility is restricted compared to that of men. Despite these findings, there is little evidence that women's health has been adversely affected. Compared to male managers, fewer female managers smoke or drink and fewer have high body mass index, high blood pressure or high cholesterol levels. Female managers are also more likely to report being in good health.

11

The British Women Managers and Professionals (With Special Focus on South Asian Immigrants)

There are currently 12 million women in the UK who are economically active. There has also been a 9 per cent increase in the number of women working full-time and a 33 per cent increase in the number of women working part-time. A significant trend in the uptake of paid employment in the UK has been a more ethnically diverse workforce. However, many differences in economic activity rates exist, not only between white women and white men, but also between ethnic groups themselves (Bhavnani, 1994). These employment patterns not only reflect race and sex discrimination, but also ways in which they can be affected by the influence of domestic and cultural responsibilities (Brah, 1993, 1996). The overall economic activity rates of working age Caucasian males is 73 per cent compared to 55 per cent Caucasian females. For men of Indian origin it is 76 per cent and for men of Pakistani/ Bangladeshi origin it is 69 per cent. In contrast, 54 per cent of Indian women are economically active and only 27 per cent of Pakistani/ Bangladesh women (Labour Force Survey, 1997). However, working age ethnic minority women are more likely to work full-time (63 per cent) than part-time (25 per cent) in comparison to white women with dependent children, 62 per cent of whom work part-time (Bhavnani, 1994).

There are high rates of employment for British South Asian women in professional and managerial work (West and Pilgrim, 1995). These women also tend to be married or have other family roles in relation to extended families. Many Asian women have direct caring responsibilities for elders and family responsibilities for their husbands' families: these family responsibilities extend to wider community responsibilities, and are different both in kind and in complexity from those of many white women. However, not all British Asian women live in such extended families, and to assume that they do, is to reflect stereotypical views (Brah, 1996; Warrier, 1994). An increasing number are living in nuclear families and are becoming "couple focused" (Bhachu, 1991). Even if they are living in nuclear families, Asian women are likely to experience pressure from kin and community members, albeit from a distance. Thus, while there may be similarities of experience for working Asian women, they are not a homogenous group. There may also be similarities of experience between British South Asian women and their white counterparts on the basis of their social class, in that their values may be similar to white middle-class women. Nevertheless, ethnicity will almost certainly impact on women's experiences of paid work and the family.

What has been highlighted is that assumptions in work-family debates appear to be gendered and culture biased. The notion of the "family" in existing literature is eurocentric in its focus overlooking the significance of extended families in some communities. Most of the literature also views the experiences of South Asian communities from a male perspective. It therefore needs to be broadened to take account of gender and ethnicity. Previous research on race and gender has been ethnocentric in its focus by failing to report the position of South Asian women in Britain as affected by cultural issues and different forms of patriarchy in employment and the household (Bhopal, 1997). The experiences of minority working women, living in dominant white cultures, highlight the way they are exposed to the national culture as well as their own ethnic culture (Lewis et al., 1992). For South Asian women, such experiences can result in conflicts between their domestic and work responsibilities and identities. In order to arrive at an understanding of the complexities of dual-role experiences of South Asian women, it is necessary to take account of different ethnic and cultural factors (Shams, 1994).

This is especially the case where it is the women who are constantly struggling with oppressive cultural traits. In Asian cultures women are given a secondary and submissive position within authoritarian and patriarchal family structures, and this is made legitimate by claiming that it is "part of the culture" (Bhopal, 1997; Brah, 1996; Drury, 1991). In such families, patterns of communication, levels of participation, and decision making reinforce gender differentiation and the passive role of women (Ghuman, 1994; Stopes-Roe and Cochrane, 1990). It is the family not the individual, which is the basic unit in Asian communities, and this means that women's wishes and desires are expected to be in line with those of their family's traditions, honour, and welfare. Furthermore, it is most likely the women who have to make all the sacrifices in order to retain community respect. Again, in the name of culture, such oppression is legitimated (Wilson, 1978). Clearly, the exercise of cultural norms by the Asian community affects the degree of autonomy, which can be exercised by women. This is revealed by pressures exerted on young women moving from the role of "daughter" to "daughter-in-law", coinciding with the time they get married. Asian girls are given contradictory messages about their role of "daughter". On the one hand, a daughter is referred to as a goddess, while on the other hand, a daughter is a burden, a temporary guest and a duty to be discharged (usually by marriage). Newly-married Asian women have to conform to yet another set of cultural expectations and pressures about how to fulfill their prescribed roles as they move from one family to another (Merrill, 1988). At times it is almost as if women are required to change their identities as such traditional norms and values become internalised (Liebkind, 1992).

It is this cultural context that the experiences of combining work and family life for British Asian managerial or professional women can be a positive and liberating experience as a source of independence (Bhachu, 1991), or as an extension of their family roles as they contribute to the family income (Warner, 1986). On the other hand, it can lead to even greater stress if their work is unfulfilling, they have less time available and have to rely more on other family members for child care, for example (Sharma, 1986; Westwood, 1988). The pressure of achieving a satisfying family life is the most frequently cited predictor of stress for Asian women (Berger et al., 1994). The position of South Asian women in the labour market influences their position in the home, there are also links between their level of education and employment status. These, in turn, affect their experiences of patriarchy, a private form exists where "traditional" women are forced into a situation of serving the domestic and economic needs of men as a result of their marginalised position in the labour market. More educated women are in a better position to be "independent" and leave their home at the sacrifice of "public patriarchy" (Bhopal, 1997; Walby, 1990).

In addition, organisational policies and practices, including the attitudes and behaviour of colleagues, create further sources of conflict. Many of the difficulties faced in the workplace are due to being a minority in a dominant white culture and consequent clashes of expectations (Bhavnani, 1994; Davidson, 1997). One of the ways in which workplace cultures can change to take account of heterogeneity is to adopt a "managing diversity" approach, which proposes that differences and similarities between groups should be treated in the same way (Ansari and Jackson, 1995). This is a move away from an equal opportunities approach, which proposes that people in the same situation should be treated in the same way (Liff, 1995). Kandola and Fullerton's (1994) view of managing diversity is an image of organisations as a "mosaic" where pluralism is emphasised instead of assimilation and diversity is valued. The emphasis is on attracting, retaining and promoting the best people, maximising the potential of all the workforce, and gaining a competitive edge and enhancing creativity by incorporating multi-cultural insights and diverse perspectives.

There is a need to explore the implications of differing family structures (the needs of Asian employees) and expectations, and the ways in which organisations can incorporate ethnic diversity in work-family debates. It is not enough to have family-friendly policies as they are based on gendered assumptions (Lewis, 1997). The managing diversity approach emphasises the need to have a "culture of flexibility", so that every employee is in a position to fit in (Hall and Parker, 1993).

It has been suggested that the strategies used by working Asian women to resolve conflicts arising from work and family must conform to particular cultural values and expectations (Sekaran, 1992). Thus it can be seen that the work-family dilemma's of British South Asian women are likely to be different from their white colleagues in many ways, and yet the experiences of minority ethnic women are missing from the literature. A notable exception is a recent study conducted in the UK by Davidson (1997) on black and ethnic women managers. The work-family experiences of these women managers were reported to be different from their white counterparts as they faced greater role conflict living in a bicultural world, as well as experienced the "double bind" of racism and sexism affecting their career development.

This study set out to collect and analyse the accounts given by British South Asian managerial or professional working women of combining work with family responsibilities. In particular it aimed to examine their reports of:

- the problems and supports involved in combining paid work with family life;
- the perceived impact of cultural values and expectations, extended family, and community support, and attitudes and behaviours in the workplace; and
- strategies they use for managing work and family responsibilities.

The Study

Semi-structured interviews were conducted and thematically analysed with 17 British South Asian full-time managerial or professional working women.

The informants were Sikh (6), Muslim (7), Hindu (4). Their marital status was single (5), married (11), divorced (1). Nine had children and eight did not. Single women were included because they too have family responsibilities in the Asian culture (Davidson, 1997). The women were contacted via various women's organisations, community groups, and personnel managers throughout the north-west of England. An attempt was made to incorporate a diversity of experience in the UK, including those born and brought up in the UK and those not born in the UK but resident for at lease five years; those who have stayed within one community or moved to another; and women from different socio-economic backgrounds.

A qualitative approach was chosen which allowed women to speak in their own terms, incorporating issues derived from the work-family literature. Thus, semi-structured interviews were conducted, which would allow detailed analyses of patterns of cultural life through the eyes of participants within that particular culture (Ham mersley and Atkinson, 1993). The interview schedule covered a range of topics, the broad areas of discussion were: demographic information; experiences of upbringing and living/coming to UK; experiences of family life; nature of family relationships, extended family, and community; experiences of work and how this is influenced by being an Asian woman; experiences of balancing work and family roles and responsibilities. These areas were generated from general discussions with the women at the initial pilot stage of the study; as well as the existing literature and gaps, which had been identified. The questions were kept open-ended and there were also prompts where required.

A two-stage process of interviews was undertaken: five initial pilot interviews were carried out in order to gain familiarity with the issues arising. Thereafter, interviews were conducted with the respondents, which varied in their length, ranging from 20 to 135 minutes, depending on how much time the respondent actually had allocated or how willing and prepared they were to talk. Each interview was tape-recorded and transcribed verbatim at a later stage. Owing to the sensitive and personal nature of the research, issues of anonymity, confidentiality and privacy were extremely pertinent, these were assured to each informant before they agreed to participate. The interviewer was also a South Asian female. The advantages of sharing common characteristics of gender and cultural backgrounds was that by having an "insider-within" perspective, a wide prior knowledge of the issues affecting Asian women gave additional insights into the research process. As such, the interviews were more conversational in nature, where the researcher served as a source of empathy and rapport was established and maintained. This did, however, assume an automatic understanding of the women's problems as well as an anticipated kinship, which can be potentially unethical in research. There were also problems of the women not feeling free to talk with the tape-recorder on, which is a common tendency for white women as well. The status of the researcher as a young, Asian female did sometimes serve as a barrier to the professional and managerial women (Rana et al., 1998). It is speculative whether the informants would have felt as comfortable and relaxed in discussing sensitive issues at all, or even at great lengths if the interviewer was male and/or Caucasian (e.g. Anderson, 1993; Stanfield and Dennis, 1993). Structurally-based variables other than gender such as race and class have been found to affect the research process (Edwards, 1990,1993). However, it is quite clear that "gender and ethnic congruence" are positive variables in the interview process (Bhopal, 1997).

A qualitative thematic level of analysis was chosen as a coherent way of making sense of the interview material. An attempt was made to draw out salient themes from each individual interview without losing the rich and valuable data collected. These themes were drawn out for further exploration in order to ascertain the problems experienced, and supports available for British Asian women combining work and family life. A "grounded theory" approach (Glaser and Strauss, 1967) was incorporated into such a procedure, that is developing and saturating categories, producing definitions; linking themes together; developing explanations and theories and making connections to existing theories. It permits respondents to speak for themselves and allows the researcher to derive a set of themes from what is said and is known as "systematic thematic analysis" (Plummer, 1995).

Several themes emerged from the thematic analysis of the transcripts of the managerial or professional British Asian women's accounts of the problems and supports in combining work and family life. For the purpose of this paper, five themes, which highlight the over-arching influences of culture, community, extended family; and experiences of work have been identified.

Some Findings : Burdonsome Family Pressure

Many of the informants felt that their families did not appreciate the demands that they as managerial or professional women, faced in pursuing a career alongside their responsibilities at home. In fact, the women's immediate and extended families were perceived to be the biggest stumbling block in combining work and family life. For these women there seemed to be a lack of understanding in accepting their hours of work, which left them very little time to participate in domestic chores, let alone relax. Nevertheless, the women were made to feel guilty and pressurised in having to put the interests of their family before their work demands and personal welfare. Some women interpreted this constant tension at home as a form of harassment. The pressures and domestic expectations for these women at home were cultural in nature, although there are some similarities in the experiences of managerial or professional South Asian women with other white women. An example of such domestic cultural expectations is the tendency for Asian families being prepared for guests (extended family, friends from the community) visiting unexpectedly at the weekends:"

You have a heavy week at work and at weekends sometimes I just don't want to get out of bed. But you have to, because if you don't you're lazy and somebody might come to our house. So everything has to be done. And you're trying to explain to your family how pressurised your life is and you just need that one day to relax but you can't because it's going to be at the expense of getting all your family angry with you. So I feel as if seven days, every day of my life I'm pressurised. There's not one day of relaxation (Sikh, single, solicitor)."

For the British Asian managerial or professional women their home life negatively interfered with their responsibilities at work in that their weekends were more tiring and stressful. This was because they were spent, more often than not, without choice, participating in community activities with extended families, as opposed to a woman's immediate family. As such, some women were unable to work at home (by choice) in the same way as their white colleagues:"

It's still different for a woman than it is for men, and for an Asian woman - Because what I carry in terms of my whole life they don't. In terms of the family patterns we have: the cultural, extended family and community patterns. In some white families they don't really have an extended structure, they don't socialise with their families as much, so they don't have the same responsibility and commitment to their family as we do (Muslim, married, assistant company director)."

It is worth pointing out that a vicious circle of misunderstanding exists, where not only do white colleagues stereotype the experiences of South Asian women, but South Asian women themselves, in fact, reinforce stereotypes of their white counterparts.

Additional responsibilities to extended family dynamics and community

South Asian managerial or professional women may find it difficult to integrate work and family domains, in the same way as white managerial or professional women, but for them it is further complicated by the extended family dimension. There are specific cultural differences between South Asian women and their white colleagues. One major source of difference is the common tendency of living in a wider extended family structure, which entails additional commitments. That is, living with or very near, to their in-laws and their families, as well as to the Asian community (based on religious affiliation) to whom they can be made to feel accountable. The influence of the Asian community in terms of enforcing value judgements of the women's actions and behaviours can interfere with their work role. Frequently, weekends are occupied by having to entertain guests at their house, or visiting the extended family and friends. It is important to examine these extended family and community dynamics in terms of reducing stress at work (which is carried forward from the home) and promoting gender equality.

Several informants discussed situations where there are expectations to visit and do things for in-laws even when living as a nuclear family. These were not always necessarily apparent, but were presumed by their in-laws:

"Because I have to work really late I think my husband's family find that hard. They can't understand why I can't come to their house on a Saturday because I have to go to work. I have to be there every weekend, which is hassle because you can't get anything else done. Your housework, your shopping, meeting your friends, it just goes out of the window" (Sikh, married, co-ordinator of Asian women's association).

Alternatively, there were some informants who chose not to allow themselves to be affected by their extended family structure and Asian community:

"There's 150 immediate members of the family because his dad's side is such a big family, so they have close links with their social events. But I don't go to weddings. Not that I don't want to, I just can't, I'm just so tired on my days off, if I've got Sunday off I just want to stay at home sit in bed watching TV and do my own thing (Sikh, married, social worker)."

In other situations where women attempt to break away from the influence of their community, as it is viewed to negatively interfere with their work life, this can have detrimental consequences for them:

"I also go to a lot of programmes in the community but we don't go with any men, even if it's just a colleague from work. I'm really reluctant because people say what is she doing with a man, it is a big pressure. There was one incident when I did go with a man and it had consequences for me because my brother-in-law was there, he told my sister and there was a big row (Muslim, divorced, community development officer)."

Work-family priorities and "superwoman syndrome"

The expectations and values in workplace cultures may conflict with the values and expectations of work and family for South Asian women. The experience of time and having to work long hours as a sign of commitment appears to be difficult for South Asian women as for many other women, as they have an additional burden to prove their competence, especially as they face barriers to their career progression. The pressure of having to fulfil multiple work and family roles and responsibilities was particularly difficult for the managerial or professional women. This is also a problem with which white managerial or professional women are faced. In certain situations they felt confused about their priorities and oppressed by the choices available to them. For those women who did not succumb to making a choice between work priorities over family priorities they attempted to balance multiple roles and responsibilities. This was discussed in terms of the "superwoman syndrome", which has been used more generally to describe the experiences of many career women (e.g. Ferree, 1990). But for South Asian women they are also accountable to their wider extended family and community. In contrast, some of the women decided to prioritise their career progression (that is, work life) before looking after their children (that is, family life). However, this was not for the same reasons as other white women. British Asian working women felt a greater need to prove themselves so as to be accepted as a true professional by their colleagues at work in view of their race and gender. In extreme cases some feared the risk of being sacked:

"Your job was always at risk, so you had to do extra. You had to make sure that no matter what happened, your kids are ill or whatever, you still begged the neighbours to make sure you got to the clinics on time. I have not taken any time off at all, my job has always been more important (Hindu, married, general practitioner)."

These minority of ambitious and career-minded women did not consider themselves to be "typical" Asian women at work. However, such a primacy of work over family interests was sometimes at the expense of the care of their children. It is not just white managerial or professional women who are faced with such a dilemma. Some informants regretted it in retrospect because they were seen to be deviating from Asian cultural norms:

I think women these days tend to be very strong, they want to go to work part-time and spend time with their children. I think I would've always liked to have done that but it didn't even occur to me to have asked. It was almost like there was no way because I wanted to keep that job and I wanted to progress, the kids were just something that I would have to handle, which maybe is wrong" (Sikh, married, process advisor for water utilities board).

Stereotypes of roles and responsibilities at work

The persistence of stereotypes by British society, which view ethnic minorities as being inferior to the dominant white culture appear to be carried forward in the workplace. For example, Asian women can be perceived to be incapable of performing their job effectively in comparison to their white colleagues. This can make it even harder for managerial or professional women to prove themselves at their workplace. There seems to be a tendency for white colleagues not seeing beyond racial and gender differences. By doing so, they fail to appreciate individual abilities. For these managerial or professional women a way of dealing with these situations is to appear confident and outspoken"

Some people they think "Oh my god an Asian woman's not going to know anything". They can be quite patronising to you because they feel that you don't understand what they're saying. But as soon as I open my mouth then they know they can't mess with me!" (Sikh, married, co-ordinator of Asian women's association).

Where white colleagues perpetuate the segregation between themselves and their Asian colleagues, the root of this seems to be a failure in recognising cultural differences. Instead, greater emphasis can be given to reinforcing differences merely on the basis of race, where differences perceived to exist are overemphasised. Some of the informants discussed this in terms of a "colour-blind approach", which was adopted by their white colleagues as a result of their cultural incompetence. Some informants believed that this ignorance was mainly perpetuated by older white males:

"There are some ignorant white males within the network that I meet. There was one occasion where we'd organised a seminar and provided lunch and I'd got a few "samosas and pakoras" in. And the older white bloke came up to me and said, "Oh they're very tasty, did you make them?" Those sorts of typical things still happen (Muslim, married, assistant company director)."

Another informant resented the "generalist" approach adopted by white colleagues where differences within and between Asian cultures fail to be appreciated:

"They just refuse to understand, they paint us with the same brush, that's generalist. But we're different to them in many ways. They think if they've met one Asian person they've met the whole of mankind" (Muslim, single, branch manager).

"Other informants acknowledged the tendency of white colleagues clumping all Asians together. This was most likely to occur when no conscious efforts were made to acknowledge religious and culture differences between Asian people:"

...they automatically assume that I won't eat pork but I'm not a Muslim. So there are certain stereotypes that people try and fit you into" (Hindu, married, assistant recruitment officer)."

As such, the competence of British Asian working women can be misunderstood by white colleagues. Jokes which play on these stereotypes and demean particular groups, can be one of the biggest obstacles in managing diversity in a multicultural workforce. Some informants explained how they dealt with such dilemmas:

"I think to a certain extent you feel pressurised to act English... You feel more pressure not to put yourself down but you make Indian jokes if you see someone who is a typical Asian, before the English man gets a chance to say anything. It shows to them that everybody just thinks that Indians are Indians and we're so backward (Sikh, single, solicitor)."

For those women who had a strict family upbringing, it was felt appropriate to make the necessary adaptations to the nature of the job and structure of the organisation. Even if this meant changing their dress sense to wearing English clothes in order to fit into the environment in line with their managerial or professional status:

"Our father's got a sense of traditional values. I wear trousers for work now that's because I'm in senior management. Before I was a manager, I used to wear shalwar kameez to work. But then I realised that because of the position I was in, it was affecting the staffs interpretation of how they saw me. I also felt that I was moving away from my traditional sense of values. So I made the conscious decision that I needed to adapt because it did make a difference, in terms of the nature of the work that I do; first impressions hit hard. I'm working very much in a white, middle-class structure and culture (Muslim, single, branch manager)."

Other informants also found it very difficult to work in an "English man's world" where certain expectations were not welcomed by them. The possibility of sexual advances being made to women at work is something that women in general may experience. However, for South Asian women they appear to be more protective as their culture engrains the oppressive nature of the roles and behaviours of women:"

I never believed in flirting with anybody but that is often expected of you, I always talked about my husband and my children. I put up that barrier I think so they knew that they cannot make any advances at me (Hindu, married, teacher)."

There were also positive experiences of British Asian working women, where their race and gender was an advantage for them.

It is evident that there is a lack of Asian role models, particularly in managerial or professional occupations. These British Asian women did not feel they were any different to other white colleagues. However, this was dependent on how they portrayed themselves. There was a general consensus among the informants that there was no reason to be treated differently if they lived and dressed like everyone else (that is, the dominant white population). Again, the importance of asserting a confident position was emphasised: "I use the fact that I'm an Asian woman as a definite positive thing. When they asked me why I felt I should get the job I said it was to provide a positive role model for those typical stereotypes of not being capable to teaching maths. Sometimes they might get a bit shocked about how blatant and rude I can be because they don't really expect it (Muslim, single, secondary school teacher)."

Experiences of discrimination

It appears to be more difficult for British Asian managerial or professional women to assert themselves in view of their gender, ethnicity and socio-economic status. We would define it as a form of "triple discrimination". These experiences can be detrimental to an individual's identity, where such effects are intrinsically intertwined. The tendency of Asian women being typecast to lower level occupations was experienced by many of the informants. As such, they can be stereotyped by others of what their position is assumed to be. As such, these women experienced problems in asserting their professional status: ...There are people I've come across who will say things to me because they've assumed straight away that I'm a typist or something. If I've sat on a management team of two white men then most probably people who don't know will wonder who I am. You can tell it by the way they treat you. Then once they know they're kind of surprised. It's just how people stereotype that an Asian woman cannot get to those levels (Muslim, married, assistant manager)."

These women also experienced problems in that their work was not given the same priority as their older white male colleagues:

"I've had experiences of two white older women who just don't give my work the same priority and I'm sick of it. Being a younger

Asian woman it's very difficult for them. There are all those different relationships and experiences at work which you're confronting all the time. But I do feel that you have to deal with them otherwise it becomes unbearable (Muslim, married, assistant manager)."

Other informants felt that their white colleagues received preferential treatment in comparison to them. As a result, British Asian women felt the need to work harder, which at times led to feelings of being taken for granted. Faced with such competition, several informants felt that it was harder to prove themselves as individuals with positive abilities to offer. This was resented by the following woman:

"I feel I probably do more than other people would do for our executive director, which I'm not given credit. So it's difficult because I feel as though I'm not taken for who I am as opposed to an Asian woman. One always wants to believe that you're here by virtue than design (Muslim, single, branch manager).

"Some of the informants in the study resented their white employers incorrectly inferring their competence, or rather their incompetence. Through the process of discrimination, Asian employees can be segregated and pigeonholed into certain categories of what their white employers assume their abilities to be. On some occasions, they are considered only to be capable of responding to the needs of Asian clients, and are therefore allocated to be responsible for Asian users of the services they are employed to provide. As a consequence, they fail to be utilised effectively in organisations. Several informants recognised that employers were in fact actively being racist. This may actually serve as a negative step forward for Asian people where it goes against their chances of being employed. One informant explained the vicious circle Asian employees may find themselves in:"

...When I first came here, because I was an Asian face, people said to me there's so much you can do with the Asians. And I thought why are you trying to isolate people, why are you trying to separate them from the general population? This was my theory of cultural incompetence, that everybody should be treated the same (Gujarati, single, dietician).

"The implications involved in pushing for equal opportunity policies and practices were also acknowledged. Another informant pointed out the way they were merely "tokenistic" and served to be counter-productive:"

I do not believe in bringing people in just to redress a balance. I serve a purpose being an Asian woman because I've got the solid academic background behind me and it looks good for them to have somebody there. There have been occasions where they've felt it looks good to have an Asian person and I've fought it off (Muslim, single, branch manager)."

With regards to recognising cultural diversity at work, all of the informants felt that potential barriers do exist in that white and Asian cultures conflict with each other. Where more importance is given to British religious occasions and events as it is the dominant work culture:"

The work culture is dominated by the white culture, so of course it's going to conflict. It doesn't often recognise other cultures, and the commitments they have. It only recognises the Christmas periods, but not the Eid or Diwali periods (Muslim, married, assistant company director)."

Discussion implications of research and future direction

Even though the roles of women are becoming diverse in the increasingly multicultural society of Britain in the 1990s, the roles demands, values, and expectations of South Asian women differ in emphasis from white women. For British South Asian women their family structures incorporate diverse cultural norms and expectations. The complexities of such roles and responsibilities make it more difficult for them to combine work and family life. It is clear that the managerial or professional status of their work does not necessarily make it easier for these British South Asian women, as culture plays such a dominant role in their experiences. Their social mobility does not really alleviate their already inferior position. "Asianness" seems to be a negative trait from which they cannot themselves, which is not, compensated for by their professionalism Instead, they are subjected to a triple form of discrimination on the basis of their race, gender, and social status.

It can therefore be more difficult for South Asian women to prove themselves in their career, where they are constantly confronting and challenging stereotypes of their roles and responsibilities. Certain stereotypes and cultural issues can be due to religious constraints (West and Pilgrim, 1995). However, over-emphasis is given to such constraints by white colleagues, who demonstrate their cultural ignorance by attributing all differences to religious values and beliefs.

The major cultural issue seems to be one that leads to particular differences in family patterns and associated commitments, which are more apparent for the women in South Asian families than the men. There is a tendency for Asian people to be, characterised as collectivist, with a strong commitment to their immediate family, when in fact that so-called "family" goes much wider to include husband's families, friends and the religious community (Stopes-Roe and Cochrane, 1990; Tayeb, 1988). These narrow definitions of the family are used in debates within organisations which fail to acknowledge the interrelated nature of extended family dynamics and links with the wider community.

It is clear that young Asian men are not subject to the same cultural expectations and pressures as Asian women. Asian community, and South Asian men in particular, need to be helped to understand the difficulties for the women in having to keep so many people happy, and to support them instead of perpetuating gender differences between them. The gender inequalities in the treatment and expectations of men and women reinforce conflicting views prescribed by the Asian culture and community.

Economically active British Asian mothers, like Western mothers, find themselves caught between two conflicting sources of pressure: to find adequate childcare while working as well as being a "good" mother and worker (e.g. Warner, 1986). The Asian community and extended family can be seen as supportive in terms of childcare assistance; conversely it can be seen as sustaining traditional gender roles. Many white women also rely on family members for their childcare needs (Brannen et al., 1994). Contrary to popular myths, which imply that all women in professional jobs find it easier to combine work and family life as they can afford to buy childcare, British South Asian working women may actually share the problems of many other non-Asian women living in nuclear families. This is because many British South Asian working women do not automatically have the assistance of older female relatives with their childcare needs.

At home there is a lack of understanding of the demands of the British South Asian women's careers from their families, there by not allowing them time to relax, especially where they are preoccupied with their additional extended family responsibilities and commitments at weekends. These pressures of fulfilling multiple work-family roles combined make the women feel very guilty and confused about what their priorities should be, not only for themselves, but also so that they conform to cultural expectations of their immediate family, extended family and community members. These feelings of accountability exist even if British South Asian women do not live with their husband's family, Such cultural expectations may not always be apparent but are presumed by their in-laws. Value judgements about a woman's actions and behaviour are constantly interpreted by their extended families and community, so that they are reminded to do things for them in the name of preserving family honour and traditions, as well as retaining respect in their community. Clearly these responsibilities can have an impact on the individual well-being of British South Asian working women.

In addition to the nature of their differing family structures and expectations as distinct from their white colleagues, British South Asian women also face problems in the workplace. The lack of congruence between home and work cultures have been discussed in terms of experiencing a "culture clash", in so far as the British and Asian women's family experiences were challenged by conflicting beliefs and values by the dominant corporate culture (Carr-Ruffino, 1995). The persistence of segregating ethnic and white cultures makes it harder for British South Asian women to prove their abilities at work, let alone asserting their managerial or professional status. In such situations the importance of an assertive and confident personality is highlighted as a positive attribute. What is required in these situations is a mutual process of adaptation and accepting employees on an individual basis according to the nature of the job and structure of the organisation.

The findings of the women's experiences of combining work and family life have led us to see little advantage to them of any potential "bicultural synthesis" of the norms and values of British Asian cultures. Combining cultures could be a valuable asset as it might enable access to different cultural resources, which may be used flexibly in different contexts (Bell, 1990; Drury, 1991). Instead, it appears there is a "bicultural fracturing" of cultures. Issues of subordinate minority cultures integrating into majority cultures as opposed to being treated as separate categories are particularly pertinent to the experiences of South Asian women combining work and family life. The debate as to whether ethnic minorities do feel different from the dominant society making it justifiable to be treated differently seems to be far from settled. However, the most salient aspects of the women's accounts suggest that it is more the dominant population's failure to be culturally aware or senaitive towards ethnic minorities. White work colleagues tend to generalise the experiences of British South Asian working women which shows their cultural incompetence in failing to recognise the heterogeneity within and between Asian cultures.

Furthermore, it should not be assumed that British South Asians are to be treated as a homogenous group. To assume so will only serve to reinforce and perpetuate their inferior position in society. Instead, it is important to use their accounts in order to suggest ways British society (particularly employers and the women's own families and communities) can become aware of their experiences, as shaped and determined by the Asian culture. In the work domain, discrimination, sex-role stereotyping, and social isolation is experienced by British South Asian women (Bhatnagar, 1988). The women in-this study did not feel that any drastic measures or changes to existing policies and practices which are distinct from those applying to white colleagues needed to be proposed. Instead, they suggested that greater efforts should be made towards ensuring greater equality on the basis of recognising individual differences and accepting diversity. It is necessary for British society in general to be educated to appreciate the differences in British South Asian women's experiences.

In the workplace, should Asian women be treated the same or differently to white women? In the present study, South Asian managerial or professional women tended to have a low sense of entitlement in comparison to their white counterparts. This was mainly because it affected their occupational attainment. They felt the need to work twice as hard to prove their competence as they did not want family issues to affect their career progression. There appears to be parallel issues of sameness and difference, which reflect debates about gender, that is whether women would like to be treated the same as men. Some South Asian women were quite adamant that they should not be treated differently from other white women. As such there was not a need for organisational cultures to apply specific policies to exist for them. However, there was ambiguity whether South Asian women felt entitled to ask for things specifically because of religious (ethnic) or family (gendered) needs. Some South Asian women would have preferred to adapt their work for their family needs but were hesitant to ask. It is, therefore, debatable whether family needs should be interpreted as benefits or rights. In addressing issues about workplace culture change to accommodate work and family, it is important to recognise that the work-family experiences of South Asian women are different. In order to incorporate gender and ethnic diversity it is important to contextualise their experiences as affected by the wider socio-economic political context, as well as extended family and community dynamics.

The practical implications of the research are related to recognising cultural diversity at work. There is scope for raising cultural awareness, but it is important to ensure that diversity reduces rather than enhances the effects of stereotypes (Kandola and Fullerton, 1994). A starting point for enhancing the quality of interaction in the workplace is a "celebration" of diversity and the bringing together of what is best in different cultures. One of the positive outcomes of this research points to the advantages of having Asian women role models as one way of moving beyond stereotypes of their capabilities Some of the managerial or professional women challenge stereotypical images of British South Asian women, their working lives, and related community issues. It is important to revisit oppressive images of South Asian women as submissive, passive, oppressed and dominated by men (Brah, 1993; Shams, 1994), and reveal instead a powerful picture of the changes in the organization of Asian family life in Britain in some parts of the community. An increased awareness about these changes is of considerable significance to employers as well as in relation to other families and the wider community. The debate is far from settled about how managerial or professional women juggle work and family commitments. It is evident that some of the women's accounts draw attention to the ways in which cultural background an blur these boundaries even more. However, many families respond effectively to such complex demands. A lot of the accounts provide a compelling picture of changing aspirations among South Asian managerial or professional women (e.g. Rana, 1998).

This study has provided an insight into the cultural tensions that are inherent in the experiences of British South Asian managerial or professional women combining work and family life. This has clear implications for the workplace. It is, therefore, important for employers to understand the work-family experience of South Asian women. This is especially so, in light of the r cent shift away from traditional equal opportunities approaches towards recognising and managing cultural divers~rnaches which pay attention to individual differences among employees (Henderson, 1994; Liff, 1995). The first stage to promoting an overall organisational culture change in favour of an acceptance of diversity, with an emphasis on cultural sensitivity, is to listen to the experiences of the workforce. To do so, is to begin the process of empowerment at work.

11.1 A Comparison of French and British Women Professionals

According to a recent report entitled 'Women in Professional Occupations In France and Britain', published by the European Commission, exclusionary practices by people still play an important part in frustrating women's access to professional careers, despite the removal of formal barriers to equality.

The report examines the first state of a project of the same name, which delves into the issue of gender relations in Britain and France. It sums up the project's first year of efforts to gather detailed background information concerning education, training and qualifications for the professions of accountancy, law, banking and pharmacy in the two countries. This project is funded by the EC the Economic and Social Research Council of Britain and the

Universities of Kent, Aston and Solford. It will run up to September 1992.

Although similar proportions of French and British women are in employment, French women are much more likely to work full-time and to have continuous employment careers than their British counterparts. The authors point to evidence that these differences. in employment patterns may be due to state policies and societal differences. In the UK, for example, strong trade unions, particularly at the level of organisation and workplace, have hindered women, said the report... Weaker unions in France, on the other hand, have contributed to strong state labour protection. 'The universalist provisions of French labour law have not been denied to women,' the report said."

The French state sought to protect the health of mothers and infants through policies such as maternity leave and provisions for the care of children of working mothers. The UK attempted to improve the health of infants by excluding their mothers from the labour force, the report said. 'In Britain, the working mother was for long held to put the health of her Infant at risk."'

"When looking at the specific professions outlined in detail in the study, French women have progressed further than British women in accountancy and more French women have trained for the law.

Banking system have reached the upper echelons of management; and more women qualify as pharmacists in France than in Britain. 'The data suggest, however, that, even where women have reached initial qualification levels equal to those of men, the presence of occupational segregation by gender is still very evident..."

12

Women Managers of Eastern Europe

The situation of women managers in Eastern Europe varies from country to country. We have highlighted only on a few countries in the region.

The Russian Scene

Education occupies a prominent place in the contemporary discussions of the revival of national consciousness and the economy in Russia. Recognizing education as "the driving force behind efforts at reform in all phases of life" (OECD, 1998, p. 14), Russian scholars, policy makers, and politicians have unanimously endorsed the project of democratizing schools and universities and cultivating the values of a civil society. Given the fact that educational reform calls for a radical redefinition of values and practices, it comes as no surprise that much of the literature on the subject is concerned with the hardships and pain of transformation (Davydov, 1997; Holmes et al., 1995). What is surprising, however, is that the research focuses primarily on the students and teachers, leaving other participants in the reform, such as administrators, out of the scope of scholarly attention. This study attempts to fill in this gap in Russian educational studies by directing its attention to the problems surrounding the life and work of women administrators in higher education institutions.

The place of women in Russian higher education

Recent surveys estimate that women occupy less than a third of all faculty positions in Russian universities and institutes, even though the proportion of women faculty members may be well over a third in legal, business, pedagogical, medical, and arts institutions (Levin Stankevich and Savelyev, 1996). The State Committee on Statistics (Goskosmtat) is registering a steady expansion in the number of women scientists, teachers, and educators (Koval, 1995), which is taking place simultaneously with two important processes in the Russian system of higher education. First, the profession of college professor is losing its prestige owing to low salaries that are forcing universities to expand their recruitment pools (Davydov, 1997). Sadly, women are entering universities as men are moving out into more lucrative and prestigious jobs. Second, the establishment of new programmes and departments (particularly in law, economics, and business) in response to the demands of the market and the emergence of new types of educational institutions (colleges and academies) have created new opportunities for employment both for men and for women (Lugachyov et al., 1997). Combined with the fact that teaching has traditionally been perceived as a legitimate female occupation, these two trends will continue to contribute to the increase in the numbers of women undertaking careers in higher education.

Until several years ago, the highest level of university administration was entirely in male hands. The first woman rector in the history of Russian universities was appointed in 1995 (Bain et al., 1998). In Russia, as in many other European countries, women are disproportionately over-represented at the lower levels of the institutional hierarchy and under-represented at the top. For example, at Moscow State University, perhaps the most readily available institution for study, women comprise 67 percent of instructors and 17 percent of full professors, 15 percent of department chair people, 5 percent of directors of research units, and 6 percent of laboratory heads (Morozova, 1994). The scarcity of data on women administrators in universities across the country makes these women virtually personae incogniti. How do they succeed in the male-dominated academy? How do they resolve the conflicts between their private and public identities? How do the current changes in society at large affect their personal understanding of their roles as mothers, wives, scholars, and administrators? These are the major questions the article addresses in analyzing and interpreting the results of in-depth interviews with women administrators.

Interpretative Framework: Discourses on motherhood and profession in Russia

Drawing on a post-structuralist theoretical perspective, the researcher approached women's stories of motherhood, marriage, and career as testimonies of their becoming subjects in particular kinds of discourses. Following the Foucaultian conceptualization of power as a form or technique which "categorizes the individual..., attaches him to his own identity, imposes a law of truth on him" (Foucault, 1982, p.212), the study intended to uncover the ways in which women comply with and resist the norms and "laws of truth" of the dominant discourses on motherhood and profession.

The contemporary discourses on the private and public roles of women in Russia reflect, in Irina Jurna's words, "mirrored stereotypes" of the socialist era (1995). While, during the existence of the Soviet Union, women were viewed primarily as labouring units and then as mothers, the present ideological demand is reversed, requiring women to return to their "natural" duties as transmitters of national culture and language and reproducers of the nation. Moreover, whereas the roles of a wife and a man's partner inscribed in the traditional heterocentric pattern can be contested by women who opt for personal independence and development, "the axiom that 'EVERY woman is ABOVE ALL ELSE a mother"' remains virtually unchallenged (Kay, 1997, p.89).

This reversal on the societal value scale of the identities of women has resulted in a recasting of the hierarchy of causes to which women are conditioned to subscribe. Although during the Soviet era, the "'right to work' was extended more as a responsibility than [as] empowerment" (Holmgren, 1995, p.19), the present-day discourses on gender fail or rather do not intend to redeem the empowering aspect of professional development for women. Consequently, active and meaningful participation in the public sphere lost the status of a rightful cause for women, leaving it to men to devote themselves to the causes of political and economic reform.

The data portion of the research consists of nine in-depth interviews with Russian women administrators in higher education. The sample consists of seven directors of research and educational centres and two chairwomen of university departments. The three-to four-hour interviews took place in Russia (Moscow, St. Petersburg, and Barnaul) in 1998.

The age of the respondents ranged from late thirties to mid-fifties. At the time of the interview, all nine women had adolescent or adult children and were either married or divorced. All respondents held a kandidat nauk degree (candidate of science), roughly the equivalent of a Western PhD. Before becoming administrators, eight of the interviewees had been faculty members at different universities and had come mostly from the fields of the social sciences. One woman with a background in the hard sciences had worked both in academic and industrial settings. The three excerpts cited in this study were selected to illustrate some of the difficulties and contradictions arising from the attempts of women to make meaning of their private and public identities.

The names of the respondents cited below are codified (eg : LL)

Women as Mothers

By choosing to combine motherhood with the pursuit of a career, the respondents positioned themselves in the margins of the normative discourse on motherhood that prohibits women from investing in identities outside the private sphere. This marginalization had a punitive effect on the women, invoking in them a sense of guilt for not living up to the ideal. A self-characterization as "an abnormal, crazy mother trying to read books and nurse the baby" (LL, mid-thirties) was a common image in the narratives. In addition, the attempts of the women to explain their motherhood through the framework of the Russian cultural heritage marked their narratives with a tinge of religiosity, which, according to studies (Lagunova, 1996), is generally typical of the world view of Russian women having higher education qualifications.

In the Foucauldian conceptualization, the norm of motherhood, as with any regulatory norm, presupposes an agency to resist by providing space for change without threatening the livelihood of dominant discourses. Since the norm operates through the constant reiteration of itself, the subject may resist it by entering the practice of reiteration, disrupting it, and redefining the norm from the inside of discourse (Butler, 1990). The following example of a respondent illustrates her role as a mother.

"I do not consider myself a bad mother. Even from the point of view of stereotypes. Everything is so confused nowadays in Russia that there are no stereotypes anymore. The good mother is a wife of a good husband who makes money. Then she has a role of a good mother: to stay at home and to raise children. If she doesn't have such [a] husband, the good mother is the one who, despite all circumstances, can earn money to give her child an education. (NN, mid-thirties)

NN subverts the stereotype through its own reiteration and questions the norm by displaying the impossibility of its implementation. The good mother is the one who stays at home raising and educating children, which is impossible for NN, a divorced woman who has to earn money outside her home in order to raise and to educate her children. For a divorced woman, being a good mother is possible only on the condition that she become a bad mother. The inner contradiction of the normative stereotype exposed in this excerpt allows NN to use the opened space to renegotiate the norm. Her commitment to work becomes legitimized along with her role as a mother, while the dominant discourse on motherhood is kept largely intact: motherhood remains to be defined within the framework of heterosexuality and marriage.

Women as Bosses

The identity construction of professional women is obstructed by numerous often mutually exclusive prohibitions of certain attitudes and types of behaviour. As the interviews show, women are berated for displaying stereotypically feminine qualities of kindness and nurturing and at the same time punished for showing the opposite masculine qualities of firmness and aggressiveness. Nevertheless, the respondents talked about making a conscious effort to attend to the emotional needs of their subordinates, describing relations in the work place in terms of affection, support, and inclusiveness, affirming the values of women's "ethics of justice and care" (Gilligan, 1993). Surfacing in the narratives of all respondents, this female ideal of human communication is often opposed to the masculinized rules of behaviour in the public world. In the following excerpt, NN reconstructs this polarization in her response to the question about differences between men's and women's ways of exercising power:

Everything is dictated by the social structure and the rules of life, not by gender. It was the same with communism. It was the same when the democrats came to power and wanted to give everything to everybody. Then it turns out that, no, everything is structured in the same way. Possibly it is the question of power.

One respondent said : ..."I know many women who made careers.... I know those who compete withhold information if something is happening. Such petty games. (NN, mid-thirties)"

This excerpt illustrates more than simple disappointment with certain women leaders who emulate masculine patterns of organizational behaviour. By comparing negative examples of female leadership with the political world of discredited communists and democrats, she virtually denounces competition as a negative feature of the public world. NN's attitude appears to be consistent with the studies of Western scholars who point out that Russians perceive competition negatively (Jurna, 1995). However, it is important to understand why competition has acquired such negative assessment on the part of women (and all Russians for that matter) after more than seventy years of their relatively unquestioned participation in the socialist competition of the Soviet era.

The explanation requires revisiting the nuances of translation. In the Russian language, there are two words that can be translated by English-speaking researchers as "competition." The first one, **sorevnovaniye**, has a positive connotation implying equal and fair competition with the purpose of achieving benefit for all. The second word, **konkurentsia**, is used mainly to describe capitalist competition and bears a negative connotation. The second word is the one that is used most often in the narratives. Thus, the respondents refer to the immoral and cruel aspect of the capitalist market, thereby making a value judgement. With its focus on extreme individualism and disregard for the needs of others, competition simply falls out of the value system of women.

The Fantasy of a Superwoman

The attempts to reconcile private and public identities may result in the creation of a fantasy of a superwoman as the projection of the ideal self. As Henrietta Moore points out, the "fantasies of identity are invariably linked to fantasies of power and agency in the world" (1994, p. 66). In the excerpt below, SS attempts to unite her various roles into one comprehensive self-portrait that ultimately reaches phantasmic proportions. She responds:

"And what is the career for? It depends on what goal in life you set. If you set a goal to be happy and if you understand happiness as the desire to excel in cooking. dancing, politics, and dissertation defenses, in other words, if you answer the question. "what is the meaning of life?" with "it is in realization ... of all your potential", then I would have hanged myself if I had been locked in a room. But if I had been deprived of my children, my husband, my relatives, and friends, even of the opportunity to bake cakes, which I love, to knit, and to work on the furniture, I would not have liked it either. (SS, mid-fifties)"

What makes this fragment remarkable is not the scope of enumerated activities, but SS's decision to mention them all in the first place. Telling her story from the position of power and authority, SS had to look back at her personal features and previous events, rearrange then into a coherent sequence, and give them a new meaning as markers on the path to success. Although, as she told the interviewer later, she does not habitually engage in all the enumerated domestic activities, some of which (like baking cakes and knitting) are stereotypical markers of a good housewife, she found it important that they be recorded too, for they redeem her as a woman according to the dominant discourses on womanhood.

Interestingly enough, in her analysis of the public images of successful Russian women, Olga Voronina (1994) noticed a similar tendency to emphasize the culinary skills of women as a proof of their "real nature". Thus, in a curious way, the excerpt presents a construct of a successful woman as she should be seen from the point of view of a complete realization of woman's capabilities. This construct is also a fantasy—a phantasmic identity receiving much investment on the part of the respondent because it renders her most powerful.

Conclusion

As accounts of successful career making. the women stories lying at the basis of this analysis are reflections of personal struggle and achievement in the world of academe. However, these personal experiences have a profound political significance for the growing number of women faculty members and administrators in Russian universities and institutes. Building their careers at a time when the structure and organizational principles of universities are being transformed under the pressures of the market economy, these women have to find their voices in the male-centred culture of academe and in the individualistic orientation of emerging capitalism. The situation is further complicated by the rise of the national revivalist thinking with its patriarchal agenda of returning women to their "proper" place in the home.

The conflicting demands imposed on women by the dominant discourses on motherhood profession reflect the continuous polarization and gendering of the private and public spheres in the Russian Federation. In this respect, the stories of women administrators offer a positive lesson of resistance. They suggest that as long as the masculine orientation of the university remains unchallenged, a phantasmic superwoman will remain the only legitimate identity to which professional women can aspire.

12.1 Situation in Poland

The Women's Studies Conference, which took place in Lodi, Poland, on May 17-21, 1993 has highlighted the status of Polish women in general and that of the Polish women managers in particular. The number of men in management in Poland is much higher than the number of women in management. This is due to the combination of women's biological and professional roles.

Women function in a society permeated by sex stereotypes that women managers must overcome on their path to success. The traditional attitude of Polish women, for whom the family is generally the basic criterion determining their social functions, plays an important role as well. For most women, employment is simply another duty that they must carry out in their role of mother and wife. The postwar employment of women in Poland increased their duties but failed to change their social roles. Thus, women are aware that they have the right to work but not to direct or manage their social lives.

13

The Asian Women Managers

Western women managers working in Asia may find themselves doing business in cultures in which women are secondary to men and don't have equal status in the workplace. In Japan, for example, sexual harassment, withholding paychecks, and abrogating contracts are common treatment toward women, even at the managerial level.

"I think that the biggest drawback for businesswomen in Japan is that it's difficult for them to participate on an equal footing in the after-hours activities," says a Japanese consular official.

"The 'social grease' of Japanese business is harder for them to access. They can't afford expensive dinners and parties; golf games aren't going to be offered. But foreign business women in Japan face the same problems that foreign businessmen in Japan face. Being a foreigner is more of an issue than being a woman or a man."

Another Japanese official suggests that expatriate women managers in Japan seek women of equivalent rank and position and then behave like them in professional situations. "That way, the women will be considered polite and appropriate and still get their business done."

Still, acceptance of women in Asian business is growing. As economies develop, there's a greater need for the best and brightest, no matter what the gender. In fact, one woman manager's experience confounds the stereotypes.

"Asia has a bad rap about being sexist," says Sea-Land's Manciagli. "Before I went, I read some books and adjusted my style. I didn't feel discrimination, sexism, or harassment. I was chosen because I had marketing expertise."

But, Manciagli adds, she was often asked who was watching her children. "Asians are very direct," she says. "Family is important. They'd get a real kick when I'd answer, 'My husband.'"

Manciagli says that her own role as an expatriate was unusual for a woman. "I traveled all over. The position was new and involved work with all of the core Asian countries."

Before a sales meeting in Japan, she was warned that customers might not talk to her or look at her, or that they might fall asleep. "I heard all of the horror stories. But they didn't happen. I just drank up all the knowledge I could."

Clifford Clarke of Clarke Consulting Group says that one of his clients, a woman expert working in Japan who was vice-president of human resources for the Bank of America, found that Japanese male employees opened up and shared their problems with her more readily than they did with her male American counterparts. Consequently, says Clarke, she became a great source of information on Japanese men in the workplace—though she says that the Japanese men probably wouldn't have been as open with her if she had higher status; then, they would have felt competitive. And the men's behavior became more sexist in the after-hours social scene, in which a lot of Japanese men conduct business.

Clarke says that other women experts report that they had to prove themselves with every Japanese man in the workplace, no matter what their credentials. Conversely, a man's reputation in Japan precedes him; he doesn't have to prove himself repeatedly.

Some women experts also say that Asian men tend to have great difficulty reporting to women. Unfortunately, when these men seek transfers to other departments, male American experts often support the move. Clarke says that Japanese men simply don't know how to behave when working with a woman (especially one of a different ethnicity) for the first time in their lives. They actually don't know what to say.

Interestingly, Clarke says that he has heard many times that on a continuum of communication styles, American men are at one end, Japanese women are at the other end, and Japanese men and American women fall close together in between. Like American women, Japanese men tend to be supportive, respectful, tactful, and indirect in their communication styles. And they express themselves with feelings as well as facts.

Clarke points out that it's unfair to expect Asian men to adapt immediately to working with women experts. The men need training and development in less threatening situations, such as behavior modeling.

13.1 The Status of Women Administrations in Bangladesh

The effective performance of government is crucial to most developing countries as the state usually plays a dominant role in development. However, state organizations are often viewed as inefficient and inflexible with acute problems of management development. They are confronted with inadequate/outdated institutional structures, characteristically with too few managers, and lack of a coherent personnel development policy. Too often it has been assumed that managers can pick up managerial knowledge on an on-the-job basis but it is increasingly recognized that there is a need for specific training to facilitate the acquisition of the skills and attitudes necessary for their increased effectiveness. However, training alone is not enough; what has been learnt must be effectively transferred to the trainee's work situation.

At the same time, governments increasingly recognize the importance of involving female managers more fully in senior roles, for reasons of equity and to tap unused reservoirs of human potential. Many international agencies now support management training and development programmes, which focus on the needs of women at work.

Thus, professional programmes have been designed and offered to women focusing on organizational analysis, policy and skills, and including issues associated with gender sensitivity within the organization as well as good governance and effective administrative processes. In 1994, a three-year programme was commissioned by the Overseas Development Administration (ODA) for 45 female civil servants from Bangladesh to participate in a specifically designed management training and development programme. This paper is based on the study of the 14 female managers who participated in the first phase of this international programme in 1994. It aims to assess the value and effectiveness of the use of attachments in similar organizations in the UK and is based on the results obtained. The question of transfer of skills and ways and means of improving the training process are posed and dealt with accordingly.

Finally, pertinent conclusions are drawn and practical recommendations are made.

Women and development in Bangladesh

Like many other developing countries, women in Bangladesh have traditionally been invisible and excluded from most development activities. They have been doubly disadvantaged by the country's poverty and by culturally determined attitudes towards women. To an outsider, Bangladeshi women may appear to be "unemployed" but in reality they make a significant economic contribution in family enterprises and the informal sector. In recent years there has been a shift in attitude towards women in paid employment as necessity forces more women to join the formal labour force. However, women on the whole are still hampered from full participation by lack of educational opportunities at all levels from basic literacy to higher education. The majority of women who receive any education still do so through the informal system, although efforts have recently been made to encourage girls' and women's participation in the formal education sector by, for example, reserving 50 per cent of primary vacancies for female teachers and at the same time encouraging women to be trained as qualified teachers.

Female managers in the civil service

There has been widespread concern in the aid community about the performance of the Government of Bangladesh: that it is neither efficient nor sufficiently accountable. Much hope is vested in Bangladeshi women civil servants by the development agencies who see them as potential prime movers in the process of consolidation and reform which is needed to build an effective civil service to support parliamentary democracy as well as promote sustainable development. As the public sector is significant in Bangladesh's development there is a need for it to set the standard in terms of women's employment and training. Currently, the ratio of women to men in the Bangladeshi civil service is 1:10, hence at officer level a women has to compete with at least ten men within her work team. Although women have been employed, particularly in education and health, since independence in 1971, they have only been allowed to enter the senior administrative cadre in the last ten years. Moreover, their appointment is subject to a quota (10 per cent), which although guaranteeing a minimum number of women, may also in practice be acting as a ceiling. There are 276 women in the administrative cadre, equivalent to 6.5 per cent of the total, the majority of whom are functioning in assistant secretarial positions and none above deputy secretary level. Most of these women (who are incidentally all graduates and come from families who believe in female education) are still faced with problems arising from the unacceptability of women working outside the home environment and distant postings away from family.

The working problems encountered by women of the administrative cadre are many. These include:

- apprehension of getting posted in remote areas;
- absence of a day-care centre;
- lack of separate rest room facilities;
- unavailability of an individual room in which to work;
- negative attitudes towards them by male colleagues;
- doubts of superior officers about the capabilities (for work) of women officers; superiority complexes of their male colleagues;
- tendency to treat women officers in a gender-biased fashion;
- comments that male officers are more efficient than women officers;
- the absence of a congenial working environment;
- having to perform the dual role of housewife and government officer without the required support system;
- non co-operation of male colleagues and family members;
- absence of security when having to work after hours in vacated offices;
- societal backwardness (women not accepted as government administrators/officers by the public).

Overall, the United Nations Development Programme (UNDP) study concluded that training is a key issue—notably gender awareness—in light of the new roles that women are assuming in government service. Mandatory gender awareness training has been recommended for all officers, both male and female. Moreover, the need for further networking has been encouraged and developed.

Women in senior management: phase one

For some years, Bradford University in UK has been conducting programmes to enable women in developing countries to enter senior roles in management and public life. In 1994, a three-year programme commissioned by ODA for women civil servants from Bangladesh began. Forty-five study fellows from the administrative cadre of the Ministry of Establishments attended courses in Bradford over three years, of which the first group of 14 (see Table I) went in 1994. The intention was to enable female managers in senior posts to compete for the most senior grades in the civil service and have a significant impact on policy making and the implementation of good governance in Bangladesh.

As part of the training it was felt that short work placements with senior women in local and national government departments would be very valuable for the female Bangladeshi civil servants in obtaining a perspective on the working experience of women managers in the UK and to compare administrative practice. Due to time constraints, these would last for two weeks and take place halfway through the course, i.e. during weeks six and seven. The women later had further opportunity to compare working practices and women's situations in a post-course study visit to Malaysia.

It must be noted that the position of these senior managers is vastly different from the (predominantly male) managers on which western literature is based: they are from a developing country, they work in the public sector and they are women. In the case of the Bangladeshi women, their own training needs analysis showed that their situation is largely shaped by being female managers in a particular cultural setting. For example, they identified as weaknesses: shyness, submissiveness, religious feeling, lack of courage, and conservativeness. They were prone to ascribe to themselves weaknesses, which were issues over which they had no control or which suggested the influence of negative feedback from male colleagues, e.g. being tactless, too talkative, inefficient. Indeed, it has been said that the resistance to women's changing roles in developing economies can be gauged from the attitudes of men to women managers.

Placements and management development

There are numerous strategies available to management developers to enhance the learning process involved in developing managers. In order to ensure that Bangladeshi women could experience the role of senior female managers first hand, placements were considered the most suitable strategy for this aspect of their training. Placements of two weeks were sought mainly in local government and the civil service, as these together broadly correspond to the Bangladeshi civil service. As one of the women's functions is to be magistrates, Bradford Magistrates Court and Bradford Law Centre were also approached. Within these organizations senior female managers were identified to accept the responsibility for these study fellows. The response was very positive and study fellows were placed with a total of ten organizations.

These points were discussed with managers from the placement organizations and individual programmes were then devised combining elements of job shadowing and special programmes.

The original intention was that placement would relate to the women's current work in Bangladesh. However, since all the women work as generalists, there were wider benefits to be gained from observing good administrative practice considering that they would mostly be transferred to other ministries on returning to Bangladesh. Several of the women already had quite a wide experience, having held a variety of posts in ministries/divisions and field offices throughout the country because of the policy of quite rapid transfers—a trend which is likely to continue. Most of the placements were within walking/local transport distance of the university but six study fellows travelled in pairs to London, Bristol and Hull. In most instances the women were paired for language, mutual support and reflection and this seemed to work well.

Main results

A post-placement evaluation was carried out by questionnaire and interview/discussion with both the study fellows and placement organizations. This highlighted interesting and significant issues. Although some of the women were fearful about setting off for their placements, by the end they had obviously gained tremendously in confidence. For example, this was evident from their own interpretation and enhanced English language skills. Some of the women felt that the placement had been the most valuable part of the course; all agreed it had been a useful and helpful experience. In a video workshop later in the course, several women spoke passionately of what they had seen and learnt and how they would incorporate their new knowledge in their work in Bangladesh, e.g. introducing more efficient office practices.

All had gained an insight into the ways of working in UK organizations and were impressed by well-managed meetings and the speed with which files were dealt with and the relationships between different organizations, e.g. local and national government, councils and non-government organizations (NGOs), social services and the courts. They noted the informal relations between colleagues here and were inspired by the skills and assertiveness of the women managers they met. They drew parallels between women here and in Bangladesh being impeded by a glass ceiling but felt that male colleagues here had a more open attitude to women managers.

At the Ministry of Agriculture, Fisheries and Food (MAFF) for example, the women gained useful knowledge relating to their work, e.g. contrasting UK and Bangladeshi agricultural policy and integrating environmental concerns and conservation strategies. One woman commented:

"Although MAFFs policies regarding agricultural production are very different—they are looking for ways to reduce it and we are always trying to increase production—I was very interested in farming systems, use of fertilizer and environmental balance and these I will try to introduce in my country."

Some job "fits" were near perfect, for example the "thana nisbahi" officers (TN 0) (district officers) who went to local councils. One woman said:

"I was very impressed with what I saw there. I want to use this experience to improve our way of working in Bangladesh—the organizational structure, planning and ways of conducting meetings."

Issues and improvements

Several issues emerged which have implications for the training phases of such programmes. Three were:

(1) The women felt that shadowing was no longer effective after a few days and they found programmes prepared specifically for them more helpful. This obviously relies on the resources of the organization to be able to do this—a good solution was a form of "serial shadowing" of several different managers in the organization. This seemed to work well without over pressuring our key contact person, for example in Bradford Social Services.

(2) As the strongest candidates were sent further afield, it was actually observed that more difficulties were experienced with placements closest to base, although proximity made it easier to resolve problems as they arose. Whereas there were no problems with punctuality in London and Bristol, this did create difficulty with some placements within walking distance/local public transport and greatly diminished the value of the placement to both parties.

(3) The women were paired in such a way as to overcome language problems but in one case where this was not possible, lack of English language skills did inhibit the effectiveness of the placement to some degree due to difficulties in communication.

Transfer of managerial skills

What is of most importance is how useful the placement experience, and indeed the whole training course, will be in the trainee's future work in their own organization in Bangladesh. Research has shown that ultimately the success of training mainly depends on the commitment of the trainee's organization. The literature suggests that in many cases supervisors are not interested in the outcome of the training, do not use the skills acquired or even ask for a report. When individuals try to introduce small improvements learned from training, they are often rebuffed.

Even worse, a high proportion of trainees were immediately transferred on return. This is particularly unfortunate where placements were chosen in equivalent organizations in order for the trainee to gain insights and information directly relevant to their usual work. Another implication is that the new boss may not be committed to training which they did not plan for and will probably not have considered how to incorporate the newly acquired skills. Indeed, they may be more concerned that the woman quickly fits in to her new work situation. More information regarding these issues will be gathered in follow-up visits.

Another aim of the programme was that women would not only become more effective in their own work, but that they would create a network of support among themselves and for other women. These and other issues need to be further investigated for the training and development programme to achieve its goals fully.

The women managers who co-ordinated the placements reported that they enjoyed the experience of working with their Bangladeshi counterparts very much, except where there were particular problems, e.g. with communication. Often they were surprised at how effective a learning experience it was for them. Even in a city like Bradford, with a significant population originating from the Indian subcontinent (including a Bangladeshi community) some organizations found it quite a humbling experience to learn first-hand from a practitioner what problems they face in other countries. Most wanted to learn much more about Bangladesh and the women's roles.

Sometimes it was evident that the women trainees had made an impact throughout the organization. For example, in one city council directorate, when the researcher telephoned, the receptionists spoke warmly of the trainee based on the seventh floor: "Do you mean Salma? We all love Salma, its really nice having her here".

In several of the organizations, more people than originally planned were keen to be involved in the placement and extra visits and attendance at functions were added.

In some instances a form of solidarity developed through the realization that women in the UK and in Bangladesh share similar problems. For example, these included adjusting to the norms of male behaviour and being expected to work early in the morning or later into the evening, despite family responsibilities, which normally fall on women. As the placement went on, the study fellows often became involved in other social activities. Some real friendships were developed, which continued while the study fellows were in the UK, and hopefully in the future.

Conclusions

Clearly all the Bangladeshi women enjoyed the placements and felt they were a very valuable part of the course. Several of them later used their experience as the basis of the research paper they produced as part of the programme in Bradford. This was not required, as they could choose any topic, hence it implies the usefulness and relevance of the placement experience. The senior female managers in placement organizations also found it very worthwhile and several indicated their willingness to host study fellows again in the future.

Based on the results of the first placement it is felt that the programme could be further enhanced in these ways:

- In recognition of the placement organization's desire to learn more about Bangladesh, e.g. the women's work or culture, the study fellows could run an informal information session in the placement organization and perhaps material, e.g. slides and artefacts, could be brought with them from Bangladesh for this purpose.
- The placement organization generally requested more information before the placement and this will probably be approached in a more systematic way in future possibly with a general meeting and more appropriate background reading.

The organizations also wanted more information about the women they would be hosting. This can possibly be addressed by starting matching at the pre-course meetings in Bangladesh, but one still needs to spend some time with the women in Bradford before making final decisions. This would also mean identifying the placement organization much earlier.

The evaluation of placements needs to be given more thought. As the Bangladeshi women write in quite a formal style it is difficult to glean much from written evaluations and by chance a later video workshop gave a fuller insight into their experiences on placement. Maybe the placement ought to be made later in the course when the women are more confident in the situation.

The period on placement in UK organizations inspired the female Bangladeshi senior managers who felt that it contributed to their development as managers, particularly in the area of people-related skills and administrative efficiency and that it would improve their effectiveness when back at work. Certainly, what has been learnt from this phase of the programme will enchance the effectiveness of future placements.

14

Women Managers of Africa : The Case of Nigeria

The research that has been done in the United States indicates that males and females perceive successful managers as possessing characteristics that are generally ascribed more to men than women. In this study, a sample of 70 Nigerians was used to investigate the impact of gender on attitudes toward women managers. By using the Women As Managers scale, the results indicate that Nigerian women have more positive attitudes toward women managers than their male counterparts. The implications of the results are discussed for two types of multinational firms.

An argument can be made, and supported by considerable research, that the discouraging plight of women in management is a result of negative stereotypes held about them. The number of women in management positions is influenced by the perceptions of men who have traditionally dominated the upper echelons of business organizations (Heilman, 1995).

Sex-role stereotyping of managerial work can result in the perception that females are less capable or qualified than males to hold managerial positions. It may also hinder the entry of women into the upper hierarchies of business organizations.

Multinational enterprises (MNEs) need to pursue women as capable managers and encourage "sex neutral" policies in recruiting and training them. To do so, they must first ascertain: (1) the attitudes of the women to be recruited, and (2) the likelihood that males will accept women as peers in the workplace and not discriminate in terms of hiring and promoting them (Brenner & Tomkiewicz, 1982).

The role and attitude toward women in management has been well documented for developed countries (e.g., Heilman et al., 1989). In fact, at least two or more countries in every major continent except Africa have been discussed in the literature (e.g., Antal &

Krebsbach-Gnath, 1987; Izraeli, 1987; Lansing & Ready, 1988; Renshaw, 1987; Steinhoff Tanaka, 1987). While, most of the countries in Africa are poor, there are a couple of nations like Nigeria and South Africa with promising future potential.

Nigeria is a country on the west coast of Africa with a population estimated close to 100 million people, and abundant natural resources. As a member of the Organization of Petroleum Exporting Countries (OPEC), Nigeria is the fourth largest producer with about two million barrels of oil per day. In addition, some have suggested that if a success story like South Korea's is ever to be told in Africa, it will most likely happen in Nigeria ("Anybody Seen," 1993).

Procedure and Participants

The sample consisted of 70 participants (43 males and 27 females) who were conveniently chosen from the southwestern part of Nigeria in 1993. Most of the respondents were potential future business managers (i.e., college students majoring in business). The participants completed the questionnaire without compensation in the presence of one of the researchers. It included 47 post-secondary students, 14 government employees, 4 bank employees, and 5 in miscellaneous occupations. About four percent of the participants were below 20 years of age; 43 percent between 20 and 24; 31 percent between 25 and 29; 16 percent between 30 and 34; and 6 percent were 35 or over. In terms of education, the percentage of respondents with less than college, some college, and bachelor's degree or better were 8.6,75.7, and 15.7 percent respectively.

Measure

The Peters, Terborg, and Taylor's (1974) Women As Managers (WAMS) scale was administered. The 21-item questionnaire explores the perceptual problems that women may encounter in the workplace. Respondents indicated whether they agreed or disagreed with each questionnaire item on a 7-point scale from "strongly agree" to "strongly disagree." Scores can range from 21 to 147, with the highest scores indicating more favorable attitudes toward women as managers. The WAMS scale was chosen because it has been used extensively in previous studies that have attempted to measure attitude toward women managers, especially in the

United States. The psychometric properties of the scale were detailed in Peters et al. (1974). Terborg, Peters, Ilgen, and Smith (1977) presented evidence to support the construct validity of the scale, and Ilgen and Moore (1983) verified its reliability. The reliability estimate (Cronbach alpha) for the WAMS scale in this study was .73.

Result

Mean scores were calculated for the WAMS scale items. The means were also compared to determine if any statistically significant differences existed between attitude toward women managers for male and female Nigerians Significant differences for gender effects were tested using one-way analysis of variance (ANOVA).

There were thirteen statistically significant differences between means on the WAMS scale (items 2, 3, 4; 6, 8, 9, 11, 12, 16, 17, 18, 19, and 20) for this sample of Nigerians. The total mean scores on all items for males (88,1) and females (108.2) were also significantly different ($F = 37.8$; $p<.0001$). These findings suggest in general that, Nigerian females appear to have more positive attitudes toward women managers than their male counterparts.

The results also appear to indicate that there are some significant differences in the attitude of Nigerian men and women toward women managers. In certain situations, Nigerian females may face obstacles in dealing with their male counterparts. The possibility of this incongruency of attitudes has also been found to exist in the United States. In comparison to previous studies, the mean scores for Nigerian men and women are lower than for their U.S. counterparts (e.g., Tomkiewicz & Adoyemi-Bello, 1995).

One unique aspect of the results is that Nigerian women appear to believe that they may not be competitive enough to be successful in the business world (i.e.. scale item number 20). This is the first result of its kind using the WAMS scale. The administration of the scale cross-culturally, the relatively small sample size, and the statistical significance of the difference in means at the .05 level however, limit any generalization without further replication of the study.

In Retrospect

Some of the major human resources management challenges confronting multinational enterprises are how to effectively attract, select, and retain effective personnel regardless of their gender and place of origin (Dowling, Schuler, & Welch, 1994). In international business, multi-domestic companies are those who primarily emphasize local responsiveness in their global operations. Each subsidiary has considerable autonomy and its own set of value creation activities. Therefore, among other things, multi-domestic firms develop individual recruiting and hiring policies. The results of this study suggest that multinationals that are organized as multi-domestic firms and desire to promote global egalitarianism in the hiring and promotion of women may be confronted with some difficulty in Nigeria. This may be due in part to the fact that top management positions are dominated by men who appear in general to have less favorable attitudes toward women.

Conversely, because transnational firms focus simultaneously on realizing location and experience curve economies, local responsiveness, and internal transfer of core competencies worldwide, they may be in a better position to aid in the recruiting and promotion of Nigerian women. The hiring and promotion of female managers in Nigeria may be further enhanced if it is true that expatriate women managers face less obstacles than their indigenous counterparts (Adler. 1993). Therefore, it may be necessary for the transnational firm to use expatriate female managers in Nigeria in order to facilitate the development of indigenous female managers. Finally, the need to globally promote the hiring and promotion of women means that more studies of the present nature may be needed in international business.

Table 14.1

Gender Differences in Mean Ratings on Attitude toward Women as Managers Scale

Women As Managers Scale item	Male n=43 Mean	Female n=27 Mean	P
2. Women have the objectivity required to evaluate business situations properly	4.0	5.2	<.05
3. [*] Challenging work is more important to men than it is to women	2.4	3.5	<.05
4. Men and women should be given equal opportunity for participation in management training programs	5.2	6.1	<.05
6. [*] On the average, women managers are less capable of contributing to an organization's overall goals than are men.	4.0	5.4	<.01
8. The business community should someday accept women in key managerial positions	5.4	6.1	<.05
9. Society should regard work by female managers as valuable as work by male managers.	4.8	6.0	<.01
11. The possibility of pregnancy does not make women less desirable employees than men.	3.3	4.7	<.01
12. Women would no more allow their emotions to influence their managerial behavior than would men.	3.5	4.7	<.01
16. [*] Women are less capable of learning mathematical and mechanical skills than are men.	3.8	5.0	<.05
17. [*] Women are not ambitious enough to be successful in the business world.	4.7	6.2	<.001

Women As Managers Scale item	Male n=43 Mean	Female n=27 Mean	P
18. Women cannot be assertive in business situations that demand it.	4.2	5.3	<.01
19. Women possess the self confidence required of a good leader.	4.2	5.5	<.01
20. Women are not competitive enough to he successful in the business world.	5.6	4.5	<.05
MEAN TOTAL SCORE	88.1	108.3	<.001

[*] Items scored in reverse

15

The Situation in Latin America : A Pilot Study of Mexico

There is a striking absence of information on women managers in Latin America despite the fact that, in the past decade, studies of women managers in non-English speaking countries have proliferated. A pilot study on women managers within the context of gender relations and managerial ideology in Mexico analyzes several factors that enable a select group of senior-level Mexican women to hold influential positions. The findings suggest that women have a nontraditional Mexican management style and successfully manage the work-family interface. Nevertheless, women still encounter obstacles to their advancement such as discrimination and stereotyping.

Select References

A Gayle & Sleven Ballard, "Speaking Out: Perceptions of Women managers in the Public Service", Review of Public Personnel Administration, Colombia; Winter 1996.

ADAMS, E. F. A multivariate study of subordinate perceptions of and attitudes toward minority and majority managers. Journal of Applied Psychology, 1978, 63, 277-88.

Alison, Taylor, "Glass Ceilings and Stone Walls: Employment equity for women in Ontario School boards", Gender and Education, June 1995, Vol. 7, Issue 2.

ALLPORT, G. W. The Nature of prejudice. Cambridge, MA: Addison-Wesley, 1954.

ALVESSON, M., & BILLING, Y. D. Gender and organization: Towards a differentiated understanding. Organization Studies, 1992, 13/12, 73-102).

Anonymous, "Black women among group dissatisfied with prospects for advancement Study", Jet (Chicago, Mar 2, 1998).

Brett, J.M., & Stroh, L.K. (1994). Turnover of female managers. In M.J. Davidson & R.J. Burke (Eds.), Women in management: Current research issues (pp 55 64) London UK Paul Chapman Publishing.

Brockner, J. (1988). The effects of work layoffs on survivors: Research, theory, and practice. In B.M. Staw & L.L. Cummings (Eds.), Research in organizational behavior (Vol.10, pp.213-255). Greenwich, CT: JAI Press. Cascio, W.F. (1993). Downsizing: What do we know? What have we learned? Academy of Management Executive, 7 (1), 95-104. Fed up Executive women confront midlife crisis. (1995). For tune, 134, 60-86.

David R. "Women Demolish more Career Barriers", Christian Science Monitor, 6/6/2001, Vol. 93, Issue 134.

Dipti Bhatnagar & Ranjini Swami, "Attitudes toward women as managers: Does interaction make a difference?", Human Relations (New York", Nov. 1995.

Goffee, R, & Nicholson, N. (1994). Career development in male and female managers: Convergence or collapse? In M.J. Davidson & R.J. Burke (Eds.), Women in management: Current research & issues (pp.80-92). London, UK: Paul Chapman Publishing. Gutek, B.A , Cohen, A.G., &

Konrad, A.M. (1990). Predicting social-sexual behavior at work: A contact hypothesis. Academy of Management Journal, 33, 560-577 Hochschild, A. (1989). The second shift. New York, NY: Avon Books.

HARTMANN, H. I. The family as the locus of gender, class, and political struggle: The example of housework. Signs, 1981, 6, 366-394.

HARVEY, J. New technology and the gender divisions of labor. In G. Lee and R. Loveridge (Eds.), The manufacture of disadvantage. Milton Keynes, Philadelphia: Open University Press, 1986, pp.72-82.

HEILMAN, M. E., & MARTELL, R. E. Exposure to successful women: Antidote to sex discrimination applicant screening decisions? Organizational Behavior and Decision Processes, 1986, 37, 376-390.

Heli K. Lohtinen & Flona N. Wilson, "Women and power in organizations", Executive Development (Bradford, 1994).

HENNING, M., & JARDIM, A. The management women. Garden City, New York: Anchor Press, 1977.

IOWARD, J. A., & SHETH,. N. The theory of buyer behavior. New York: Wiley, 1969.

JACOBSON, M. B., & EFFETZ, J. Sex roles and leadership perceptions of the leaden and the led. Organizational 3 Behaviour and Human Performance, 1974,12, 383-397.

James C Johnson & Diane J Meelure, "Job Satishfaction of Logistics Managers: Female versus Male Perspectives", Transportation Journal, Fall 1999, Vol. 39, Issue 1, p.5.

JOHNSON, R. C., THOMSON, C. W., B FRINCKE, G. Word values, word frequency and visual duration thresholds. Psychological Review, 1960, 67, 332-342.

KANTER, R. M. Men and women of the corporation. New York: Basic, 1977. (a)

KANTER, R. M. Some effects of proportion on group life: Skewed sex ratios and responses to token women. American Journal of Sociology, 1977, 82(5), 965-990.

LOTT, B. The devaluation of women's competence. Journal of Social Issues, 1985, 41(4), 43-60.

MACCOBY, E. E. The development of sex differences. Stanford, CA: Stanford University Press, 1W6.

Maddock S , & Parkin, D. (1994). Gender cultures: How they affect men and women at work. In M.J. Davidson & R.J. Burke (Eds.), Women in management Current research issues (pp.29-40). London, UK: Paul Chapman Publishing.

Maddock, E. E., & JACKLIN, C N he psychology of sex differences. Stanford, CA: Stanford University Press, 1974.

MAIER, N. R. Male versus female discussion leaders. Personnel Psychology, 1970, 23, 455-461.

Marshall J. (1995). Women managers moving on: Exploring career and life choices. London, UK: Routledge. McKinley, W., Sanchez, C.M., & Schick, A.G. (1995) Organizational downsizing: Constraining, cloning, learning. Academy of Management Executive, 9 (3), 32-42. Noer, D.M. (1993). Healing the wounds: Overcoming the trauma of layoffs and revitalizing downsized organizations. San Francisco, CA: Jossey-Bass.

MARTIN, P. Y., HARRISON, D., &DINITTO, D. Advancement for women in hierarchical organizations: A multilevel analysis of problems and prospects. He Journal of Applied Behavioural Science, 1983, 19 (1), 19-33.

Monica Tomiak, Gene F. Gentleman & Jette Maurice, "Health and gender differences between middle and senior managers in Canadian Public Service", Social Science & Medicine.

Nancy J. Ader & Dafna N. Izraeli, "Where in the world are the women exectutives?", Business Quarterly (London, Autumn 1994).

"NAFE NET-WORKER: Paris Conference Reports on the status of women-owned Business", Executive Female, Sep/Oct 1997, Vol.20, Issue 5, p. 58.

NIEVA, V. F., & GUTEK, B. A. Sex effects on evaluation. Academy of Management Review, 1980, 5 (2), 267-276.

OSBORN, R. N., & VICARS, W. M. Sex stereotypes: An artifact in leader behaviour and subordinate satisfaction analysis? Academy of Management Journal, 1976, 19, 439-449.

PETERS, L. H., TERBOGH, J. R., & TAYNOR, J. Women as managers scale: A measure of attitudes towards women in management positions. JSAS Catalogue of Selected Documents in Psychology, 1974, No.505.

PODMORE, D., & SPENCER, k Gender and disadvantage among a professional elite. In G. Lee and R. Loveridge (Eds.), The manufacture of disadvantage. Milton Keynes, Philadelphia: Open University Press, 1986, pp.20-32.

RAG INS, B. R., & COTTON, J. L. Easier said than donę: Gender differences in perceived barriers to gaining a mentor. Academy of Management Journal, 1991, 34 (4), 939-951.

Rekha Karambayya, "Caught in the crossfire: Women and Corporate Restructuring", Revue Canadienne des Sciences developments l'Administration, (Montreal), Dec. 1998.

Rhonda & Richards, "Winners at Work", Essence, March 1996, Vol. 26, Issue II, p. 74.

Rochelle Sharpe, "As Leaders, Women Rule", Business Week, 11/20/2000, Issue 3708, p.47.

Rosin, H.M , & Korabik, K (1995). Organizational experience and propensity to leave: A multivariate investigation of men and women managers. Journal of Vocational Behavior, 46, 1-16.

Rosin, H.M , & Korabik, K. (1991). Workplace variables, affective responses, and intention to leave among women managers. Journal of Occupational Psychology, 64, 317330.

Schwartz, EN (1989, 3anuary February). Management women and the new facts of life. Harvard Business Review, 1, pp. 65-76.

SCHWARTZ, F. N. Women as a business imperative. Harvard Business Review, 1992, March-April, 105-113. SPENCE, H. A. Job market signalling, Quarterly Journal of Economies, 1973, 87, 356-368.

Stroh, L K , Brett, J.M., & Reilly, A H. (1993). Turned over, or turned off? A comparison of male and female turnover. Paper presented at the meeting of the Society for Industrial and Organizational Psychology, San Francisco, CA. White, B., Cox, C., & Cooper, C. (1992). Women's career development: A study of high flyers Oxford, UK Blackwell.

TAJFEL, H. The social psychology of minorities, London, Minority Rights Group, Report No. 38, 1978.

TAYLOR, M. S., & ILGEN, D. R. Sex discrimination against women in initial placement decisions: A laboratory investigation. Academy of Management Journal, 1981, 24, 859-865.

WEBER, R., & CROCKER, J. Cognitive processes in the revision of stereotypic beliefs. Journal of Personality and Social Psychology 45, 961-977,1983.

YODER, J. D. An academic woman as a token: A case study. Journal of Social Issues, 1985, 41(4), 61-72.

ZAJONC, R. B. Attitudinal effects of mere exposure. Journal of personality and Social Psychology, 1968, Monograph Supplement, 9, 1-27.

Part II

An Extended Bibliography

I
THEORETICAL CONCERNS ABOUT WOMEN ADMINISTRATORS AND PROFESSIONALS

Ader, Nancy J; Izraeli, Dafna N; Where in the world are the women executives? Business Quarterly; London; Autumn 1994; Vol. 59, No. 1, p. 89.

Adler, N. J. and Izraeli, D.N. Women in Management Worldwide. Armonk, NY: Sharpe, Inc., 1988.

Anonymous; Developing Women Managers : Current issues and good practice", Equal Opportunities International; Patrington; 1995; pp. 36-50.

Ardener, Shirley, ed. Perceiving Women. New York: Wiley, 1975.

Barber, Jill. Sisterhood Betrayed: Women in the Workplace and the All About Even Complex. New York: St. Martin's Press, 1991.

Bergman, B. R. The Economic Emergence of Women. New York: Basic Books, 1986.

Bielby, W. T. and Baron, J. N. "A Woman's Place is With Other Women: Sex Segregation Within Firms," (in) Sex Segregation in the Workplace: Trends, Explanations, Remedies, edited by B. F. Reskin. Washington, DC: National Acad. Press, 1984, pp.27-55.

Blau, F. D. Discrimination Against Women: Theory and Evidence, (in) Labor Economics: Modern Views, edited by W. Darity, Jr. Boston: Kluwer-Nijhoff, 1984, pp.53-89.

Blau, F. D. Occupational Segregation by Gender: A Look at the 1980s. Presented at Annual Meeting Am Econ. Assoc., New York, 1988.

Blau, F. D. and Beller, A. H. Trends in Earning Differentials By Gender, 1971-1981. Ind. Labor Relation. Rev. Vol. 41 1988, pp. 513-29.

Blaxall, M., and Reagan, B. eds. Women and the Workplace: The Implications of Occupational Segregation. Chicago: University of Chicago Press, 1976.

Bridges, W. P., and Miller, B. Sex and Authority in the Workplace. A Replication and Critique. Am. Social. Rev. Vol. 46, 1981, pp. 677-83.

Brown, C. and Pechman, J. A. Gender in the Workplace. Washington, D. C.: The Brookings Institution, 1987.

Chafets, J. S. Sex and Advantage: A Comparative, macro-Structural Theory of Sex Stratification. New Jersey: Rowman and Allenheld, 1984.

Cockburn, C. Brothers: Male Dominance and Technological Change. London: Pluto Press, 1983.

Collins, Nancy W. Women Leading: Making Tough Choices on the Fast Track. Lexington, Mass.: S. Greene Press, 1988.

Colwill, N. The New Partnership: Women and Men in Organizations. Palo Alto, CA: Mayfield Publishing Company, 1982.

Coontz, Stephanie and Henderson, Peta, eds. Women's Work, Men's Property: The Origins of Gender and Class. London: Verso, 1986.

Cooper, Cary L. and Davidson, Marilyn J., eds. Women in Management: Career Development for Managerial Success. London: Heinemann, 1984.

Crompton, R. and Jones, G. White Collar Proletariat: Deskilling and Gender in Clerical Work. London: Macmillan, 1984.

Dalton, Dan. R. and William D. Todor. "Gender and Workplace Justice: A Field Assessment." Personnel Psychology, Volume 38, No. 1, Spring, 1985, pp. 133-152.

Dex, S. The Sexual Division of Work. New York: St. Martin's, 1985.

Dipboye, R. L. "Problems and Progress of Women in Management." Working Women: Past, Present, Future. Washington, D. C.: Bureau of National Affairs, 1987, pp. 118-153.

Donneli, S., and Hall, J. "Men and Women as Managers: A Significant Case of No Significant Difference." Organizational Dynamics, 1980, pp. 60-76.

Eisenstein, H. Contemporary Feminist Theory. Boston, MA: Twayn Publishers, 1983.

England, P. "Assessing Trends in Occupational Sex-Segregation, 1900-1976, (in) Sociological Perspectives on Labor Markets, edited by I. Berg. New York: Academic Press, 1981, pp. 273-295.

Epstein, C.F. "Encountering the Male Establishment: Sex-Status Limits on Women's Careers in the Professions.: American Journal of Sociology, Volume 75, 1970, pp. 965-982.

Epstein, Cynthia F. "Encountering the Male Establishment: Sex-Status Limits on Women's Careers in the Professions," (in). The Professional Woman, edited by Athene Theodore. Boston: The Schenkman Publishing Company, 1971.

Epstein, C.F. Women's Place: Options and Limits in Professional Careers. Berkeley: Univ. Calif, 1971.

Ezell, H. F. et al. "Women Entering Management: Differences in Perceptions of Factors Influencing Integration" Group and Organizational Studies, Vol. VIII, No. 2, June, 1982, pp. 243-253.

Fenn, Margaret. Making it in Management: A Behavioral Approach for Women Executives. Englewood Cliffs, N.J.: Prentice-Hall, 1978.

Fidell, L. and DeLamater, J,. eds. Women in the Professions: What's All the Fuss About. Beverly Hills: Sage, 1971.

Frank, H. H., ed. Women in the Organization. Philadelphia: University of Pennsylvania Press, 1977.

Fukami, C. "Women in Management: Separation or Integration?" (in). Women and Men in Organizations: Teaching Strategies, edited by Dorothy M. Hai. Washington.: The Organizational Behavior Teaching Society, 1984.

Gamarnikow, Eva, ed. Gender, Class, and Work. London: Heinemann, 1983.

Gilson, Edith. Unnecessary Choices: The Hidden Life of the Executive Woman. New York: W. Morrow, 1987.

Glickman, Albert S., ed. The Changing Composition of the Workforce: Implications for Future Research and its Application. New York: Plenum Press, 1982.

Gutek, B.A. Sex and the Workplace. San Francisco, CA: Jossey-Bass, Inc., 1985.

Gutek, B.A., & Dunwoody, V., Eds. Women in Work: Volume II. Newbury Park, CA: Sage Publications, 1987, pp. 261-265.

Gutek, B.A., Nakamura, C. Y., Gahart, M., Handschumacher, J. W., & Russell, D. "Sexuality in the Workplace." Basic and Applied Social Psychology, Vol. I. 1980 pp. 255-265.

Hai, D.M. Women and Men in Organizations: Teaching Strategies. Washington. D.C.: George Washington University, 1985.

Harriman, A. Women/Men/Management. New York: Praeger Publishers, 1985.

Harlan, Anne. Moving Up: Women in Managerial Careers: Final Report. Wellesley; MA: Wellesley College, Center for Research on Women, 1981.

Hearn, Jeff and Sheppard, Deborah L., eds. The Sexuality of Organization. Newbury Park, CA: Sage Publications, 1990.

Hearn, J. "Sexism, Men's Sexuality in Management: The Seen Yet Unnoticed Case of Men's Sexuality." Sexuality, Power and Organization Theory. Symposium conducted at the annual meeting of the Academy of Management. San Diego, 1985.

Henning, M., & Jardim, A. The Managerial Woman. New York: Pocket Books, 1978.

Henning, H., & Jardim, A. The Managerial Woman. Garden City, NY: Anchor Press/Doubleday, 1977.

Highman, Edith L. The Organization Woman: Building a Career - An Inside Report. New York, NY: Human Sciences Press, 1985.

Heese-Biber, S. Women at Work. Palo Alto, CA: Hayfield Publishing Co., 1984

Hoffman, Carl & Reed, John Shelton. "Sex Discrimination? - The XYZ Affair." Public Interest, Vol. 62, 1981, pp 21-39.

Horgan, D.D. "Management Development. Women" Journal of Business and Psychology 3 (3) : 1989, pp. 200-313.

Jelinek, M., & Adler, N.J. "Women: World-class Managers for Global Competition." Academy of Management Executive, 1988, pp. 11-20.

Kanter, R.M. Men and Women of the Corporation. New York: Basic Books, 1977.

Kanter, R.M. "The Impact of Hierarchical Structure on the Work Behavior of Women and Men." Soc. Probl. 23: 1976, pp. 415-30.

Kirkham, K. "Managing Diversity in Organizations: Teaching About Majority Group Behavior." Presentations at the Twelfth Annual Organizational Behavior Teaching Conference, University of Virginia, 1985.

Kranz, Harry. The Participatory Bureaucracy: Women and Minorities in a More Representative Public Service. Lexington, MA: Lexington Books, 1976.

Krefting, L.A. Berger, P.K. Wallace, M.J. "The Contribution of Sex Distribution, Job Content and Occupational Classification to

Job Sex-typing." Journal of Vocational Behavior, Volume 13, 1978, pp. 181-191.

Kreps, Juanita. Sex in the Market Place: American Women at Work. Baltimore and London: John Hopkins Press, 1971.

Lipman-Blumen, J. "The Vicarious Achievement Ethic and Non-Traditional Roles for Women." Presented at Annual Meeting East. Sociol. Soc., New York, 1973.

Lipman-Blumen, J. Gender Roles and Power. Englewood Cliffs, NJ: Prentice-Mall, Inc., 1984

Loring, Rosalind & Wells, Theodora. Breakthrough: Women into Management. (New York: Van Nostrand Reinhold Co., 1972

Lunneborg, Patricia W. Women Changing Work. New York: Bergin & Garvey, 1990.

Marshall, Judi. Women Managers: Travellers in a Male World. Chichester, New York: Wiley, 1984.

Marshall, K. Who are the Professional Women? Ottawa: Statistics, Canada, 1987.

McCarty, Paulette A. "Effects of Feedback on the Self-confidence of Men and Women." Academy of Management Journal, Vol. 29, No 4., 1986, pp. 840-847.

Martin, Y.N., Harrison, D., and Dinitto, D. "Advancement for Women in Hierarchical Organizations: A Multilevel Analysis of Problems and Prospects.: Journal of Applied Behavioral Science 19(1), 1983, pp. 19-33.

Matthaaei, J.A. An Economic History of Women in America: Women's Work, the Sexual Division of Labor, and the Development of Capitalism. New York: Schocken Books, 1982.

McKeen, Carol A. Work Experiences and Career Success of Managerial and Professional Women. Kingston, Ont.: Queen's University, School of Business. 1990.

McRae, Susan, ed. Keeping Women in: Strategies to Facilitate the Continuing Employment of Women in Higher Level Occupations: London: Policy Studies Institute, 1990.

Melia, Jinx. Breaking into the Boardroom: When Talent and Hard Work Aren't Enough. New York: Putnam, 1986.

Miller, Jon, (1986). Pathways in the Workplace: Effects of Gender and Race on Access to Organizational Resources. Cambridge, MA: Cambridge University Press, 1986, p. 84.

Morrison, A.M., White, R.P., & Van Velsor, E. Breaking the Glass Ceiling; Can Women Reach the Top of America's Largest Corporations? Reading, MA: Addison-Wesley, 1987.

Murphy, Irene L. Public Policy on the Status of Women: Agenda and Strategy for the 70s. Lexington, Mass: Lexington Books, 1973.

Oppenheimer, V.K. The Sex-Labeling of Jobs. ind. Relat. Volume 7, 1968, pp. 219-34.

Nicholson, Nigel. Managerial Job Change: Men and Women in Transition. New York: Cambridge University Press, 1988.

Powell, Garv N. Women and Men in Management: The New Dynamics. Beverly Hills, CA: Sage Publications, 1988.

Ramsford, E.H. & Miller, J. Race, Sex, and Feminist Outlooks. American Journal of Sociology, 48, 1983, pp. 46-59.

Reskin, Barbara F. and Hartmann, Heidi I., eds. Women's Work, Men's Work: Sex Segregation on the Job. Washington, D.C.: National Academy Press, 1986.

Rizzo, Ann-Marie. The Integration of Women in Management: A Guide for Human Resources and Management Development Specialists. New York: Quorum Books, 1947.

Rose, Suzanna & Larwood, Laurie. Women's Careers: Pathways and Pitfalls. New York: Praeger, 1988.

Rosenfeld, R. "Women's Occupational Careers: Individual and Structural Explanations." Sociology of Work and Occupations, 6, 1970, pp. 283-311.

Schneider, Stephen A. The Availability of Minorities and Women for Professional and Managerial Positions, 1970-1985. Philadelphia: Industrial Research Unit, Wharton School, university Pennsylvania, 1977.

Shuch, Milton L., ed. Women in Management. Indianapolis: Bobbs-Merrill Educational Pub., 1981.

Simpson, Richard L., & Simpson, Ida. "Women and Bureaucracy in the Semi-Professions," The Semi-Professions. New York: The Free Press, 1969, pp. 196-197, 231, 239.

Sinclair, Amanda. Women in Management: Advantage Through Diversity. Parkville, Victoria, Australia: University of Melbourne, Graduate School of Management, 1988.

Sitterly, C. A Woman's Place: Management. Englewood Cliffs, NJ: Prentice-Hall, 1988.

Slavin, Sarah, ed. The Politics of Professionalism, Opportunity, Employment, and Gender. New York: Haworth Press, 1987.

Spencer, Anne & Podmore, David, eds. In A Man's World: Essays on Women in Male-dominated Professions. London: Tavistock, 1987.

Standley, K., & Soule, B. N Women in Male-dominated Professions: Contrasts in their Personal and Vocational Histories." Journal of Vocational Behavior, 4, 1974, pp. 245-258.

Stead, B.A. Women in Management. Englewood Cliffs, NJ: Prentice-Hall, Inc., 1978.

Strober, M. "Toward a General Theory of Occupational Sex Segregation: The Case of Public School Teaching. Sex Segregation in the Workplace: Trends, Explanations, Remedies. Washington, DC: National Academy Press, 1984, pp. 144-56.

Terborg, J.R., & Olgen, D.R. "A Theoretical Approach to Sex Discrimination in Traditionally Masculine Occupations. Organizational Behavior and Human Performance, Volume 13, 1975, pp. 352-76.

Terborg, J.R. "Women in Management: A Research Review. Journal of Applied Psychology, Volume 62, 1977, pp. 647-664.

Theodore, Athena. "The Professional Woman: Trends and Prospects," The Professional Woman. Cambridge, Mass: Schenkmann, 1971, pp. 1-35.

Thompson, Ann McKay. Management Strategies for Women: or, Now That I'm Boss, How Do I Run This Place? New York: Simon and Schuster, 1980.

White, L.K., & Brinkerhoff, D.B. "The Sexual Division of Labor: Evidence from Childhood." Social Forces, 60, 1981. pp. 170-181.

Wolf, W.C., & Fligstein, N.D. "Sex and Authority in the Workplace: The Causes of Sexual Inequality." American Sociological Review, 44, 1970. pp. 235-252.

Yogev, Sara. "Judging the Professional Woman: Changing Research, Changing Values." Psychology of Women Quarterly, Vol. 7(3), 1983, pp 219-239.

II
ANTICIPATORY SOCIALIZATION OF WOMEN TOWARD MANAGERIAL AND PROFESSIONAL CAREERS

Alper, T. G. "Achievement motivation in College Women: A Now-you-see-it-now-you-don't Phenomenon." American Psychologist, 1974, 29, pp. 194-203.

Almquist, E.M. "Sex Stereotypes in Occupational Choice: The Case of College Women." Journal of Vocational Behavior, 1978, 5, pp. 13-21.

Almquist, E.M., and Angrist, S. "Career Salience and Atypicality of Occupational Choice Among College Women. Journal of Marriage and the Family, 1970, 32, pp. 242-249.

Almquist. E.M., Angrist, S.S., and Michelsen, R. "Women's Career Aspirations and Achievements. College and Seven Years After." Sociology of Work and Occupations, 1980, 1, pp. 367-384.

Andrew, Caroline, Cecile Coderre, & Ann Denis. "Stop or Go: Reflections of Women Managers on Factors Influencing. Their Career Development." Journal of Business Ethics, Volume 9, Number 4,5, April/Nay 1990, pp. 361-367.

Angle, J., Wissmann, D.A. "Gender, College Major, and Earnings." Sociol. Educ., 1981, 54, pp. 25-33.

Bachman, J.G., Bare, D.E., and Frankie, E.I. Correlates of Employment Among High School Seniors. Ann Arbor: Institute for Social Research, University of Michigan. 1986

Bartol, K. and Manhardt, P.J. "Sex Differences in Job Outcome Preferences: Trends Among Newly Hired College Graduates. Journal of Applied Psychology, 1979, 64, pp. 477-482.

Beller, A.H. "Occupational Segregation by Sex: Determinants and Changes." Journal of Human Resources, 1982, 17, pp. 371-91.

Betz, N.E. and Fitzpatrick, L.F. The Career Psychology of Women. Orlando, FL: Academic. 1987.

Betz, N.E. and Hackett, G. "The Relationship of Career Related Self-Efficacy Expectations to Perceived Career options in College Men and Women." Journal of Counseling Psychology, 1981, 28, pp. 399-410.

Blau, P.M., Gustad, J.W., Jesson, R. Barnes, H.S., and Wilcox, R.C. "Occupational Choices: A Conceptual Framework." Industrial and Labor Relations Review, 1956, 9, pp. 531-537.

Bridges, J.S. "College Females Perceptions of Adult Roles and Occupational Fields for Women." Sex Roles, 1987, 16, pp. 591-604.

Bridges, J.S., and Bower, M.S. "The effects of perceived job availability for Women on College Women's Attitude Toward Prestigious Male-dominated Occupations." Psychology of Women Quarterly, 1985, 9, pp. 265-277.

Brief, A.P. and Aldag, R.J. "Male-female. Differences in Occupational Values Within a Majority Group." Journal of Vocational Behavior, 1975, 6, pp. 305-314.

Chusmir, L.H. "Motivation of Managers: Is Gender a Factor?" Psychology of Women Quarterly, 1985, 9, pp. 153-159.

Cowan, G. and Moore L. "Female Identity and Occupational Commitment." Paper presented at the meeting of the American Psychological Association, Denver, April 1971.

Cherry, F. and Deaux, K. "Fear of Success Versus Fear of Gender-inappropriate Behavior." Sex Roles, 1978, 4, pp. 97-101.

DeFleur, M.L. "Children's Knowledge of Occupational Roles and Prestige: Preliminary Report." Psychol. Rep. 1963. 13, p. 760.

Eccies, J.S. "Gender Roles and Women's Achievement-related Decisions." Psychology of Women Quarterly, 1987, 11, pp.135-172.

Florentine, R. "Increasing Similarity in the Values and Life Plans of Male and Female College Students? Evidence and Implications." Sex Roles, 1988, 18, pp. 143-158.

Foster, L.W. and Kolinko, T. "Choosing to be a Managerial Woman: An Examination of Individual Variables and Career Choice." Sex Roles, 1979, 5, pp. 627-34.

Fowlkes, M.R. Behind Every Successful Man: Wives of Medicine and Academe. NY: Columbia Univ. Press, 1980.

Fox, L.H., Tobin, D. and Brody, L. "Sex-role Socialization and Achievement in Mathematics." (in) Sex-Related Differences in Cognitive Functioning: Developmental Issues, ed. M.A. witting, A.C. Peterson, pp. 303-32. New York: Academic Press, 1979.

Garrison, H.H. "Gender Differences in the Career Aspirations of Recent Cohorts of High School Seniors." Soc. Probl. 1979, 27, pp. 170-85.

Gomez-Jejia, L.R. "Sex Differences During Occupational socialization". Academic Management Review, 1983, 26, pp. 492-99. Harmon, L.W. "Anatomy of Career Commitment in Women." Journal of Counseling Psychology, 1970, 17, pp. 77-80.

Harris, C.T. and Earle, J.R. "Gender and Work Values: Survey Findings From a working-Class Sample." Sex Roles, 1986, 15, pp. 487-494.

Harley, R.E. "Children's Concepts of Male and Female Roles." Merrill-Palmer Quarterly, 1960, 6, pp. 83-91.

Herzog, A. Regula. "Sex Role Attitudes Among High School Seniors; Views About Work and Family Roles." Ann Arbor, Mich: Survey Research Center, Institute for Social Research, University of Michigan, 1982.

Herzog, A.R. "High School Seniors' occupational Plans and Values: Trends in Sex Differences 1976 through 1980." Sociology of Education, 1982, 55, pp. 1-13.

Hollenbeck, John R., Ilgen, Daniel R., Ostroff, Cheri; and Vancouver, Jeffrey B. "Sex Differences in occupational Choice, Pay, and Worth: A Supply-side Approach to Understanding the Male-female Wage Gap." Personnel Psychology, Winter 1987, 40:4, pp. 715-743

Holstrom, V.L and Beech, L.R. "Subjective Expected Utility and Career Preferences." Organizational Behavior and Human Performance." 1973, 10, pp. 201-207.

Homer, M. "Sex Differences in Achievement Motivation and Performance in Competitive and Non-Competitive Situations." PhD dissertation. Ann Arbor, MI: University of Michigan.

Hout, M. and Morgan, W.R. "Race and Sex Variations in the Causes of the Expected Attainments of High School Seniors. An. J. Social. 1975, 81, pp. 364-94

Jensen, Marlene. Women Who Want to be Boss: Business Revelations and Success Strategies From Americans Top Female Executives. Garden City, NY: Doubleday, 1987

Kohlbert, L. "A Cognitive-Developmental Analysis of Children's Sex Role Concepts and Attitudes." (in) the Development of Sex Differences, ed. E.E. Maccoby, 1966, pp. 82-173. Stanford: Stanford University Press.

Kollock, P., Blumstein, P., and Schwartz, P. "Sex and Power in Interaction: Conversational Privileges and Duties. 1985, 50, pp. 34-46.

Kriedberg, G., Butcher, A.L., and White, K.M. "Vocational Role Choice in Second-and Sixth-Grade Children." Sex Roles, 1978, 4, pp. 175-81.

Kuzioski, J. "Token Women: Comment on Spangler, Gordon and Pipkin." Am. J. Sociol., 1979, 84, pp. 1438-39.

Laska, S.B. and Micklin, M. "The Knowledge Dimension of Occupational Socialization: Role Models and Their Social Influence." Youth Soc., 1979, 10, pp. 360-78.

Lemkau, J.P. "Women in Male-Dominated Professions. Distinguishing Personality and Background Characteristics." Psychology of Women Quarterly, 1983, 8, pp. 114-165.

Lesser, G.S. "Achievement Motivation in Women." (in) Human Motivation, ed. D.C. McClelland, R.S. Steele, 1973, Morristown, NJ: Gen. Learning.

Levine, A. and Crumrine, J. "Women and the Fear of Success: A Problem in Replication." Am. J. Sociol. 1975, 80, pp. 964-74.

"Lipman-Blumen, J. and Tickamyer, A.R. "Sex Roles in Transition: A Ten-year Perspective." Ann. Rev. Sociol. 1975, 1, pp. 197-338.

Lueptow, L.B. "Sex-typing and Change in the Occupational Choices of High School Seniors, 1964-1975." Sociol. Educ. 1981, 54, pp. 16-324.

Lueptow, L.B. "Social Change and Sex-role Change in Adolescent Orientations Toward Live, Work, and Achievement: 1964-1975." Soc. Psychol. Q., 1980, 43, pp. 48-59.

Lueptow, L.B. "Social Structure, Social Change and Parental Influence in Adolescent Sex-Role Socialization: 1964-1975. J. Marriage Fam. 1980, 42, pp. 930103.

McClendon, M.J. 1976. The Occupational Status Attainment Process of Males and Females. Am. Sociol. Rev., 1976, 41, pp. 52-64.

Macke, A.S., HudisHudis, F.M. and Larrick, D. "Sex-Role Attitudes and Employment Among Women: Dynamic Models of Continuity and Change." (in) Women's Changing Roles at

Home and on the Job. Spec. Rep. No. 26 ed. J. Sawhill, 1978, pp. 199-54. Washington, DC: Natl. Comm. Manpower Policy.

McKenzie, Ward. "Family Centered Case Management With Sexually Aggressive Youth." Olympia: Washington, Region III, Division of Children, Youth, and Family Services, Dept. of Social and Health Services, 1987.

Mai-Dalton, R.R., and Sullivan, J. "The Effects of Manager's Sex on the Assignment to a Challenging or a Dull Task and Reasons for the Choice." Acad. Mgmt. J., 1981, 24, pp. 603-12.

Marini, M.M. "Sex differences in the Determination of Adolescent Aspirations: A Review of Research." Sex Roles 1978, 4, pp 723-53.

Marini, M.M. and Greenberger, E. "Sex Differences in Occupational Aspirations and Expectations." Sociol. Work occup. 1978, 5, pp. 147-78.

Marshall, G.N.; Lang, E.L. "Optimism, self-mastry, and symptoms of depression in women professionals." Journal of Personality & Social Psychology, July 1990, Vol. 59 Issue 1, p. 132, 8p.

Meyer, J.H. "Influence of Alumni Careers and Students' Educational Pathways on Animal Science Undergraduate Teaching Programs." J. Anim. Sci, Volume 68, Number 10, October 1990, pp. 3056-3068.

Mintz, R. and Patterson, C.H. "Marriage and Career Attitudes of Women in Selected College Curriculums." Vocational Guidance Quarterly, 1969, 17, 213-217.

Mureell, Audrey J. and Frieze Hanson, Irene. "Aspiring to Careers in Male-and Female-Dominated Professions." Psychology of Women Quarterly, 1991, 15,pp. 103-126.

Nemerowicz, Gloria Morris. Children's Perceptions of Gender and Work Roles. New York: Praeger, 1979.

Nordholm, L.A. and Westbrook, M.T. "Career Selection, Satisfaction, and Aspirations Among Female Students in Five Health Professions." Australian Psychologist, 1981, 16, pp. 63-78.

O'Leary, V. "Some Attitudinal Barriers to occupational Aspirations of Women." Psychological Bulletin, 1974, 81, pp. 809-826.

O'Leary, V. "Some Attitudinal Barriers to occupational Aspirations in Women." Psychological Bulletin, 1981, 8, pp 809-826.

Papalia, D. E., and Tennent, S.S. "Vocational Aspirations in Preschoolers a Manifestation of Early Sex Role Stereotyping. Sex Roles, 1975, 1, pp. 197-199.

Parcel, T.L. and Mueller, C.W. Ascription and Labor Markets: Race and Sex Differences in Earnings. New York: Academic Press, 1983.

Pietrofesa, J.K., and Schlossberg, N.K. "Counselor Bias and the Female Occupational Role." (in) Counselor Bias and the Female occupational Role, ed. N. Glazer-Malbin and H.Y. Waehrer, pp. 219-221. Chicago: Rand McNally, 1972.

Polachek, S.W. "Sex Differences in College Major." Ind. Labor Relat. Rev. 1978, 31, pp. 498-508.

Power, G.N. "Teaching Women and Men in Organizations Course: Issues for the Male Teacher." (in) Women and Men in Organizations: Teaching Strategies. ed. Dorothy M. Hai. Washington: The Organizational Behavior Teaching Society.

Roos, P.A. and Reskin, B.F. "Institutional Factors Contributing to Sex Segregation in the Workplace. (in) Sex Segregation in the Workplace: Trends, explanations, Remedies, ed. B.F. Resdin, pp. 235-260. Washington, DC: Nati. Acad. Press, 1984.

Schneider, Stephen A. The Availability of Minorities and Women for Professional and Managerial Positions, 1970-1985. Philadelphia: Industrial Research Unit, Wharton School, University of Pennsylvania, 1977.

Sewell, W. H., Hauser, R.M., and Wolf, W.C. "Sex Schooling and Occupational Status.: Am. J. Sociol. 1980, 8, pp. 551-583.

Shann, M.H. "Career Plans of Men and Women in Gender-Dominant Professions." Journal of Vocational Behavior, 1983, 22, pp. 343-356.

Smith, M.D. and Self, G.D. "The Congruence Between Mothers' and Daughters' Sex-role Attitudes: A Research Note." J. Marriage Fam. 1980, 42, pp. 105-109.

Snizek, W.E. and Mayer, L. "Cosmopolitanism and Localism Among Undergraduate College Students; A Study in Anticipatory Socialization." Acta Sociological, 1984, 27, pp. 19-29.

Spitze, G.D. "Role Experiences of Young Women: A Longitudinal Test of the Role Hiatus Hypothesis." Journal of Marriage and the Family, 1978, 40, pp. 471-479.

Stake, J.E. "Motives for Occupational Goal Setting Among Male and Female College Students." Journal of Applied Psychology, 1978, 63, pp. 617-622.

Stein, A.H. and Bailey, M. "The Socialization of Achievement Orientation in Females," Psychological Bulletin, 1973, 80, pp. 345-366.

Stein, A.H. and Bailey, M.M. "The Socialization of Achievement Motivation in Females." (in) Women and Achievement, ed. M.T.S. Mednick, S.S. Tangri, and L.W. Hoffman. Washington, DC: Hemisphere, 1975, pp. 151-157.

Tangri, S.S. "Determinants of Occupational Role Innovation Among College Women.: Journal of Social Issues, 1972, 28(2), pp. 177-199.

Turner, B.F. and Mccaffrey, J.H. Socialization and Career Orientation Among Black and White College Women." Journal of Vocational Behavior, 1974,5, pp. 307-319.

Veroff, J., Wilcox, S. and Atkinson, J.W. "The Achievement Motive in High School and College Age Women." Journal of Abnormal and Social Psychology, 1953, 48, pp. 108-109.

Voydanoff, P. "Work-Family Life Cycles." Paper presented at the Workshop on Theory Construction and Research Methodology, National Council on Family Relations. 1980.

Wagman, M. "Sex and Age Difference in Occupational Values." Personnel and Guidance Journal, 1965, 44, pp. 258-262.

Walker, Henry A. "Gender Differences in Role Differentiation and organizational Task Performance." Ann. Rev. Sociol. 1986, 12, pp. 255-275.

White, L.K. and Brinkerhoff, D.B. "The Sexual Division of Labor: Evidence From Childhood." Soc. Forces, 1981, 60, pp. 170-181.

Winters, A.S. and Frankel, J. "Women's work Role as Perceived by Lower Status White and Black Female Adolescents." Adolescence, 1984, 19, pp 403-415.

Yogev, S. "Do Professional Women Have Egalitarian Relationships?" Journal of Marriage and the Family, 1981, 43, pp. 865-871.

III
PROFESSIONAL SOCIALIZATION OF WOMEN ACROSS ORGANIZATIONS

Buono, Anthony F., & Kamm, Judith B. "Marginality and the Organizational Socialization of Female Managers," Human Relations 36, 12, 1983, pp. 1125-1140.

Cabin, John. Internships in Foreign and Defense Policy: A Complete Guide for Women (& Men) Prepared by Women in International Security. MD: Seven Locks Press, 1990.

Hai, D.M. "Teaching 'Women in Management' Courses; Current Issues." Exchange: The Organizational Behavior Teaching Journal, 7(4), 1982, pp. 38-40.

Josefowitz, N. "Teaching Managerial Skills to Women: The Issues of All-female vs. Mixed-sex Group Groups." Women and Men in Organizations: Teaching Strategies. Washington: The Organizational Behavior Teaching Society, 1984.

Marini, M.M., & Brinton, M.C. "Sex Typing in Occupational Socialization." Sex Segregation in the Workplace: Trends, Explanations, Remedies. Washington, D.C.: National Academy Press, 1984, pp. 157-170.

McKinney Kellogg, D., Spelman, D., & Crary, M. "Introducing Women in Management Issues in an OB Course." The Organizational Behavior Teaching Review, IX (3), 1984, pp. 83-95.

Posner, Barry Z. "Female and Male Socialization Experiences: An Initial Investigation." Journal of Occupational Psychology. Vol. 58(1), 1985, pp. 81-85.

Rosenthal, Patrice, Gender differences in managers' casual explanations for their work performance : A study in two organizations. Journal of Occupational and Organizational Psychology;Leicester; June 1996, Guest, David; Vol. 69, pt. 2.

Weiss, C.S. "The Development of Professional Role Commitment Among Graduate Students." Human Relations, 34, 1981, pp. 13-31.

IV
BARRIERS AGAINST THE UPWARD MOBILITY OF WOMEN MANAGERS AND PROFESSIONALS

Becker, Mary E., Daniel R. Fischel, & Edward P. Lazear. "Barriers Facing Women in the Wage-Labor Market and the Need for Additional Remedies: A Reply to Fischel and Lazear/ Comparable Worth: A Rejoinder." University of Chicago Law Review, Volume 53, Number 3, Summer 1986, pp. 934-952.

Campbell, Myrtle V. A Study of Perceived Barriers and Strategies to Career Advancement for Selected Female Administrators in Indiana. Thesis, Indiana University, 1984.

Carney, Larry S. & Charlotte G. O'Kelly. "Barriers and Constraints to the Recruitment and Mobility of Female Managers in the Japanese Labor Force." Human Resource Mgmt. Volume 26, Number 2, Summer 1987, pp. 193-216.

Clynch, Edward J. and Gaudin, Carol A. "Sex in the shipyards: An Assessment of Affirmative Action Policy," Public Administration Review, 1982, 42, pp. 114-120.

Corse, Sara J. "Pregnant Managers and Their Subordinates: The Effects of Gender Expectations On Hierarchical Relationships." Journal of Applied Behavioral Science, Volume 26, Number 1, 1190, pp. 25-47.

Culletn, Dallas. "Career Barriers: Do We Need More Research?" Journal of Business Ethics (Netherlands), Volume 9, Number 4,5, Apr/May 1990, pp. 353-359.

Davidson, M.J. and Cooper, C.L. "She Needs a Wife: Problems of Women Managers." Leadership and organization Development Journal, 1984, 5(3), pp.1-30.

Forbes, Benjamin J. James E. Piercy. & Thomas L. Hayes. "Women Executives: Breaking Down Barriers?" Business Horizons, Volume 31, Number 4, Nov/Dec 1988, pp. 6-9.

Jacobson, Aileen. Women in Charge: Dilemmas of Women in Authority. New York: Van Nostrand Reinhold, 1985.

Jacobson, Sarah Williams, Women in Management : Trends, Issues, and Challenges in Mangerial Diversity; Competitive Frontiers : Women Managers in a Global Economy. Academy of Managment Review, Mississippi State; July 1995, Vol. 20, Issue 3, p.741.

Jardim, Anne & Margaret Hennig. "The Last Barrier: Breaking into the Boys' Club at the Top." Working Woman, Volume 15, Number 11, November 1990, pp. 130-134, 164.

McKibben, Jenny. "Powerful Barrier to Equality." Industrial Society (UK), December 1990, pp. 16-17.

O'Leary, V.E. "Some Attitudinal Barriers to occupational Aspirations in Women." Psychological Bulletin, 1974, 81, pp. 809-826.

Phelps, Norman L. "Senior Self-Image: Breaking the Age Barrier." Marketing Communications, Volume 11, Number 3, March 1986, pp. 55-58.

Pilotta, Joseph J. ed. Women in organizations: Barriers and Breakthroughs. Prospect Heights, IL: Waveland Press, 1983.

Quinn, Lawrence R. "After 20 Years Women Face the Same Barriers. Executive Financial Woman, Volume 2, Number 6, Winter 1987, pp. 21-25.

Ragins, Belle Rose. "Barriers to Mentoring: The Female Manager's Dilemma."Human Relations, January, 1989 42, pp. 1-22.

Robinson, Joseph Arnold. "Women Managers: Aids and Barriers in their Career Paths, Performance and Advancement." DAI 35/10A, p 6310.

Rossi, A.S. "Barriers to the Career Choice of Engineering, Medicine, or Science Among American Women." (in) Women and the Scientific Professions, ed. J.A. Mattfeld and C.G. Van Aken. Cambridge, Mass: MIT Press, 1965.

Schwarts, Eleanor Brantley. The Sex Barrier in Business. Atlanta: Georgia State University, 1971.

Stamp, Gillian. "Some Observations on the Career Paths of Women." Journal of Applied behavioral Science, Volume 22, Number 4, November 1986, pp. 385-396.

Thomas, Louella, & Willie E. Hopkins. "The Continuing Struggle of Women in Management: 15 the End in Sight?" Management Quarterly, Volume 26, Number 4, Winter 1985/1986, pp 37-43.

Wilson, Reginald. "Women of Color in Academic Administration: Trends, Progress, and Barriers." Sex Roles, July 1989, 21, pp. 85-97.

· V
RECRUITMENT OF WOMEN INTO MANAGERIAL SYSTEMS

Acker, Joan and Donald R. Van Houten, "Differential Recruitment and Control: The Sex Structuring of Organizations," (in) Administrative Science Quarterly, Volume 19, Number 2, June 1974. pp. 152-163.

Arvey, R.D. "Unfair Discrimination in the Employment Interview: Legal and Psychological Aspects." Psychological Bulletin, Number 86, 1979, pp. 736-765.

Baude, Annika. "A Dialogue that Might Yet Take Place: A Female Researcher Talks to Personnel Managers About Recruitment Processes." International Studies of Management & Organization, Volume 19, Number 4, Winter 1989/1990, pp. 51-76.

Beehr, T.A. and D.C. Gilmore. "Applicant Attractiveness as a Perceived Job-relevant Variable in Selection of Management Trainees." Academy of Management Journal, Number 25, 1982, pp. 608-618.

Brenner, O.C. and J. Tomkiewicz. "Job Orientation of Males and Females: Are Sex Differences Declining?" Personnel Psychology, Number 32, 1979, pp 741-750.

Cash, T.F., B. Gillen and D.S. Burns. "Sexism and 'Beautyism' in personnel Consultant Decision Making." Journal of Applied Psychology, Number 62, 1977, pp. 301-310.

Cann, A., W. Siegfried, and L. Pearce. "Forced Attention to Specific Applicant Qualifications; Impact of Physical Attractiveness and Sex of Applicant Biases." Personnel psychology. Number 34, 1981, pp. 65-75.

Dipboye, R.L., R.D. Arvey, and D.E. Terpstra. "Sex and Physical Attractiveness of Raters and Applicants as Determinants of Resume Evaluations." Journal of Applied Psychology, Number 62, 1977, pp. 288-294.

Dipboye, R.L., H.L. Fromkin, and K. Wiback. "Relative Importance of Applicant Sex, Attractiveness and Scholastic Standing in Evaluation of Job Applicant Resumes." Journal of Applied Psychology, Number 60, 1975. pp. 39-43.

Ferris, G.R. and D.C. Gilmore. "Effects of Mode of Information Presentation, Sex of Applicant, and Sex of Interview on Simulated Interview Decisions." Psychological Reports, Number 40, 1977, p 566.

Firth, M. "Sex Discrimination in Job Opportunities for Women." Sex Roles, Number 8, 1982, pp. 891-901.

Gardner, Donald G. and Chris J. Berger. "The Effects of Sex Stereotypes, Amount of Relevant Information, and Awareness of Organizational Selection practices on Sex Discrimination for a Managerial position." West Lafayette, IN: Institute for Research in the Behavioral, Economic, and Management Sciences, Krannert Graduate School of Management, Purdue University, 1980.

Gerdes, E.P. and D.M. Garber. "Sex Bias in Hiring: Effects of Job Demands and Applicant Competence." Sex Roles, Number 9, 1983, pp. 307-320.

Gordon, F.E. and M.H. Strober, ed. Bringing Women into Management, New York: McGraw-Hill, 1975.

Hammer, W.C., J.S. Kim, L. Baird and W.J. Bigoness. "Race and Sex as Determinants of Ratings by Potential Employers in a Simulated work-Sampling Task." Journal of Applied Psychology, Number 59, 1974, pp. 705-711.

Hartford, C.T. "The Aptitude Index Battery Use with Minority Groups and Women." Life Insurance Marketing and Research Association, Research Report, 1975.

Heilman, M.E. and L.R. Arauwatari. "When Beauty is Beastly: The Effects of Appearance and Sex on Evaluations of Job Applicants for Managerial and Non-managerial Jobs." Organizational Behavior and Human Performance, Number 23, 1979, pp. 360-372.

Karambayya, Rekha, Caught in the crossfire : Women and corporate restructuring. Revue Canadienne des Sciences de I'Administration; Montreal; December 1998, Vol. 15, n.4, pp. 333-338.

Katz, David. "Sex Discrimination in Hiring: The Influence of Organizational Climate and Need for Approval on Decision Making Behavior." Psychology of Women Quarterly, Volume 11, March 1987, pp. 11-20.

Kirnan, Jean Powell, John A. Farley, and Kurt F. Geisinger. "The Relationship Between Recruiting and Source, Applicant Quality and Hire Performance: An Analysis by Sex, Ethnicity, and Age." Personnel Psychology, Volume 42, Number 2, 1989, pp. 293-308.

Levinson, R.M. "Sex Discrimination and Employment Practices: An Experiment with Unconventional Job Inquiries. Soc. Probl. Volume 22, 1975, pp. 533-543.

Pavan, Barbara Nelson. "Job Search Strategies Utilized by Certified Aspiring and Incumbent Female and Male Public School Administrators." Paper presented at the annual meeting of the American Educational Research Association, New Orleans, April 1988.

Rose, G.L. and P. Andiappan. "Sex Effects On Managerial Hiring Decisions." Academy of Management Journal, Number 21, 1978, pp. 104-112.

Rosen, B. and T.H. Jerdee. "Effects of Applicants' Sex and Difficulty of Job on Evaluations of Candidates for Managerial Positions." Journal of Applied Psychology, Number 59, 1974, pp. 511-512.

Rosen, B. and T.H. Jerdee. "Influence of Sex Role Stereotypes on Personnel Decisions." Journal of Applied Psychology, Number 59, 1974, pp. 9-14.

Taylor MS, Ilgen Dr. "Sex Discrimination Against Women in Initial Placement Decisions: A Laboratory Investigation." Academy of Management Journal, Number 24, 1981, pp. 859-865.

VI
PERFORMANCE EVALUATION OF WOMEN MANAGERS AND PROFESSIONALS

Abramson, P. E., P. A. Goldbert, J.H. Greenberg, & U.M. Abramson. "The Talking Platypus Phenomenon: Competency Ratings as a Function of Sex and Professional Status." Psychology of Women Quarterly, Number 2, 1978, pp. 114-124.

Adams, J., R.F. Priest, R.W. Rice, & H.T. Prince. "Effects of Rater Attitudes and Attributes on Female and Male Leaders' Effectiveness." 1980 Biannual AMEED Psychology Symposium, Washington, DC, October, 1980.

Arvey, R.D. "Sex Bias in Job Evaluation Procedures." Personnel Psychology, Number 39, 1986, pp. 315-335.

Arvey, R.D., E.M. Passino, & J.W. Lousbury. "Job Analysis Results as Influenced by Sex of Incumbent and Sex of Analyst." Journal of Applied Psychology, Number 62, 1977, pp. 411-416.

Ash, P. and L. Crnic. Validation Study of the Midwest Industrial Management Association's Job Evaluation Plan for Production and Related Jobs. Chicago: Midwest Industrial Management Association, 1974.

Ash, P. "The Reliability of Job Evaluation Rankings." Journal of Applied Psychology, Number 32, 1948, pp. 313-320.

Bellak, A.O., M.W. Bates, & D.M Glasner. "Job Evaluation: Its Role in the Comparable Worth Debate." Public personnel Management, Number 12, 1983, pp. 418-424

Bemmels, B. "The Effect of Grievants' Gender on Arbitrators' Decisions." Industrial and Labor Relations Review, Number 41, 1988, pp. 251-262.

Bemmels, Brian. "Gender Effects in Discipline Arbitration: Evidence From British Columbia," Academy of Management Journal, Volume 31, Number 4, 1988, pp. 699-706.

Brief, A.N. and M.J. Wallace. "The Impact of Employee Sex and Performance on the Allocation of Rewards: The Case of a Job With an Neutral Sex Type." Journal of Psychology, Number 92, 1976, pp. 25-34.

Butterfield, D.A. and G.N. Powell. "Effect of Group performance, Leader Sex, and Rater Sex on Ratings of Leader Behavior."

Organizational Behavior and Human Performance, Number 28, 1981, pp. 129-141.

Brown, B. and F. Geis. "Turning Lead into Gold: Evaluations of Men and Women Leaders and the Alchemy of Consensus." Journal Pers. Soc. Psychol, Number 46, 1984, pp. 811-824.

Cash, T.F., B. Gillen, & D.S. Burns. "Sexism and 'Beautyism' in Personnel Consultant Decision Making." Journal of Applied Psychology, Number 28, 1977, pp. 80-55.

Dalton, D.R. and W.D. Todor. "Gender and Workplace Justice: A Field Assessment." Psychology, Number 38, 1985, pp. 133-151.

Deau, K. and J. Taynor. "Evaluation of Male and Female Ability: Bias Works Two Ways." Psychological Reports, Number 31, 1973, pp. 20-31.

Die, Ann H.; Theodore Debbs, & James L. Walker. "Managerial Evaluations by Men and Women Managers." The Journal of Social Psychology, Volume 130, December 1990, pp. 763-769.

Dobbins, Gregory H. "Effects of Gender on Leaders' Responses to Poor Performers: An Attributional Interpretation." Academy of Management Journal, Volume 28, Number 3, 1985, pp. 597-598.

Doverspike, D. and G.V. Barrett. "An Internal Bias Analysis of a Job Evaluation Instrument." Journal of Applied Psychology, Number 69, 1984, pp. 648-662.

Frank1 F.D. and J. Drucker. "The Influence of Evaluatee's Sex on Evaluation of a Response of a Managerial Selection Instrument." Sex Roles, Number 3, 1977, pp. 59-64.

Frasher, J.M., R.S. Frasher, & F.B. Wims. "Sex-role Stereotyping in School Superintendents' Personnel Decisions." Sex Roles, Number 8, 1982, pp. 261-268.

Frieze, I.H., J.E. Olson, & D.C. Good. "Perceived and Actual Discrimination in the Salaries of Male and Female Managers." Journal of Applied Social Psychology, Number 20, 1990, pp. 46-67.

Gold, Una O.C. & Judith K. Pringle. "Gender-Specific Factors in Management Promotion." Journal of Managerial Psychology, Volume 3, Number 4, 1988, pp. 17-22.

Grams, R. and D.P. Schwab. "An Investigation of Systematic Gender-related Error in Job Evaluation." Acad. Mgt. J., Number 28, 1985, pp. 179-290.

Gupta, N. T.A. Beehr, & G.D. Jenkins. "The Relationship Between Employee Gender and Supervisory-subordinate Cross-ratings." Proceedings of the Academy of Management, Number 40, 1980, pp. 396-400.

Hall, F.S. and D.T. Hall. "Effects of Job Incumbents' Race and Sex on Evaluations of Managerial Performance." Academy of Management Journal, Number 19, 1976, pp. 476-481.

Harlan, A. and C.L. Weiss. "Sex Differences in Factors Affecting Managerial Career Advancement." (in) Women in the Workplace, P.A. Wallace, ed. Boston: Auburn House, 1982, pp. 59-100.

Hartmann, H.I. "Internal Labor Markets and Gender: A Case Study of Promotion. (in) Gender in the Workplace, C. Brown & J. A. Pechnan, ed. Washington, DC: Brookings Institute, 1987, pp. 59-105.

Heilman, M. E. and M.H. Stopeck. "Being Attractive, Advantage or Disadvantage? Performance-based Evaluations and Recommended Personnel Actions as a Function of Appearance, Sex and Job Type." Organ. Behav. Hum. Decision Process, Number 35, 1985, pp. 202-215.

Heilman, M.E. and L.R. Saruwatari. "When Beauty is Beastly: The Effects of Appearance and Sex on Evaluations of Job Applicants for Managerial and Non-managerial Jobs." Organ. Behav. Hum. Perform., Number 23, 1979, pp. 360-72

Katx, M.G. and L. A. Messe. "A Sex Difference in the Distribution of Over sufficient Rewards. Paper presented at the Midwestern Psychological Association, Chicago, 1973.

Larwood, L., P. Rand, & A.D. Hovanessian. "Sex Differences in Response to Simulated Employee Discipline Cases." Personnel Psychology, Number 32, 1979, pp. 539-550.

Larwood, L. and J. Blackmore. "Sex Discrimination in Manager Selection: Testing Predictions of the Vertical Dyad Linkage Model." Sex Roles, Number 4, 1978, pp. 359-367.

Lee, D. and K. Alvares. "Effect of Sex on Descriptions and Evaluations of supervisory Behavior in a Simulated Industrial Setting. "Journal of Applied Psychology, Number 28, 1970, pp. 390-395.

Lee, D.M. and K.M. Alvares. "Effects of Sex on Descriptions and Evaluations of Supervisory Behavior in a Simulated Industrial Setting." Journal of Applied Psychology, Number 62, Volume 4, 1977, pp. 405-410.

L'Heureux-Barrett, Tara, & Janet L. Barnes-Farrell. "Overcoming Gender Bias in Reward Allocation: The Role of Expectations of Future Performance." Psychology of Women Quarterly, Number 15, 1991, pp. 127-139.

Lewis7 C.T. "Assessing the Validity of Job Evaluation." Public Personnel Management, Number 18, Volume 1, Spring 1989, pp. 45-63.

Lillestol, Jane Marie Brush. "Effect of Applicant's Sex, organizational Level of Job and Sex of Personnel Manager of Evaluations of Candidates for Managerial Positions in Retail Merchandising." DAI Volume 38/OEA, 1977, p. 3601.

Mai-Dalton, Renate & Jeremiah J. Sullivan. "The Effects of Manager's Sex on the Assignment to a Challenging or a Dull Task and Reasons for the Choice." Academy of Management Journal, Volume 24, Number 3, 1981, pp. 603-612.

Mai-Dalton, R.R., S. Feldman-Summers, & T.R. Mitchell. "Effect of Employee Gender and Behavioral Style on the Evaluations of Male and Female Banking Executives." Journal of Applied Psychology, Number 64, 1979, pp. 221-226.

Mischel, H.N. "Sex Bias in the Evaluation of Professional Achievements." Journal of Educational Psychology, April 1974, pp. 157-166.

Mobley, W.H. "Supervisor and Employee Race and Sex Effects of Performance Appraisals: A Field Study of Adverse Impact and Generalizability." Academy of Management Journal, Number 25, 1982, pp. 598-606.

Mount, M.K. and R.A. Ellis. "Impacts of Pay Level, Job Gender and Job type on Job Evaluation Ratings." Paper presented at the annual meeting of the academy of Management, San Diego, August 1985.

Mount, Michael K. & Rebecca A. Ellis. "Investigation of Bias in Job Evaluation Ratings of Comparable Worth Study Participants." Personnel Psychology, Number 1, Spring 1987, pp. 85-96.

Naughton, T.J. "Effect of Female-linked Job Titles on Job Evaluation Ratings." Journal of Management, Number 14, Volume 4, December 1988, pp. 567-578.

Nieva. V.F. and B.A. Gutek. "Sex Effects on Evaluation." Academy of Management Review, Number 5, 1980, pp. 267-276.

Offermann, L.R. "Visibility and Evaluation of Female and Male Leaders." Sex Roles, Number 14, Volume 9/10, 1986, pp. 533-543.

Olson, J.E. and I.M. Frieze. "Income Determinants of Women in Management." (in) Women and Work: An Annual Review, edited by A.H. Stromberg, L. Larwood & B.A. Gutek, Beverly Hills, CA: Sage, 1987.

Olson, C.A. and B.E. Becker. "Sex Discrimination in the Promotion Process." Industrial and Labor Relations Review, Number 36, 1983, pp. 624-641.

Peters, L.M., E.J. O'Connor, J. Weckley, A. Pooyan, B. Frank, & B. Erenkratz. "Sex Bias and Managerial Evaluations A Replication and Extension." Journal of Applied Psychology, Number 69, 1984, pp. 349-352.

Pluakos, Elaine & Kenneth N. Wexley. "The Relationship Among Perceptual Similarity, Sex, and Performance Ratings in Manager-Subordinate Dyads." Academy of Management Journal, Volume 26, Number 1, 1983, pp. 129-139.

Ragins, Belle Rose. "Power and Gender Congruency Effects in Evaluations of Male and Female Mangers." Journal of Management, Volume 15, Number 1, March 1989, pp. 65-76.

Reis, H. & L. Jackson. "Sex Differences in Reward Allocations: Subjects, Partners, and Tasks." Journal of Personality and Social Psychology, Number 59, 1981, pp. 9-14.

Rose, G. "Sex Effects on Effort Attributions in Managerial Performance Evaluations." Organizational Behavior and Human Performance, Number 21, 1978, pp. 367-378.

Rosen, B. & M.F. Mericle. "Influence of Strong Versus Weak Fair Employment Policies and Applicant's Sex on Selection Decisions and Salary Recommendations in a Management Simulation." Journal of Applied Psychology, Number 64, 1979, pp. 435-439.

Rosen, B. and T.H. Jerdee. "The Influence of Sex-Role Stereotypes on Evaluations of Male and Female Supervisory Behavior." Journal of Applied Psychology, Number 57, Volume 1, 1973, pp. 44-48.

Rosen, B. and T. Jerdee. "Influence of Sex Role Stereotypes on Personnel Decisions." Journal of Applied Psychology, Number 59, 1974, pp. 9-14.

Rosen, B. & T.H. Jerdee. "Effect of Applicant's Sex and Difficulty of Job on Evaluations of Candidates of Managerial Positions." Journal of Applied Psychology, Number 59, 1974, pp. 511-512.

Rosen, B. & T.H. Jerdee. "Effects of Employee's Sex and Threatening Versus Pleading Appeals on Managerial Evaluations of Grievances." Journal of Applied Psychology, Number 60, 1975, pp. 442-445.

Scase, Richard, Robert Goffee, & Anna Mann. "Women Managers: 1. Room at the Top/2. Destroying the Myths." Management Today, March 1987, pp. 64-67.

School, Richard W. & Elizabeth Cooper. "The Use of Job Evaluation to Eliminate Gender Based Pay Differentials." Public Personnel Management, Volume 20, Number 1, Spring, 1991, pp. 1-12.

Schwab, D.P. & R. Grams. "Sex-related Errors in Job Evaluation: A Real World Test." Journal of Applied Psychology, Number 70, 1985, pp. 533-539.

Schwab, D.P. "Job Evaluation Research and Research Needs." (in) Comparable Worth: New Directions in Research, edited by Heidi Hartmann, Washington: National Academy Press, 1985.

Stephenson, Beth Broadhurst. "Sex Bias in Management Evaluation." DAI Number 42-09B, 1981, p 3859.

Stewart, L.P., & W.B. Gudykunst. "Differential Factors Influencing the Hierarchical Level and Number of Promotions of Male and Females Within An Organization." Acad. Mgmt. J. Number 25, 1982, PP. 586-597.

Stumpf, S.A., & M. London. "Management Promotions: Individual and Organizational Factors Influencing the Decision Process." Academy of Management Review, Number 6, 1981, pp. 539-549.

Walsh, James, et.al. "The Effects of Gender on Assessment Center Evaluations." Journal of Occupational Psychology, Volume 60, Number 2, 1987, pp. 305-309.

Walker, J.E., C. Tausky, & D. Oliver. "Men and Women at Work: Similarities and Differences in Work Values Within Occupational Groupings." Journal of Vocational Behavior, Number 21, 1982, pp. 17-36.

Wexley, K.N., E.D. Pulasko. "Sex Effects on Performance Ratings in Manager-subordinate Dyads: A Field Study." Journal of Applied Psychology. Number 67, 1982, pp. 433-439.

VII
WOMEN & MEN ADMINISTRATORS: VARIATIONS IN LEADERSHIP ATTRIBUTES

Anderson, Lynn R. & Margaret McLenigan. "Sex Differences in the Relationship Between Self-monitoring and Leader Behavior." Small-Group-Behavior, Volume 18, Number 2, May 1987, pp. 147-167.

Bartol, Kathryn M. Male and Female Leaders in Small Work Groups: An Empirical Study of Satisfaction, Performance, and Perceptions of Leader Behavior. East Lansing: Michigan State, 1973.

Beckstrom, Sharon Lee. "Men and Women Managers' Perceptions About Successful Managers: Implications for Management Training and Development." DAI, Volume 50/08A, p. 2561, 1989.

Bourantas, Dimitris and Nancy Papalexandris. "Sex Differences in Leadership: Leadership Styles and Subordinate Satisfaction." Journal of Managerial Psychology, Volume 5, Number 5, 1990, pp. 7-10.

Bozzi, Vincent. "Assertiveness Breeds Contempt." Psychology Today, Volume 21, September 1987, p 15.

Brenner, O.C., Josept Tomkiewicz, & Virginia E. Schein. "The Relationship Between Sex Role Stereotypes and Requisite Management Characteristics Revisited." Academy-of-Management Journal, Volume 32, Number 3, September 1989, pp. 662-669.

Bushardt, Stephen C., Aubrey Fowler, & Regina Caveny. "Sex-Role Behavior and Leadership: An Empirical Investigation." Leadership & Organization Development Journal, Volume 8, Number 5, 1987, pp. 13-16.

Cannings, Kathleen and Claude Montmarguette. "Managerial Momentum: A Simultaneous Model of the Career Progress of Male and Female Managers." Industrial & Labor Relations Review, Volume 44, Number 2, January 1991, pp. 212-228.

Childress, Georgia P. "Myths and Realities of Women in Management." Organization Development Journal, Volume 4, Number 1, Spring 1986, pp. 44-48.

Chonko, Lawrence B. "Machiavellianism: Sex Differences in the Profession of Purchasing Management." Psychological Reports, Volume 51, Number 2, October 1982, pp. 645-646.

Dion, Kenneth L, & Regina A. Schuller. "Ms. and the Manager: A Tale of Two Stereotypes." Sex-Roles, Volume 22, Number 9-10, May 1990, pp. 569-577.

Feuer, Dale. "How Women Manage." Training, Volume 25, Number 8, August 1988, pp. 23-31.

Fields, Suzanne. "Flirting With the Feminist Mystique." Business Month, Volume 136, Number 5, November 1990, pp. 11-12.

Fierman, Jaclyn. "Do Women Manage Differently?" Fortune, Volume 122, Number 15, December 17, 1990, pp. 115-118.

Francis, David R., Women demolish more career barriers. Christian Science Monitor, 6/6/2001, Vol. 93 Issue 134, pl, Op. 2 Charts,

Gomez-Mejia, Juis R. "Women's Adaptation to Male-Dominated Occupations." International Journal of Manpower, Volume 11, Number 4, 1990, pp. 11-16.

Grant, Jim. "Women as Managers: What They Can Offer to Organizations." Organizational Dynamics, Volume 16, Number 3, Winter 1988, pp. 56-63.

Hale, Sylvia M. "The Documentary Construction of Female Mismanagement." Canadian Review of Sociology and Anthropology; Volume 24, Number 4, 1987, pp. 489-513.

Heilman, Madeline E., Caryn J. Block, Richard F. Martell, & Michael C. Simon. "Has Anything Changed? Current Characterizations of Men, Women, and Managers." Journal of Applied Psychology, Volume 74' Number 6, December 1989, pp. 935-942.

Hildebrandt, Herbert William. A Managerial Profile: The Woman Manager. Ann Arbor, MI: Graduate School of Business Administration, University of Michigan, 1985.

Kidwell, Jeaneen M., Robert E. Stevens, & Art L. Bethke. "Differences in Ethical Perceptions Between Male and Female Managers: Myth of Reality?" Journal of Business Ethics, Volume 6, August 1987, pp. 489-493.

Korabik, Karen. "Androgyny and Leadership Style." Journal of Business Ethics (Netherlands) Volume 9, Number 4,5, Apr/May 1990, pp. 283-292.

Kormondy, Elizabeth Ann. "The Effects of Sex Role Stereotypes and Sex Role Orientation on the Casual Attributions Made By Male and Female Managers in Same and Cross-Sex Manager-Subordinate Situations." DAI Volume 43/063, 1987.

Lumpkin, James R. & Keith R. Tudor. "Effect of Pay Differential on Job Satisfaction: A Study of the Gender Gap." Journal of Purchasing & Materials Mgmt., Volume 26, Number 3, Summer 1990, pp. 25-29.

Mathison, David L. "Sex Differences in the Perception of Assertiveness Among Female Managers." Journal of Social Psychology, Volume 126, Number 5, October 1986, pp. 599-606.

Metcalf, Beverly A. "Male and Female Managers: AN Analysis of Biographical and Self-Concept Data. Special Issue: Women and Work." Work and Stress, Volume 1, Number 3, Jul-Sep 1987, pp. 207-219.

Moore, Loretta Marie. Distinguishing Characteristics of Women Managers. DAI 38/113, 1977, p. 200.

Ottaway, Richard N. & Deepti Bhatnagar. "Personality and Biographical Differences Between Male and Female Managers in the United States and India. Special Issue: Women's occupational Plans and Decisions." Applied Psychology An International Review, Volume 7, Number 2, April 1988, pp. 201-212.

Palmer, David D. "Personal Values and Managerial Decision: Are There Differences Between Women and Men?" College Student Journal, Volume 17, Number 2, summer 1983, pp. 124-131.

Parker, Barbara & Leonard H. Chusmir. "A Generational and Sex-Based View of Managerial Work Values." Psychological Reports, Volume 66, Number 3 (pt 1), June 1990, pp. 947-950.

Parker, Sydney Ruth. "The Yin and the Yang: Do Women Managers Have the Best of Both Worlds? A Comparative Study of the Masculinity and Femininity of Managers." DAI Volume 37/06B, 1976, p. 104.

Powell, Gary N. "One More Time: Do Female and Male Managers Differ?" Academy of Mgmt Executive, Volume 4, Number 4, August 1990, pp. 68-75.

Powell, Gary N. Women & Men in Management. Newbury Park, CA: Sage Publications, 1988.

Rosener, Judy B. "Ways Women Lead." Harvard Business Review, Volume 68, Number 6, Nov/Dec 1990, pp. 119-125.

Rowney, J.I.A. & A.R. Cahoon. "Individual and Organizational Characteristics of Women in Managerial Leadership." Journal of Business Ethics (Netherlands), Volume 9, Number 4,5, Apr/May 1990, pp. 293-316.

Schein, Virginia E. "Sex Role Stereotyping, Ability and Performance: Prior Research and New Directions." Personnel Psychology, Number 31, 1978, pp. 87-94.

Schmidt, Warren H. Managerial Values in Perspective. New York: AMA Membership Publications Division, American Management Associations, 1983.

Schul, Patrick L., Steven J. Remington & Rober L. Berl. "Assessing Gender Differences in Relationships Between Supervisory Behaviors and job-related Outcomes in the Industrial Sales Force." Journal of Personal Selling & Sales Management, Volume 10, Number 3, Summer 1990, pp. 1-16.

Sharma, Sarla. "Psychology of Women in Management: A Distinct Feminine Leadership.: Equal Opportunities International (UK), Volume 9, Number 2, 1990, pp. 13-18.

Smeltzer, Larry R. & James D. Werbel. "Gender Differences in Managerial Communication: Fact or Folk-Linguistics?" Journal of Business Communication, Volume 23, Number 2, Spring 1986, pp. 41-50.

Statham, Anne. "The Gender Model Revisited: Differences in the Management Styles of Men and Women." Sex Roles1 Volume 16, April 1987, pp. 409-429.

Weber, Elizabeth. "Characteristics of Selected Women Managers: Personal, Educational and Career." DAI Volume 39/06A, 1976, p 3317.

Westman, Mina & Dalia Etzion. "The Career Success/Personal Failure Phenomenon as Perceived in Others: Comparing Vignette of Male and Female Managers." Journal of Vocational Behavior, Volume 37, Number 2, October 1990, pp. 209-224.

VIII
ROLE PERCEPTIONS OF MANAGERIAL WOMEN AND ROLE EXPECTATIONS OF OTHERS

Adams, Jerome, Robert W. Rice, & Debra Instone. "Follower Attitudes Toward Women and Judgments Concerning Performance by Female and Male Leaders." Academy of Management Journal, Number 27, September 1984, pp. 636-643.

Barnett, John H. & Marvin J. Karson. "Managers, Values, and Executive Decisions: An Exploration of the Role of Gender, Career Stage, Organizational Level, Function, and the Importance of Ethics, Relationships and Results in Managerial Decision-Making." Journal of Business Ethics (Netherlands), Volume 8, Number 10, October 1989, pp. 747-771.

Bass, B.M., J. Krusell, & R.A. Alexander. "Male Managers' Attitudes Toward Working Women." American Behavioral Scientist, Number 15, 1971, PP. 221-236.

Bhatnagar, Deepti, Swamy, Ranjini; Attitudes toward women as managers : Does interaction make a difference? Human Relations; New York, November 1995, Vol. 48, Issue 11, p. 1285.

Beutell, Nicholas J. "Correlates of Attitudes Toward American Women as Managers." Journal of Social Psychology, Volume 124, Number 1, October 1984, pp. 57-63.

Brenner, O.C., & Nicholas J. Beutell. "The Effect of Birth Order and Gender on American Managers' Attitudes Toward Female Managers." The Journal of Social Psychology, Number 129, February 1969, pp. 57-64.

Broverman, I. K., S.R. Vogel, D.M. Broverman, F.E. Clarkson, & P.S. Rosenkrantz. "Sex Role Stereotypes: A Current Appraisal." The Journal of Social Issues, Number 28, 1972, pp. 59-76.

Butterfield, D.A., & G.N. Powell. "Effects of Group Performance, Leader Sex, and Rater Sex on Ratings of Leader Behavior." organizational Behavior and Human Performance. Number 28, 1981, pp. 129-141.

Cohen, S.L., K.A. Bunker, A.L. Burton, & P.O. McManus. "Reactions of Male Subordinates to the Sex-role Congruency of Immediate Supervision." Sex Roles, Number 4, 1973. pp. 297-311.

Corse, Sara J. "Pregnant Managers and Their Subordinates: The Effects of Gender Expectations on Hierarchical Relationships." The Journal of Applied Behavioral Science, Volume 26, Number 1, 1990, pp. 25-47.

Deutsch, F.M., & F.T.L. Leong. "Male Response to Female Competence. N Sex Roles, Number 9, 1983, pp. 79-91.

Dubono, P. "Attitudes Toward Women Executives: A Longitudinal Approach." Academy of Management Journal, Number 28, 1985, pp. 235-239.

Dubono, P., J. Costas, H. Cannon, C. Wanker, & H. Emin. "An Empirically keyed Scale for Measuring Managerial Attitudes Toward Women Executives." Psychology of Women Quarterly, Number 3, 1979, pp. 357-364.

Enriquez-White, Celia. "Attitudes of Hispanic and Anglo Women Managers Toward Women in Management." DAI Number 43/08A, 1982, p. 2512.

Frank, Ellen J. "Business Students' Perceptions of Women in Management." Sex Roles, Volume 19, Number 1-2, July 1988, pp. 107-113.

Garland, H., & K.H. Price. "Attitudes Toward Women in Management and Attributions for Their Success and Failure in a Managerial Position." Journal of Applied Psychology, Number 62, 1977. pp. 29-33.

Giacalone, Robert A. & Stephen B. Knouse. "Men's Attitudes Toward Woman and Symbolic Association-Disassociation with Female Managers." Basic and Applied Social Psychology, Volume 9, Number 4, December 1938, pp. 289-300.

Gulhati, K. "Attitudes Toward Women Managers - Comparison of Attitudes of Male and Female Managers in India." Economic and Political Weekly, Volume 25, Number 7-8, 1990, pp. M41-M48.

Gutek, B.A., & C.Y. Nakamura. "Gender Roles and sexuality in the World of Work," (in) Changing Boundaries: Gender Roles and Sexual Behavior, edited by E.R. Allgeier & N.B. McCormick, Palo Alto, Calif: Mayfield, 1932, pp. 182-201

Hall, D.T. "A Model of Coping with Role Conflict: The Role Behavior of College Educated Women." Administrative Science Quarterly, Number 17, 1972, pp. 471-486.

Hall, Francine S., & Douglas T. Hall. "Dual Careers - How Do Couples and Companies Cope with the Problems?" Organizational Dynamics, Spring 1978, pp. 57-77.

Herman, J.B. & K.K. Gylistrom. "Working Men and Women" Inter-and-intra Role Conflict." Psychology of Women Quarterly, Number 1, 1977, pp. 319-333.

Jacobson, M.B., & J. Effertz. "Sex Roles and Leadership: Perceptions of the Leaders and the Led." Organizational Behavior and Human performance, Volume 12, Number 3, 1974, pp. 383-396.

Kahne, H. "The Women in Professional Occupations: New Complexities for Chosen Roles." Journal of the National Association for Women Deans, Administrators, and Counselors, Volume 39, Number 4, Summer 1976, pp. 179-185.

Kaley, M.M. "Attitudes Toward the Dual Role of the Married Professional Woman." American Psychologist, Volume 26, Number 3, March 1971, pp. 301-306.

Koberg, Christine S., & Leonard H. Chusmir. "Relationship Between Sex Role Conflict and Work-related Varianles: Gender and Hierarchical Differences." Journal of Social Psychology, Volume 129, Number 6, December 1989, pp. 779-791.

Liden, Robert C. "Female Perceptions of Female and Male Managerial Behavior Sex Roles, Volume 12, February 1985, pp. 421-432.

McBroom, Patricia. The Third Sex: The New Professional Woman. New York: W. Morrow, 1986.

Martin, J. "The Suppression of Gender Conflict in Organizations: Deconstructing the Fissure Between Public and Private. " Paper presented at the national meetings of the Academy of Management, Anaheim, CA, August, 1988.

Marchall, J. Women Managers. Travellers in a Male World. Chichester: Wiley, 1948.

Mayes, S.S. "women in Positions of Authority." Signs: Journal of Women in Society and Culture, Volume 4, Number 3, 1979, pp. 556-568.

Miller, Annetta & Pamela Kruger. "Good-bye Sexist Pig - Say Hello to the New Old Boy." Working Woman, Volume 15, Number 4, April 1990, pp. 94-96.

Miller, J., S. Labovits, & L. Fry. "Inequities in the Organizational Experience of Women and Men.31 Social Forces, Number 54, 1975, pp. 365-381.

Newgarden, Peggy. "Establishing Affirmative Action Goals for Women." Public Admin. Review, Volume 36, Number 4, July/ August 1976, pp. 369-374.

Nieva, V.F., & B.A. Gurtek. Women and Work: A Psychological Perspective. New York: Praeger, 1981.

Nuss, Shirley. Women in the World of Work: Statistical Analysis and Projections to the Year 2000. Geneva: International Labour Office, 1989.

Nyquist, L.V., & J. T. Spence. "Effects of Dispositional Dominance and Sex Role Expectations on Leadership Behaviors." Journal of Personality and Social Psychology. Number 50, 1986, pp. 87-93.

Orth, C.D., & F. Jacobs. "Women in Management: A Pattern for Change." Harvard Business Review, Volume 49, Number 4, 1971, pp. 139-147.

Palley, M.L., & M.B. Preston, editors. Race, Sex, and Policy Problems. Lexington, MA:D.C. Heath, 1979.

Petty, M.M., & R.H. Miles. "Leader Sex-role Stereotyping in a Female Dominant Work Culture." Personnel Psychology, Number 29, 1976, pp. 393-404.

Post, Linda Currey. "View from the Top: Women Executives in Communication." Communication World, Volume 4, Number 3, February 1987, pp. 17-19.

Powell, G. "Sex-role Identity and Sex: An Important Distinction for Research on Women in Management." Basic and Applied Social Psychology, Volume 3, 1982, pp. 67-79.

Reif, W.E., J.W. Newstrom, & R.M. Monczka. "Exploding Some Myths About Women Managers." California Management Review, Volume 27, Number 4, 1975, pp. 72-79.

Rizzo, Ann-Marie. "Perceptions of Membership and Women in Administration: Implications for Public Organizations."

Administration and Society, Volume 10, Number 1, May 1978, pp. 33-48.

Rochelle, As Leaders, Women Rule, Women executive - Rating of; Performance standards, Women; Business Women, Business Week, 11/20/2000 Issue 3708, p. 74, 6p, 1 Chart, 3c.

Rosen, B., M.E. Templeton, & K. Kirchline. "First Few Years on the Job: Women in Management." Business Horizons, Volume 24, Number 12, 1981, pp. 26-29.

Rosen, B., & T.H. Jerdee. "Influence of Sex-role Stereotypes on Personnel Decisions." Journal of Applied Psychology, Number 59, 1974, pp. 9-14.

Schwartz, F.N. "Management Women and the New Facts of Life." Harvard Business Review, Volume 89, Number 1, Jan/Feb., 1989, pp. 65-76.

Smart, Mollie S., & Russell C. Smart. "Paired Prospects: Dual-Career Couples on Campus." Academe, Volume 76, Number 1, Jan/ Feb. 1990. pp. 33-37.

Spencer, Anne, & David Podmore, editors. In a Man's World: Essays On Women in Male-doRinated Professions. London: Tavistock, 1987.

Stead, J., editor. "Women's Bureau, U.S. Department of Labor, Employment Standards Administration. The Myth and the Reality." Women in Management, Englewood Cliffs: prentice-Hall, Inc., 1978.

Steinberg, Jill A. Climbing the Ladder of Success in High Heels: Backgrounds of Professional Women. Ann Arbor, MI:UMI Research Press, 1984.

Sutton, Charlotte D. & Kris K. Moore. "Attitudes Toward Executive Women: Do They Differ Geographically?" Personnel Administrator, Volume 31, Number 5, May 1986, pp. 75-88.

Symons, G.L. "Careers and Self-concepts: Managerial Women in French and English Canada," (in) Work in the Canadian Context (2nd ed.) edited by K. Lundy & B. Warme. Toronto: Butterworth, 1986.

Terborg, J.R., & P. Shingledecker. "Employee Reactions to Supervision and Work Evaluation as a Function of Subordinate and Manager Sex." Sex Roles, Number 9, 1983, pp. 813-824.

Terborg, James R. "Integration of Women into Management Positions: A Research Review." Paper presented at the 84th Annual Meeting of the American Psychological Association, Washington, DC, September 3-7, 1976.

Trempe, J., A. Rigny, & R. Haccoun. "Subordinate Satisfaction with Male and Female Managers: Role of Perceived Supervisory Influence." Journal of Applied Psychology, Volume 70, Number 1, 1985, pp. 44-47.

Veilleus, France, & Francine Tougas. "Male Acceptance of Affirmative Action Programs for Women: The Results of Altruistic or Egoistical Motives?" International Journal of Psychology, Volume 24, Number 4, 1989, pp. 485-496.

Ware, Roger; Studebaker Cooper, & J. Jerilyn. "Attitudes Toward Women as Managers With Regard to Sex, Education, Work, and Marital Status. "Psychological Reports, Volume 65, Number 1, August 1989, pp. 347-350.

Watson, Carol. "When a Woman is the Boss: Dilemmas in Taking Charge." Group & organization Studies, Volume 13, Number 2, June 1988, pp. 163-181.

Williams, Christine L. Gender Differences at Work: Women and Men in Nontraditional occupations. Berkeley: University of California Press, 1989.

Wong, P.T.P., G. Kettlewell, & C.F. Sproule. "On the Importance of Being Masculine: Sex Role Attribution and Women's Career Advancement." Sex Roles, Number 12, 1985, pp. 757-769.

Yohalem, Alice M. The Careers of professional Women: Commitment and Conflict. Montclair, N.J.: Allanheld, Osmun, 1979.

IX

THE FAMILY ENVIRONMENT OF WOMEN MANAGERS

Amaral, Thomas M. "Selected Functions of Social Support Among a Sample of Managerial and Professional Women." Doctoral Thesis, Indiana University, 1984.

Amaro, Hortensia, Nancy F. Russo, & Julie Johnson. "Family and Work Predictors of Psychological Well-being Among Hispanic Women Professionals. Special Issue: Hispanic Women and Mental Health." Psychology of Women Quarterly, Volume 11, Number 4, December 1987, pp. 505-521.

Brothers, Joyce. The Successful Woman: How You Can Have a Career, a Husband, and a Family — and Not Feel Guilty About It. New York: Simon and Schuster, 1988.

Cannings, Kathy. "Family Commitments and Career Success: Earnings of Male and Female Managers." Industrial Relations (Canada), Volume 46, Number 1, Winter 1991, pp. 141-158.

Cole, Jonathan R. & Harriet Zuckerman. "Marriage, Motherhood and Research performance in Science." Scientific American Volume 256, February 1987, pp. 119-125.

Corse, S.J. "The Effect of Manager's Pregnancy on Subordinates' Behavior and Reactions to Her: An Interactional Study using Conflictual Role Plays." Doctoral Dissertation, University of Maryland, 1987.

Corse, Sara H. "Pregnant Managers and Their Subordinates: The Effects of Gender Expectations on Hierarchical Relationships." The Journal of Applied Behavioral Science, Volume 26, Number 1, 1990, pp. 25-47.

Davidson, Marilyn J. & Gary L. Cooper. "Executive Women Under Pressure. Special Issue: Occupational and Life Stress and the Family." International Review of Applied Psychology, Volume 35, Number 3, July 1986, pp. 301-326.

Diamond, Harriet Ann. "Suicide by Women Professionals." DAI 38/lOB, 1977, p. 5009.

Farley, L. The Woman in Management: Career and Family issues. Ithaca, NY:ILR Press, 1983.

Fogarty, Michael Patrick; Rhona Rapoport & Robert N. Rapoport. Sex, Career and Family; Including an International Review of Women's Roles. Beverly Hills, Calif: Sage Publications, 1971.

Gilson, Edith. Unnecessary Choices: The Hidden Life of the Executive Woman. New York: Paragon House, 1989.

Gray, Janet Dreyfus. "The Married Professional Woman: An Examination of Her Role Conflicts and Coping Strategies." Psychology of Women Quarterly, Volume 7, Number 3, Spring 1983, pp. 235-243.

Gray, J.D. "Role Conflicts and Coping Strategies in Married Professional Women." Doctoral Dissertation, University of Pennsylvania, 1979.

Hantrais, Linda. Managing Professional and Family Life: A Comparative Study of British and French Women. Aldershot, Hants, England; Brookfield, Vt., USA: Dartmouth, 1990.

Heckman, N.A., R. Bryson, & J.B. Bryson. "Problems of Professional Couples: A Content Analysis." Journal of Marriage and the Family, Number 39, 1977, pp. 323-330.

Kaley, M.M. "Attitudes Toward the Dual Role of Married Professional Women." American Psychologist, Number 26, 1971, pp. 301-306.

Katz, M. "Role Conflict Exercises for Combining Family and Career." The organizational Behavior Teaching Review., Volume IX, Number 3, 1984, pp. 98-99.

O'connell, L., M. Betz, & S. Kurth. "Plans for Balancing Work and Family Life: Do Women Pursuing Nontraditional and Traditional Occupations Differ?" Sex Roles, Number 20, 1989, pp. 35-45.

Pines1 A. & D. Kafry. "Tedium in the Life and Work of Professional Women As Compared with Men." Sex Roles, Volume 7, Number 10, 1981, pp. 963-977.

Polegato, R., & R.G. Barras. "Geographically Separated Dual-career Families." Business Quarterly, Volume 49, Number 1, 1984, pp. 145-150.

Parelius, A.P. "Change and stability in College Women's Orientations Toward Education, Family, and Work." Soc. Probl., Number 22, 1975, pp. 420-432.

Poloma, M. "Role Conflict and the Married Professional Woman," (in) Toward a Sociology of Women, edited by C. Safilios-Rothschild, Lexington, Mass: Xerox Coll., 1972, pp. 189-198.

Poloma, M.M., & T.N. Garland. "The Married Professional Woman: A Study in the Tolerance of Domestication." Journal of Marriage and the Family, Number 33, 1971, pp. 531-540.

Rogan, H. "Executive Women Find it Difficult to Balance Demands, of Job, Home.N Wall Street Journal, October 30, 1984, pp. 35, 55.

Rosen, B., T.H. Jerdee, & T.L. prestwich. "Dual-Career Marital Adjustment: potential Effects of Discriminatory Managerial Attitudes." J. Marriage Fam., Number 37, 1975, pp. 565-572.

Rosin, Hazel M. & Karen Korabik. "Marital and Family Correlates of Women Managers' Attrition from Organizations." Journal of Vocational Behavior, Volume 37, Number 1, August 1990, pp. 104-120.

Sales, E., & I.H. Frieze. "Women and Work: Implications for mental Health," (in) Women and Mental Health Policy, edited by L.E. Walker, Beverly Hills, CA:Sage, 1983, pp. 229-246.

Shaw, L.B., & T. O'Brien. "Introduction and Overview," (in) Dual Careers: A Decade of Change in the Lives of Mature Women, edited by L.B. Shaw. Washington, DC: US Dept. Labor, 1981. pp. 1-61.

Stoess, Alfred William. "Conformity Behavior of Managers and Wives of Managers in Wife-Oriented and Non-Wife-Oriented Companies." DAI 28/OEA, 1967, p. 1940.

Stoner, Charles R. & Richard I. Hartman. "Family Responsibilities and Career Progress: The Good, the Bad, and the Ugly." Business Horizons, Volume 33, Number 3, May/June 1990, pp. 7-14.

Stoner, Charles R., Richard I Hartman, & Raj Arora. "Work/Family Conflict: A Study of Women in Management." Journal of Applied Business Research, Volume 7, Number 1, Winter 1990-1991, pp. 67-74.

Taylor, Alex, III. "Why Women Managers Are Bailing Out." Fortune, Volume 114, Number 4, August 18, 1986, pp. 16-23.

Treuille, Beverly Benz. Managing It All: Time-Saving Ideas for Career, Family, Relationships & Self. New York: Master Media, 1988.

Wicks, J.W., & R.L. Workman. "Sex-role Attitudes and the Anticipated Timing of the Initial Stages of Family Formation Among Catholic University Students." J. Marriage Fam., Number 40, 1978, pp. 505-516.

Wilcox, John. "Mommy Track, Daddy Track." Training & Development Journal, Volume 43, Number 9, September 1989. pp. 12-14.

Wiley, Mary G. & Arlene Eskilson. "Gender and Family/Career Conflict: Reactions of Bosses." Sex-roles, Volume 19, Number 7-8, October 1988, pp. 445-466.

X
DISCRIMINATORY PRACTICES TOWARD WOMEN ADMINISTRATORS AND PROFESSIONALS

Fraser, Ian. "Discrimination and All that Hoc Ha!" Public Service Review, 13:23, 1976, pp. 1, 10.

Heilman, M.E., & Guzzo, R.A. "The Perceived Cause of Work Success as a Mediator of Sex Discrimination in Organizations." Organization Behavior and Human performance, 21: 1978, pp. 346-357.

Heilman, M.E. "Sex Bias in Work Settings: The Lack of Fit Model." Research in Organization Behavior, Vol.5: 1983, pp. 269-298. Greenwich Conn: JAI Press.

Heilman, M.E. "Occupational Sex Discrimination: A Review." Handbook of Human Sexuality. Englewood.Cliffs, N.J.: prentice-Hall, 1979.

Osterman, p. "Sex Discrimination in professional Employment; A Case Study. Industrial and Labor Relations Review, 32, 1979, pp. 451-464.

Peitchinis, Stephen G. Women at Work: Discrimination and Response. Toronto, Ont.: McClelland & Stewart, 1989.

Reed, C.M. & Cohen, L.J. "Anti—nepotism Rules: The Legal Rights of Married Co-workers." public personnel Management, 18(1): 1989, pp. 37-44.

Steward, L.P., & Gudykun5t, W.B. "Differential Factor Influencing the Hierarchical Level and Number of promotions of Males and Females Within an organization." Academy of Management Journal, 25: 1982, pp. 586-597.

Terborg, J.R., & Ilgen, D.R. "A Theoretical Approach to Sex Discrimination in Traditionally Masculine Occupations." Journal of organizational Behavior and Human performance, 13: 1975, pp. 352-376.

XI
SEXUAL HARASSMENT OF WOMEN MANAGERS

Allegretti, J.G. "Sexual Harassment by Nonemployees: The Limits of Employer Liability." Employee Relations Law Journal, Volume 9, 1983, pp. 98-112.

Anonymous, "Sexual Harassment on the job." Women in Business, Jul/Aug 91, Vol. 43 Issue 4, p4, 1/6p.

Daidridge, K., & G. McLean. "Sexual Harassment: How Much of a problem Is It.. Really?" Journal of Business Education, Number 56, 1980, pp. 294-297.

Baxter, Jr., R.H. "Judicial and Administrative protections Against Sexual Harassment in the Workplace." Employee Relations Law Journal, Number 7, 1982, pp. 587-593.

Collins, E.g., & T.B. Blodgett. "Sexual Harassment: Some See it. Some Won't." Harvard Business Review, Volume 59, Number 2, 1981, pp. 76-95.

Crary, Marcy. "Managing Attraction and Intimacy at Work." Org. Dynam., Spring 1987, pp. 26-41.

Faley, R.H. "Sexual Harassment: A Critical Review of Legal Cases with General Principles and Preventive Measures." Personnel Psychology, Number 35, 1982, pp. 583-600.

Farley, L. Sexual Shakedown: The Sexual Harassment of Women on the Job. New York: McGraw-Hill, 1978.

Ford, Robert C. & Frank S. McLaughlin. "Sexual Harassment at Work.": Business Horizons, Volume 31, Number 6, Nov/Dec, 1988, pp. 14-19.

Franklin, Phyllis, et al. Sexual and Gender Harassment in the Academy: A Guide for Faculty, Students, and Administrators. New York: Modern Language Association of America, 1981.

Gutek, Barbara A., Aaron Groff Cohen, & Alison M. Konrad. "Predicting Social-Sexual Behavior at Work: A Contact Hypothesis." Academy of Management Journal, Volume 33, Number 3, 1990, pp. 560-577.

Gutek, B.A. Sex and the Workplace: The Impact of Sexual Behavior and Harassment on Women, Men, and Organizations. San Francisco: Jossey-Bass, 1985.

Gutek, B.A., & B. Morasch. "Sex-ratios, Sex Role Spillover, and Sexual Harassment of Women at Work." Journal of Social Issues, Volume 38, Number 4, 1982, pp. 55-74.

Konrad, A.M., & B.A. Gutek. "Impact of Work Experiences on Attitudes Toward Sexual harassment." Administrative Science Quarterly, Number 31, 1986, pp. 422-438.

Leeds Trade Union and Community Resource and Information Centre. Sexual Harassment of Women at Work. Leeds: TUCRIC, 1983.

Levarge, Paul. "Sexual Harassment in the Workplace." Chemical Engineering, Volume 93, March 3, 1986, pp. 107-108.

Linenberger, P. "What Behavior Constitutes Sexual Harassment?" Labor Law Journal, Volume 4, 1983, pp. 238-247.

MacKinnon, C. Sexual Harassment of Working Women: A Case of Sex Discrimination. New Haven, Conn: Yale University Press, 1979.

McIntosh, J. "Sexual Harassment. You Tell Us It's Not a Joke." Cosmopolitan, October 1982.

McIntyre, Douglas I. and James C. Renick. "Sexual Harassnent and the States as Policy-makers and Employers." State Government, Volume 56, Number 4, 1983, pp. 128-133.

McIntyre, Douglas I. and James C. Renick. "Protecting Public Employees and Employers from Sexual Harassment." Public personnel Management Journal, Volume 11, Fall 1982, pp. 282-292.

McLaughlin, Paul. "The Case of the Amorous Associates: Is There a Diplomatic Way to Squelch a Senior Colleagues' Unwelcome Attentions?" Canadian Business, Number 63, January 1990, pp. 79-82.

Mingle, John D. "Sexual Harassment." Chemical Engineering Progress, Volume 83, March 1987, pp. 21-24.

Morral, Katherine. "Office Love Kindles Mixed Feelings." Savings Institutions, Volume 109, Number 4, April 1988, pp. 64-65.

Murrell, Audrey J.; Olson, Josephine E.; Frieze, Irene Hanson; Sexual harassment and gender discrimination: a longitudinal study of women managers, The Journal of Social Issues [H.W. Wilson - SSA] Spring 1995, Vol. 51, pp. 139-49.

Powell, Gary N. & Lisa A. Mainiero. "What Managers need to Know About Office Romances." Leadership &

organization Development Journal, Volume 11, Number 1, 1990, pp. i-iii.

Powell, G.N., C.A. Benzinger, A.A. Bruno, T.N. Gibson, M.L. Pfeiffer, & T.P. Santopietro. "Sexual Harassment as Defined by Working Women." Paper presented at the 41st Annual Meeting of the Academy of Management. San Diego, 1981.

Quinn, Robert E. & Patricia L. Lees. "Attraction and Harassment: Dynamics of Sexual Politics in the Workplace." Ong Dynamics, Autumn, 1984, pp. 35-46.

Quinn, R. "Coping With Cupid: The Formation, Impact, and Management of Romantic Relationships in organizations." Administrative Science Quarterly, Number 22, 1977, pp. 30-45.

Ross, Cynthia S., & Vicki A. Green. "Sexual Harassment: A Liability Higher Education Must Face." The Journal of the College and University Personnel Association, Volume 34, Spring 1983.

Sederis, Virginia D. "Sexual Harassment in State Government: A Dirty Little Secret," (in) State Government: CQ's Guide to Current Issues and Activities 1985-86, edited by Thad L. Beyle, Washington: congressional Quarterly Press, 1984.

Tangri, S.S., M.R. Burt, & L.B. Johnson. "Sexual Harassment at Work: Three Explanatory Models." Journal of Social Issues, Volume 38, Number 4, 1982, pp. 33-54.

Terpstra, D.E., & D.D. Baker. "The Identification and Classification of Reactions to Sexual Harassment." Journal of organizational Behavior, Volume 10, Number 1, January 1989, pp. 1-14.

Terpstra, David E., & Douglas D. Baker. "Outcomes of Sexual Harassment Charges." Academy of Management Journal1 Volume 31, Number 1, 1988, pp. 185-194.

Terpstra, David E., & Susan E. Cook. "Complainant Characteristics and Reported Behaviors and Consequences Associated with Formal Sexual Harassment Charges." Personnel Psychology, Volume 38, Number 3, Autumn 1985, pp. 559-574.

U.S. Merit Systems Protection Board, Office of Merit Systems Review and Studies. Sexual Harassment in the Federal Workplace: Is it a problem? Washington: Government Printing Office, March 1981.

Waks, J.W., & M.G. Starr. "The Sexual Shakedown in Perspective: Sexual Harassment in its Social and Legal Contexts." Employee Relations Law Journal, Number 7, 1982, pp. 567-586.

Westoff, Leslie Aldridge. Corporate Romance: How to Avoid It, Live Through It, or Make It Work For You. New York: Times Books, 1985.

XII
SALARY DIFFERENCES BETWEEN MEN AND WOMEN MANAGERS AND PROFESSIONALS

Ashenfelter, O., & T.H. Hannan. "Sex Discrimination and Market Competition: The Case of the Banking Industry." Q.J. Econ. Number 101, 1986, pp. 149-173.

Bridges, W.P., & R.A. Berk. "Determinants of White Collar Income: An Evaluation of Equal Pay for Equal Work." Soc. Sci. Res. Number 3, 1974, pp. 211-234.

Blau, F.D. Equal Pay in the Office. Lexington, Mass: Heath, 1977.

Cooper, Elizabeth A. & Gerald V. Barrett. "Equal Pay and Gender: Implications of Court Cases for Personnel Practices." Academy of Mat. Rev. Volume IX, Number 1, 1984, pp. 84-94.

Cowley, Geoffrey. "Comparable Worth: Another Terrible Idea." Bureaucrat, Volume 13, Spring 1984, pp. 16-19.

Dombrowski, Cathy. "Comparable Worth Emerging as Women's Issue of the '80s." American City & Country. Volume 100, July 1985, p. 62.

England, Paula. "Evaluating Work and Comparable Worth." Ann. Rev. Social, Number 14, 1988, pp. 227-248.

Frieze, Irene 'Perceived and Female Volume 20, H., Josephine E. Olson, & Deborah C. Good. and Actual Discrimination in the Salaries of Male Managers." Journal of Applied Social Psychology,, Number 1, Jan. 1990, pp. 46-67.

Halaby, C.N. "Sexual Inequality in the Workplace: An Employer-specific Analysis of Pay Differences." Soc. Sci. Res. Number 8, 1979. pp. 79-104.

Lorber, L.A., J.R. Kirk, S.L. Samuels, & D.J. Spellman. Sex and Salary: A Legal and personnel Analysis of Comparable Worth. Alexandria. VA: American Society for personnel Administrators, 1985.

Luksetich, W.A. "Market power and Sex Discrimination i white Collar Employment." Rev. Soc. Econ., Number 37, 1979, pp. 211-224.

Mahoney, T.A., & RH. Blake. "Occupational Pay as a Function of Sex Stereotypes and Job Content." Paper presented at the

Annual Meeting of the National Academy of Management, Atlanta, August 1979.

Mahoney, T.A., & R.H. Blake. "Organizational Pay as a Function of Sex Stereotypes and Job Content." Paper presented at the Annual Meeting of the National Academy of Management, Atlanta, August 1979.

Malkiel, B.G., & J.A. Malkiel. "Male-female Pay Differentials in professional Employment." Am. Econ. Rev., Number 63, 1973, pp. 693-705.

Olson, J.E., & I.H. Frieze. "Income Determinants for Women in Management," (in) Women and Work: An Annual Review, Volume 2, edited by A.H. Stromberg, L. Larwood, & B.A. Gutek. Beverly Hills, CA: Sage, 1987, pp. 173-206

Rosenbaum, J.E. "Jobs, Job Status, and Women's Gains From Affirmative Action: Implications for Comparable Worth," (in) Comparable Worth: New Directions for Research, edited by H.I. Hartmann, Washington, DC: National Acad. Press, 1985, pp. 116-136.

Pfeffer, J., & A. Davis-Blake. "The Effect of the Proportion of Women on Salaries: The Case of College Administrators." Admin. Sci. Q., Number 32, 1987, pp. 1-24.

Seigelman, L., H.B. Muward, & J.M. Shepard. "The Salary Differential Between Male and Female Administrators: Equal Pay for Equal Work?" Academy of Management Journal, Number 25, 1982, pp. 664-671.

Smith, Sharon P. "Government Wage Differentials by the Sex." Journal of Human Resources1 Volume 11, Number 2, Spring 1976, pp. 185-199.

Stratton, Brad. "Pay Not Equal for Women." Quality Progress, Volume 21, September 1988, pp. 27-29.

Tompkins, Jonathan. "Comparable Worth and Job Evaluation Validity." Public Administration Review, Volume 47, Number 3, May-June 1987, pp. 254-158.

Treiman, D.J., & H.I Hartman. "Women, Work, and Wages: Equal Pay for Jobs of Equal Value. Washington, DC: National Academy Press, 1981.

Van Alstyne, Carol. "Women and Minorities in Administration of Higher Education Institutions: Employment Patterns and Salary Comparisons." Washington: College and University Personnel Association, 1977.

XIII
MINORITY WOMEN ADMINISTRATORS AND PROFESSIONALS

Bell, Ella Louise, "The Bicultural Life Experience of Career-oriented Black Women." Journal of Organizational Behavior, Volume 19, November 1990, p. 459.

Brief, A.P., & R.T. Aldag. "Male and Female Differences in Occupational Attitudes Within Minority Groups." Journal of Vocational Behavior, Number 6, 1975, pp. 305-314.

Brown, Andolyn V. "Black Female Administrators in Higher Education: A Survey of Demographic Data, Previous Work Experiences, Characteristics of Present Positions and Characteristics of Employing Institutions." Doctoral Thesis, Bowling Green State University, 1980.

Carlson, L.A., and C. Swartz. "The Earnings of Women and Ethnic Minorities 1959-1979." Industrial and Labor Relations Review, Volume 41, Number 4, July 1988, pp. 530-546.

Carroll, C.M. "Three's A Crowd: The Dilemma of the Black Women in higher Education, (in) Academic Women on the Move, edited by A. Ross & A. Calderwood, New York: Russell Sage, 1973, pp. 173-186.

Dugger, K. "Social Location and Gender Role Attitudes: A Comparison of Black and White Women." Gender and Society, Number 2, 1988, pp. 425-448.

Epstein, C.F. "Positive Effects of the Multiple Negative: Explaining the Success of Black Professional Women," (in) Changing Women in a Changing Society, edited by J. Huber, Chicago: university of Chicago, 1973, pp. 150-173.

Epstein, C. "positive Effects of the Double Negative: Explaining the Success of Black professional Women." American Journal of Sociology, Number 78, 1973, pp. 912-935.

Epstein, C.F. "positive Effects of the Multiple Negative: Explaining the Success of Black Professional Women." American Journal of Sociology, Number 78, 1973, pp. 173-184.

Glover, Robert W. et al. "Minority Women, Professional Work." Manpower, Volume 7, Number 7, 1975, pp. 8-12.

Gump, J.P. "Reality and Myth: Employment and Sex-role Identity in Black Women," (in) The Psychology of Women: Directions in Research, edited by J. Sherman & F.L. Denmark, New York: Psychological Dimensions, 1980, pp. 349-380.

Gump, J.P., & L.W. Rivers. "A Consideration of Race in Efforts to End Sex Bias," (in) Issues of Sex Bias and Sex Fairness in Career Interest Measurement, edited by Esther E. Diamond, Washington, DC: National Institute of Education, 1975.

Hemmerick, Steve. "Minorities Statute Hits 4 Managers." Pensions & Investments, Volume 19, Number 7, April 1, 1991, pp 1, 45.

Hood, Angelicue Lewis. "A Comparative Analysis of the Developmental Experiences and Tasks of Black and White Women Managers." DAI 50/061, 1989, p. 189.

Lewis, D.K. "A Response to Inequality: Black Women, Racism, and Sexism." SIGNS: Journal of Women in Culture and Society, Number 3, 1977, pp. 339-361.

McNeely, R.L. "Predictors of Job Satisfaction Among Three Racial/ Ethnic Groups of Professional Female Human Service Workers." Journal of Sociology and Social Welfare, Volume 14, Number 4, December 1987, pp. 115-136.

Morrison, Ann M. "Women and Minorities in Management." American Psychologist, Number 45, February 1990, pp. 200-208.

Nkomo, Stella M. & Taylor Cos. "Gender Differences in the Upward Mobility of Black Managers: Double whammy or Double Advantage?" Sex Roles, Volume 21, December 1989, pp.825-839.

Nkomo, S. "Uncharted Journey: Minority Women in Management." Paper presented at the National Meetings of the Academy of Management, Anaheim, CA, August 1988.

Purvear, G.R., & M.S. Mednick. "Black Militancy, Affective Attachment1and the Fear of Success in Black College Women." J. Consult. Clin. Psychol., Number 42, 1974, pp. 263-266.

Semyonoy, M., & V. Kraus. "Gender, Ethnicity and Income Inequality: The Israeli Experience." International Journal of Comparative Sociology, Number 24, 1983, pp. 258-272.

Sims-Wood, Janet L. Black Women in the Employment Sector. Monticello, IL: Vance Bibliographies, 1979.

Williams, Audrey. "Research on Black Women College Administrators: Descriptive and Interview Data." Sex Roles, Number 21, July 1989, pp. 99-112.

XIV
MANAGERIAL WOMEN IN CROSS-NATIONAL PERSPECTIVE

Adler, Leonore Loeb, editor. Women in Cross-cultural Perspective. Praeger Publishers,

Adler, Nancy J. "Women in Management Worldwide." International Studies of Management & Organization, Volume 16, Number 3/4, Fall 1986/Winter 1987, pp. 3-32.

Adler, Nancy J. & Dafna N. Izraeli, editors. Women in Management Worldwide. Armonk, NY: M.E. Sharpe, 1988.

Adler, Nancy J. "Pacific Basin Managers: A Gaijin, Not a Woman." Human Resource Management, Volume 26, Number 2, Summer 1987, pp. 169-191.

Adler, Nancy J. "Women in International Management: Where Are They?" CA Mat Rev., Volume XXVI, Number 4, Summer 1984, pp. 78-89.

Ahmad, Karuna. "The Trishankus: Women in the Profession in India," sociological Bulletin, Mar/Sept. 1984, pp. 75-90.

Andors, P. "The Four Modernizations and Chinese Policy on Women." Bulletin of Concerned Asian Scholars, Volume 31, Number 2, April/June 1981, pp. 44-57.

Andrew, Caroline, Cecile Coderre, & Ann Demis. "Stop or Go: Reflections of Women Managers on Factors Influencing Their Career Development." Journal of Business Ethics (Netherlands), Volume 9, Number 4,5, April/Maya 1990, pp. 361-367.

Antal, A.B., & C. Krebsbach-Gnath. "Women in Management: Unused Resources in the Federal Republic of Germany." International Studies of Management & Organization, Volume XVI, Number 3-4, 1986/87, pp.133-151.

Anonymous, Women's International Network News, Winter 92, Vol. 18 Issue 1, p 71, 1/2p.

Anonymous, Nafe net-worker, Business Women; National Association for Female Executives, "Executive Female, Sep/Oct 97, Vol. 20 Issue 5, p 58, 4p, 2c.

Armstrong, Pat. "Is There Still a Chairman of the Board?" Journal of Management Development (UK), Volume 8, Number 6, 1989, pp 6-16.

Asplund, Gisele. Women Managers: Changing Organizational Cultures. Chichester, NY: Wiley, 1988.

Barad, M. & T. Weinshall. "Women as Managers in Israel." Public Administration in Israel and Abroad. Jerusalem: Israel Institute of Public Administration; 1967, pp. 78-87.

Brimelow, E. "Women in Civil Service." Public Administration Volume 59, Fall 1981, pp. 313-335.

Chan, A. "Women Managers in Singapore: Citizens for Tomorrow's Economy," (in) Women in Management Worldwide, edited by N.J. Adler & D. Izraeli, Armonk, NY: M.E. Sharpe, 1987.

Chaturvedi, Geeta. Women Administrators of India: A Study of the Socio-economic Background and Attitudes of Women Administrators of Rajasthan. Jaipur: RBSA Publishers, 1985.

Clark, Roger. "Contrasting Perspectives On Women's Access to Prestigious Occupations: A Cross-National Investigation." Social science Quarterly, Volume 72, Number 1, March 1991.

Cooper, Cary L., editor. Practical Approaches to Women's Career Development: A Report on the Conference at St. Hugh's College, Oxford, on Septesher 16-17, 1981. Moorfoot, Sheffield: Training Services, Manpower Services Commission, 1983.

Coyle, A. "The Limits of Change: Local Government and Equal Opportunities for Women." Public Administration (UK), Volume 67, Number 1, spring 1989, pp. 39-50.

Crapol, Edward P., editor. Women and American Foreign Policy: Lobbyists, Critics, and Insiders. New York: Greenwood Press, 1987.

Davidson, Nicol & Margaret Croke. The United Nations and Decision-making: The Role of Women. New York: UNITAR, 1978.

Davis, Nancy J. & Robert V. Robinson, "Men1s and Women's Consciousness of Gender Inequality: Austria, West Germany, Great Britain, and the United States." American Sociological Review, Volume 56, February 1991, pp. 72-84.

Effroni, L. Promotions and Wages in the Israeli Public Service -Are Women Discriminated Against? Jerusalem: The Institute of Labor and Welfare Research, 1980.

Epstein, C.F. "Women and Elites: A Cross-National perspective," (in) Access to Power: Cross-National Studies of Women and Elites, edited by C.F. Epstein & R.L. Coser. London: Allen & Unwin, 1981.

Erwee, Ronel. "South African Women: Changing Career Patterns." International Studies of Management & Organization, Volume 16, Number 3/4, Fall 1986/Winter 1987, pp. 174-189.

Erwee, R. "South African Women: Changing Career Patterns," (in) Women in Management Worldwide, edited by N.J. Adler, & D.N. Izraeli. Armonk, NY: M.E. Sharpe, 1988, pp. 213-225.

Ferrari, S. "The Italian Woman Executive." Management International Review, Volume 17, Number 1, 1977, pp. 13-21.

Fogarty, Michael Patrick. Women in Top Jobs, 1968-1979. London: Heinemann Educational Books, 1981.

Fogarty, Michael Patrick. Women and Top Jobs: The Next Move, London: P.E.P., 1972.

Gleeson, James Joseph. The Feared No Evil: The Woman Agents of Britain's Secret Armies, 1939-45. London: R. Hale, 1976.

Gray, Michael. "The Cost of Equality: U.K. Ruling May Carry $50 Billion Tab." Pensions & Investments, Volume 18, Number 6, May 28, 1990.

Hammond. V. "Women in Management in Great Britain." (in) Women in Management Worldwide, edited by N.J. Adler and D.N. Izraeli. Armonk, NY: M.E. Sharpe, 1988, pp. 168-185.

Hanmer, Jalna. Women and Social Work: Towards a Women-centered Practice. Chicago, IL: Lyceum Books, 1989.

Harris, Philip R. & Dorothy L. Harris. "Women Managers and professionals Abroad" Journal of Managerial Psychology (UK) Volume 3, Number 4, 1988, pp i-ii.

Hildebrandt, Herbert W. & Jinyun Liu. "Chinese Women Managers: A Comparison with Their U.S. and Asian Counterparts." Human Resource Management, Volume 27, Number 3, Fall 1988, pp. 291-314.

Hutton, Joseph Bernard. Women Spies. London, New York: W.H. Allen, 1971.

Izraeli, Daffla N. "WomenIs Movement into Management in Israel." International Studies of Management & organization. Volume 16, Number 3-4, Fall 1986/Winter 67, pp. 76-107.

Jelinek, Mariann & Nancy J. Adler. "Women: World-Class Managers for Global Competition." Academy of Management Executive, Volume 2, Number 1, February 1988, pp. 11-19.

Junior Chamber of Commerce for London. Women Executives: Their Training and Careers. London: London Chamber of Commerce, 1966.

Kay, Margarita Artschwager. "Health and Illness in the Barrio: Women's Point of View." DAI 33/03B, University of Arizona, 1972, p. 991.

Komanyi, Margit Ilona. "The Real and Ideal Participation in Decision-making of Iban Women." DAI 33/lOB, New York University, 1973, p 4631.

Kraisonswasdi, Napasri. Women Executives: A Sociological Study in Role Effectiveness. Jaipur: Rawat Publications, 1989.

Lam, M. Natalie. "Management Training for Women: International Experiences and Lessons for Canada." Journal of Business Ethics (Netherlands), Volume 9, Number 4,5, April/May 1990, pp. 385-406.

Lansing, Paul & Kathryn Ready. "Hiring Women Managers in Japan: An Alternative for Foreign Employers." California Management Review, Volume 30, Number 3, Spring 1988, pp. 112-127.

Maria, Strykowska, "Women in management in Poland", Women's Studies International Forum [H.W. Wilson - SSA]; Jan/Feb 1995.

Muller, Helen J; Rowell, Monica; "Mexican women managers : An emerging profile" Human Resource Management; New York; Winter 1997, Vol. 36, n. 4.

Narasimban, G. & L. Iyer. "Attitudes Towards Women Managers." Economic and Political Weekly, Volume 25, Number 44, 1990, pp. 2451-2452.

Nicholson, Nigel & Michael A. West. Managerial Job Change: Men and Women in Transition. Great Britain: Cambridge University Press, 1988.

Olivares, Federica. 1'Women in Management in Italy: More Than an Emerging Issue." Equal Opportunities International (UK), Volume 6, Number 1, 1987, pp. 6-10.

Osaka, M.M. "Dilemmas of Japanese Professional Women." Social Problems; Number 26, 1978, pp. 15-25.

Padan-Eisenstark, D. "Are Israeli Women Really Equal? Trends and Patterns of Israeli Women's Labor Force Participation: A Comparative Analysis." Journal of Marriage and Family, Number 35, 1973, pp. 538-545.

Place, Helen. Women in Management: A New Zealand Study, Takapuna: Motivation, Inc., 1981.

Political and Economic Planning. Women In Top Jobs: Four Studies in Achievement. London: Allen & Unwin, 1971.

Quince, Annabelle & Russell D. Lansbury. "Two Steps Forward but Going Nowhere? Women and Management in Australia." Employee Relations (UK), Volume 10, Number 6, 1988, pp. 26-31.

Rairikar, B.R. Problems of Women Executives: With Reference to the City of Bombay. Bombay: Lala Lajpatrai Institute, 1978.

Rana Baljit Kaur etc., British South Asian women managers and professionals : experiences of work and family, Women in Management Review; Bradford; 1998, Vol. 13, n. 6, p. 221.

Renshaw, J. "Women in Management in the Pacific Islands: Exploring Pacific Stereotypes." International Studies of Management & Organization, Volume XVI, Number 3-4, 1986/87, pp. 152-173.

Roy, Manisha. "Ideal and Compensatory Roles in the Life Cycle of Upper Class Bengali Women." DAI 33/04B, University of California-San Diego, 1972.

Saisho, Yuriko. Women Executives in Japan: How I Succeeded in Business in a Male-dominated Society. Tokyo, Japan: YURI International, Inc., 1981.

Schreff ler, Roger. "Moving to Management: Japanese Women in Automotive Management." Automotive Industries, Volume 167, July 1987, pp. 54-56.

Schuler, Margaret, editor. Empowerment and the Law: Strategies of Third World Women. Washington, DC: OEF International, 1986.

Singh, D. "Women Executives in India." Management International Review, Volume 20, Number 2, 1980, pp. 53-60.

Smith, Peter & Rosemary Stewart. "Relative Career Progress of men and Women Graduates in NHS General Administration." Public Administration, Number 61, Autumn 1983, pp. 318-323.

Springer, J.F., & R.W. Gable. "Modernization and Sex Roles: The Status of Women in 'he Thai Bureaucracy." Sex Roles1 Volume 7, Number 7, July 1981, pp. 723-730.

Steinhoff, P.G., & K. Tanaka. "Women Managers in Japan," (in) Women in Management Worldwide, edited by N.J. Adler & D.N. Izraeli. Armonk, NY: M.E. Sharpe, 1988, pp. 103-121.

Steinhoff, Patricia G. & Kazuko Tanaka. "Women Managers in Japan." International Studies of Management & Organization, Volume 16, Number 3/4, Fall 1986/Winter 1987, pp. 108-132.

Symons, Gladys L. "Coping with the Corporate Tribe: How Women in Different Cultures Experience the Managerial Role." Journal of Management, Volume 12, Number 3, Fall 1986, pp. 379-390.

Anonymous, "Women managers in Asia", Training & Development; Alexandria; April 1996; Vol. 50, n. 4, p. 37.

Tatiana, Suspitsina, Mothers, Bosses and Superwomen : The Construction of Identities of Russian Woman Administrators in Higher Education. Higher Education in Europe, July 2000, Vol. 25, Issue 2, p 207, 6p.

Tremain, Elizabeth J. Evelene: The Troubleshooter was a Lady. Lincoln, Neb: Foundation Books, 1985.

de Vaus, David. "Gender and Work Orientation." Work and Occupations, Volume 18, Number 1, February 1991, pp. 72-93.

Waddington, P.A.J. The Training of prison Governors: Role Ambiguity and Socialization. London: Croom Helm, 1983.

Whitley, R. "Women, Business School and the Reproduction of Business Elites: Britain and France," (in) Access to power: Cross-national Studies of Women and Elites, edited by C. Epstein & R. Coser. London: Allen & Unwin, 1981, pp. 185-192.

Year, E, D. Moore, & G. Fishelson. To Be Deprived and Complacent: Fairness Judgments of Earnings Among Israeli Women. Tel-Aviv: Foerder Institute for Economic Research, 1984.

XV
WOMEN MANAGERS IN CORPORATE WORKPLACE

American Institute of Certified Public Accountants. "Upward Mobility of Women Special Committee: Report to the AICPA Board of Directors." New York: American Institute of Certified Public Accountants, 1988.

Anderson, Robert L. & Kathleen P. Anderson. "A Comparison of Women in Small and Large Companies. I' American Journal of Small Business, Volume 12, Number 3, Winter 1988, pp. 23-33.

Brief, A.P., & R.L. Oliver. "Male-female Differences in Works Attitudes Among Retail Sales Managers." Journal of Applied Psychology, Number 61, 1976, pp. 526-528.

Cameron, Gary Charles. "A Study of the Values of Male and Female Managers in Banking and Insurance in Nebraska." DAI 40/03A, 1979, p 1581.

Cline, Carolyn Garrett. The Velvet Ghetto: The Impact of the increasing Percentage of Women in Public Relations and Business Communication. San Francisco: IABC Foundation, 1986.

Dawkins, Lola B. "Women Executives in Business, Industry, and the Professions." Thesis: University of Texas, 1962.

Devanna, Mary Anne. Male/Female Careers - the First Decade: A Study of MBAs. New York: Columbia University, Graduate School of Business, 1984.

Fagenson, E.A. "Women in Organizations: Not Made for Top Corporate Positions?" Presented at the Academy of Management Conference, Boston, 1984.

Fernandez, John P. Racism and Sexism in Corporate Life: Changing Values in American Business. Lexington, MA: Lexington Books, 1981

Fillmore, Many Dingee. Women MBAs: A Foot in the Door. Boston, MA: G.K. Hall, 1987.

Forgionne, Guisseppi A. & Vivian E. Peeters. "The Influence of Sex on Managers in the Service Sector." California Management Review, Volume 25, Number 1, Fall, 1982, pp. 72-83.

Fraser, Edie; editor. Risk to Riche$: Women and Entrepreneurship in America: A Special Report. Washington, DC: Institute for Enterprise Advancement, 1986.

Freeman Sue Joan Mendelson. Managing Lives: Corporate Women and Social Change. Amherst: University of Massachusetts press, 1990.

Gallese, Liz Roman. "Corporate Women on the Move; Here are the Women to Watch in Corporate America." Business Month, Volume 133, Number 4, April 1989, pp. 30-56.

Gallese, Liz Roman. Women Like Us: What is Happening to the Women of the Harvard Business School, Class of '75 - The Women Who Had the First Chance to Make it to the Top. New York: Morrow, 1985.

Ghiloni, B.W. "The Velvet Ghetto: Women, Power, and the Corporation," (in) Power Elites and Organization, edited by

G.W. Domhoff & T.R. Dye. Sage Focus Editions, Volume 28, Newbury Park, CA: Sage publications, 1987, pp. 21-36.

Hardesty, Sarah. success and Betrayal: The Crisis of Women in Corporate America. New York: Watts, 1986.

Hardesty, Sarah. Success and Betrayal: The Crisis of Women in Corporate America. New York: Simon & Schuster, 1987.

Harragan, Betty Lehan. Games Mother Never Taught You: Corporate Gamesmanship for Women. New York, NY: Warner Books, 1981.

Helgensen, Sally. The Female Advantage: Women's Ways of Leadership. New York, NY: Doubleday Currency, 1990.

Hill, Roy. "Women-Cwned Companies Finally Start Making Their Mark." International Management (UK), Volume 41, Number 5, May 1986, pp. 66-70.

Hooks, Karen L. Alternative Work Schedules and the Woman CPA: A Report on Used Perception and Career Impact. Chicago, IL: the American Womanls Society of Certified public Accountants, 1989.

Jamison, Charles N. Jr. "So You Want to Be a Corporate Star." Essence, Volume 21, March 1991, pp. 65-66.

Kanter, R.M. Men and Women of the Corporation. New York: Basic Books, 1977.

Keown, Charles F. "Success Factors for Corporate Woman Executives." Group and organizational Studies, Volume 7, Number 4, December 1982, pp. 445-456.

Knapp, Michael C. "openness of Large public Accounting Firms to Female and Minority Managers.11 Sociology and Social Research, Volume 73, April 1989, pp. 149-152.

Kozmetsky, Ronya. Women in Business: Succeeding as a Manager, Professional, or Entrepreneur. Austin, TX: Texas Monthly Press, 1989.

Levy, Liz. "Women in Marketing: Equal But Superior." Marketing (UK)< July 27, 1989, pp. 24-25.

Loden, Marilyn. "Feminine Leadership: It Can Maker Your Business More Profitable." Vital Speeches, Volume 52, Number 15, May 15, 1966, pp 472-475.

McLane, Helen J. Selecting, Developing, and Retaining Women Executives: A Corporate Strategy for the Eighties. New York: Van Nostrand Reinhold Co., 1980.

Missirian, A.K. The Corporate Connection: Why Women Need Mentors to Reach the Top. Englewood Cliffs, NJ: Prentice-Hall, 1982.

Mitchell, Charlene. The Right Moves: Succeeding in a Man's World Without a Harvard MBA. New York: Macmillan, 1985.

Orth, C.D. & F. Jacobs. "Women in Management: Pattern for Change" Harvard Business Review, Volume 49, Number 4, 1971, pp. 139-147.

Patrick, Patricia Ann. "An Investigation of the Progress and Problems of Women in Managerial Positions in Business and Other Institutions in the New Orleans Area. Doctoral Thesis, University of Mississippi, 1979.

Schwartz, Eleanor Brantley. The Sex Barrier in Business. Atlanta: Georgia State University, 1971.

Silverstone, Rosalie. "Women in Accountancy: Ten Years On." Accountancy (UK), Volume 106, Number 1165, September 1990, pp. 70-73.

Struggs, Callie Foster. Woman in Business. Mescuite, TX: Ide House, 1981.

Struggs, Callie Foster. Woman in Contemporary Business. Mesquite, TX: Ide Mouse, 1982.

Sutton, Charlotte D. & Richard W. Woodman. "Pygmalion Goes to Work: The Effects of Supervisor Expectations in a Retail Setting." Journal of Applied Psychology, Volume 74, Number 6, December 1989, pp. 943-950.

Symons, G.L. "Coping With the Corporate Tribe: How Women in Different Cultures Experience the Managerial Role." Journal of Management, 1986.

Symons, G. "Women's Occupational Careers in Business: Managers and Entrepreneurs in France and in Canada." International Studies of Management & Organization, Volume XVI, Number 3-4, 1986/87, pp. 61-75.

Taylor, Marilyn L., Mariane Odiogov, & Eileen Morley. "Experienced American Professional Women in Overseas Business Assignments." Academy of Management Proceedings, Volume 33, 1975, pp. 454-456.

Vernon-Gerstenfeld, Susan. "Affirmative Action in Nine Large Companies: Field Study." Personnel, Volume 62, April 1985, pp. 54-60.

Williams, Monci Jo. "Women Beat the Corporate Game." Fortune, Volume 118, Number 6, September 12, 1988, pp. 128-138.

Winkow, Linda. "How Women and Minorities are Reshaping Corporate America." Vital Speeches1 Volume 57, Number 8, February 1, 1991, pp. 242-244.

XVI
WOMEN ADMINISTRATORS IN ACADEMIC SETTINGS

Astin, H.S. The Woman Doctorate in America. New York: Russell Sage Foundation, 1969.

Bernard, J. Academic Women. University Park: Pennsylvania University Press, 1964.

Berry, Margaret C., editor. Women in Higher Education Administration: Book of Readings. Washington, DC: National Association for Women Deans, Administrators and Counselors, 1979.

Bruce, Willa. "Dual Career Couples in the University: Policies and problems." Paper presented at the 74th Annual Conference of the National Association for Women Deans, Administrators and Counselors, Nashville, TN, March 21-25, 1990.

Budig, G.A., M.F. Hammond, & J.D. Bailey. "The place of Women in Departments of Higher Education Administration." Phi Delta Kappan, Volume 65, Number 9, May 1984, p 625.

Centra, J.A. Women, Men and the Doctorate. Princeton, NJ: Educational Testing Service, 1975.

Chamberlain, Mariam K., editor. Women in Acadene: Progress and Prospects. New York: Russell Sage Foundation, 1988.

Coursen, David. Women and Minorities in Administration: School Leadership Digest. Arlington VA: National Association of Elementary School principals, 1975.

Curby, Vicki Morgan. Women Administrators in Higher Education, Their Geographic Mobility. Washington, DC: National Association for Women Deans, Administrators, and Counselors, 1980.

Fox, M.F. "Sex, Salary, and Achievement: Reward-dualism in Academia." Sociol. Educ. Number 54, 1981, pp. 71-84.

Gilliam, Vicki Lynn. "Selection and Promotion Practices for Women in Texas Public School Administration." Doctoral Dissertation, Baylor University, 1986.

Graham, P.A. "Women in Academe" (in) Toward a Sociology of Women, edited by C. Safilios-Rothschild, Lexington, KY: Xerox, 1972.

Howard, Suzanne. Why Aren't Women Administering our Schools?: The Status of Wolen Public School Teachers and the Factors Hindering Their Promotion into Administration. Arlington, VA: National Council of Administrative Women in Education, 1975.

Hughes, H.M. "Maid of All Work or Departmental Sister-in-Law? The Faculty Wife Employed On Campus," (in) Changing Women in a Changing Society, edited by J. Huber, Chicago: University Chicago, 1973, pp. 5-11.

Hullhorst, Alice J. "A Comparative Study of the Career Aspirations, Job Seeking Patterns, and Career Patterns of Male and Female Doctoral Recipients in Educational Administration." Doctoral Dissertation, Western Michigan University, 1984.

Jones, Effie H. Women & Minorities in School Administration. Arlington, VA: Office of Minority Affairs, American Association School Administrators, 1988.

Jones, Jane Louise. A Personnel Study of Women Deans in Colleges and Universities. New York: Columbia University, 1928.

Kaufman, D.R. "Associational Ties in Academe: Some Male and Female Differences." Sex Roles, Number 4, 1978, pp. 9-21.

Kemp, Joann. Perceptions of Leader Behavior of Selected Women Physical Education Administrators Microform. Eugene, Ore.: Microform Publications, 1977

Leonard, Rebecca. "Managerial Styles in Academe: Do Men and Women Differ?" Paper presented at the Annual Meeting of the Southern Speech Communication Association, Austin, TX, April 7-10, 1981.

Lyman, Kathleen. "Advancing in School Administration: A Pilot Project for Women." Harvard Educational Review, Feb. 1980, pp. 25-35.

Lynch, Kathleen Kelley. "Grounding Research in Experience: A Case Study of Women Administrators." Paper presented at the Annual

Meeting of the American Educational Research Association, San Francisco, CA, March 27-31, 1989.

National Council of Administrative Women in Education. Wanted -More Women in Educational Leadership. Washington, 1985.

Nolan, Mary Ann Cascic. "The First Year: Women in the Principalship." A paper presented at the annual meeting of the American Educational Research Association. Washington, DC, April 20-24, 1987.

Oritiz, F.I. "career patterns in Education: Women, men and Minorities in public School Administration." NY: Praeger, 1982.

Parkhouse, Bonnie L. The Woman in Athletic Administration: Innovative Management Techniques for Universities, Colleges, Junior Colleges, High Schools, and State High Schools Associations. Santa Monica, CA: Goodyear Publishing Co., 1980.

Pavan, Barbara Nelson, & Judith McCloud D'Angelo. "Gender Differences in the Career Paths of Aspiring and Incumbent Educational Administrators." Paper presented at the Annual Meeting of the American Educational Research Association, Boston, MA, April 16-20, 1990.

Pierro, Lou M. "The Perceptions of Sex Discrimination Held By Women Administrators in Higher Education." Doctoral Thesis, Indiana University, 1986.

Rometo, Lorraine Kinces. "Women Administrators in Pennsylvania's Public Schools - overcoming Barriers to Recruitment and promotion." Doctoral Dissertation, Temple University, 1983.

Rossi, A.S., & A. Calterwood, editors. Academic Women on the Move. New York: Russell Sage Foundation, 1973.

Schmuck, Patricia A. "Deterrents to Women's Careers in School Management." Sex Roles, Volume 1, Number 4, December 1975, pp. 339-354.

Short, Paula M. et al. "Women Professors of Educational Administration: A profile and Salient Issues." Paper presented at the Annual Meeting of the American Educational Research Association, San Francisco, CA, March, 1989.

Sturtevant, Sarah Martha & Harriet Hayes, editors. Deans at Work: Discussions by Eight Women Deans of Various Phases of Their Work. New York: Harper & Brothers, 1930.

Tinsley, Adrian, Cynthia Secor, & Sheila Kaplan, editors. Women in Higher Education Administration. San Francisco: Jossey-Bass, 1984.

Trivedi, R.K., & D.N. Rao. "Regular Recruits to the IAS: A Study." Journal of the National Academy of Administrations, Number 3 July, 19E0.

Vitiello, Carol Irma. "Agnes Samuelson: A Profile and Analysis of the Administrative Career of An Iowa Educator. It Doctoral Dissertation, The University of Iowa, 1984.

Waring, Richard W. "How to Save Our Catholic Colleges: A Guide for Trustees, Administrators, Alumni, and Religious Orders." Perrysbert, OH: The Fiscal and Personnel Resources of Catholic Colleges, 1989-90.

Weissman, M.M., K. Nelson, J. Hacknan, C. Pincus, & B. Prusoff. "The Faculty Wife: Her Academic Interests and Qualifications." (in) Academic Women on the Move, edited by A. Rossi, & A. Calderwood, New York: Russell Sage, 1973, pp. 187-195.

Wheeler, Karen J. & Martha W. Tack. "Male and Female College Presidents: Leadership Behaviors and Attitudes." Paper presented at the Annual Meeting of the American Research Association, San Francisco, CA, March 27-31, 1989.

Whitaker, Kathryn S. & Kenneth Lane. "Is A Woman's Place in School Administration?" School Administrator, Volume 47, Number 2, February 1990, pp. 8-12.

Williams, Audrey. "African American Women and Affirmative Action." Sex Roles, Volume 21, Number 1-2, July 1989, pp. 99-112.

Williams, Dorothy Ellen. "Assessing the Upper-Level Female Administrator in Public School Districts of Texas: A Profile of Characteristics, Processes, and Training." Doctoral Dissertation, Texas A&M University, 1985.

Wilson, Reginald. Women of Color in Academic Administration: Trends, Progress, and Barriers." Sex Roles, Number 21, July 1989, pp. 85-97.

XVII
WOMEN IN POLICE LEADERSHIP

Balkin, Joseph. "Why policemen Don't Like Policewomen." Journal of Police Science and Administration. Number 16, March 1988, pp. 29-38.

Block, P. et al. "Policewomen On Patrol, Major Findings." Washington, D.C., The police Foundation, 1973. pp. 1-60.

Bouza, A.V. "Women in policing." FBI Law Enforcement Bulletin, Volume XLIV, Number 9, September 1975, p.5.

Carrier1 John. The Campaign for the Employment of Women as police Officers. Aldershot, Hants, England: Aebury; Brookfield, VT: Gower publishing Co., 1988.

Feinman, Clarice. Women in the Criminal Justice System. New York: Praeger, 1985.

Fooner, Michael. Women in Policing: Fighting Crime Around the World. New York: Coward, McCann & Geoghegan, 1976.

Gamire, Barnard. "Female Officers in the Department." FBI Law Enforcement Bulletin, Volume XLIII, Number 6, June 1974, p. 13.

Grant, Rosemary. "Heading for the Top - The Career Experiences of a Group of Women Deputies in One Lea." Gender and Education, Volume 1, Number 2, 1989, pp. 113-125.

Higgins, Lois. "Historical Background of policewomen's Service," Journal of Criminal Law & Criminology, Volume XLI, Number 6, March-April, 1951, pp. 822-823.

Knoohuizen, Ralph. Women in police Work in Chicago. Evanston, IL: Chicago Law Enforcement Study Group, 1974.

Koenig, Esther, J. "An overview of Attitudes Toward Women in Law Enforcement." public Admin. Review, Volume 36, Number 4, 1978, pp. 267-270.

Lunneborg, Patricia W. Women Police officers: Current Career Profile. Charles C. Thomas, 1989.

Lord, Lesli Kay. "A Comparison of Male and Female Peace Officers' Stereotypic Perceptions of Women and Women Peace Officers." Journal of Police Science and Administration, Number 14, June, 1986, pp. 83-97.

McCormack, Robert. "Interview: Catherine B. Frank, Executive Administrator of New Jersey State Association of Chiefs of Police." Law Enforcement News, September 9, 1985, pp.

Milton, Catherine. "Women in Policing 9-11." Washington, DC Police Foundation, 1972, pp. 13-15.

Owings, Chloe. Women Police: A Study of the Development and Status of the Women Police Movement. Montclair, NJ: Patterson Smith, 1969.

Perlstein, Gary R. "Certain Characteristics of Policewomen." Police, Volume XVI, Number 5, January 1972, p. 46.

Perlstein. "Policewomen and Policemen: A Comparative Look.: The Police Chief, Volume XXXIX, Number 3, March 1972, p. 74.

Price, B.R. "A Study of Leadership Strength of Female Police Executives." Journal of Police Science and Administration, Volume II, Number 2, June 1974, p. 219.

Prince, John J. "A Pilot Study to Select and Prepare Underprivileged Minorities and Women for Employment in Law Enforcement." Journal of Police Science and Administration, Volume 10, September 1982, pp. 350-356.

Rafter, Nicole Hahn & Elizabeth Anne Stanko, editors. Judge, Lawyer, Victim, Thief: Women, Gender Roles and Criminal Justice. Boston:Northeastern University Press, 1982.

Sherman, L.J. "An Evaluation of Policewomen on Patrol in a Suburban Police Department." Journal of Police Science & Administration, Volume III, Number 4, December 1975, pp. 434-438.

Sherman Lewis J. "A Psychological View of Women in Policing." Journal of Police Science and Administration, Volume I, Number 4, December 1973, p. 387.

Sichel, Joyce L. et al. Women On Patrol: A Pilot Study of Police performance in New York City. Washington: Dept. of Justice, Law Enforcement Assistance Administration, National Institute of Law Enforcement and Criminal Justice, 1978.

Singleton, Sarah M. "Gender Bias Skews Justice for Women." Trial Volume 26, February 1990, pp. 39-41.

Townsey, Roi Diane. "Black Women in American Policing: An Advancement Display." Journal of Criminal Justice, Volume 10, November/December 1982, pp. 455-468.

Walsh, Anthony. "Gender-Based Differences: A Study of Probation Officers' Attitudes About, and Recommendations For, Felony Sexual Assault Cases." Criminology, Volume 22, August 1984, pp. 371-387.

Weinshall, Teddy. "Does Military Service Help Women into Management?" Women in Management Review (UK) Volume 3, Number 1, 1987, pp. 38-44.

Weisheit, Ralph S. "Women inn the State Police: Concerns of Male and Female Officers." Journal of Police Science and Administration Volume 15, June 1987, pp. 137-144.

Wexier, Judie Gaff in and Deana Dorman Logan. "Sources of Stress Among Women Police Officers." Journal of Police Science and Administration, Volume 11, March, 1982, pp. 46-53.

XVIII
WOMEN IN MILITARY LEADERSHIP

Adams, J. "Attitudinal Studies on the Integration of Women at West point." Minutes DACOWITS. Phoenix, November 1990.

Adams, Jerome. "Women at West point: A Three-Year Perspective." Sex Roles Volume 11, September 1984, pp. 525-541.

Barkalow, Carol and Andrea Raab. In the Men's House: An Inside Account of Life in the Army by One of West Point's First Female Graduates. New York: Poseidon Press, 1990.

Baxter, Douglas Clark. Servants of the Sword: French Intendants of the Army, 1630-70. Urbana, IL: University of Illinois Press, 1976.

Binkin, Martin and Shirley J. Back. Women and the Military, Washington, DC: Brookings Institution, 1977.

Cheatham, Harold E. "Integration of Women into the U.S. Military. Sex Roles, Volume 11, Number 3, 1984, pp. 141-153.

Cooper, Helen M., Adrienne Auslander Munich, & Susan Merrill Squier, editors. Arms and the Woman: War, Gender, and Literary Representation. Chapel Hill: University of North Carolina Press, 1989.

Dienstfrey, Stephen J. Women Veterans' Exposure to Combat. Armed Forces and Society, Volume 14, Number 4, Summer 1988, pp. 549-558.

Dorn, Edwin. Who Defends America?: Race, Sex, and Class in the Armed Forces. Washington, D.C.: University Press of America, 1989.

Dunivin, Karen 0. "Gender and perceptions of the Job Environment in the U.S. Air Force." Armed Forces and Society, Volume 15, Number 1, Fall 1988, pp. 71-91.

Earley, Charity Adams. One Woman's Army: A Black officer Remembers the WAC. College Station: Texas A&M University Press, 1989.

Elshtain, Jean Bethke, and Sheila Tobias, editors. Women, Militarism, and War: Essays in History, Politics, and Social Theory. Totowa, N.J.: Rowman & Littlefield, 1990.

Ferber, M.A., & H.M. Lowry. "Women: The New Reserve Army of the Unemployed." Signs: J. Women Cult. Soc. Spring, 1976, pp. 213-232.

Galloway, Judith M. "The Impact of the Administration of Women to the Service Academies on the Role of the Woman Line Officer." American Behavioral Scientist, Volume 19, Number 5, May/June 1976, pp. 647-664.

Goldman, N. "The Changing Role of Women in the Armed Forces." (in) Changing Women in a Changing Society, edited by J. Huber, Chicago: University of Chicago, 1973, pp. 130-149.

Goldman, Nancy Loring, editor. Female Soldiers: Combatants or Noncombatants? Historical and Contemporary Perspectives. Westport, Conn. Greenwood Press, 1982.

Goldman, Nancy. "The Utilization of Women in the Armed Forces of Industrialized Nations." Sociological Symposium, Number 18, 1977, pp. 1-23.

Goldman, Nancy. "The Utilization of Women in the Armed Forces of NATO Countries." Military Review, Volume 54, Number 10, October 1974.

Good, Jane E. & Karl M. Klein. "Women in the Military Academies: US Navy." The Physician and ports medicine. Volume 17, Number 1, February 1989, pp. 99-102.

Hacker, Barton C. and Sally L. Hacker. "Military Institutions and the Labor Process: Non-economic Sources of Technological Changes, Women's Subordination, and the Organization of Work." Technology and Culture, Volume 28, October 1987, pp. 743-775.

Harrell, Karen Fair. Women in the Armed Forces: A Bibliography, 1970-1980. Monticello, IL: Vance Bibliographies, 1980.

Holm, Jeanne. Women in the Military: An Unfinished Revolution. Novato, CA.: Presidio Press, 1982.

Klick, Jean E. "Utilization of Women in the NATO Alliance," Armed Forces and Society, Number 4, Summer 1978, pp. 673-678.

Macdonald, Sharon, Pat Holden & Shirley Ardener, editors. Images of Women in Peace and War: Cross-Cultural and Historical Perspectives. Madison, WI: University of Wisconsin Press, 1988.

Matsakis, Aphrodite. Vietnam Wives: Women and Children Surviving Life with Veterans Suffering Post Traumatic Stress Disorder. Kensington, MD: Woodbine House, 1988.

Norman, Elizabeth M. Women at War: The Story of Fifty Military Nurses Who Served in Vietnam. Philadelphia: University of Pennsylvania Press, 1990.

Office of the Assistant Secretary of Defense. Military Women in the Department of Defense, Volume 1, Washington, DC: Office of the Secretary of Defense, 1983.

Russell, Mark S. The Female Veteran Population. Washington, DC: Veterans Administration, Office of Reports and Statistics, 1983.

Rustad, Michael. Women in Khaki: The American Enlisted Woman. New York: Praeger, 1982.

Segal, Mady Wechsler and David R. Segal. "Social Change and the Participation of Women in the American Military." (in) Research in Social Movements, Conflicts and Change, edited by Louis Knesbert, Greenwich, CN:JAI Press, Volume 5, 1983, pp. 235-258.

St. John Williams, Noel T. Judy O'Grady and the Colonel's Lady: The Army Wife and Camp Follower Since 1660. Washington: Brassey's Defence Publishers, 1988.

Stanley, Sandra Carson & Mady Wechsler Segal. "Military Women in NATO: An Update." Armed Forces and Society, Volume IV, Number 3, Summer 1988, pp. 559-585.

Thomas, Patricia. The Role of Women in the Military: Australia, Canada, The United Kingdom, and the United States. San Diego, CA: U.S. Naval personnel Research and Development Center, 1978.

Thomas, Patricia J. "Women in the Military: American and the British Commonwealth: Historical Similarities." Armed Forces and Society, Volume 4, Summer 1978, pp. 623-646.

Tziner, Aharon. and Shimon Dolan. "Validity of an Assessment Center for Identifying Future Female Officers in the Military." Journal of Applied Psychology, Number 67, December 1982, pp. 728-736.

United States. "Joint Resolution to Authorize the Establishment of a Memorial on Federal Land in the District of Columbia and Its Environs to Honor Women Who Have Served in the Armed Forces of the United States." Washington: U.S. Government Printing Office, Superintendent of Documents, 1987.

United States Congress/House Committee on Armed Services: Military Personnel and Compensation Subcommittee. "Benefits for Former Spouses of Military Members." Hearing Before the Military Personnel and Compensation Subcommittee of the Committee on Armed Services, House of Representatives, ninety-seventh

Congress, first session. Washington D.C. U.S. Government Printing Office, 1983.

United States Congress/House Committee on Armed Services: Military Personnel and Compensation Subcommittee. "Women in the Military." Hearings before the Military Personnel and Compensation Subcommittee of the Committee on Armed Services, House of Representatives, One Hundredth Congress, first and second sessions, Washington: U.S. Government Printing Office: 1988.

United States Congress/House Committee on Armed Services: Military Personnel and Compensation Subcommittee. "Women in the Military." Hearing before the Military Personnel and Compensation Subcommittee of the Committee on Armed Services, House of Representatives, One Hundred First Congress, second session, Washington: U.S. Government Printing Office, 1990.

United States General Accounting Office. "Civilianizing Certain Air Force Positions Could Result in Economies and Better Use of Military Personnel." Report to the Secretary of the Air Force, Washington: U.S. General Accounting Office, 1982.

United States General Accounting Office. "Using Civilian personnel for Military Administrative and Support Positions, Can More Be Done?" Washington: General Accounting Office, 1978.

United States General Accounting Office. "Women in the Military: More Military Jobs Can Be Opened Under Current Statutes." Report to Congressional Recuesters, Washington: General Accounting Office, 1988.

Wells, Wandakay. Demographic and Socioeconomic Data on Female Veterans. Washington, DC: Office of Information Management and Statistics, Statistical Policy and Research Service, Research Division, 1985.

Williams, T. Harry. Americans at War: The Development of the American Military System. Baton Rouge: Louisiana State University Press, 1960.

Woelfel, J.C., J.M. Savell, B.E. Collins & P. M. Bentler. 19A Preliminary Version of a Scale to Measure Sex-role Attitudes in the Army." Research Memorandum, Volume 76, Number 3, U.S. Army Research Institute for the Behavior and Social Sciences1 February 1976.

Yarbrough, Jean. "The Feminist Mistake: Sexual Equality and the Decline of the American Military." Policy Review, Number 33, Summer 1985, pp. 48-52.

XIX

WOMEN IN VOLUNTARY ORGANIZATION LEADERSHIP

Conklin, Elizabeth Nancy. "Women's Voluntary Associations in French Montreal: A Study of Changing Institutions and Attitudes." DAI 33.lOB, 1972, (. 4628.

Daniels, A.K. "Invisible Careers: Women Civic Leaders from the Volunteer World. Chicago: University of Chicago Press, 1988.

Daniels, Arlene Kaplan, et al. The Place of Volunteerism in the Lives of Women: Analysis of Four Types of Volunteer Service: Community Leaders of Pacific City, Equality for Women, Pacific Family Planning, Hospital Volunteers at Urban Medical Center. Evanston, IL: Program on Women at Northwestern University, 1975.

Edwards, Patricia, et al. "Women, Work, and Social Participation." A paper presented at the Annual Meeting of American sociological Association, Toronto, Canada, 1981.

Gold, D. "Women and Volunteerism" (in) Women in Sexist Society, edited by V. Gornick & B. Horan, New York: Mentor, pp. 384-400.

Goodrich, Norma Lorre. Priestesses. New York: Harper perennial, 1990.

Goodrich, Norma Lorre. Priestesses. New York: F. Watts, 1989.

Lichstenstein, Marsha. "Some Correlates of the Amount of Volunteer Activity in a Sample of Elite Women: The Relative Effect of Previous Volunteer Experiences and Socio-personal Characteristics." Doctoral Thesis, Rutgers University, 1983.

Mcpherson, J.M. & L. Smith-Lovin. "Women and Weak Ties: Differences by Sex in the Size of Voluntary Organizations." Am. J. Sociol. Number 87, 1982, pp. 883-904.

Morgan, John H. Women Priests: An Emerging Ministry in the Episcopal Church, 1975-1985. Bristol, IN: Wyndham Hall Press, 1985.

Public Management Institute. Nonprofit Management Skills for Women Managers. San Francisco, CA: Public Management Institute, 1980.

Robertson, Olivia. Ordination of a Priestess. Enniscorthy: Cesara Publications, 1977.

Sanders, Audrey. "The Value of Volunteer Work in the Lives of Thirty Suburban Women." Thesis, Adelphi University, 1979.

Schram, Vicki Ruth. "Determinants of Volunteer Work Participation by Married Women." Doctoral Thesis, University of Illinois at Urbana-Champaign, 1980.

Snider, Martha Amn. "Wife/Mother Role Adjustment and Other Managerial Strategies Related to a Community Leadership Volunteer Demand." Doctoral Thesis, Oregon State University, 1985.

Sommers, David. Women in Organizations: An Analysis of the Role and Status of Women in American voluntary Organizations. Washington, DC: B'nai B'rith International, 1983.

XX
WOMEN IN LIBRARY ADMINISTRATIVE SYSTEMS

Ballard, Robert. Equal Pay for Equal Work: Women in Special Libraries. New York: Special Libraries Association, 1981 Bennett, George E. Librarians in Search of Science and Identity: The Elusive profession. Metuchen, NJ: Scarecrow Press, 1988.

Braunagel, Judith S. "Job Mobility of Men and Women Librarians and How It Affects Career Advancement." American Libraries, Number 10, December 1979, pp. 643-647.

Dale, Doris Cruger. Career Patterns of Women Librarians with Doctorates. Champaign, IL: University of Illinois, Graduate School of Library Science, 1980.

Dickson, Katherine Murphy. "Women Librarians Re-entering the Work Force." American Library Association, Committee on the Status of Women in Librarianship; Principal Investigator, Chicago: American Library Association, 1985.

Douglass College. Preconference on the Status of Women in Librarianship. Douglass College, 1974.

Fennell, Janice C. A Profile of Women Directors of the Largest Academic Libraries in the United States: An Analysis and Description. Unpublished PhD dissertation, The Florida State University, 1978.

Heim, Kathleen M. On Account of Sex: An Annotated Bibliography on the Status of Women in Librarianship, 1977-1981. Chicago: American Library Association, 1984.

Heim, Kathleen, editor. The Status of Women in Librarianship: Historical, Sociological, and Economic Issues. New York: Neal-Schuman publishers, 1983.

Houser, Lloyd J. The Search for a Scientific Profession: Library Science Education in the U.S. and Canada. Metuchen, NJ: Scarecrow Press, 1978.

Irvine, Betty Jo. Sex Segregation in Librarianship: Demographic and Career Patterns of Academic Library Administrators. Westport, CN: Greenwood Press, 1985.

Lundy, Kathryn Renfro. Women View Librarianship: Nine Perspectives. Chicago: American Library Association, 1980.

Myers, Margaret & Mavra Scarborough, editors. 'I Women in Librarianship: Melvil's Rib Symposium." Proceedings of the Eleventh Annual Symposium. New Brunswick, N.J.: Bureau of Library and Information Science Research, Rutgers University Graduate School of Library Service, 1975.

Passet, Joanne Ellen. "Quest for a Profession: The Origins of Library Education in Indiana. PhD Thesis, Indiana University, 1988.

Shuter, Janet, editor. Women and Librarianship. Bradford, West Yorkshire, England: MCB University Press, 1984.

Taylor, Marion R. "Mobility and Professional Involvement in Librarianship" (in) The Status of Women in Librarianship, edited by Kathleen M. Heim. New York: Neil-Schuman Publishers, 1983, pp. 321-344.

University of Michigan, School of Library Science. Women in the Library Profession: Leadership Roles and Contributions, Ann Arbor, MI: University of Michigan, 1971.

Wall, Celia. "Self-Concept: An Element of Success in the Female Library Manager." Journal of Library Administration, Volume 6, Number 4, Winter 1985/86, pp. 53-65.

Weibel, Kathleen and Kathleen M. Heim, editors. The Role of Women in Librarianship, 1876-1976: The Entry, Advancement, and Struggle for Equalization in One Profession. Phoenix: Oryx Press, 1979.

Weingand, Darlene E., editor. Women and Library Management: Theories, Skills, and Values. Ann Arbor, MI: Pierian Press, 1982.

XXI
WOMEN IN SOCIAL SERVICE ADMINISTRATION

Austin, Carol D., et al. "Experiences of Women as Social Welfare Administrators." Social Work, Volume 30, Mar/Apr 1985, pp. 173-179.

Chafetz, Janet Saltzmen. "Women in Social Work." Social Work, Volume 17, September 1972, pp. 12-19.

Cherniss, Cary. Professional Burnout in Human Service Organizations. New York: Praeger, 1980.

Curlee, M.B. & F.B. Raymond. "The Female Administrator: Who Is She?" Administration in Social Work, Volume 2, Number 3, Fall 1978, pp. 307-318.

Dominelli, Lena. Feminist Social Work.. Houndmills, Basingstoke, Hampshire: Macmillan; New York: New York University Press, 1989.

Ezell, H.F. & C.A. Odewahn. "An Empirical Inquiry of Variables Impacting Women in Management in Public Social Science Organizations." Administration in Social Work, Volume IV, Number 4, Winter 1980, pp. 53-70.

Fanshel, D. "Status Differentials: Men and Women in Social Work. Social Work, Volume 21, 1975, pp. 448-454.

Hanlan, M.S. "Women in Social Work Administration: Current Role Strains." Administration in Social Work, Volume I, Number 1, 1977, pp. 259-265.

Hanmer, Jalna. Women and Social Work: Towards a Woman-centered Practice. Chicago, IL: Lyceum Book5, 1989.

Haynes, Karen S. Women Managers in Human Services. New York: Springer Publishing Co., 1989.

Haynes, Karen S. "Sexual Differences in Social Work Administrators' Job Satisfaction." Journal of Social Service Research, Spring/Summer Volume 6, Number 3-4, 1983, pp. 57-74.

Kerson, Toba. "Strategies for Success: Women in Social Service Administration." Administration in Social Work, Fall, 1979, pp. 313-326.

Kravetz, Diane & Katherine L. Pollock. "Experiences of Women as Social Welfare Administrators." Social Work Number 30, Mar/Apr. 1985, pp. 173-179.

Kravetz, D. & C.D. Austin. "Women's Issues in Social Service Administration." Administration in Social Work, Volume VIII, Number 4, Winter 1984, pp. 25-38.

Kunkel, Dale, editor. Sexual Issues in Social Work: Emerging Concerns in Education and Practice. Honolulu: University of Hawaii, School of Social Work, 1979.

Maccoby, Eleanor R., editor. The Development of Sex Differences. Stanford, CA: Stanford University Press, 1966.

Marchant, Helen & Betsy Wearing, editors. Gender Reclaimed: Women in Social Work. Sydney, NSW: Hale & Iremonger, 1986.

Pugh, Joanne, editor. Nonprofit Management Skills for Women Mangers. San Francisco, CA: Public Management Institute, 1980.

Scotch, C. Bernard. "Sex Status in Social Work: Grist for Women's Liberation." Social Work, Volume 16, July 1971, pp. 5-12.

Sibley, D. "Invisible Women? The Contribution of the Chicago School Social Service Administration to Urban Analysis." Environment and Planning, Volume 22, June 1990, pp. 733-745.

XXII
WOMEN PROFESSIONALS IN MEDIA

Abrahamson, Phyllis Leslie. Sob Sister Journalism. New York: Greenwood Press, 1990.

Beasley, Maruine Hoffman. The First Women Washington Correspondents. Washington: George Washington University, 1976.

Beasley, Maurine Hoffman. "Pens and petticoats: The Story of the First Washington Women Correspondents." DAI 35/09A, 1974, p. I 6085.

CARIMAC. Women and Media Decision-making in the Caribbean. CARIMAC/Unesco Seminar, September 28-30, 1981, Kingston, Jamaica.

Consumers' Association of Penang. Abuse of Women in the Media. Penang, Malaysia: Consumers' Association of Penang, 1982.

Craft, Christine. Too Old, Too Ugly, and Not Deferential to Men. Rocklin, CA: Prima Pub. and Communications, 1988.

Crean, S.M. Newsworthy: The Lives of Media Women. Toronto, Canada: Stoddart, 1985.

Edwards, Julia. Women of the World: The Great Foreign Correspondents. Boston: Houghton Mifflin, 1988.

Fox, Margery Q. Power and Piety. "Women in Christian Science." DAI/34/07B, 1973, p. 3060.

Gallagher, Margaret. Unequal Opportunities: The Case of Women and the Media. Paris: Unesco Press, 1981.

Gelfman, Judith Schlein. "Women in Television News: The On-Air Woman Newscaster in New York." DAI 35/04A, 1974, p. 2209.

Goldreich, Gloria. What Can She Be? A Newscaster. New York: Lothrop, Lee & Shepard, 1973.

Harris, Betty Clayton. The Role of Women on Indiana Newspapers, and in Other Media, 1876-1976. Muncie, IN: Woman's Press Club of Indiana, 1977.

Holly, Susan Marie. Women in Weekly Newspaper Management. Bloomington, IN: Center for New Communications, School of Journalism, Indiana University, 1978.

Jakes, John. Great Women Reporters. New York: Putnam, 1969.

Jelinek, Mariann. "Career Management and Women." (in) Women, Communication, and Careers, edited by Marianne Grewe-Partsch and Gertrude J. Robinson, New York: Saur publishing, Inc. 1980.

Logie, lona R. "Careers for Women in Journalism: A Personnel Study of 881 Women Experienced as Salaried Writers in Journalism, Advertising, Publicity, and Promotion. PhD dissertation, Columbia University, ADD, 1939.

McLendon, Winzola. Don't Quote Me: Washington Newswomen and the Power Society. New York: Dutton, 1970.

Paisner, Daniel. The Imperfect Mirror: Inside Stories of Television Newswomen. New York: Morrow, 1989.

Ogan, Christine L. "On Their Way to the Top? Men and Women Middle-Level Newspaper Managers." Paper presented at the 62nd Annual Meeting of the Association for Education in Journalism, Houston, Texas, August 5-8, 1979.

Pokrywczynski, James and John Crowley. "Job Satisfaction Among Women in Advertising." AEIMC Convention, 1988.

Ross, Ishbel. Ladies of the Press. New York: Arno Press, 1974.

Rouse, Ewart. "Women Dominate Ad Field: Hiring Trend Reflects Nature of Work Force," Yakima Herald Republic, June 15, 1986, p. E#

Sanders, Marlene. Waiting for Prime Time: The Women of Television News. Urbana: University cf Illinois Press, 1988.

Schlipp, Madelon Golden. "Great Women of the Press. Carbondale: Southern Illinois University Press, 1983.

Soderlund, Walter C. "Gender in Canadian Local Television News: Anchors and Reporters." Journal of Broadcasting & Electronic Media. Volume 33, Spring 1989, pp. 187-196.

Theus, Kathryn T. "Gender Shifts in Journalism and Public Relations." Public Relations Review, Volume 11, Spring 1985, pp. 42-50.

Whittaker, Susan. "Relative Effectiveness of Male and Female Newscasters." Journal of Broadcasting. Volume 20, spring 1976, pp. 177-184

XXIII
WOMEN IN THE LEGAL PROFESSIONS

Abramson, Jill. Where They Are Nov: The Story of the Women of Harvard Law 1974. Garden City, NY: Doubleday, 1986.

Brown, Drollene P. Belva Lockwood Wins Her Case. Niles, IL: A Whitman, 1987.

Chester, Ronald. Unegual Access: Women Lawyers in a Changing America. South Hadley, NA: Bergin & Garvey Publishers, 1985.

Continuing Legal Education. Women and Rainmaking: The Secrets and Skills of Client Development. Boston, MA: Continuing Legal Education, 1990.

Couric, Emily, editor. Women Lawyers: Perspectives on Success. New York, NY: Law & Business/Harcourt Brace Jovanovich, 1984.

Davis, Nary Lee. Women in the Legal Professions. Minneapolis, MN: T.S. Denison, 1976.

Epstein, Cynthia Fuchs. Women in Law. Garden City, NY: Anchor Press/Doubleday, 1983.

Epstein, C. F. "Women Lawyers and Their Profession: Inconsistency of Social Controls and Their Consequence for Professional Performance." (in) The Professional Woman edited by A. Theodore, Cambridge, MA: Schenkman, 1971, pp. 669-684.

Feiden, Karyn. Negotiating Time: New Scheduling Options in the Legal Profession. San Francisco, CA: New Ways to Work, 1986.

Fenten, D.X. Ms.-Attorney. Philadelphia: Westminster Press, 1974.

Goldreich, Gloria. What Can She Be? A Lawyer. New York: Lothrop, Lee & Shepard Co, 1973.

Grossblat, Martha & Bette H. Sikes. Women Lawyers: Supplementary Data to the 1971 Lawyer Statistical Report. Chicago: American Bar Foundation, 1973.

International Federation of Women Lawyers. Souvenir Album on the Occasion of the 15th Convention of the International Federation of Women Lawyers, Tehran, Iran, April 8-14, 1969.

Jack, Rand. Moral Vision and professional Decisions: The Changing Values of Women and Men Lawyers. New York: Cambridge University Press, 1989.

Kenvin, Helene Schwartz. Lawycring. New York: Farrar, Straus and Giroux, 1976.

McHugh, Mary. Law and the New Woman. New York: Watts, 1975.

Morello, Karen Berger. The Invisible Bar: The Woman Lawyer in America, 1638 to the Present. Boston: Beacon Press, 1988.

Morello, Karen Berger. The Invisible Bar: The Woman Lawyer in America, 1638 to the Present. New York: Random House, 1986.

National Commission on the Role of Fillipino Women. San Miguel, Manila1 Philippines: National Commission on the Role of Filipino Women, 1982.

New Jersey Supreme Court. Task Force on Women in the Courts: Report of the First Year. Newark, NJ: The Task Force, 1984.

Stover, Robert V. Making it and Breaking it: The Fate of Public Interest Commitment During Law School. Urbana, IL: University of Illinois Press, 1989.

Thielens, Wagner. The Socialization of Law Students: a Case Study in Three Parts. New York, NY: Arno Press, 1980.

Warsaw, Janine N. editor. Women Trial Lawyers: How They Succeed in Practice and in the Courtroom. Englewood Cliffs, NJ: prentice-Hall, 1987.

Swiger, Elinor Porter. Women Lawyers at Work. New York: Messner, 1978.

XXIV
WOMEN ENGINEERS AND SCIENTISTS

"Surveying Metalworking's Gender Gap." Tooling & Production, 72 Volume 52, September 1996, pp. 59-60-.

Abir-Am, Pnina G. & Dorinda Outram, editors. Uneasy Careers and Intimate Lives: Women in Science, 1789-1979. New Brunswick: Rutgers University Press, 1987.

Ainley, Marianne Gosztonyi, editor. Despite the Odds: Essays on Canadian Women and Science. Montreal: Vehicule Press; Buffalo, NY: U.S. distributor, University of Toronto Press, 1990.

Armstrong, Sue. "Female Circumcision: Fighting a Cruel Tradition." New Scientists, Volume 129, February 2, 1991, pp. 42-47.

Arnold, Lois. Four Lives in Science: Women's Education in the Nineteenth Century. New York, NY: Schocken Books, 1984.

Asbrand, Deborah. "Women in Engineering Serve as Role Models to Fight Image of Male-dominated Profession." EDN, Volume 31, May 15, 1986, pp. 271-275.

Attas, Isabelle. "Women's Work. Engineering (London, England), Volume 229, September 1989, pp. 51-53.

Baum, Eleanor. "Recruiting and Graduating Women: The Underrepresented Student." IEEE Communications Magazine, Volume 28, December 1990, pp. 47-50.

Bailyn, L. "Experiencing Technical Work: A Comparison of Male and Female Engineers.' Human Relations, Number 40, 1987, pp. 299-312.

Berchtold, Gladys Beaman (interview). ASTM Standardization News, Volume 14, January, 1986, pp. 26-30.

Brown, J.M. "A Woman in the World of Engineering." IEEE Transactions on Education, Volume E-18, 1975, pp. 3-10.

Bugliarello, George et al, editors. Women in Engineering: Bridging the Gap Between Society and Technology. Chicago, IL: University of Illinois at Chicago Circle, 1972.

Chen, Katherine T. "A Canny Manager of Boeing's Electronics R & D.: IEEE Spectrum, Volume 27, September, 1990, pp. 44-45.

Cole, J. R., and H. Zuckerman. "Marriage, Motherhood and Research Performance in Science." Scientific American, February 1987, pp. 119-125.

Committee on the Education and Employment of Women in Science and Engineering, office of Scientific and Engineering Personnel, National Research Council. Climbing the Ladder: An Update on the Status of Doctoral Women Scientists and Engineers. Washington, DC: National Academy Press, 1983.

Crane, Janet G. "Women in the Industry." Tappi Journal, Volume 71, July 1988, pp. 46-52.

David, Deborah Sarah. "Career Patterns and Values: A Study of Men and Women in Science and Engineering." Thesis, Columbia University, 1971.

Denning, John. "The Hazards of Women's Work." New Scientist, Volume 105, January 17, 1985, pp. 12-15.

Dresseihaus, Mildred S. "Women Graduate Students." Physics Today, Volume 391 June 1986, pp. 74-75.

Erickson, Judith. "Women in the Workplace." Professional Safety, Volume 32, February 1987, pp. 30-37.

Fitzpatrick, J.L. & T. Silverman. "Women's Selection of Careers in Engineering: Do Traditional-Nontraditional Differences Still Exist? Journal of Vocational Behavior1 Number 34, 1989, pp. 266-278.

Freeman, Joan. A Passion for Physics: Memoirs of a Woman Physicist. Bristol, England; Philadelphia, PA: A Huger, 1991.

Fritz, Ann. "Problems of Women Managers." Machine Design, Volume 60, September 8, 1988, pp. 109-112.

Gardner, R.E. "Women in Engineering: The Impact of Attitudinal Difference: On Educational Institutions." Engineering Education, Number 67, pp. 233-240.

Ginzberg, Eli. Technology and Employment: Concepts and Clarifications. Boulder: Westview Press, 1986.

Gof f, Alice Charlotte. Women Can be Engineers. Youngstown, OH, 1946.

Grady, Judith R. "Bridging the Gender Gap." IEEE Spectrum, Volume 21, November 1984, pp. 87-88.

Grondin, Deirdre. "Research, Myths and Expectations: New Challenges for Management Educators.~' Journal of Business Ethics (Netherlands), Volume 9, Number 4,5, Apr/May 1990, pp. 369-372.

Haas, Violet B. et al, editors. Women in Scientific and Engineering Professions. Ann Arbor, MI: University of Michigan 74 Press, 1984.

Hacker, Sally. Pleasure, Power, and Technology: Some Tales of Gender, Engineering, and the Cooperative Workplace. Boston: Unwin Hyman, 1989.

Harmon, Margaret. Ms. Engineer. Philadelphia, PA: Westminster Press, 1979.

Helson, R. "Women Mathematicians and the Creative Personality." Journal of Consulting and Clinical Psychology, Number 36, 1971, pp. 210-220.

Henriques, Nikki. "Women in Computing: Escape From the Female Ghetto." New Scientist, Volume 103, August 9, 1984. Volume 103, pp. 17-19.

Her::enberg, Caroline L. Women Scientists from Antiquity to the Present: An Index. West Cornwall, CT: Locust Hill Press, 1986.

Honigl Jack. Women and IT." Computer Data (Canada), Volume 14, Number 4, April 1989, pp. 1-2.

Howard, Jean Ross. A Salute to Women in Aerospace. Washington: U.S. Department of Transportation, Federal Aviation Administration, Office of General Aviation, 1976.

International Conference of Women Engineers and Scientists. Proceedings. Torino, Italy: AIDIA Secretariat, 1971.

Jagacinski, Carolyn M. "Engineering Careers: Women in a Male-Dominated Field." Psychology of Women Quarterly, Volume 11, 1987, pp. 97-110.

Jagacinski, C.M. & W.K. LeBold. "A Comparison of Men and Women Undergraduates and Professional Engineers." Engineering Education, Number 72, 1981, pp. 213-220.

Johnson, Maryfran. "Career Boosters for Women." Computer world, Volume 24, Number 50, December 10, 1990, p. 95.

Kalindia, Uniya and Prasad Ram, editors. "Role of Women Scientists in Social Transformation & Nation Building: Edited Abstract of Proceedings of the Seminar on Role of Women Scientists in Social Transformation and Nation Building, New Delhi, April 27-28, 1988.

Keenan, Tony, Time Newton, & Chris Logue. "Sex Discrimination in Practice. Experiences of Female Professior al Engineers."

Electronics and Power, Volume 30, November/December 1984, pp. 882-884.

Kosheleva, Inna. Women in Science. Ctranslated from the Russian by Frances Longnan. Moscow: Progress Publishers, 1983.

Langbein, Laura Irwin. Profile of IEEE Women Members: Their Salaries, Demographics, Attitudes Toward the Workplace, and professional Status. New York, NY: The Institute of Electrical and Electronics Engineers.

Lankford, John and Rickey L. Slavings. "Gender and Science: Women in American Astronomy, 1855-1940." Physics Today, Volume 43, March 1990, pp 58-ES.

Lewis, Patricia. "Na Escape From Sexist Science." New Scientist, Volume 113, March 19, 1987, p. 58.

Manthorpe, Catherine. "Feminists Look at Science." New Scientist, Volume 105, March 7, 1985, pp. 29-31.

Mascone, Cynthia Fabian. "Engineering a Two-Career Lifestyle." Chemical Engineering, Volume 95, September 12, 1988, pp. 101-102.

McAfee, N. "Brighter Prospects for Women in Engineering." Engineering Education, Number 64, 1974, pp. 23-25.

Mcllwee, Judith Samson. Women in Engineering: Gender, Power, and Workplace Culture. Albany, NY: State University of New York Press, 1992.

McLane, Helen J. "Listen, Please!" Chentech, Volume 14, October 1984, pp. 584-586.

Meyer, J.H. "Influence of Alumni Careers and Students' Educational Pathways on Animal Science Undergraduate Teaching Programs." Journal of Animal Science, Volume 68, Number 10, October 1990, pp. 3056-3068.

Michel, Jean. Women in Engineering Education. Paris: Unesco, 1988.

Musella, Marianne A. "What Women Engineers Want—What Women Engineers Can Do." Chemical Engineering, Volume 97, October 1990, pp. 207-208.

National Research Council. Committee on the Education and Employment of Women in Science and Engineering. "Women Scientists in Industry and Government: How Much Progress in the 1970's?" Washington, D.C." National Academy of Sciences, 1980.

National Research Council. Committee on the Education and Employment of Women in Science and Engineering. "Climbing the Academic Ladder: Doctoral Women Scientsts in Academe." Washington, D.C.:" National Academy of Sciences, 1979.

National Science Foundation. Women and Minorities in Science and Engineering. Washington: National Science Foundation, 1982.

Northrup, Herbert R. "Professional Women in R&D Laboratories." Research-Technology Management. Volume 31, Number 4, Jul/Aug, 1988, pp. 44-52.

Oliver, Mary Jo. Women in Non-Traditional Aviation and Space Careers: An Overview. Washington: Department of Transportation, Federal Aviation Administration, Office of Aviation Policy, 1979.

O-Maoldomhnaigh, Micheal & Vera Ni-Mhaolain. "The Perceived Expectation of the Administrator as a Factor Affecting the Sex of Scientists Drawn by Early Adolescent Girls. "Research-in-Science-and-Technological-Education, Volume 8, Number 1, 1990, pp. 69-74.

Ott, M.D. "Retention of Men and Women Engineering Students." Research in Higher Education, Number 9, 1978, pp. 127-150.

Palca, Joseph. "Women Left Out at NIH." Science, Volume 248, June 29, 1990, pp. 1601-1602.

Parrish, John B. "Women Continue to Rise in the Professions." Chemical Engineering Progress, Volume 84, January 1988, pp. 50-56.

Pearl, Amy, Martha E. Pollack and Eve Riskin. "Becoming a Computer Scientist." Communications of the ACM, Volume 33, November 1990, pp. 47-57.

Pepin, Lucie. "Women in the Workplace—Some Occupational Hazards." Professional Safety, Volume 31, January 1986, pp. 36-39.

Perrucci, Carolyn Cummings. The Female Engineer and Scientist: Factors Associated with the Pursuit of a Professional Career. Springfield, VA: National Technical Information Service, 1969.

Perrucci, C.C. "Minority Status and the Pursu.t of Professional Careers. Women in Science and Engineering." Social Forces, Number 49, 1970, pp. 245-259.

Richter, Derek editor. Women Scientists: The Road to Liberation. London: Macmillan, 1982.

Rossi, A.S. "Barriers to the Career Choice of Engineering, Medicine, or Science Among American Women." (in) Readings on the Psychology of Women, edited by J.M. Bardwick. New York: Harper & Row, 1972, pp. 72-82.

Rossi, A.S. "Women in Science: Why So Few: "(in) Toward a Sociology of Women, edited by C. Safilios-Rothschild, Lexington, MA: Xerox Coil, 1972, pp. 141-153.

Rubin, Debra K, "Women Take on Construction (owners and executives)." Engineering News-Record, Volume 217, October 16, 1986, pp. 24-29.

Ruina, Edith. Women in science and Technology: A Report on the Workshop on Women in Science and Technology. Cambridge, MA: MIT Press, 1973.

Setzer, Steven W. "Putting the Shoe on the Other Foot." ENR, Volume 225, August 2, 1990, p. 44C18.

Shelley, Suzanne. "Women Engineers: The Playing Field Isn't Level." Chemical Engineering, Volume 96, Number 12, December 1989, pp. 47-48.

Skeldon, Paul. "Who Wants to be and Engineer?" Process Engineering, Volume 72, January 1991, pp. 76-77.

Sloan, M.E. "Opportunities for Women in Engineering." IEEE Transactions on Education. Number E-18, 1975, pp. 1-2.

United States Congress/House Committee on Government Operations, Government Activities and Transportation Subcommittee. "Discrimination Against Blacks and Women at Federal Aviation Administration, Air Traffic Control Facility, O'Hare Airport: Hearing Before a Subcommittee of the Committee on Government

Operations, Mouse of Representatives, One Hundredth Congress." Washington, D.C.: U.S. Government Printing Office, 1988.

Veglahn, Nancy. Women Scientists. New York, NY: Facts on File, 1991.

Verheyden-Hilliard, Mary Ellen. Engineer from the Comanche Nation, Nancy Wallace. Bethesda, MD: Equity Institute, 1985.

Verheyden-Hilliard, Mar,~ Ellen. Scientist and Astronaut, Sally Ride. Bethesda, MD: Equity Institute, 1985.

Verheyden-Hilliard, Mary Ellen. Scientist from Puerto Rico, Maria Cordero hardy. Bethesda, MD: Equity Institute, 1985.

Vetter, B.M. "Women Scientists and Engineers: Trends in Participation." Science, Number 214, 1981, pp. 1313-1321.

Voelcker, John. "An Engineering Manager Who Thrives on Challenge (Computer Society president-elect Helen Wood)." IEEE Spectrum, Volume 26, October 1989, pp. 39-42.

Voice, Isabel Perry. "Women Safety Manager Profiles and Success Factors." DAI 44/04A, p. 1187, 1983.

Wallsgrove, Ruth. "When Women Take Over." New Scientist, Volume 113, January 22, 1987, p. 58.

Walton, Anne. "Attitudes Toward Women Scientists." Chemtech, Volume 16, July 1986, pp. 396-401.

Wheal, Chris. "Leading Lady of the Left (Barbara Switzer)." The Engineer (London, England) Volume 271, December 13-27, 1990, p. 42.

White, M.S. "Psychological and Social Barriers to Women in Science." Science, Volume 170, Number 3956, 1970, pp. 413-417.

Yost, Edna. Women of Modern Science. Westport, CN: Greenwood Press, 1984.

Zahm, John Augustine. Woman in Science. Notre Dame, IN: University of Notre Dame Press, 1991.

Zientara, Marguerite. Women, Technology & Power: Ten Stars and the History They Made. New York, NY: AMACON, 1987.

Zuckerman, Harriet; Jonathan R. Cole and John T. Bruer, editors. The Outer Circle: Women in the Scientific Community. New York: Norton, 1991.

XXV
WOMEN IN PUBLIC ADMINISTRATION

Burns, Ruth Ann & Diane Rathbard Margolis. Women in Public Service. Prepared for the U.S. Department of Housing and Urban Development. Washington: Office of Policy Development and Research, 1980.

Daley, Dennis M. "Differing Perceptions Between Men and Women Over Personnel Management Practices: Gender-related Differences Among Iowa Public Employees." Public Personnel Management, Volume 13, Number 3, Fall 1984, pp. 345-354.

Duerst-Lahti, Georgia. "But Women Play the Game Too: Communication Control and Influence in Administrative Decision Making." Administration & Society, Volume 22, Number 2, August 1990, pp. 182-205.

Duerst-Lahti, Georgia. "Gender Power Relations in public Bureaucracies." Doctoral dissertation, University of wisconsin-Madison, 1987.

Fine, Marlene, G.; Fern L. Johnson, and M. Sallane Ryan. "Cultural Diversity in the Workplace." Public personnel Management, Volume 19, Number 3, Fall 1990, pp. 305-310.

Gallas, Nesta M. "Women in public Administration." Public Administration Review, Volume 36, July/August 1976.

Kranz, Harry. The participatory Bureaucracy: Women and Minorities in a More Representative public Service. Lexington, MA: Lexington Books, 1976.

Lacy, Gwynette Precia Ford. "An Evaluation of Attitudes Toward Women as Managers in a Government Setting." Doctoral Thesis, University of Wisconsin, Madison, 1979.

Leader, S.G. "The policy Impact of Elected Women Officials." (in) The Impact of the Electoral Process, edited by L. Maisel & J. Cooper. Beverly Hills, CA: Sage, 1977.

Lepper, Mary M. "The Status of Women in the U.S., 1976: Still Looking for Justice and Equity." Public Administration Review, Volume 36, Number 4, July/August, 1976, p. 366.

Lopez-Lee, David. "Organizational Representatives; An Operational Imperative for the personnel Function." public personnel Management, September-October, 1979, pp. 287-293.

Lovrich, Nicholas and Charles Jones." Affirmative Action; Women Managers and performance Appraisal: Simultaneous Movement in Conflict Directions?" Review of public personnel Administration, Volume 3, Number 3, Summer 1983, pp. 3-20.

Lynn, Naomi B. and Richard E. Vaden. "Toward a Non-Sexist personnel Opportunity Structure: The Federal Executive Bureaucracy." public personnel Management, July-August, 1979, pp. 209-215.

Neuse, Steven M. "Professionalism and Authority: Women in public Service." public Administration Review, Volume 38, Number 5, September/October 1978, pp. 436-441.

Rader, Martha H. "Evaluating a Management Development Program for Women." Public Personnel Management1 May-June, 1979, pp. 138-145.

Riccucci, N.M. Women, Minorities, and Unions in the Public Sector. Contributions in Labor Studies, Number 28. Westport, CT: Greenwood Press, 1990.

Rubin, Marilyn Marks. "Women in ASPA: the Fifty-year Climb Toward Equality." Public Administration Review, Volume 50, March/April 1990, pp. 277-297.

Samuels, Catherine. The Forgotten Five Million: Women in Public Employment. New York: Women's Action Alliance, Inc. 1975.

Slack, James D. "Affirmative Action and City Managers: Attitudes Toward Recruitment of Women." Public Administration Review, Volume 47, Number 2, Mar/Apr, 198, pp. 199-206.

Van Wagner, Karen and Cheryl Swanson. "From Machiavelli to Ms.: Differences in Male-Female Power Styles," Public Administration Review, January-February, 1979, pp. 66-72.

XXVI
WOMEN IN FEDERAL ADMINISTRATION

Arvis, Paul F. "Factors Affecting the Recruitment and Advancement of Women to Managerial Positions in Federal Agencies." Doctoral Thesis, American University, 1973.

Association of American Foreign Service Women. A World of Difference: A Collection by American Foreign Service Women. Fairfax, VA: Association of American Foreign Service Women Writers' Group, 1987.

Calkin, Homer L. Women in American Foreign Affairs. Washington: Department of State, 1977.

Calkin, Homer L. Women in the Department of State: Their Role in American Foreign Affairs. Washington: Office of the Deputy Under Secretary for Management., 1978.

Graebner, W. "Uncle Sam Just Loves the Ladies: Sex Discrimination in the Federal Government, 1917." Labor History Volume 21, Number 1, Winter 1979-80, pp. 75-85.

Gunas, Peter J. III. "The Department of Labor's Glass-ceiling Initiative." Employment Relations Today, Volume 17, Winter 1990-91, pp. 277-280.

Harrison, Pat. American Women of Achievement. New York: Chelsea House, 1991.

Howard, Lawrence. "Civil Service Reform: A Minority and Women's Perspective." Public Administration Review. Volume 38, Number 4, July/August 1978, pp. 305-308.

Hutton, Joseph Bernard. Women in Espionage. New York: Macmillan, 1972.

Kellough, J. Edward. "Federal Agencies and Affirmative Action for Blacks and Women." Social Science Quarterly, Volume 71, March, 1990, pp. 83-92.

Kellough, J. Edward. "Integration in the Public Workplace: Determinants of Minority and Female Employment in Federal Agencies." Public Administration Review. Volume 50, September/October 1990, pp. 557-566.

Lewis, Gregory B. "Gender and Promotions: Promotion Chances of White Men and Women in Federal White-collar Employment." The Journal of Human Resources, Volume 21, Summer 1986, pp. 406-419.

Lewis, Gregory B. "Race, Sex, and Supervisory Authority in Federal White-Collar Employment," Public Administration Review, Volume 46, January/February 1986, pp. 25-30.

Lewis, Gregory B. "Progress Toward Racial and Sexual Equality in the Federal Civil Service." Public Administration Review, Volume 48, May/June 1988, pp. 700-707.

Long, James E. "Employment Discrimination in the Federal Sector.: Journal of Human Resources, Volume 11, Number 7, Winter 1976, pp~. 86-97.

Newsom, David D. "Relationship Between US Diplomats and Foreign Policy and the Media." Gannett Center J. Volume 3, Fall 1989, pp. 175-187.

Skurzynski, Gloria. Safeguarding the Land: Women at Work in Parks, Forests, and Rangelands. New York: Harcourt Brace Jovanovich, 1981.

Steeward, Debra. "Women in Top Jobs: Am opportunity for Federal Leadership." Public Administration Review, Volume 36, July/August 1976, PP. 357-364.

Taylor, Patricia A. "Income Equality in the Federal Civilian Government.: American Sociological Review, Volume 44, June 1979, PP. 468-479.

U.S. Civil Service Commission. Study of Employment of Women in the Federal Government, 1974.

United States Congress/House Committee on Government Operations-Government Activities and Transportation Subcommittee. "Discrilination Against Blacks and Women at Federal Aviation Administration, Air Traffic Control Facility, O'Hare Airport: Hearing before a subcommittee of the Committee on Government Operations, House of Representatives, One Hundredth Congress, second session, June 20, 1988.

Washington:United States Government Printing Office, 1988.

Walther, Regis H. Orientations and Behavioral Styles of Foreign Service Officers. New York: Carnegie Endowment for International Peace, 1965.

"Washington State Task Force on Gender and Justice in the courts." Final Report of the Washington State Task Force on Gender and Justice in the Courts. Qlvmpia, WA: Office of the Administrator for the courts, 1989,

XXVII
WOMEN IN STATE ADMINISTRATION

Briley, K.D. Status of Women in Kentucky State Agencies. Frankfort: Legislative Research Commission, 1972.

Carroll, Susan J. "The Recruitment of Women for Cabinet-level Posts in State Government: A Social Control Perspective." The Social Science Journal, Volume 21, Januarv 1984, pp. 91-107.

Gerrard, Meg, June Oliver, & Martha Williams. "Women in Management: Proceedings of the Conference Women and Men, Colleagues in Management? The University of Texas at Austin, May 16-17, 1975." Austin, TX: Center for Social Work Research, School of Social Work University of Texas at Austin, 1976.

Governor's Commission on the Status of Women. A Statistical Survey of Vermont Women in Five Areas of Leadership: State Government, Education, Banking, and Insurance, Judiciary, Health. Montpelier, VT: Governor8s Commission on the Status of Women, State of Vermont, 1985.

Gutek, B.A., C.Y. Nakamura, M. Gahart, J.W. Handschumacher & D. Russell. "Sexuality in the Workplace." Basic and Applied Social Psychology, Volume 1, 1980, pp. 255-265.

Gutek, B.A. & V. Dunwoody. "Understanding Sex in the Workplace," (in) Women and Work: An Annual Review, edited by A.H. Stromberg, L. Larwood, & B.A. Gutek, Volume 2, Newbury Park, CA: Sage Publications, 1987, pp. 249-269.

Harrison, A. Women in Kentucky State Government, 1940-1980. Frankfort: State Library, 1981.

Hildebrandt, Herbert William. A Managerial profile: The Woman Manager. Ann Arbor, MI: Division of Research, Graduate School of Business Administration, University of Michigan, 1985.

Johnson, Alicia. "New York State is Finding Jobs for Women." Management Review, Volume 77, May 1988, p.2.

Kentucky Legislative Research Commission. Salary Differentials Between Men and Women in Kentucky State Government. Frankfort: Kentucky Legislative Research Commission, 1983.

Kleeman, Katherine E. "Women in State Government: Looking Back, Looking Ahead. The Journal of State Government, Sep/Oct 1987, pp. 199-203.

Lacy, Gwynette Precia Ford. "An Evaluation of Attitudes Toward Women As Managers in a Government Setting." DAI 41/09A, p. 4116, 1979.

Mohapatra, Manindra, et al. "Public Service Values of Women and Minority Public Administrators: An Empirical Study of Kentucky State Public Managers. Paper presented at the Annual Meeting of the Indiana Academy of Social Sciences, Bloomington, Indiana, October 5, 1990.

Moore, G. "Women in the Ol-boy Network: The Case of New York State Government (in) Power Elites and Organizations edited by G.W. Domhoff, & T.R. Dye. Sage Focus Editions, Volume 20, Newbury park, CA: Sage Publications, 1987, pp. 63-84.

Radin, Beryl A. "Leadership Training for Women in State and Local Government." Public personnel Management, Volume 9, March/April 1980, pp. 52-57.

Rehfuss, John A. "A Representative bureaucracy: Women and Minority Executives in California Career Service." Public Administration Review, Volume 46, September/October 1986, pp. 454-460.

Rizzo, Ann-Marie. "Patterns of Person-group Relationships for Female and Male Mid-Level Managers in Three Governmental Agencies. DAI 36/bA, p. 6950, 1974.

Ross, Cvnthia and Robert England. "Stat. Governments' Sexual Harassment Policy Initiatives. "Public Administrative Review, Volume 47, Number 3, May/June 1987, pp. 259-262.

Sigelman, Lee. "The Curious Case of Women in State and Local Government." Social Science Quarterly, Volume 56, Number 4, March 1976, pp. 591-604.

Williams, Almano Duclo. "State Administrators' Attitudes Toward the Political Environment: The Impact of Gender." Mai 27/04, p. 459, 1989.

Williams, M. Lee. "Gender Differences and Public Sector Managers: Women's Perceptions of Equality in State Government." Paper presented at the International Communication Association Convention, Dublin, Ireland, June 24-28, 1990.

Young & Company, Arthur. A Comparable Worth Study of State of Michigan Job Classifications. Lansing: Office of Women and Work, Michigan Department of Labor, 1981.

XXVIII
WOMEN IN LOCAL ADMINISTRATION

Burns, R.A. Women in Municipal Management. Urban Data Service Report, Volume 12, Number 2, February 1980, pp. 1-12.

Cayer, N. Joseph. "Minorities and Women in Sate and Local Governments: 1973-75." Public Administration Review, Volume 40, September/October 1980, p. 446.

Coyle, Angela. "The Limits of Change: Local Government and Equal Opportunities for Women." Public Administration, Volume 67, Spring 1989, pp. 39-50.

Edson, S.K. Pushing the Limit: The Female Administrative Aspinamt. Albany: SUNY, 1988.

EEOC, Minorities and Women in State and Local Government 1975, Volume 1: United States Summary. Washington, DC: Government Printing Office, 1977.

Grant, J. "On How I Chose to Become a Feminist Planner." Town Planning Quarterly, Volume 62, Number 20, March 1981, pp.

Holley, Leta F. "Women in Executive and Managerial Positions in Omaha, Nebraska." Doctoral Thesis, University of Colorado, 1960.

Kaplan, Jane Rachel. "Sexism in Planning: A Woman Examines a Man's perception of Planning." Practical Planner, Volume S, Number 3, September 1978, pp. 35-37.

Nduom, Papa Kwesi. "Women in Municipal Management: Milwaukee Municipal Work Force." DAI 44/bA, 1982, p. 269.

Saltzstein, Alan and Grace Saltzstein. "The Reality of Equal Employment Compliance in Municipalities." State and Local Government Review, Volume IX, Number 3, September 1977, pp. 80-84

Shaul, Marnie S. "The Status of Women in Local Governments: An International Assessment." Public 'Administration Review, Volume 42, November/December 1982, pp. 491-500.

Sigelman, Lee. "The Curious Case of Women in State and Local Government." Social Science Quarterly, Volume 57, March 1976, pp. 591-604.

Slack, J.D. "Affirmative Action and City Managers: Attitudes Toward Recruitment of Women." Public Administration

Review, Volume 47, Number 2, March/April 1987, pp. 199-206.

Welch, Susan et al. "Correlates of Women's Employment in Local Governments." Urban Affairs Quarterly, Volume 18, June 1983, pp. 551-564.

XXIX
WOMEN PROFESSIONALS IN HEALTH CARE SYSTEMS

American Medical Association. Maternity Leave for Residents. Chicago, IL: American Medical Association, 1984.

Bernstein, Anne E. Women Treating Women: Case material from Women Treated by Female Psychoanalysts. New York, NY: International Universities Press, 1984.

Blackwell, Elizabeth. Pioneer Work in Opening the Medical profession to Women: Autobiographical Sketches. New York, NY: Schocken Books, 1977.

Bowman, Marjorie A. Stress and Women Physicians. New York, NY: Springer-Verlag, 1985.

Caplovitz, David. Student-faculty Relations in Medical School: A Study of Professional Socialization. New York, NY: Arno Press, 1980.

Carlton, Wendy. "In Our Professional Opinion...": The Primacy of Clinical Judgment Over Moral Choice. Notre Dame, IN: University of Notre Dame Press, 1978.

Christ, Louis W.A.C. Medical Students' Socialization Before and While at Medical School with particular Reference to Career Choice Changes. Ottawa: Canton University, 1971.

Davies, Gaye. "Managing Organizational Change: Strategies for the Female Health Care Supervisor." Health Care Supervisor, Volume 8, Number 4, July 1990, pp. 9-14.

Dempsey-Polan, Laura. "Women: Once and Future Leaders in Health Administration." Hospital and Health Services Administration, Volume 33, Number 1, Spring 1988, pp. 89-98.

DeMund, Mary. Women Physicians of Colorado. Denver, CO: Range Press, 1976.

Gardner, Elizabeth. "Information Bridge-Builder." Modern Healthcare, Volume 19, Number 52, December 29, 1989, p. 58.

Gill, Thelma. "Women as Managers: Implications for Occupational Therapy." British Journal of Occupational Therapy, Volume 49, Number 12, December 1986, pp. 385-388.

Greene, Carol. Elizabeth Blackwell, First Woman Doctor. Chicago, IL: Childrens Press, 1991.

Gulabacanda, Santabai. Sanganyajoge/Atmakathana. Pune: Srividya Prakasana, 1988.

Haas, Jack. Becoming Doctors: The Adoption of a Cloak of Competence. Greenwich, CN: JAI Press, 1987.

Hamilton, Jane Meier. Survival Skills for the New Nurse. Philadelphia, PA: Lippincott, 1986.

Hardy, Margaret E. Role Theory: Perspectives for Health professionals. New York, NY: Appleton-Century-Crosts, 1978.

Jacox, Ada Kathryn. "The Nurse's Cap: A case Study of Administrator - Nurse Conflict." DAI 31/06A, 1969, p. 3056.

Kang, Gay E. A Social-evolutionary Investigation of Factors Affecting Female Employment in the Medical profession. East Lansing, MI: Michigan State University, 1983.

Leserman, Jane. Men and Women in Medical School: How They change and Mow They Compare. New York, NY: Praeger, 1981.

Lorber, Judith. Women Physicians: Careers, Status, and Power. New York, NY: Tavistock Publications, 1984.

Moldow, Gloria. Women Doctors in Gilded-Age Washington: Race, Gender, and Professionalization. Urbana, IL: University of Illinois Press, 1987.

Myers, Loretta C. Socialization of Neophyte Nurses. Ann Arbor, MI: UMI Research Press, 1982.

Nebel, Diane. "Women in Environmental Health; Where They Have Been and Where They are Today." Journal of Environmental Health, Volume 52, September/October, 1988, pp. 24-25.

Ott, Mary Diederich. Women's participation in First-Professional Degree Programs in Medicine, Dentistry, Veterinary Medicine, and Law, 1969-70 Through 1974-75. Washington, DC: U.S. Dept. of Health, Education, and Welfare, Education Division, National Center for Education Statistics, 1976.

Parker, Beulah. The Evolution of a Psychiatrist: Memoirs of a Woman Doctor. New Haven: Yale University Press, 1987.

Perrone, Bobette. Medicine Women, Curanderas, and Women Doctors. Norman, OK: University of Oklahoma Press, 1989.

Sanders, H.R., J.M. Barnes, J.M. duplessis, A.G. Muller, and J.E. Mostert. "Aspects of Work of Women Medical Doctors in the Cape Province. A Preliminary Investigation." S. Afr. Med.

Journal, Volume 78, Number 10, November 17, 1990, pp. 598-602.

Schmalenberg, Claudia. coping with Reality Schock: The Voices of Experience. Wakefield, MA: Nursing Resources, 1979.

Schmude, Judy G. "The Gender Factor in Hospital Administration: An Analysis of the Relationship of the Strength of Attitudes Toward Women in Hospital Administration." DAI 45/02A, 1983, p. 373.

Shapiro, Eileen & Leah M. Lowenstein, editors. Becoming a Physician: Development of Values and Attitudes in Medicine. Cambridge, MA: Ballinger Publishing Co, 1979.

Shepherd, Marvin Dean. "Analysis of Practice Patterns, Stereotyping of Women as Managers and Perceptions of Women in Pharmacy by Men and Women Pharmacy School Graduates." DAI 42/013, 1980, p. 151.

Shuval, Judith T. Entering Medicine: The Dynamics of Transition: A Seven Year Study of Medical Education in Israel. Oxford, NY: Pergamon Press, 1980.

Simpson, Ida Harper. From Student to Nurse: A Longitudinal Study of Socialization. New York, NY: Casbridge University Press, 1979.

Smith, Elizabeth. A Woman With a Purpose: The Diaries of Elizabeth Smith, 1872-1884. Toronto; Buffalo: University of Toronto Press, 1980.

Steinsholt, I.M, E. Rygh & J. Thesen. "Women Physicians. Developmental Tendencies in Specialization and Career Patterns." Tidsskr-Nor-Laegeforen, Volume 110, Number 25, October 20, 1990. pp. 3255-3259.

Vertinsicy, Patricia A. The Eternally Wounded Woman: Women, Doctors, and Exercise in the Late Nineteenth Century. New York, NY: St. Martin's Press, 1990.

Walsh, Mary Roth. "Doctors Wanted, No Women Need Apply": Sexual Barriers in the Medical Profession, 1835-1975. New Haven: Yale University Press, 1977.

Wehl, Yaakov. House Calls to Eternity: The Story of Dr. Selma Wehl, Heroine of Medical Practice and Torah living. Brooklyn, NY: Mesorah Publications, 1987.

XXX
WOMEN SOCIAL SCIENTISTS

Bell, Cohn. "The SSRC: Restructured and Defended," (in) Social Researching: Politics, Problems, Practice, edited by Cohn Bell and Helen Roberts, London; Boston: Routledge & K. Paul, 1984.

Bowman, Kathleen. New Women in Social Sciences. Mankato, MN: Creative Education; Chicago: Childrens Press, 1976.

Collins, H.M. "Researching Spoonbending," (in) Social Researching: Politics, Problems, practice, edited by Cohn Bell and Helen Roberts, London: Routledge and K. Paul, 1984.

Deegan, Mary Jo. editor. Women in Sociology: A Bio-Bibliographical Sourcebook, Lincoln, Nebraska: Greenwood Press, 19—.

Finch, Janet. "It's Great to Have Someone To Talk to," (in) Social Researching: politics, problems, practice, edited by Cohn Bell and Helen Roberts, London: Routledge and K. Paul, 1984.

Fitzpatrick, Ellen F. Endless Crusade: Women Social Scientists and Progressive Reform. New York: Oxford University Press, 1990.

Frankenberg, Ronald. "Incidence or incidents: political and Methodological Underpinnings of a Health Research Process in a Small Town," (in) Social Researching: politics, Problems, practice, edited by Cohn Bell and Helen Roberts, London: Routledge and K. Paul, 1984.

Graham, Hilary. H Surveying Through Stories," (in) Social Researching: politics, problems, practice, edited by Cohn ~ell and Helen Roberts, London: Routledge and K. Paul, 1984.

Hamer, Jalna and Diana Leonard. "Negotiating the problem: The DHSS and Research on Violence in Marriage," (in) Social Researching: politics, Problems, practice, edited by Cohn Bell and Helen Roberts, London: Routledge and K. Paul, 1984.

Harding, Sandra. Feminism and Methodology: Social Science Issues. Bloomington, IN: Indiana University Press, 1987.

James, Nicky. "A Postscript to Nursing," (in) Social Researching: Politics, Problems, Practice, edited by Cohn Bell and Helen Roberts, London: Routledge and K. Paul, 1984.

Jenkins, Richard, "Bringing it All Back: An Anthropology in Belfast," (in) Social Researching: Politics, Problems, Practice, edited by Cohn Bell and Helen Roberts, London: Routledge and K. Paul, 1984.

Platt, Jennifer. "The Affluent Worker Re-Visited," (in) Social Researching: Politics, problems, Practice, edited by Cohn Bell and Helen Roberts, London: Routledge and K. Paul, 1984.

Roberts, Helen. "Putting the Show on the Road," (in) Social Researching: politics, problems, Practice, edited by Colin Bell and Helen Roberts, London: Routledge and K. Paul, 1984.

Wright, Charles Robert. "The Effect of Training in Social Research on the Development of Professional Attitudes, New York: Arno Press, 1980.

XXXI
STRATEGIES OF SUCCESS FOR WOMEN MANAGERS

American Association of University Women. Women On Their Way: Career Women in Massachusetts. Boston: AAUW, 1979.

Bern, Paula. How to Work for a Woman Boss, Even if You'd Rather Not. New York: Dodd, Mead, 1987.

Berryman-Fink, Cynthia & Virginia Eman Wheeless. "Effects of Attitudes Toward Women and Women in Management on Perceived Communication Competencies of Women Managers." Paper presented at the Annual Meeting of the Western Speech Communication Association, Seattle, WA, February 18-21, 1984.

Bhaghat, R. and M. Chassie. "Determinants of Organizational Commitment in Working Women: Some Implications for Organizational Integration." Journal of Occupational Behavior, Number 2, 1981, pp. 17-30

Bohigian, Valerie. Ladybucks. New York, NY: Dod, Mead, 1987.

Brothers, Joyce. The Successful Woman: How You Can Have a Career, a Husband, and a Family — and Not Feel Guilty About It. New York: Simon and Schuster, 1988.

Brownell, Judi. "Perceptions of Effective Listeners: A Management Study." Journal of Business Communication, Volume 27, Number 4, Fall 1990, pp 401-415.

Camnings, Kathleen and Claude Montmarquette. "Managerial Momentum: A Simultaneous Model of the Career Progress of Male and Female Managers." Industrial and Labor Relations Review, Number 44, January 1991, pp. 212-228.

Carr-Ruffino, Norma. The Promotable Woman: Becoming a Successful Manager. Belmont, CA: Wadsworth Publishing Co., 1985.

Catalyst Staff. Upward Mobility. New York: Holt, Rinehard and Winston, 1982.

Cole, Diane. Hunting the Headhunters: A Woman's Guide. New York: Simon & Schuster, 1988.

Collins, Eliza G.C. "Dearest Amanda—": An Executive's Advice to Her Daughter. New York: Harper & Row, 1984.

Collins, Nancy W. Women Leading: Making Tough Choices on the Fast Track. Lexington, MA: S. Greene Press, 1988.

Cooper, Cary L. Practical Approaches to Women's Career Development: A Report on the Conference at St. Hugh's College, Oxford, on September 16-17, 1981. Moorfoot, Sheffield: Training Services, Manpower Services Commission, 1983.

Crain, Sharie. Taking Stock: A Woman's Guide to Corporate Success. Chicago: Regnery, 1977.

Crowley, Mary C. Women Who Win. Old Tappan, NY: F.M. Revell Co., 1979.

Darwent, Charles. "New Girls' Networks." Management Today (UK) January 1990, pp. 68-69.

Dunlap, Jan. Personal and Professional Success for Women. Englewood Cliffs, NJ: Prentice-Hall, 1972.

Fenn, Margaret. Making It In Management: A Behavioral Approach for Women Executives. Englewood Cliffs, NJ: Prentice-Hall, 1978.

Fields, Suzanne. '1Flirting with the Feminist Mystique." Business Month, Volume 136, Number 5, November 1990, pp. 11-12.

Fogarty, Michael Patrick. Women and Top Jobs: The Next Move. London: P.E.P., 1972.

Foxworth, Jo. Boss Lady: An Executive Woman Talks About Making It. New York: Crowell, 1978.

Foxworth, Jo. Wising Up: The Mistakes Women Make in Business and How to Avoid Them. New York, NY: Delacorte Press, 1980.

Garland, H. & K.H. Price. "Attitudes Toward Women in Management and Attributions for Their Success and Failure in a Managerial Position." Journal of Applied Psychology, Number 62, 1977, pp. 29-33.

Garland, Howare, Karen F. Hale and Michael Burnson. "Attributions for the Success and Failure of Female Managers: A Replication and Extension." Psychology of Women Quarterly, Volume 7, Winter 1982, pp. 155-162

Gervais, Pamela Erickson, Pam Holsinger, & Kamala Bremer. "Advancement of Women's Careers in Public Service." Paper presented at the women in the Year 2000 Conference, Portland, OR, September 1986.

Grewe-Partsch, Marianne and Gertrude J. Robinson, editors. Women, Communication, and Careers. Munchen, New York: K.G. Saur, 1980.

Gummer, Burton. "The Organization Woman: Poor Copy or Catalyst for Change?" Administration in Social Work, Volume 14, Number 3, 1990, pp. 111-129.

Haccoun, D.M., R.R. Haccoun & C. Sallay. "Sex Differences in the Appropriateness of Supervisory Styles: A Non-management View." Journal of Applied Psychology, Number 63, 1978, pp. 124-127.

Halcomb, Ruth. Women Making It: Patterns and Profiles of Success. New York: Atheneum, 1979.

Heilman, M.E. & R.A. Guzzo. "The Perceived Causes of Work Success as a Mediator of Sex Discrimination in organizations." Organizational Behavior and Human Performance, Number 21, 1978, pp. 346-357.

Hersh-Cochran, Mona S. Executive Women in the Dallas/Fort Worth Metroplex: Significant Problems and Successful Strategies. Denton, TX: Department of Business and Economics, Texas Woman's University, 1987.

Higginson, M. Valliant. The Ambitious Woman's Guide to a Successful Career. New York, NY: AMACOM, 1980.

Highman, Edith L. The Organization Woman: Building a Career—An Inside Report. New York, NY: Human Sciences Press, 1985.

Hey, Judith. "Skills of Women Needed at the Top." Executive Excellence, Volume 7, Number 6, June 1990, pp. 14-15.

Hunsaker, Johanna. Strategies and Skills for Managerial Women. Cincinnati, OH: South-Western Publishing Co., 1986.

Ilich, John. Successful Negotiating Skills for Women. Reading, MA: Addison-Wesley, 1981.

Jensen, Marlene. Women Who Want to be Boss: Business Revelations and Success Strategies From America's Top Female Executives. Garden City, NY: Doubleday, 1987.

Keown, C.F. & A.L. Keown. "Success Factors for Corporate Women Executives." Group and Organization Studies, Number 7, 1982, pp. 445-456.

Kerr, Susan "Trying to Maintain a Breakneck Pace." Datamation, Volume 33, October 15, 1987, p. 131.

Korabik, Karen and Roya Ayman. "Should Women Managers Have to Act Like Men?" Journal of Management Development (UK), Volume 8, Number 6, 1989, pp. 23-32.

Kushell, E. & R. Newton. "Gender, Leadership Style, and Subordinate Satisfaction: An Experiment." Sex Roles, Volume 14, Number 3/4, 1986, pp. 203-209.

Larwood, Laurie & Mindy Kaplan. "Job Tactics of Women in Banking." Group and Organization Studies. Volume 5, Number 1, March 1980, pp. 70-78.

Levins, Marjorie R., et al. Women Achievers: A Series of Dialogues From the Womanagement Process. New York: American Telephone and Telegraph Co., 1977

Loden, M. Feminine Leadership or How To Make it in Business Without Being One of the Boys. New York: Times Book, 1985.

Long, Bonita C. "Relation Between Coping Strategies, Sex-Types Traits and Environmental Characteristics: A Comparison of Male and Female Managers." Journal of Counseling Psychology, Volume 37, Number 2, April 1990, pp. 185-194.

Loring, Rosalind K. Breakthrough: Women into Management. New York: Van Nostrand Reinhold Co., 1972.

McKeen, Carol A. Work Experiences and Career Success of Managerial and Professional Women. Kingston, Ont.: Queen's University, School of Business, Research Program, 1990.

Mead, Margaret et al. Women Achievers: A Series of Dialogues from the Womanagement Process. New York: American Telephone and Telegraph Co., 1978.

Melia, Jinx. Breaking into the Boardroom: When Talent and Hard Work Aren't Enough. New York: Putnam, 1987.

Mitchell, Charlene. The Extra Edge: Success Strategies for Women: A Woman's Guide to Total Professional Style. Washington, D.C.: Acropolis Books, 1983.

Morrison, Ann M. Randall P. White and Ellen Van Velsor. "Executive Women: Substance Plus Style." Psychology Today, Volume 21, Number 8, August 1987, pp. 18-26.

Neltom, Sharon and Karen Berney. "Women: The Second Wave — Billion-Dollar Women." Nation's Business, Volume 75, Number 5, May 1987, p. 24.

Newton, Derek A. Think Like a Man, Act Like a Lady, Work Like a Dog. Garden City, NY: Doubleday, 1979.

North, Susann. Traveling Alone: A Practical Guide for Businesswomen. New York: Sovereign Books, 1980.

Northcutt, Cecilia Ann. Successful Career Women: Their Professional and Personal Characteristics. New York: Greenwood Press, 1991.

Osborm, R.N. and W.M. Vicars. "Sex Stereotyoes An Artifact in Leader Behavior and Subordinates Satisfaction Analysis." Academy of Management Journal, Volume 19, September, 1976, pp. 439-449.

Patrick, Patricia Ann. "An Investigation of the Progress and Problems of Women in Managerial Positions in Businesses and Other Institutions in the New Orleans Area." Doctoral Thesis, University of Mississippi, 1979.

Paterson, Judith. Be Somebody: A Biography of Marguerite Rawalt. Austin, TX: Eakin Press, 1986.

Peskin, Dean B. Womaning: Overcoming Male Dominance on Executive Row. Port Washington, NY: Ashley Books, 1982.

Peters, L.H., J.R. Terborg, & J. Taynor. "Women As Managers Scale: A Measure of Attitudes Toward Women in Management Positions." JSAS Catalog of Selected Documents in Psychology, Volume 4, Number 27, Ms. 585, 1974.

Petty, M.M. & N.S. Brunning. "A Comparison of Relationships Between Subordinates' Perceptions of Supervisory Behavior and Measures of Subordinates;' Job Satisfaction for Male and Female Leaders." Acad. Mgmt. J., Number 23, 1980, pp. 717-725.

Pilotta, Joseph J., editor. Women in Organizations: Barriers and Breakthroughs. Prospect Heights, IL: Waveland Press, 1983.

Post, Linda Currey. "View From the Top: Women Executives in Communication." Communication World, Volume 4, Number 3, February 1987, pp. 17-19.

Powell, Gary N. and 0. Anthony Butterfield. "The 'Good Manager': Did Androgyny Fare Better in the 19805?" Group and organization Studies, Volume 14, Number 2, June 1989, pp. 216-233.

Rice, R.W., L.R. Bender & A.G. Vitters. 1'Leader Sex, Follower Attitudes Toward Women and Leadership Effectiveness: A Laboratory Experiment." Organizational Behavior and Hunan Performance, Volume 25, 1980, pp. 46-78.

Rich-Mccoy, Lois. Late Bloomer: Profiles of Women Who Found Their True Calling. New York: Harper & Row, 1980.

Rizzo, Ann-Marie. The Integration of Women in Management: A Guide for Human Resources and Management Development Specialists. New York: Quorum Books, 1990.

Rose, Suzanna editor. Women's Careers: Pathways and Pitfalls. New York: Praeger, 1988.

Rossman, Marge. When the Headhunter Calls: A Guide for Women in Management." Chicago: Contemporary Books, 1981.

Royal CBS Publishing editor. success Secrets: How Eighteen Everyday Women Became Fortune Builders and Famous Speakers. Glendora, CA: Royal CBS Pub., 1978.

Rynes, S. & B. Rosen. "A Comparison of Male and Female Reactions to Career Advancement Opportunities." Journal of vocational Behavior, Number 22, 1983, pp. 105-116.

Sandroff, Ronni. "Action Plan for Success." Working Woman, Volume 14, Number 10, October 1989, pp. 106-112.

Scollard, Jeannette Reddish. No-Nonsense Management Tips for Women. New York: Simon & Schuster: pocket Books, 1983.

Shockley-Zalabak, Pamela; Constance Courtney and Donald Dean Morley. "The Female Professional: perceived Communication Prof iciencies as Predictors of organizational Advancement." Human Relations, Volume 41, July 1988, pp. 553-567.

Skinner, Zenobia Middleton. "Impact, Influence, and perception of Networking Among Women Employees in the Commonwealth of Kentucky. "MAI 27/04, 1989, p. 459.

Slaney, R.B. & M. Caballero. "Changing Male Attitudes Toward Women's Career Development: An Exploratory Study." Journal of counseling Psychology, Volume 30, 1983, pp. 126-129.

Smith, Kenwyn K., Valerie M. Simmons, & Tern B. Thames. "Fix the Women." Journal of Applied Behavioral Science, Volume 25, Number 1, 1989, pp. 11-29.

Spruell, Geraldine R. "Making It, Big Time—Is It Really Tougher for Women?" Training and Development Journal, Volume 39, Number 8, Aug 1985, pp. 30-33.

Stanford, Susan M. "Attitudes Towards Women: Critical Background Predictors and the Effect of a Managerial Development and Feminist Awareness Seminar. Thesis, Northwestern University,

Stashow, Gloria. Careers in Management for the New Woman. New York: F. Watts1 1978.

Stewart, Nathaniel. The Effective Woman Manager: Seven Vital Skills for Upward Mobility. New York: Wiley, 1978.

Terborg, J.R. & P. Shingledecker. "Employee Reactions to Supervision and Work Evaluation as a Function of Subordinate and Manger Sex." Sex Roles, Volume 9, Number 7, 1983, pp. 813-824.

Tomkeiwicz, J. & O.C. Brenner. "Organizational Dilemma: Sex Differences in Attitudes Toward Women Held by Future Managers." Personnel Administrator, Number 277, 1982, pp. 62-65.

Treuille, Beverly Benz. Managing It All: Time-Saving Ideas for Career, Family, Relationships & Self. New York: MasterMedia, 1988.

Warihay, P.D. "The Climb to the Top: Is the Network the Route for Women?" Personnel Administrator, Volume 25, Number 4, 1980, pp. 55-69.

Wilkes, Mary. The Women's Edge. Marimac Publishing, 1985.

XXXII
EMPOWERMENT OF WOMEN MANAGERS AND PROFESSIONALS

Arroba, Tanya and Kim James. "Are Politics Palatable to Women Managers? How Women Can Make Wise Moves at Work." Women in Management Review (UK), Volume 3, Number 3, 1988, pp. 123-130.

Bookman, Ann & Sandra Morgen, editors. Women and the Politics of Empowerment. Philadelphia: Temple University Press, 1988.

Bools, Barbara. Power Failure: Why Women said "no" to Top Management Positions - Six Inside Stories to Help Others Say "Yes". New York: St. Martin's press, 2989.

Brass, Daniel J. "Men's and Women's Networks: A Study of Interaction Patterns and Influence in an Organization." Academy of Management Journal, Volume 28, Number 2, 1985, pp. 337-343.

Champion, Donald L. "A Comparison of Men and Women Managers on preferences for Organizational Conflict Management." Doctoral Thesis, Florida State University, 1979.

Chusmir, Leonard, H. and Barbara Parker. "Dimensions of Need for Power: personalized vs. Socialized Power in Female and Male Managers." Sex Roles Volume 11, November 1984, pp. 759-769.

Cockburn, C. Machinery of Dominance: Women, Men and Technical Know-how. London: Pluto press, 1985.

Cohen, Sherry Suib. "Beyond Macho — The Power of Womanly Management." Working Woman, Volume 14, Number 2, February 1989, pp. 77-81.

Cohen Sherry Suib. Tender Power: A Revolutionary Approach to Work and Intimacy. Reading, MA: Addison-Wesley, 1988.

Cutmore-Smith, Julya. "Exploring the Dark:' Women, power and Work." Equal Opportunities International (UK) Volume 5, Number 3/4, 1986, pp. 32-35.

Davis, Andrea R. "Power Players: Ten Afro-American Women in the Corporate World." Essence Magazine, Volume 20, March 1990, p. 71.

Dexter, C.R. "Women and the Exercise of Power in organizations: From Ascribed to Achieved Status." (in) Women and Work 1: An Annual Review edited by L. Larwood, A.H. Stromberg, and B.A Gutek, Beverly Hills, CA: Sage publications, 1985, pp. 239-258.

Duane, Michael J. "Sex Differences in Styles of Conflict Management." Psychological Reports, Volume 65, Number 3, Pt. 1, December 1989, pp. 1033-1034.

Fagenson, Ellen A "Perceived Masculine and Feminine Attributes Examined as a Function of Individuals' Sex and Level in the Organizational Power Hierarchy: A Test of Four Theoretical perspectives." Journal of Applied Psychology, Volume 75, Number 2, April 1990, pp. 204-211.

Fairhurst, G.t. & B.K. Snavely. "Majority and Token Minority Group Relationships: Power Acquisition and Communication. 11 Academy of Management Review, Number 8, 1983, pp. 292-300.

Hearn, Jeff & Wendy Parkin.Sex at Work: The Power and Paradox of Organization Sexuality. New York:. St Martin's Press, 1987.

Hirschowitz, R. The Power Motive and Its Expression in a Group of English-speaking South African Women." Pretoria: Human Sciences Research Council, 1986.

Jacobson, Aileen. Women in Charge: Dilemmas of Women in Authority. New York, NY: Van Nostrand Reinhold, 1985.

Kapalka, George M. and Juliana R. Lachenmeyr. "Sex-role Flexibility, Locus of Control, and Occupational Status." Sex-Roles, Volume 19, Number 7-8, October 1988, pp. 417-427.

Kipnis, D., S. Schmidt, & I. Wilkinson. "Intraerganizational Influence Tactics: Explorations in Getting One's Way. " Journal of Applied Psychology, Number 65, 1980, pp. 440-452.

Mainiero, L.A. "Coping with Powerlessness: The Relationship of Gender and Job Dependency to Empowerment Strategy Usage." Administrative Science Quarterly, Volume 31, 1986, pp. 633-653.

McCall, Ava Louise. "Learning to Teach: Women's Struggle for Empowerment." Doctoral Thesis, Indiana University, 1987.

Miller, Patricia M. Powerful Leadership Skills for Women. Shawnee Mission, KS: National Press Publications, 1988.

Pickering, Tonya H. and Brian H. Kleiner. "Women: Power and Advancement." Equal Opportunities International (UK), Volume 8, Number 3, 1989, pp. 24-27.

Ragins, B.R. & E. Sundstrom. "Gender and Power in Organizations: A Longitudinal Perspective, Psychological Bulletin, Number 105, 1989, pp. 51-88.

Ragins, Belle Rose. "Power and Gender Congruency Effects in Evaluations of Male and Female Managers." Journal of Management. Volume 15, Number 1, March 1989, pp. 65-76.

Ragins, B.R. "Power and Leadership Effectiveness: A Study of Subordinate Evaluations of Male and Female Leaders." Doctoral dissertation: University of Tennessee, 1987.

Salancik, G.R. & J. Pfeffer. "The Bases and Use of Power in organizational Decision Making: The Case of a University." Administrative Science Quarterly. Number 19, 1974, pp. 453-473.

Salancik, G.R. & J. Pfeffer. "Who Gets Power - and How They Hold On To It: A Strategic Contingency Model of Power." Organizational Dynamics, Volume 5, Number 3, 1977, pp. 3-21.

Sheppard, D. "Sexuality and Social Construction of Organizational Power: The Image and Self-image of Women Managers." (in) Sexuality in the Organization, edited by J. Hearn, G. Burrell, D. Sheppard, & P. Tancred-Sheriff. London: Sage, 1989, pp. 139-157.

Smith, E.L. & M. Grenier. "Sources of Organizational Power for Overcoming Structural Obstacles." Sex Roles, Number 8, 1982, pp. 733-746.

St. Yves, A. F. Contant, M. H. Freeston, J. Huard, et al. "Locus of Control in Women Occupying Middle-Management and Non-management Positions." Psychological Reports, Volume 65, Number 2, October 1989, pp. 483-486.

Suojanen, waino W. Tricia Working, Jane S. Goldner, Kelley Ort and Sherrie Cribbe. "The Emergence of the Type E Woman." Business, Volume 37, Number 1, Jan/Feb/Mar 1987, pp. 3-7.

Tewari, Harish C. "A Study of Women Managers Need for Achievement, Affiliation, and Power." DAI 39/OSA, 1977, p. 3040.

Thompson, M.E. "Sex Differences: Differential Access to Power or Sex Role Socialization?: Sex Roles, Number 7, 1981, pp. 413-424.

Tremain, Elizabeth J. Evelene: The Troubleshooter was a Lady. Lincoln, NE: Foundation Books, 1985.

Wiley, M.G. & A. Eskilson. "The Interaction of Sex and Power Base on Perceptions of Managerial Effectiveness." Academy of Management Journal, Number 25, 1982, pp. 671-677.

Winsor, Jerry L. "Sex and Power in the Office: An Overview of Gender and Executive Power Perceptions in Organizations." (in) Professional Communication in the Modern World: Proceedings of the 31st Southeast Convention of the American Business Communication Association, Hammond, LA, April 1984.

XXXIII
STRESS MANAGEMENT AND MANAGERIAL WOMEN

Adkinson, Judith A. "Promoting Women in Educational Administration: A Case Study of Conflict and Stress." Administrator's Notebook, Volume 27, Number 5, pp. 1-4, 1978.

Bartol, K.M. & M.S. Wortman, Jr. "Sex of Leader and Subordinate to Role Stress: A Field Study." Sex Roles, Volume 5, 1979, PP. 513-518.

Bowman, Marjorie A. Stress and Women Physicians. New York: Springer-Verlag, 1990.

Bromet, E.J.et al. "Epidemiology of Depression and Alcohol Abuse/ Dependence in a Managerial and Professional Work Force. Journal of Occupational Med., Volume 32, Number 10, October 1990, pp. 989-995.

Chusmir, Leonard H. and Victoria Franks. "Stress and the Woman Manager." Training & Development Journal, Volume 42, Number 10, October 1988, pp. 66-70.

Cooper, C. & M.J. Davidson. High Pressure. Working Lives of Women Managers. Glasgow: Fontanta, 1982.

Davidson, J. J. & C.L. Cooper. "Occupational Stress in Female Managers. A Comparative Study." Journal of Management Studies, Volume 21, Number 2, 1984, pp. 185-205.

Davidson, M.J. & C.L. Cooper. Stress and the Woman Manager. Oxford: Martin Robertson, 1983.

Etzion, Dalia. "Burning Out in Management: A Comparison of Women and Men in Matched Organizational Positions. Special Issue: women in Israel. Israel Social Science Research, Volume 5, Number 1-2, 1987, pp. 147-163.

Frankenhaeuser, Marianne et al. "Stress On and Of f the Job As Related to Sex and Occupational Statue in White-Collar Workers." Journal of Organizational Behavior (UK) Volume 10, Number 4, October 1989, pp. 321-346.

Hantrais, Linda. Managing Professional and Family Life: A Comparative Study of British and French Women. Aldershot, Hants, England; Brookfield, VT., USA: Dartmouth, 1990.

Jacobs, Nehama and Sarah Hardesty. "why Some Women are Dropping Out." Management Review, Volume 76, Number 6, June 1987, pp. 61-63.

Jick, Todd D. and Linda F. Mitz. "Sex Differences in Work Stress." Journal of Library Administration, Volume 7, Number 1, Spring 1986.

Johnson, Maryfran. "Life in IS: Women Under Glass." Computerworld, Volume 24, Number 49, December 3, 1990, pp. 93-95.

LaRosa, Judith J. "Executive Women and Health: Perceptions and practices. American Journal of Public Health, Volume 80, December 1990, pp. 1450-1454.

Lee, Valerie. Pregnancy in the Executive Suite. McAllen, TX: Success Publications, 1988.

Nelson, D.L. & J.C. Quick. "Professional Women: Are Distress and Disease Inevitable?" Academy of Management Review, Volume 10, 1985, pp. 206-218.

Nelson, Debra L. & James C. Quick. "Men and Women of the Personnel Profession: Some Differences and Similarities in Their Stress." Stress Medicine, Volume 5, Number 3, July-September 1989, pp. 145-152.

Nivens, Maryruth K. "Handling Conflict and Stress (Women as Their Own Worse Enemies)." Paper presented at Up the Managerial Ladder, a Conference for Women, Montgomery, AL< November 2, 1979.

Orodenker, Sylvia Z. "Family Caregiving in a Changing Society: The Effects of Employment on Caregiver Stress." Family and Community Health, Volume 12, Number 4, February 1990, pp. 58-70.

Parasuraman, S. & M. Cleek. "Sex Versus Job Role: A Study of Role Stressors, Stress Reactions, and Coping Among Managers." Eastern Academy of Management Proceedings, 1-4, 1982.

Pendergrass, Virginia E. & Nancy M. Ostrove. "A Survey of Stress in Women in Policing." Journal of Police Science and Administration, Volume 12, September 1984, pp.303-309.

Pharr, Ann E. "Effects of Stress on Women Managers in Washington, D.C." DAI 49/IIA, 1988, p. 3502.

Smith, Frances B. "Stemming the Exodus of Women Managers." Credit, Volume 16, Number 2, Mar/Apr 1990, pp. 28-29.

Smith, Kenneth et al. "Stress in AWSCPA Members." The Women CPA, July 1989, pp. 26-29.

Spilman, M.A. "Gender Differences in Worksite Health Promotion Activities. Special Issues; Worksite Health Promotion." Social Science and Medicine, Volume 26, Number 5, 1988, pp. 525-535.

XXXIV
MANAGERIAL TRAINING FOR WOMEN PROFESSIONALS

Ann, Kenneth & Michelle Saint-Germain. "Public Administration Education and the Status of Women." American Review of Public Administration, Volume 18, Number 3, September 1988, pp. 297-307.

Alban Metcalfe, Beverly. "What Motivates Managers: An Investigation by Gender and Sector of Employment." Public Administration, Number 67, Spring 1989, pp. 95-108.

Ashburn, Elizabeth Alexander. "Influences and Motivations for Black and White Women to Attain Positions in a Male-dominated Profession." Thesis, University of New York at Buffalo, 1979.

Ashridge Management College. Employee Potential: Issues in the Development of Women. London: Institute of Personnel Management, 1980.

Barbee, Margaret S. "Skill Assessment and Training for Women Managers." DAI 37/123, 1976, p. 6386.

Bartol, K.M. "Relationship of Sex and Professional Training Area to Job Orientation." Journal of Applied Psychology, Volume 61, 1976, pp. 368-370.

Bern, Sandra L. & Daryl J. Bern. "Training the Woman to Know Her Place: The Power of a Nonconscious Ideology." (in) Women's Role in Contemporary Society, 1972, pp. 101-115.

Berryman-Fink, Cynthia and Charles B. Fink. "Optimal Training for Opposite-sex Managers." Training and Development Journal, Volume 39, Number 2, February 1985, pp. 27-29.

Berryman-Fink, Cynthia. "Perceptions of Women's Communication Skills Related to Managerial Effectiveness." Paper presented at the Annual Meeting of the Communication Language and Gender Conference, Athens, OH, October 1982.

Banksby, Margaret. "In Their Own Words: The Clues to How to Develop Women Managers." Women in Management Review (UK), Volume 3, Number 2, 1987, pp. 71-77.

Brandt, Ronald S. "Coaching and Staff Development: Readings from Educational Leadership. Alexandria, VA: Association for Supervision and Curriculum Development, 1989.

Brown, M. Helen. "Women's Centres: Relationships Between Values and Action." Journal of Management Studies, Volume 27, Number 6, November 1990.

Buchanan, Estill. "The Growing Opportunities for Women in Management.: Management Review, Volume LVII, Number 8, September 1968, p. 62.

Burrow, Martha G. Developing Women Managers: What Needs To Be Done? New York: AMACOM, 1978.

Burrow, M.G. "Women-A Worldwide View of Their Management Development Needs," A special report to AMA members, New York: America Management Association, 1976.

Chanana, Karuna, editor. Socialization, Education, and Women: Explorations in Gender, Identity. New Delhi: Orient Longman, 1988.

Chusmir, Leonard H. "Job Commitment and the Organizational Woman." Academy of Management Review, Volume 7, Number 4, 1982, pp. 595-602.

Crawford, Jacquelyn S. Women in Middle Management: Selection, Training, Advancement, Performance. Ridgewood, NJ: Forkner Publishing Corporation., 1977.

Feuer, Dale. "How Women Manage." Training, Volume 25, Number S, August 1988, pp. 23-31.

Fonda, Nickie. "Single-Sex vs. Mixed-Sex Training." Journal of European Industrial Training (UK) Volume 10, Number 7, 1986, pp. 28-33.

Gomez-Mejia, Luis R. & David B. Balkin. "Can Internal Management Training Programs narrow the Male-Female Gap in Managerial Skills?" Personnel Administrator, Volume 25, Number 5, May 1980, pp. 77-83.

Gordon, F. and M. Strober, editors. Bringing Women into Management. New York: McGraw-Hill, 1975.

Gordonl Francine E. Perspectives on Bringing Women into Management. Menlo Park, CA: Stanford Research Institute, 1976.

Hammond, Valerie. "Management Training for Women." Journal of European Industrial Training (UK), Volume 10, Number 7, 1986, pp. 15-22.

Henmig, M. "Career Development for Women Executives." PhD Dis8ertation1 Harvard University, 1971.

Jacklin, C.N. & E.E. Maccoby. "Sex Differences and Their Implications for Management." (in) Bringing Women into Management, edited by F. Gordon and M. Strober. New York: McGraw-Hill, 1975, pp. 23-39.

Lavoie, Dma. "Formal and Informal Management Training Programs for Women in Canada: Who Seems to be Doing a Good Job?" Journal of Business Ethics (Netherlands) Volume 9, Number 4,5, Apr/May 1990, pp. 377-383.

Lockheed, N.E. & K.P. Hall. "Conceptualizing Sex as a Status Characteristic: Applications to Leadership Training Strategies." Journal of Social Issues, Summer 1976, pp. 111-124.

Loughran, Tim. "Corning Tries to Break the Glass Ceiling." Business & Society Review, Number 76 Winter 1991, pp. 52-55.

Manning, Marilyn Jakad. Leadership Skills for Women. Los Altos, CA: Crisp Publications, 1989.

McLane, H.S. Selecting, Developing and Retaining Women Executives. New York: Van Nostrand, 1980.

Miner, J.B. "Motivational Potential for Upgrading Among Minority and Female Managers." Journal of Applied Psychology, Volume 62, 1977, pp. 691-692.

Miner, J.B. "Motivation to Manage Among Women: Studies of Business Managers and Educational Administrators." Journal of Vocational Behavior, Volume 5, 1974, pp. 197-208.

Moses, Joel C. '1lndoctrination as a Female Political Role in the Soviet Union." Comparative Policies, Volume VIII, Number 4, July 1976, pp. 525-547.

Nowak, Margaret J. and Steven Ward. "Determinants of Women's Career Aspirations." Equal Opportunities International (UK) Volume 8, Number 6, 1989, pp. 1-6.

Parasuraman, Saroj and Magid Igbaria. "An Examination of Gender Differences in the Determinants of Computer Anxiety and Attitudes Toward Microcomputers Among Managers." International Journal of Man Machine Studies, Volume 32, Number 3, Mar 1990, pp. 327-340.

Parikh, Indira J. Management Training: Mixed Groups or Single Sex Groups. Ahmedabad, India: Indian Institute of Management,

Parrish, J.B. "Top Level Training of Women in the United States, 1900-1960." J. Nat. ASSOC. Women Deans & Couns., Volume 25, 1962, pp. 76-83.

Radin, Beryl. "Leadership Training for Women in State and Local Government." Public Personnel Management, Volume IX, Number 2, March/April 1980, pp. 55-58.

Reavley, Martha. "Who Needs Training: Women or organizations?" Journal of Management Development (UK) Volume 8, Number 6 1989, pp. 55-60.

Rothfeld, Rae. "Women in Management: Can Education Fill the Gap?" (in) Women and Management: An Expanding Role edited by D.O. Jewell, Atlanta, GA: Georgia State University Publishing Services Division, 1977.

Rothwell, Sheila. "Management Courses and Women." Ergonomics, Volume 27, Number 5, May 1984, pp. 547-556.

Schner, Joy A. & Frieda Reitman. "Effects of Employment Gaps on the Careers of M.B.A.'s: More Damaging for Men Than for Women?" Academy of Management Journal, Volume 33, Number 2, 1990, pp. 391-406.

Shockley, P.S. & C.M. Stanley. "Women in Management Training Programs: What They Think About Key Issues.'1 Public Personnel Management, Number 9, 1980, pp. 214-224.

Solomon, E.E., R.C. Bishop, & R.K. Bresser. "organizational Moderators of Gender Differences in Career Development: A Facet Classification." Journal of Vocational BEhavior, Volume 29, 1986, pp. 27-41.

Smith, Mike et al. A Development Programme for Women in Management. Aldershop, Hampshire, England; Brookfiled, VT. USA: Gower, 1984.

Staley, Constance C. and Pamela Schockley-Zabalak. "Communication Proficiency and Future Training Needs of the Female Professional: Self-Assessment vs. Supervisors' Evaluations," Human Relations, Volume 39, 1986, pp. 891-902.

Stern, Barbara B. "Women in Managerial Roles: AN Innovative Course for Women Marketing Students." Journal of Education for Business, Volume 61, Number 3, December 1985, pp. 128-131.

Steward, Nathaniel. The Effective Woman Manager: Seven Vital Skills for Upward Mobility. New York: John Wiley, 1978.

Toyne, Marguerite C. "Woman's Career Path to Management Through Effective Communication." Journal of Business Communication, Volume 15, Number 1, ????, p. 19-28.

United States Women's Bureau. College Women Seven Years After Graduation:Resurvey of Women Graduates - Class of 1957. Washington, D.C., 1966.

Waling, Ann Marie Britt. "An Analysis of Labor Force Experience and Market Work Commitment of Women Interested in Management Training." Doctoral Thesis, Purdue University, 1979.

Walt, D.E. "The Motivation for Women to Work in high-Level Professional Positions." Unpublished doctoral dissertation, American University, 1962.

Wexler, Judie G. and Vicki Quinn. "Considerations in the Training and Development of Women Sergeants." Journal of Police Science and Administration, Volume 13, Number 2, June 1985, pp. 98-105.

Wheeless, Virginia Eman, & Cynthia Berryman-Fink. "Perceptions of Women Managers and Their Communicator Competencies." Communication Quarterly, Volume 33, Number 2, Spring 1985, pp. 137-147.

Wilcox, John. "Mommy Track, Daddy Track." Training and Development Journal, Volume 43, Number 9, Sept. 1989, pp. 12-14.

XXXV
MENTORING THE WOMEN MANAGERS AND PROFESSIONALS

Barnier, L.A. "A study of the Mentoring Relationship: An Analysis of its Relation to Career and Adult Development in Higher Education and Business." Dissertation Abstracts International, Volume 42, Number 7-A, 1982, pp. 3012-3013.

Berry, P. "Mentors for Women Managers: Fast-track to Corporate success." Supervisor Management, Volume 28, Number 8, 1983, pp. 36-40.

Bowen1 D.D. "Were Men Meant to Mentor Women?" Training and Development Journal, Volume 39, Number 2, 1985, pp. 31-34.

Collins, Nancy W. professional Women & Their Mentors: A practical Guide to Mentoring for the Woman Who Wants to Get Ahead. Englewood Cliffs, NJ: Prentice-Hall, 1983.

Cook, M.F. "Is the Mentor Relationship Primarily a Male Experience?" The personnel Administrator. Volume 24, Number 11, 1979, pp. 82-86.

Fitt, L.W. & D.A. Newton. "When the Mentor is a Man and the Protegee is a Woman." Harvard Business Review, Number 59, 1981, pp. 56-60.

Hunt, D.M. & C. Michael. "Mentorship: A Career Development Training Tool." Academy of Management Review, Number 8, 1983, pp. 475-485.

Lean, E. "Cross-Gender Mentoring-Downright Upright and Good for productivity." Training and Developmental Journal, Volume 37, Number 5, 1983, pp. 60-65.

McNeer, Elizabeth J. "The Mentoring Influence in the Careers of Women ARL Directors." Journal of Library Administration, Volume 9, Number 2, 1988.

Moneer, Elizabeth J. "The Role of Mentoring in the Career Development of Women Administrators in Higher Education." PhD Dissertation, The Ohio State University, 1981, pp. 14-39.

Missirian, A. K. The Corporate Connection: Why Women Need Mentors to Reach the Top." Englewood Cliffs, NJ: prentice-Hall, 1982.

Missirian, A.K. "The Process of Mentoring in Career Development of Female Managers." PhD Dissertation, University of Massachusetts, 1980.

Noe, Raymond A. "Women and Mentoring: A Review and Research Agenda." Academy of Management Review, Volume 13, Number 1, 1988, pp. 65-78.

Phillips, Linda Lee. "Mentors and Proteges: A Study of the Career Development of Women Managers and Executives in Business and Industry, Thesis, University of California, Los Angeles, 1977.

Riley, S. & D. Wrench. "Mentoring Among Women Lawyers." Journal of Applied Social Psychology, Number 15, 1985, pp. 374-386.

Ragins, B.R. "Barriers to Mentoring: The Female Manager's Dilemma." Human Relations, Number 42, 1989, pp. 1-22.

Schrader, E.M. "Personality Characteristics of the Woman-to-woman Mentor in the Career Area." Dissertation Abstracts International, Volume 42, Number 1-B, 1981, p. 404.

Shapiro, E.C., F.P. Haseltine and M.P. Rowe. "Moving Up: Role Models, Mentors, and the Patron System." Sloan Management Review, Volume 19, Number 3, 1978, pp. 51-58.

Speizer, J.J. "Role Models, Mentors and Sponsors: The Elusive Concepts." Signs: J. Women Cult. Soc. Number 6, 1981, pp. 692-712.

Vertz, Laura L. "Women, Occupational Advancement and Mentoring: An Analysis of One Public Organization." Public Administration Review, Volume 45, May/June 1985, p. 420.

XXXVI
PROFESSION OF WOMEN ADMINISTRATORS & PROFESSIONALS

Adler, N., & Izraeli, D. (Eds.). 1988. Women in management worldwide. Armonk, NY: M. E. Sharpe.

Alimo-Metcalfe, B. (1993, "Different gender - different rules: assessment of women in management", in Barrar, P. and Cooper, C.L. (Eds.), Managing Organisations in 1992: Strategic Responses, Routledge, London.

Bartlett, K. T. 1990. Feminist legal methods. Harvard Law Review, 103: 829-888.

Billing. Y. D., & Alvesson. M. 1994. Gender, managers and organization. Berlin: Walter de Gruyter.

Blum, T., Fields, D.L. and Goodman, J. (1994, "Organizational level determinants of women in management", Academy of Management Journal, Vol.37 No.2, pp.241-68.

Bowen, D.E. and Lawler, E.E. (1992, "The empowerment of service workers: what, why, how and when?", Sloan Management Review, spring, pp.31-9.

Campion, M.A., Cheraskin, L. and Stevens, J. (1994, "Career related antecedents and the outcomes of job rotation", Academy of Management Journal, Vol.17 No.6, pp.1518-42.

Coe, T. (1992, The Key to the Men's Club - Opening the Doors to Women in Management, Institute of Management, Corby.

Collinson, D. (1991, "Poachers turned gamekeepers: are personnel managers one of the barriers to equal opportunities?", Human Resource Management Journal, Vol.1 No.3, spring.

Cooper, C.L. and Davidson, M.J. (Eds) (1984, Women in Management, Butterworth-Heinemann, Oxford.

Davidson, M. and Cooper, C.L. (1992, Shattering the Glass Ceiling: The Woman Manager, Paul Chapman, London.

Dopson, S. and Stuart, R. (1993, "Information technology, organizational restructuring and the future of middle management", New Technology, Work and Employment, Vol.8, pp.10-20.

Drath, W.H. (1990, "Managerial strengths and weaknesses as

functions of the development of personal meaning", The Journal of Applied Behavioural Science, Vol.26 No.4, pp.483-97.

Edwards, Christine; Woodall, Jean Welchman Rosemary; "Organizational change and women managers' careers: the restructuring of disadvantage?" Employee Relations; Bradford; 1996. Vol. 18, No. 5, p. 25.

Evetts, J. (1993, "Women and management in engineering: the 'glass ceiling' for women's careers", Women in Management Review, Vol.8 No.7, pp.19-25.

Flanders, M.L. (1994, Breakthrough - The Career Woman's Guide to Shattering the Glass Ceiling, Paul Chapman, London.

Fletcher. 1994. Castrating the female advantage: Feminist standpoint research and management science. Journal of Management Inquiry. 3: 74-82.

Hirsh, W. and Bevan, S. (1991, "Managerial competences and skill languages", in Silver, M. (Ed.), Competent to Manage: Approaches to Management Training and Development, Routledge, London, ch. 7.

Institute of Management (1994, National Management Salary Survey, Remuneration Economics, Kingston.

Jackson, C. and Hirsh, W. (1991, "Women managers and career progression: the British experience", Women in Management Review and Abstracts, Vol.6 No.2.

Jacobson, S.W., & Jacques, R. 1990. Of knowers, knowing and the known: A gender framework fro revisioning organizational and management scholarship. Paper presented at the annual meeting of the Academy of Management, San Franciso.

Kanter, R.M. (1977, Men and Women of the Corporation, Basic Books, New York, NY.

Larwood, L., Stromberg. A., & Gutek, B. (Eds.), 1986. Women and work. Newbury Park. CA: Sage.

Legge, K. (1987, "Women in personnel management: uphill climb or downhill slide?", in Spencer, A. and Podmore, D. (Eds), In a Man's World: Essays on Women in Male-dominated Professions, Tavistock, London.

Long, P. (1984, "Would you put your daughter in personnel management?", Personnel Management Vol.16 No.4, pp. 16-20.

Luthans, F., Rosenkrantz, S.A. and Hennessey, H.W. (1985, "What do successful managers really do? An observational study of managerial activities", Journal of Applied Behavioural Science, Vol.2 No.3, pp.255-70.

Marshall, J. (1984, Women Managers: Travellers in a Male World, Wiley, Chichester.

Monks, K. (1993, "Careers in personnel management", Personnel Review, Vol.22 No.1, pp.55-66.

Motram, R. (1987, "Problems for the user in avoiding sex bias", Occupational Psychologist, No.3, pp.6-7.

Nicolson, N. and West, M. (1988, Managerial Job Change: Men and Women in Transition, Cambridge University Press, Cambridge.

Purcell, J. and Ahlstrand, B. (1994, Human Resources Management in the Multi-divisional Company, Oxford University Press, Oxford.

Ragins, B.R. and Sundstrom, D. (1989, "Gender and power in organizations", Psychological Bulletin, Vol.105, pp.51-88.

Schick-Case, S. (1994, "Gender differences in communications and behaviour in organisations", in Davidson, M.J. and Burke, R.J. (Eds), Women in Management, Paul Chapman, London, pp.129-43.

Silver, M. (Ed.) (1991, Competent to Manage: Approaches to Management Training and Development, Routledge, London.

Storey, J. (1992, Developments in the Management of Human Resources, Blackwell, Oxford.

Tharenou, P., Latimer, S. and Conroy, D. (1994, "How do you make it to the top? An examination of influences on women's and men's managerial advancement", Academy of Management Journal, Vol.37 No 4, pp.899-931.

White, B., Cox, C. and Cooper, C.L. (1992, Women's Career Development: A Study of High Flyers, Blackwell, Oxford.

XXXVII
WOMEN AND POWER IN ORGANISATIONS

Fiona M, Lahtinen HK, Heli, KW, "Women and power in organizations", Executive Development; Bradford; 1994, Vol. 7, No. 3, pp. 16.

Hakim, C,"Job Segregation: Trends in the 1970s", Employment Gazette, December, 1981.

Hammond, "Working Women Abroad: Great Britain", Equal Opportunities International, Vol.5 No. 1,1987, pp.8-16.

Hirsh, W. and Jackson, C., "Women into Management — Issues Influencing the Entry of Women in Managerial Jobs", Paper No.158, Institute of Manpower Studies, University of Sussex, 1989.

Stamp, P. and Robarts, S., Positive Action: Changing the Workplace for Women, National Council for Civil Liberties, London, 1986.

Beechey, V. and Perkins, T., A Matter of Hours: Women, Part- Time Work and the Labour Market, Polity Press, Oxford, 1987.

Peitchinis, S.G., Women at Work: Discrimination and Response, McClelland and Stewart, Toronto, 1989.

Hammond, V. and Holton, V., A Balanced Workforce — Achieving Cultural Change for Women, Ashridge Management College, Berkhamsted, 1991.

EOC Report quoted in Personnel Today, 2-15 June 1992 p.48.

Shortridge, K., "Poverty Is a Woman's Problem", in Freeman, J. (Ed.) Women: A Feminist Perspective, Mayfield Publishing Company, Palo Alto, CA, 1986.

Henning, M. and Jardim, A., The Managerial Woman, Marion Boyars, London, 1978.

Astin, H.S., "The Meaning of work in Women's Lives: A Socio psychological Model of Career Choice and Work Behavior", The Counseling Psychologist, Vol.12, 1984, pp.117-26.

Hyde, J.S., Fennema, E. and Lamon, S.J., "Gender Differences in Mathematics Performance: A Meta-analysis", Psychological Bulletin, Vol. 107, 1990, p.139.

Kimball, M.M.,"A New Perspective on Women's Math Achievement", Psychological Bulletin, Vol.105, 1989, pp.198-214.

Jacobs, J. E. and Eccles, J.S., "The Impact of Mothers' Gender-Role Beliefs on Mothers' and Children's Ability Perception" Journal of Personality and Social Psychology, Vol.63, 1992, pp.932-44.

Stanworth, M., Gender and Schooling, Anchor Brendon Ltd, Essex, 1986.

Scase, R. and Goffee, R., "Women in Management: Towards a Research Agenda", International Journal of Human Resources Management, Vol.1 No. 1,1990, pp.107-25.

Dale, A., "Occupational Inequality, Gender and Life Cycle", Work, Employment and Society, Vol.1 No.3, 1988, pp. 326-51

Davidson, M.J. and Cooper, C., Shattering the Glass Ceiling: The Woman Manager, Paul Chapman Publishing, London, 1992.

Leavitt, J.A., Women in Management: An Annotated Bibliography, Oryz, Phoenix, AZ, 1982.

Davidson, M.J. and Cooper, C., "She Needs a Wife: Problems of Women Managers", Leadership and Organizational Development Journal, Vol.5 No.3, 1984.

Alban-Metcalfe, B., "The Effects of Socialisation on Women's Management Careers", Management Bibliographies & Reviews, Vol. 11 No.3, 1985.

Adler, N. and Izraeli, D. (Eds), Women in Management Worldwide, M.E. Sharpe, New York, NY, 1988.

Kanter, R.M., Men and Women of the Corporation, Basic Books, New York, 1989.

Institute of Directors Survey results produced in article entitled "Women at Top Hit out at Men", in Personnel Today, 24 March to 6 April 1992, p.4.

"Top Women Survey", Scottish Business Insider, May-June, 1993.

Morrison, A.M., White, R.P. and Van Velsor, E., Breaking the Glass Ceiling: Can Women Reach the Top of America's Largest Corporations? Addison-Wesley, Reading, MA, 1987.

Spencer, A. and Podmore, D. (Eds), In a Man's World: Essays on Women in Male-dominated Professions, Tavistock Publications, London, 1987.

Survey commissioned by CPM Field Marketing and reported in Personnel Today, July 1992, p.2.

Gold, U. and Pringle, J., "Management Promotions; Gender Specific Factors", Women in Management — Review and Abstracts, Vol.4 No.3, pp.5-10, published in association with the Equal Opportunities Commission, MCB University Press, Bradford, 1989.

Homans, H., "Man-Made Myths: The Reality of Being a Woman Scientist in the NHS", in Spencer, A. and Podmore, D. (Eds), In a Man's World, Tavistock Publications, London, 1987, Ch. 5.

Mintel survey reported in Personnel Today, 10 August 1993, p.4.

Angle, H.L. and Perry, J.L., "An Empirical Assessment of Organizational Commitment and Organizational Effectiveness", Administrative Science quarterly, Vol.26, 1989, pp.1-14

Powell, G.N., Posner, B.Z. and Schmidt, W.H., "Women: The More Committed Managers?", Management Review, Vol.74 No.6,1985, pp.43-5.

Powell, G.N., Women and Men in Management, Sage, Beverley Hills, CA, 1988.

Harlan, A. and Weiss, C., Moving Up: Women in Managerial Careers: Third Progress Report, Wellesley Centre for Research on Women, Wellesley, MA, 1980.

Mills, A.J. and Murgatroyd, S.J., Organizational Rules: A Framework for Understanding Organizational Action, Open University Press, Milton Keynes, 1991.

Curran, M.M., "Gender and Recruitment: People and Places in the Labour Market", Work, Employment and Society, Vol.2 No.3,1988, pp.335-51.

Rosen, B. and Jerdee, T.H., "The Influence of Sex-role Stereotypes on Evaluations of Male and Female Supervisory Behaviour", Journal of Applied Psychology, Vol.59, 1974, pp.9-14.

Schein, V.E., "Fair Employment of Women through Personnel Research", Personnel Journal, Vol.51,1972, pp.330-5.

Taylor, M.S. and llgen, D.R., "Sex Discrimination against Women in Initial Placement Decisions: A Laboratory Investigation", Academy of Management Journal, Vol.24, 1981, pp.859-65.

Heilman, M.E., "Information as a Deterrent against Sex Discrimination: The Effects of Applicant Sex and Information Type of Preliminary Employment Decisions", Organizational

Behaviour and Human Performance, Vol.33, 1984, pp.1174-86.

Lott, B., "The Devaluation of Women's Competence", Chapter 6 in Bohan, J.S. (Ed.), Seldom Seelz, Rarely Heard, Women's Place in Psychology, Westview Press, Boulder, CO, 1992.

Alimo-Metcalfe, B., "Women in Management: Organizational Socialization and Assessment Practices that Prevent Career Advancement", International Journal of Selection and Assessment, Vol.1 No.2, April 1993, pp.68-83.

Webb, J., "The Gender Relation of Assessment", in Firth-Cozens, J. and West, M.A. (Eds), Women at Work, Open University Press, Milton Keynes, 1991.

Collinson, D.L., Barriers to Fair Selection: A Multi-sector Study of Recruitment Practices, Equal Opportunities Commission Research Series, HMSO, London, 1988.

Witz, A., "Patriarchy and Professions: The Gendered Politics of Occupational Closures", Sociology, Vol.24 No.4, 1990, pp.675-90.

Kanter, R.M., "Power Failure in Management Circuits", Harvard Business Review, Vol.57 No.4, 1979, pp.65-75.

Walters, P.A., "Servants of the Crown", in Spencer, A. and Podmore, D. (Eds), In a Man's World, Tavistock Publications, London, 1987, pp.12-32.

Collinson, D.L. and Knights, D., "Men Only: Theories and Practices of Job Segregation in Insurance", in Knights, D. and Wilmott, H. (Eds), Gender and the Labour Process, Gower, Aldershot, 1986, Ch. 7.

Coyle, A., "Behind the Scenes; Women in Television", in Coyle, A. and Skinner, J. (Eds), Women and Work: Positive Action for Change, Macmillan Education, Basingstoke, 1988, Ch. 3.

Al-Khalifa, E., "Pin Money Professionals? Women in Teaching", in Coyle, A. and Skinner, J. (Eds), Women and Work: Positive Action for Change, Macmillan Education, Basingstoke, 1988, Ch. 4.

Podmore, D. and Spencer, A., "Gender in the Labour Process — The Case of Men and Women Lawyers", in Knights, D. and Wilmott, H. (Eds), Gender and the Labour Process, Gower. Aldershot, 1986, Ch. 2.

Tannen, D., You Just Don't Understand: Women and Men in Conversation, William Morrow, New York, NY, 1990.

Tavris, C., The Mismeasure of Women, Simon & Schuster, New York, NY, 1992.

Smith, D., The Everyday World as Problematic: A Feminist Sociology, Northeastern University Press, Boston, MA, 1987.

Fishman, P., in Thomson, J.L. (Ed.), Learning Liberation: Women's Response to Men's Education, Croom Helm, London, 1983.

Gilligan, C., In a Different Voice: Psychological Theory and Women's Development, Harvard University Press, Cambridge, MA, 1982.

Cassell, C.M. and Walsh, S., "Towards a Woman-friendly Psychology of Work: Gender Power and Organizational Culture", paper presented to the BPS Annual Occupational Psychology Conferences, Liverpool, 4-6 January 1991.

Cohen. B. and Fraser, N., Childcare in a Modern Welfare System, Institute of Public Policy Research. London. 1991.

Hewison, J. and Dowswell. T., Child Health Care and The Working Mother, Chapman & Hall, London, 1994.

Hackett, G. and Betz, N.E., "A Self-efficacy Approach to the Career Development of Women", Journal of Vocational Behaviour, Vol.18, 1981, pp.326-39.

Hoyles, C., "Girls and Computers", Bedford Way Papers, No.34, Institute of Education, London, 1988.

Wajcman, J., "Technology as Masculine Culture", The Polity Reader in Gender Studies, Polity Press, Cambridge, 1994.

White B., Cox, C. and Cooper, C., Women's Career Development: A Study of High Flyers, Blackwell, Oxford, 1992.

Fagenson, E., "Perceived Masculine and Feminine Attributes Examined as a Function of Individuals' Sex and Level in the Organizational Power Hierarchy: A Test of Four Theoretical Perspectives", Journal of Applied Psychology, Vol.2, 1990, pp.204-11.

Lahtinen, H.K., "Mentoring Executive Development", Executive Development, Vol.6, 1993, pp.11-15.

Vertz, L.L., "Women Occupational Advancement, and Mentoring: An Analysis of One Public Organization", Public Administration Review, Vol.45, 1985, pp.415-23.

Noe, RA., "Women and Mentoring: A Review and Research Agenda", Academy of Management Review, Vol.13, 1988, pp.65-78.

Ardold, V. and Davidson, M.J., "Adopt a Mentor — the New Way Ahead for Women Managers?", Women in Management Review & Abstracts, Vol.5,1990, pp.10-18.

Dreher, G.F. and Ash, R.A., "A Comparative Study of Mentoring among Men and Women in Managerial, Professional and Technical Positions". Journal of Applied Psychology, Vol.75, 1990, pp.539-46.

Brass, D.J., "Men's and Women's Network: A Study of Interaction Patterns and Influence in an Organization", Academy of Management Journal, Vol.28, 1985, pp.327-43.

Raggins, R.B. and Cotton, J.L., "Easier Said than Done: Gender Differences in Perceived Barriers to Gaining a Mentor", Academy of Management Journal, Vol.34, 1991, pp.939-51.

Bronstein, P., Black, L., Pfenning, J. and White, A., "Getting Academic Jobs: Are Women Equally Qualified—and Equally Successful?" American Psychologist, Vol.41, 1986, pp.318-22.

Swoboda, M.J. and Millar, S.B., "Networking-Mentoring: Career Strategy of Women in Academic Administration", Journal of NAWDAC, Vol.49, 1986, pp.8-13.

Haring-Hidore, M. and Paludi, M.A., "Sexuality and Sex in Mentoring and Tutoring: Implications for Women's Opportunities and Achievement", Peabody Journal of Education, Vol.67, 1987, pp.164-72.

Cook, E.P., Psychological Arzdrogyny, Pergamon Press, Oxford, 1985.

Wilson, F.M., Organizational Behaviour and Gender, forthcoming book to be published by McGraw Hill, 1995.

XXXVIII
GLASS CEILING FOR WOMEN PROFESSIONALS & ADMINISTRATORS

ABELLA, JUDGE ROSALIE (1984) Report of the Commission on Equality in Employment (Ottawa, Ministry of Supply and Services).

ACKER, SANDRA (Ed.) (1989) Teachers, Gender and Careers (Philadelphia, PA, Falmer Press).

ACKER, SANDRA, (in press) Gender and teacher's work, in: M. APPLE (Ed.) Review of Research in Education.

Anonymous, Women professionals still face glass ceiling. Women's International Network News, Summer 93, Vol. 19, Issue 3, p. 76. 2/3p.

APPLE, MICHAEL (1986) Teachers and Texts (New York, Routledge & Kegan Paul).

CANN, JOAN, JONES, GRACE & MARTIN, IAN (1991) Behind the rhetoric: women academic staff in colleges of higher education in England, Gender and Education, 3, pp.15-29.

FOCUS ON LEADERSHIP 1(1984) Conference Summary (Ministry of Education, Ontario).

GASKELL, JANE (1991) Education as preparation for work in Canada: structure, policy and student response, in: D. ASHTON & G. LOWE (Eds) Making Their Way: education, training and the labour market in Canada and Britain (Toronto, University of Toronto Press).

GRANT, ROSEMARY (1989) Women teachers' career pathways: towards an alternative model of 'career', in: S. ACKER (Ed.) Teachers, Gender and Careers (Philadelphia, PA, Falmer Press).

JACOBSON, STEPHEN (1989) School management: still a white man's game, Executive Educator, 11, (11), p.19. JAGGAR, ALISON (1983) Feminist Politics and Human Nature (Sussex, Harvester Press).

KENNINGTON EDSON, SAKRE (1988) Pushing the Limits, the Female Administrative Aspirant (New York, State University of New York Press).

KING, ALAN & PEART, MARJORIE (1992) Teachers in Canada: their work and quality of life. Available from the Canadian Teachers' Federation.

Leadership (1993) Supplement to American School Board Journal, 180(12), pp. A15-A17.

LEE, ENID (1990) Anti-racist education: from policy to practice (public lecture, Queen's University, Ontario).

MACKINNON, CATHARINE (1982) Feminism, Marxism, method and the state: an agenda for theory, in: N. KEOHANE, Z. ROSALDO & B. GELPI (Eds) Feminist Theory, a Critique of Ideology (Sussex, Harvester Press).

MACKINNON, CATHARINE (1987) Feminism Unmodified, Discourses on Life and Law (Cambridge, MA, Harvard University Press).

MARONEY, HEATHER JON & LUXTON, MEG (Eds) (1987) Feminism and Political Economy (Toronto, Methuen).

MILES, ANGELA & FINN, GERALDINE (Eds) (1982) Feminism in Canada, from Pressure to Politics (Montreal, Black Rose Books).

MINISTRY OF EDUCATION (1989) The Status of Women and Affirmative Action/Employment Equity on Ontario School Boards: Report to the Legislature 1988 (Toronto, Queen's Printer for Ontario).

MINISTRY OF EDUCATION (1991) The Status of Women and Employment Equity in Ontario School Boards: Report to the Legislature 1990 (Toronto, Queen's Printer for Ontario).

MINISTRY OF EDUCATION (1993) The Status of Women and Employment Equity in Ontario School Boards: Report to the Legislature 1992 (Toronto, Queen's Printer for Ontario).

OUSTON, JANET (1993) Women as managers, in: J. OUSTON (Ed.) Women in Education Management (Harlow, Longman).

PASCALL, GILLIAN (1986) Social Policy, a Feminist Analysis (London, Tavistock).

PESHKIN, ALAN (1993) The goodness of qualitative research, Educational Researcher, 22, pp.23-29.

ROSSITER, AMY (1988) From Private to Public (Toronto, The Women's Press).

SHAKESHAFT, CAROL (1987) Women in Educational Administration (Newbury Park, CA, Sage).

SMITH, DOROTHY (1987) The Everyday World as a Problematic, a Feminist Sociology (Toronto, University of Toronto Press).

TASK FORCE ON BARRIERS TO WOMEN IN THE PUBLIC SERVICE (1990) Beneath the Veneer, Vols 1-4 (Ottawa, Supply and Services Canada).

WEEDON, CHRIS (1987) Feminist Practice and Poststructuralist Theory (Oxford, Basil Blackwell).

WEILER, KATHLEEN (1988) Women Teaching for Change (South Hadley, Bergin & Garvey).

XXXIX
JOB SATISFACTION OF WOMEN MANAGERS

Diane E. Lewis, "More Women Are Becoming Family's Primary Breadwinner," Minneapolis Star Tribune (February 23, 1998), p. D2.

Robert J. Bowman, "Just Short of Perfection," Distribution (September 1997), p.29.

Martha C. Cooper and Bernard J. La Londe, "1997 Career Patterns of Women in Logistics," 1997 Annual Conference Proceedings (Oak Park, IL: Council of Logistics Management, 1998), p.99.

Barbara A. Gutek, Aaron Groff Cohen and Ann Tsui, "Reactions to Perceived Sex Discrimination," Human Relations (June 1996) pp.791-813.

Johnson. Job satisfaction of Logistics Managers: Female versus Male Perspectives. Transportation Journal, Fall 99, Vol. 39, Issue 1, p.5, 15p, 2 charts, 5 graphs Johnson, James C.; McClure, Diane.

Joseph B. White and Carol Hymowitz, "Watershed Generation of Women Executives Is Rising to the Top." The Wall Street Journal (February 10,1997), pp. Al, A6.

David D. Kirkpatrick. "Women's Presence In High-Level Jobs Weak, Study Says," The Wall Street Journal (October18. 1996), p. B 16.

Deborah Tannen: Gender and Discourse (New York: Oxford University Press, 1996): Talking 9 to 5: Women and Men in the Workplace: Language. Sex and Power (Dresden, TN: Avon Books, 1995): That's Not What I Meant: How Conversational Styles Makes or Breaks Relationships (Westminster. MD: Ballatine Books, 1991), and You Just Don't Understand (Westminster. MD: Ballatine Books, 1991).

Robert Schrank. "Two Women, Three Men on a Raft." Harvard Business Review (May-June 1994). pp. 68-80.

Steve Hamm. "Why Women Are So Invisible," Business Week (August25, 1997). p.136. and, Kathleen Reardon. "The Memo Every Woman Keeps In Her Desk," Harvard Business Review (March-April 1993). pp.16-22.

Ronald J. Burke and Carol A. McKeen. "Employment Gaps and Work and Career Satisfactions of Managerial and Professional Women," International Journal of Manpower (January 1996).

pp.47-55: Diane Dodd-McCue and Gail B. Wright, "Men, Women, and Attitudinal Commitment: The Effects of Workplace Experiences and Socialization." Human Relations (August1996). pp.1065-1091; Felice N. Schwartz, "Management Women and the New Facts of Life," Harvard Business Review (January-February 1989), pp.65-76 and Felice N. Schwartz. "Woman As A Business Imperative." Harvard Business Review (March-April 1992). pp.105-113.

See: Sally Apgar. Cheryl A. Meyer, and Jane Freedman. "Delivering the Results is the Secret to Success," in Star Tribune (July27. 1997). pp. Al. A12-14; Sandra Early, "Woman Executives: The Waiting Game, Corporate Report Minnesota (July 1997). pp. 32-50; Linda Hilelstein and Stephanie Anderson Forest. "Woman: Breaking Through." Business Week (February 17. 1997). pp.64-70; Toni Mack, "High Finance With a Touch of Theater," Forbes (May 18,1998). pp.140-154; Patricia Sellers. "Women, Sex and Power," Fortune (August 5, 1996). pp.42-56. and White and Hymowitz.

Rae Andre, "A Comparison of Career Status and Attitudes Among Men and Women in Logistics." Logistics and Transportation Review (Vol.31. No.2, 1995). p.186.

Amy Aronson. "Trendicators: A Shaky Economy. or Just Frazzled Nerves?" Working Women (April 1995). p.16.

"Nine to Five: How Workers Feel." The Wall Street Journal (September 19, 1997). p. R4.

Peter M. Lynagh. Paul R. Murphy. and Richard F. Poist. "Career-Related Perspectives Regarding Women in Logistics: A Comparative Analysis." Transportation Journal (Fall 1996). pp.36-37.

See: Aaron Bernstein. "Who Says Job Anxiety is Easing?" Business Week (April 7,1997), p.38; Kenneth Labich. "Kissing Off Corporate America." Fortune (February 20,1995), pp.44-52. and Betsy Morris, "Executive Women Confront Midlife Crisis," Fortune (September 18,1995), pp. 60-86.

Stephanie Armour, "Management Loses Its Allure," USA Today (October15, 1997), pp. B1-2; Keith H. Hammond and others, "Work and Family," Business Week (September 15, 1997), pp.96-99; Keith H. Hammond and Gabrielle Saveri, "Accountants Have

Lives, Too, You Know," Business Week (February 23, 1998), pp.88-90; Sue Shellenbarger, "More Execs Resigning For Family Time," Minneapolis Star Tribune (March 15, 1998), p. D5, and Jon Tevlin, "Report Says Workers Need More Family Time," Minneapolis Star Tribune (April 15, 1998), pp. Al, All.

Sarah Hardesty and Nehama Jacobs, Success and Betrayal: The Crisis of Women in Corporate America (New York: Franklin Watts, 1986).

Martha C. Cooper and Bernard J. La Londe, "1997 Career Patterns of Women in Logistics," 1997 Annual Conference Proceedings of the Council of Logistics Management (Oak Brook, IL: Council of Logistics Management, 1998), p.112.

Peter M. Lynagh, Paul R. Murphy, and Richard F. Poist, "Women's Views Regarding Employment in Transportation and Logistics: A Status Report," Journal of Transportation Law, Logistics and Policy (Winter 1998), p.170.

Diane Dodd-McCue and Gail B. Wright, "Men, Women and Attitudinal Commitment: The Effects of Workplace Experiences and Socialization," Human Relations (August 1996), pp.1065-1091, and Diane E. Lewis, "Disenchanted Women Give Up Careers To Stay Home," Minneapolis Star Tribune (April 6, 1998), p. D7.

Ronald J. Burke and Carol A. McKeen, "Employment Gaps and Work and Career Satisfactions of Managerial and Professional Women," International Journal of Manpower (January 1996), pp.47-55; Ronald J. Burke and Carol A. Mc Keen, "Employment Gaps, Work Satisfaction and Career Advancement Among Women Chartered Accountants," Journal of Managerial Psychology (July 1995), pp.16-21, and Stephanie Lee, "CEOs: Moving Toward Employee Awareness," Trusts and Estates (November 1996), p.8.

Janet L. Bokemeier and William B. Lacy, "Job Values, Rewards, and Work Conditions As Factors in Job Satisfaction Among Men and Women," The Sociological Quarterly (Vol.28, No.2, 1986), pp.189-204; Faye Crosby, Jacqueline Golding, and Andrea Resnick, "Discontent Among Male Lawyers, Female Lawyers, and Female Legal Secretaries," Journal of Applied Social Psychology (Vol.13, No.1, 1983), pp.183-190; Louis W. Fry and

Sue Greenfeld, "An Examination of Attitudinal Differences Between Policewomen and Policemen," Journal of Applied Psychology (Vol.65, No.1, 1980), pp.123-126; Joel Lefkowitz, "Sex-Related Differences in Job Attitudes and Dispositional Variables: Now You See Them,..." Academy of Management Journal (April 1994), pp. 323-349; Bilha Mannheim, "Male and Female Industrial Workers: Job Satisfaction, Work Role Centrality, and Work Place Preference," Work and Occupations (November 1983), pp.413-436; E. Sharon Mason, "Gender Differences in Job Satisfaction," Journal of Social Psychology (April 1995), pp.143-151; Jo Phelan, "The Paradox of the Contented Female Worker: An Assessment of Alternative Explanations," Social Psychology Quarterly (Vol.57, No. 2, 1994), pp.95-107; Thomas J. Phelan and Jo Carol Phelan, "Higher Education and Early Life Outcomes," Higher Education (Vol.12, 1983), pp.665-680; Reba Rowe and William E. Snizek, "Gender Differences in Work Values," Work and Occupations (May 1995), pp.215-229; Judy A. Siguaw and Earl D. Honeycutt, Jr. "An Examination of Gender Differences in Selling Behaviors and Job Attitudes," Industrial Marketing Management (Vol.24, 1995), pp.45-52, and Dianne B. Smith and Walter T. Plant, "Sex Differences in the Job Satisfaction of University Professors," Journal of Applied Psychology (Vol.67, No.2, 1982), pp.249-251.

Kenneth H. Forsythe, James C. Johnson, and Kenneth C. Schneider, "Traffic Managers: Do They Get Any Respect?" Journal of Business Logistics (Vol.11, No.2, 1990), pp.89-91.

Bernard J. La Londe, James M. Masters, Arnold B. Maltz, and Lisa R. Williams, "Traffic Managers: A Discipline in Transition," Transportation Journal (Winter 1991), p.58.

Anna Wilde Mathews, "Logistics Firms Flourish Amid Trend in Outsourcing," The Wall Street Journal (June 2, 1998), p. B6, and Robert Walters, "Scrambling for Jobs," Distribution (January1996), p.27.

Laurie Joan Aron, "Logistics: From Assembly Line to Comer Office," Inbound Logistics (July 1995), p.32.

Lisa Harrington, "The Outsourcing Decision: Step By Step," Inbound Logistics (June 1995), pp.18-24.

F.M. Andrews and S.B. Withey, Social Indicators of Well-Being: America's Perceptions of Lije Quality, (New York: Plenum Press,

1976). The psychometric properties of this scale are examined in Joan R. Rentsch and Robert P. Steel, "Construct and Concurrent Validations of the Andrews and Withey Job Satisfaction Questionnaire," Education and Psychological Measurement (Vol.52, No.2, 1992), pp.357-367.

Robert P. Steel and A.J. Mento, "The Participation-Performance Controversy Reconsidered: Subordinate Competence as a Mitigating Factor," Group and Observational Studies (Vol.12, 1987), pp.411-423 and R.W. Rice, D.A. Gentile, and D.B. McFarlin, "Facet Importance and Job Satisfaction," Journal of Applied Psychology (Vol.76, 1991), pp.31-39.

John A. Byrne, "Jack: A Close-Up Look at How America's #1 Manager Runs GE," Business Week (June, 8 1998), p.105

XXXX
WOMEN MANAGERS & PROFESSIONALS IN US & CANADA

Anonymous. Black women among group dissatisfied with prospects for advancement: study Jet; Chicago; Mar 2, 1998.

Fireman, Jaclyn, "Do Women Manage Differently," Fortune, Vol.122, No.12, December 17,1990, pp.112-113.

Gallese, Liz Roman, "Why Women Aren't Making It To The Top," Across the Board, Vol.28, No.4, April 1991, pp.18-22.

Helgensen, Sally, The Female Advantage: Women's Way's of Leadership, Doubleday/Currency, New York, 1990.

Rosener, Judy B., "Ways Women Lead," Harvard Business Review, Vol.68, No.6, November/December 1990, pp.119-125.

Stoner, Charles R. and Hartman, Richard I., "Family Responsibilities and Career Progress: The Good, The Bad, and The Ugly," Business Horizons, Vol. 33, No.6, 1988., pp.49-54.

Fields, Suzanne, "Flirting with the Feminine Mystique, Business Month, Vol. 136, No. 5, November 1989, pp. 11-12.

Barber, Daniel M. (1988). "Newly Promoted City Managers." Public Administration Review 48 (May/June): 694-699. Blau, Francine D. and Wallace E. Hendricks (1978). "Occupational Segregation By Sex: Trends and Prospects." Journal of Human Resources 14 (Sept): 197-210. Bose, Christine E. and Peter H. Rossi (1983). "Gender and Jobs: Prestige Standings of Occupations as Effected by Gender." American Sociological Review 48 (June): 316-330. Bullard, Angela M. and Deil S. Wright (1993). "Circumventing the Glass Ceiling: Women Executives in American State Governments." Public Administration Review 53 (May/June): 189-202. Cayer, N. Joseph and Lee Siegelman (1980). "Minorities and Women in State and Local Government: 1973-1975." Public Administration Review 39 (Sept/Oct): 443-450. Cunningham, Joy Pierson (1992). "Fostering Advancement for Women and Minorities." Public Management 74:20-25. Elliot, Robert E. (1986). "The Fairness of Veteran's Preference in a State Merit System: The Employee's Point of View." Public Personnel Management 15 (Fall): 311-323. Equal Employment Opportunity Commission (1988). Annual Report on the Employment of Minorities, Women, and People With Disabilities in the Federal Government: Fiscal Year 1988. Washington D.C.: U. S. Government Printing Office.

Gottfried, Frances (1988). The Merit System and Municipal Civil Service: A Fostering of Social Inequity. Westport, CT: Greenwood Press. Guy, Mary E. (1993). "Three Steps Forward, Two Steps Back: The Status of Women's Integration Into Public Management." Public Administration Review 53 (July/August): 285291. Hays, Steven W. and Richard C. Kearney (1992). "State Personnel Directors and the Dilemmas of Workforce 2000: A Survey." Public Administration Review 52 (July/August): 380388. Hopkins, Anne H. (1980). "Perception of Employment Discrimination in the Public Sector." Public Administration Review 39 (March/April): 131-137. Huckle, Patricia (1985). "Whatever Happened to Affirmative Action? Employment of.

Women in Los Angeles City Department of Water and Power." Revieo of Public Personnel Administration 6 (Fall): 44-58. Kornegay-Clarke, Norma (1986). "Why Upward Mobile is Tough for High Tech Women." Personnel 65 (March): 9-12. Kovach, Kenneth A. (1985)."Sex Stereotyping by Tomorrow's Executives." Personnel 64 (Dec): 14-20. Lepper, Mary M. (1976). "The Status of Women in the United States in 1976: Still Looking for Justice and Equality." Public Administration Review 36 (July/Aug): 365-369. McClendon, McKee J. (1976). "The Occupational Status Attainment Process of Males and Females." American Sociological Reviezo 41 (Feb): 52-64. Neuse, Steven M. (1978). "Professionalism and Authority: Women in Public Service." Public Administration Review 37 (Sept/Oct): 43640. Rehfuss, John A. (1986). "A Representative Bureaucracy? Minority and Women Executives in California Career Services." Public Administration Review 46 (Sept/Oct): 454-459. Rosenfeld, Rachel A. (1980). "Race and Sex Differences in Career Dynamics." American Sociological Review 45 (Aug): 583-609. Slack, James D. (1987). "Affirmative Action and City Managers: Attitude Toward Recruitment of Women." Public Administration Review 46 (March/April): 199-206. Tummala, Krishna K. (1987). "Veteran's Preference in the State of Montana: Equal Employment or Affirmative Action?" Puhlic Personnel Administration 16(Summer): 159-169. U.S. Department of Commerce (1989). Facts on Working Women. Washington, D.C.: U. S. Government Printing Office. U.S. Merit Systems Protection Board (1994). Working for America: An Update. Washington D.C.: U. S. Government Printing Office. U.S. Merit Systems Protection Board

(1990). Working for America: A Federal Employee Survey. Washington D.C.: U.S. Government Printing Office. Vertz, Laura L. (1985)."Women, Occupational Advancement, and Mentoring: An Analysis of One Public Organization." Public Administration Review 45 (May/June):415-423. Ward, Patricia A., Peter F. Orazem and Steffen W. Schmidt (1992). "Women in Elite Pools and Elite Positions." Social Science Quarterly 73 (March): 31-45.

Tomiack, Monica; Gentleman, Jane F.; Jette, Maurice; Health and gender differences between middle and senior managers in the Canadian Public Service Social Science & Medicine [H.W. Wilson – SSA]; Nov 1997.

Lawn-Day, Gayle A; Ballard, Steven; Speaking out: Perceptions of women managers in the public service Review of Public Personnel Administration; Columbia; Winter 1996, Vol. 16, No. 1, p. 41.

Richards, Rhonda Women in the professions – United States Essence, Mar 96, Vol. 26, Issue 11, p. 74, 4p, 1bw.

XXXXI

WOMEN ADMINISTRATORS & PROFESSIONALS IN UK IN A MULTICULTURAL PERSPECTIVE

Anderson, M.L. (1993), "Studying across difference: race, class, gender in qualitative research", in Stanfield, J.H. and Dennis, R.M. (Eds), Race and Ethnicity in Research Methods, Sage, London, pp. 39-52.

Ansari, K. and Jackson, J. (1995), Managing Cultural Diversity at Work, Kogan Page, London.

Bell, E.L (1990), "The bicultural life experience of career-oriented black women", Journal of Organisational Behaviour, Vol.11, pp.459-77.

Berger, P.S., Delcampo, R.L., Herrera, R.S. and Wiegel, R.R. (1994), "'Family / work roles' in relation to perceived stress: do gender and ethnicity matter?", Journal of Family and Economic Issues, Vol.5 No.13, Fall, pp.223-42.

Bhachu, P. (1991), "Culture, ethnicity and class among Punjabi Sikh women in 1990's Britain", New Community, Vol.17 No.3, April, pp.401-12.

Bhatnagar, D. (1988), "New paradigms for research and action", Sex Roles, Vol.18, pp.343-55.

Bhavnani, R (1994), Black Women in the Labour Market: A Research Review, Equal Opportunities Commission,

Bhopal, k. (1997), Gender, Race and Patriarchy. A Study of South Asian Women, Ashgate, Aldershot.

Brah, A. (1993), "Race and culture in the gendering of labour markets: South Asian young women and the labour market" New Community, Vol.19 No.3, pp.441-58.

Brah, A. (1996), Cartographies of Diaspora. Contesting Identities, Routledge, London.

Brannen, J., Meszaros, G., Moss, P. and Poland, G. (1994), Employment and Family Life, A Review of Research in the UK (1980-1994), Institute of Education, University of London, London.

Carr-Ruffino, N. (1995), Managing Diversity. People skills for a Multicultural Workplace, International Thomson Publishing, USA.

Davidson, M. (1997), The Black and Ethnic Minority Woman Manager. Cracking the Concrete Ceiling, Paul Chapman, London.

Department of Education and Employment (1997), Separate Tables: Statistics on Women and Men in Education, Training and Employment, DEE.

Drury, B. (1991), "Sikh girls and the maintenance of an ethnic culture", New Community, Vol.17 No.3, April, pp. 387-99.

Edwards, R. (1990), "Connecting method and epistemology: white women interviewing black women", Women's International Forum, Vol.13, pp.477-90.

Edwards, R. (1993), "An education in interviewing. Placing the researcher in the research", in Renzetti, C.M. and Lee, R.M. (Eds), Researching Sensitive Topics, Sage, Newbury Park, CA.

Ferree, M. (1990), "Beyond separate spheres", Journal of Marriage and the Family, Vol.52, pp.860-84.

Ghuman, P. (1994), Coping with Two Cultures: British Asian and Indo-Canadian Adolescents, Multilingual Matters Ltd, Clevedon.

Glaser, B. and Strauss, A. (1967), The Discovery of Grounded Theory: Strategies for Social Research, Aldine, New York, NY.

Hall, D.T. and Parker, V.A. (1993), "The role of workplace flexibility in managing diversity", Organisational Dynamics, Vol.21, pp.5-18.

Hammersley, M. and Atkinson, P. (1993), Ethnography, Principles in Practice, Routledge, London.

Henderson, G. (1994), Cultural Diversity in the Workplace. Issues and Strategies, Praeger, Westport, CT.

Kandola R.S. and Fullerton, J. (1994), Managing the Mosaic. Diversity in Action, Institute of Personnel and Development, London.

Labour Force Survey(1997), Quarterly Bulletin, No.22, December, Office for National Statistics.

Lewis, S. (1997), "Family friendly employment practices: a route to changing organisational culture or playing at the margins?", Gender, Work and Organization, Vol.4 No.1.

Lewis, S., lzraeli, D.N. and Hootsmans, H. (Eds) (1992), Dual-earner Families: International Perspectives, Sage Publications, London.

Liebkind, K. (1992), "Ethnic identity - challenging the boundaries of social psychology", in Breakwell, C. (Ed.), Social Psychology of Identity and the Self-concept, Surrey University Press..

Liff, S. (1995), Managing Diversity: New Opportunities for Women, Industrial Relations Research Unit, University of Warwick.

Merrill J. (1988), "Self poisonings by Asians", Update, Vol.37, pp.931-4

Plummer, K (1995), "Life story research", in Smith, J.A., Harre, R. and Van Langenhove, L. (Eds), Rethinking Methods in Psychology, Sage Publications, London.

Rana, B. (1998), "Challenging stereotypes of British Asian women's experiences of work and family life: Kalminder Kaur", Community, Work and Family, Vol.1 No.1, pp.91-3.

Rana, B., Reid, P., Smithson, J. and Sullivan, C. (1998), "Representing the same: Issues of reflexivity in black feminist research", Methodological Issues in Qualitative Research: Dilemma's, Choices and Solutions, IOD Occassional Paper, 1>/98; Interpersonal Organisational Development Research Group, Manchester.

Sekaran, U. (1992), "Middle class, dual earner families and their support systems in urban India", in Lewis, S., Izraeli, D.N. and Hootsmans, H. (Eds), Dual Earner Families: International Perspectives, Sage, London.

Shams, M. (1994), "Cultural diversity, dual-roles and well-being: a research note", in Bolaria, B.S. and Bolaria, R. (Eds), Racial Minorities, Medicine and Health, Fernwood Publishing, Halifax Nova Scotia; Social Research Unit, Department of Sociology, University of Saskatchewan, Saskatoon, Saskatchewan.

Sharma, U. (1986), Women's Work, Class and Urban Household. A Study of Shimla, North India, Tavistock Publications, London.

Stanfield, J.H. and Dennis, R.M. (Eds) (1993), Race, Ethnicity in Research Methods, Sage, London.

Stopes-Roe, M. and Cochrane, R. (1990), Citizens of This Country: The Asian British, Multilingual Matters Ltd, Clevedon.

Tayeb, M.H. (1988), Organisations and National Culture: A Comparative Analysis, Sage Publishing Ltd, London.

Walby, S. (1990), Theorising Patriarchy, Basil Blackwell, Oxford.

Warner, S. (1986), "Marriage, maternity, and female economic activity. Gujarati mothers in Britain", in Westwood, S. and Bhachu, P. (Eds) (1988), Enterprising Women, Ethnicity, Economy, and Gender Relations, Routledge, London.

Warrier, S. (1994), "Gujarati Prajapatis in London: family roles and sociability networks", in Ballard, R. (Ed.), Desh Pardesh. The South Asian presence in Britain, Hurst and Co., London, pp.191-213.

West, S. and Pilgrim, S. (1995), "South Asian women in employment: the impact of migration, ethnic origin and the local economy", New Community, Vol.21 No.3, pp.357-78.

Westwood, S. (1988), "Workers and wives: continuities and discontinuities in the lives of Gujerati women", in Westwood, S. and Bhachu, P. (Eds), Enterprising Women, Ethnicity, Economy, and Gender Relations, Routledge, London.

Wilson, A. (1978), Finding a Voice: Asian Women in Britain, Virago Ltd, London.

XXXXII
WOMEN ADMINISTRATORS & PROFESSIONALS IN THE AFRO-ASIAN REGIONS

ASIAN SCENE

Jayes, J. and Pulparampil, J., "Trainers' perceptions of the factors which influence the transfer of learning: an Indian case study", Journal of Public Sector Management, Vol.2 No. 1, 1990.

Amos-Wilson, P., "Same but different? What the West can learn from developing countries about management training for women", in Vizcario, C. (Ed.), Gender, leadership and Women, Ministry of Social Affairs, Madrid, 1994.

Hollway, W., "Women into senior management: a training programme for women about gender issues in management and careers", Development and Project Planning Centre, Bradford, New Series Discussion Paper no.23.

Bangladesh: Strategies for Enhancing the Role of Women in Economic Development, World Bank, 1990.

Kenny, Oriel, "Placements in management training for Bangladeshi civil servants Women in Management Review; Bradford; 1995, Vol.10, No.4, p.1.

Khan, S., The Fifty Percent Women in Development and Policy in Bangladesh, University Press Limited, Dhaka, Bangladesh, 1988.

Gulhati, K., "Attitudes toward women managers", Economic and Political Weekly, 17-24 February 1990, pp.41-8.

Youker, R.," Lessons form evaluations in Africa for external funding bodies", in Davies, J., Easterby-Smith, M., Mann, S. and Tanton, M. (Eds), The Challenge to Western Development, Routledge, London, 1989.

AFRICAN PERSPECTIVE

Adeyemi-Bello, Tope; Tomkiewicz, Joseph M. The attitudes of Nigerians towards women managers. Journal of Social Behaviour & Personality, Dec 96, Vol. 11 Issue 5, p 133, 7p,1 chart.

Adler N J (1988) Women class managers for global competition. Academy of Management Executive, 2, 11-19.

Adler, NJ. (September, 1993). Women managers in a global economy. HR magazine, 52-55.

Antal, A.B., & Krebsbach-Gnath, C. (1987). Women in management: Unused resources in the Federal Republic of Germany. International Studies of Management and Organization, 16, 133-151.

Anybody seen a giant? (1993, August 21). The Economist, 328, 3-14.

Brenner, OC., & Tomkiewicz, J. (1982). Sex differences in attitudes toward women and managerial success. Mid-Atlantic Journal of Business, 21, 27-32.

Brenner, O.C., Tomkiewicz, J., & Schein, V.E. (1989). The relationship between sex role stereotypes and requisite management characteristics revisited. Academy of Management Journal, 32, 662-669.

Copeland, C.L., Driskell, J.E., & Salas, E. (1995). Gender and reactions to dominance. Journal of Social Behavior and Personality, 10, 53-68.

Dowling, P.J., Schuler, R.S., & Welch, D.E. (1994). International dimensions of human resource management (2nd ed.). Belmont, CA: Wadsworth Publishing Company.

Dubno, P. (1985). Attitudes toward women executives: A longitudinal approach. Academy of Management Journal, 28, 235-669.

Fierman, J. (July, 1990). Why women still don't hit the top. Fortune, 30, 40-62 (non-consecutive).

Heilman, M.E. (July, 1995). Sex stereotypes and their effects in the workplace: What we know and what we don't know. Journal of Social Behavior and Personality, 10, 3-26.

Heilman, M.E., Block, C.J., Martell, R.F., & Simon, M.C. (1989). Has anything changed? Current characterizations of men, women, and managers. Journal of Applied Psychology, 74, 935-942.

Ilgen, D.R., & Moore, C.F. (1983). When reason fails: A comment on the reliability and dimensionality of the WAMS. Academy of Management Journal, 20, 89100.

Izraeli, D.N. (1987). Women's movement into management in Israel. International Studies of Management and Organization, 16, 76-107.

Lansing, P., & Ready, K. (1988). Hiring women managers in Japan: An alternative for foreign employers. California Management Review, 30, 112-127.

Peters, L.H., Terborg, J.R., & Taylor, J. (1974). Women as managers scale (WAMS): A measure of attitude toward women in management positions. Catalogue of Selected Documents in Psychology, 4, 27. [Available from Select Press, P.O. Box 37, Corte Madera, CA 94976; 415/924-1612; $18.00.]

Powell, G.N., & Butterfield, D.A. (1979). The "good manager": masculine or androgynous? Academy of Management Journal, 22, 395-403.

Powell, G.N., & Butterfield, DA. (1986). The "good manager": Does androgyny fare better in the 1980's? Presented at the Annual Meeting of the Academy of Management, Chicago, Illinois.

Renshaw, J.R. (1987). Women's movement into management in Israel, International Studies of Management and Organization, 16, 152-173.

Schein, V.E. (1975). Relationships between sex role stereotypes and requisite management characteristics among female managers, Journal of Applied Psychology, 60, 340-344.

Schein, V.E. (1978). Sex role stereotyping, ability, and performance: Prior research and new directions, Personnel Psychology, 31, 259-268.

Steinhoff, P.O., & Tanaka, K. (1987). Women managers in Japan. International Studies of Management and Organization, 16, 108-132.

Terborg, J.R., Peters, L.H., Ilgen, D.R., & Smith, F. (1977). Organizational and personal correlates of attitudes toward women as managers. Academy of Management, 20, 89-100.

Tomkiewicz, J.E. & Adeyomi-Bello T. (1995). A cross-sectional analysis of the attitudes of Nigerians and Americans toward women managers. Journal of Social Personality and Behavior, 10, 189-198.

Crandall, R. (Ed.). (1996). Handbook of gender research [Special issue]. Journal of Social Behavior and Personality, Vol.11, No.5, 133-139.

XXXXIII
WOMEN MANAGERS & PROFESSIONALS IN RUSSIA

BAIN O. B., ZAKHAROV, I. A., and NOSOVA N. B. From Certrally Mandated to Locally Demanded Service: The Russian Case, Higher Education 35 (1998) 49-67

BUTLER, J. Gender Trouble: Feminism and the Subversion of Identity. London: Routledge, 1990.

DAVYDOV, I.S. "Higher Education: Present Conditions, Problems, Solutions", Russian Education and Society 39 12 (1997): 5-19.

FOUCAULT, M. "Afterword: The Subject and Power", in, M. FOUCAULT, H. L. DREYFUS, and P. RABINOW, eds. Beyond Structuralism and Hermeneutics. Chicago: University of Chicago Press, 1982.

GILLIGAN, C. In a Different Voice: Psychological Theory of Women's Development. Cambridge, MA: Harvard University Press, 1993.

HOLMES, B., READ, G., and VOSKRESENSKAYA, N. Russian Education: Tradition and Transition. New York: Garland, 1995.

HOLMGREN, B. "Bug Inspectors and Beauty Queens: The Problems of Translating Feminism into Russian", in, E. E. BERRY, ed. Post communism and the Body Politic. New York: New York University Press, 1995.

JURNA, I. "Women in Russia: Building a Movement", in, A. SCHULER, ed. From Basic Needs to Basic Rights: Women's Claim to Human Rights. Washington, DC: Women, Law, and Development International, 1995.

KAY, R. "Images of an Ideal Woman: Perceptions of Russian Womanhood through the Media, Education, and Women's Own Eyes", in, M. BUCKLEY, ed. Post-Soviet Women: From the Baltics to Central Asia. Cambridge: Cambridge University Press, 1997.

KOVAL, V. "Women and Work in Russia", in, V. KOVAL, ed. Women in Contemporary Russia. Providence: Breghahn Books, 1995.

LAGUNOVA, E. "Obrazovannaya zhenshchina: dominanti sud'by" [The Educated Woman: The Dominants of Destiny], in, Y. ZHUKOVA, ed. Feministskaya teoria i praktika: Vostok-Zapad [Feminist Theory and Practice: East-West]. St. Petersburg: Peterburgskii Tsentr Gendernikh Problem, 1996.

LEVIN-STANKEVICH, B. L., and SAVELYEV, A. "The Academic Profession in Russia", in, P. G. ALTBACH, ed. The International Academic Profession: Portraits of Fourteen Countries. Princeton: The Carnegie Foundation for the Advancement of Teaching, 1996.

LUGACHYOV, M., MARKOV, A., TIPENKO, N., and BELYAKOV, S. "Structure and Financing of Higher Education in Russia", in, P. G. HARE, ed. Structure and Financing of Higher Education in Russia, Ukraine and the European Union. Bristol, Pennsylvania: Jessica Kingsley, 1997

MOORE, H. A Passion for Difference: Essays in Anthropology and Gender. Cambridge: Polity Press, 1994.

MOROZOVA, M. Y. "Gender Stratification in Russian Higher Education: The Matrioshka Image", in, S.S. LIE, L. MALIK, and D. HARRIS, eds. The Gender Gap in Higher Education. London: Kogan Page, 1994.

OECD. Russian Federation. Series in Reviews of National Policies for Education. Paris: Organization for Economic Co-operation and Development, 1998.

VORONINA, O. "Virgin Mary or Mary Magdalene? The Construction and Reconstruction of Sex During the Perestroika Period", in, A. POSADSKAYA, ed. (K. CLARK, trans.) Women in Russia: A New Era of Russian Feminism. London: Verso, 1994.

Index

Additional responsibilities to extended family dynamics 171
Africa 9, 205, 206
Ambivalence of women towards power and competition 34
American Women 13
Annual Salary Compared 101
Asia 4, 9
Asian Communities 164, 165, 171
Asian Women 163, 164
Asian Women Managers 193
Attitudes towards women as Managers 68

Bangladesh 195, 196, 198, 199, 204
Bangladeshi Women 199, 201, 202, 204
Barriers to Women's Power 24
Barriers to Women's Progress 22
Better career opportunities 104
Britain 21, 183
British Asian Cultures 181
British Asian Managerial & Professional Women 165, 167, 170, 171, 176
British Asian Women 169
British Asian Working Women 174, 175, 176, 177, 179, 180, 181
British South Asian Women 163, 164, 166, 172, 178, 182, 183
British Women 8
British Women Managers & Professionals 163
Burdonsome Family Pressure 169

Canada 143
Career Advancement Opportunities 92
Career benefits: Male 89
Career benefits & Negatives 94, 100
Career Choice Satisfaction 88
Career development at PSU 54
Career Paths 49
Career Planning 43
Careers in Middle Management 77
Centres of Managerial Power 4
Challenges and Remedies for Women executives 21
Change in Gender ratio 135
Changes in Managerial roles & Styles 42
Changes in specialist Carreer Paths 52
Changing Career Paths 42
Child care arrangements 30
Communist States 5
Comparison of French and British Women Professionals 183
Comparison of Male and Female logistician 86
Corporate restructuring and Reduction of jobs 103
Cross-sex mentoring 32, 33

Denmark 29
Design and Implementation 154
Devaluation of Women's Competence 27
Differences in men's and women's Behaviour 28
Differences in Personality Development 61
Discrimination in employment 143
Dual Career Relationship 10
Dual-income Families 82

Eastern Europe 5, 185
Eastern European Communist Countries 4
Employment Equity 144
Employment Equity in Practice 152
Employment Equity initiatives 105

Employment Equity Policy in Canada 160
Employment Equity Programmes 154, 156, 157
Equal Employment Opportunity 115, 116, 120
Equal Opportunity Act 1975, U.K. 30
Equal Opportunity at PSU 56, 57
Equal Opportunity Policies 40, 44
Equity as "reverse discrimination" 161
Europe 9
European Countries 186
Excellent Career Advancement Opportunities 89
Experiences of discrimination 176
Experiences of Gender Inequity 147
Explaining Women Mangers Careers 38

Fantasy of a Superwoman 190
Fast-Paced Work Enviornment 92
Federal Employee Comparability Act 119
Female Bangladeshi Civil Servants 198
Female Managers in Civil Service 196
Female Nigerians Significant differences 207
Female: Career Benefits 91
Feminine Principles of leadership 133
Feminine Skills 27
Feminine Qualities 34
Feminization of Workforce 48
Flexible working hours 30
Flexitime and Part-time work 30
Focus on ecology of Leadership 132
France 4, 29, 183
French Unions 5
Full-time working Women 136

Gender Based Difference 101
Gender-Based pay inequality 82
Gender differences 62, 72, 81, 82, 87
Gender differences in Mean rating on attitude towards women as Mangers scale 209
Gender Discrimination 59, 61
Gender Diversity 8
Gender Perception of Glass Ceiling 87
Gender roles 28
Gender Socialization 23
Glass ceiling Effect 96
Global Competition 8, 12
Graduate Mangement programmes 55

Health Status of Canadian Women Mangers 162
Helping Women in their Caeers 29
Hiring Local Women Managers 10
Hong Kong 5, 7

India 5
Indonesia 5
Influx of Women transformed Workplaces in 1990's 133
Internal Labour Market 47, 48
Israel 5, 7
Israeli Women 7

Japan 9, 193, 194
Japanese Women 9, 194
Job mobility 112
Job Satisfaction of Women Managers 81
Job Segregation 30

Latin America 211
Law banning gender discrimination 136

Malaysia 5, 7, 198
Male-Dominated Administrative Enviornment 160
Male-Dominated Occupations 66

Male-Dominated Organizations 63
Male Vs-female Job Satisfaction 87
Management Development at PSU 54
Management Development Programmes 55
Managerial Profession for Women 37
Market for mangerial Labour 40
Maxican Management style 211
Mexico 211
Men of Bangladeshi Origin 163
Men of Indian Origin 163
Men of Pakistani Origin 163
Middle East 9
Minority Women Mangers 140
Motherhood and Profession in Russia 186

Negative Perceptions of Women 23, 25
New Style of successful Women Managers 130
Nigeria 205, 208
Nigerian Women 205, 207, 208
Nontraditional jobs for Women 138
North America 4, 11
North American Firms 9
North American Women 10, 11

1997 OECD Conference in Paris 13
Occupation Preference 94

Patriarchal Social Structures 156
Pay gap 136
People's Republic of China 4
Place of Women in Russian Higher Education 185
Placement and Management Development 199
Poland 5, 192
Polish Women Mangers 192
Primacy of Women's Domestic Role 29
Profession's Ruling Elites 24
Profiles of Successful Managers in U.S. 128
Promotion Strategy 31
Proportion of Women mangers 6
Psychology of sex differences 61

Remuneration compared to men 61
Royal Commission an equality in employment 143
Rules that Militate against Women 26
Russia 5, 185, 187
Russian Women 187, 188, 191

Scarcity of Black Women Managers 140
Scope of Equity Policy 156
Scottish Business Women 24
Seizing the power 124
Sex differences in leadership 62
Sex-role expectations 64
Sex-segregated jobs 23
Sexual Harassment and discrimination in the workplace 117, 118, 120
Sexual Harassment and Pay Inequalities 23
Shared Characteristics and work Patterns make 131
Shared Characteristics for successful Women Mangers 131
Singapore 5
Situation in Poland 192
Social attitude Towards women Managers 61
South Africa 6, 206
South Asian Female 168
South Asian Immigrants 163
South Asian Men 179
South Asian Women 170-172, 175, 178, 179, 181, 182
South Korea 206
Soviet Union 5

Special treatment for Women 152
Status of Women Administration in Bangladesh 195
Status of Women Administrators 3
Status of Women in Educational Administrators 144
Stereotypes of roles and responsibilities at work 173
Stigmatized difference 61
Structural and attitudinal Barriers 30
Struggle for equal benefits 126

Talent Hungry recruiters 76
Traditional Carreer Paths 56
Traditional Sex-role attitudes 23, 29
Transfer of managerial skills 201
Transnational Corporations 8

Under representation of Women in Management Position 116
Understanding Discrimination 61
Unequal gender relations 153
United Nations Development Programme (UNDP) 197

Western Europe 4, 5
Women Administrators and Professionals of USA 115
Women and development in Bangladesh 196
Women as Bosses 189
Women as Mothers 188
Women Civil Servants 198
Women Enterpreneurs in Business Enterprises 13
Women Executives of Canada 143
Women in Educational leadership 145
Women in Local Management 5
Women in low paid jobs 23
Women in Managerial Positions 67
Women in Senior Management 198
Women in South Africa 6
Women into Management Posts 25
Women in U.K. 38
Women Managers in Africa 205
Women Managers of Eastern Europe 185
Women Managers Outshine their Male Counterparts 75
Women Managers Worldwide 8
Women Situation in Latin America 211
Women's Limited Progress 59
Women's Movement into Mangement 3, 6
Women's Perception of Workplace Conditions 120
Work-family Conflicts 103, 118
Work-family Priorities 172
Work patterns for successful women Managers 131

Yugoslavia 5

Zimbabwe 5, 6